Visual QuickStart Guide

DIRECTOR 6

For Macintosh

ANDRE PERSIDSKY

Peachpit Press

Visual QuickStart Guide
Director 6 for Macintosh
Andre Persidsky

Peachpit Press
2414 Sixth Street
Berkeley, CA 94710
510/548-4393
800/283-9444
510/548-5991 (fax)

Find us on the World Wide Web at: http://www.peachpit.com
Peachpit Press is a division of Addison Wesley Longman

Cover design: The Visual Group

ISBN 0-201-68895-6

9 8 7 6 5 4 3 2 1

Printed and bound in the United States

♻ Printed on recycled paper

Thank you.

Jeremy Judson, Roslyn Bullas, and the rest of the staff at ***Peachpit Press***.

Table of Contents

Table of Contents

Chapter 5: **Animating Sprites**

Chapter 6: **Control Panel**

Table of Contents

Chapter 7: **Paint Window**

Table of Contents

Table of Contents

Introduction

Macromedia's Director is a powerful and extensive multimedia development tool. Use it to create animation, interactive movies, marketing presentations, technical simulations, and even full scale commercial productions such as entertainment titles for CD-ROM. The multimedia productions that you can synthesize with Director's powerful features are endless.

This book teaches the fundamentals of using Director, and covers the latest version 6 features. You will learn all the steps involved in creating a **movie**—the term used to describe any multimedia piece created in Director. You will learn how to create and assemble cast members in cast windows. How to animate cast members on the stage and build your movie frame-by-frame using the score window. How to create and edit cast members in the paint window. You will learn how to control movie playback, set scene transitions, alter color palettes, and add interactive controls to your movies using **Lingo**—Director's scripting language. You will learn about all the tools and techniques that Director supports for creating animation. Coverage on **Xtras** is also provided.

In the *Visual QuickStart Guide* format, this book provides step-by-step instructions, supported by numerous screen shots and tips. Where necessary, concise explanations are given. The emphasis is to get you up and running as quickly as possible through practical examples.

Chapter 2 provides an overview of the steps involved in creating a simple Director movie. Once you have mastered the basic techniques, the multimedia presentations you can create are limitless!

The Director screen and main windows

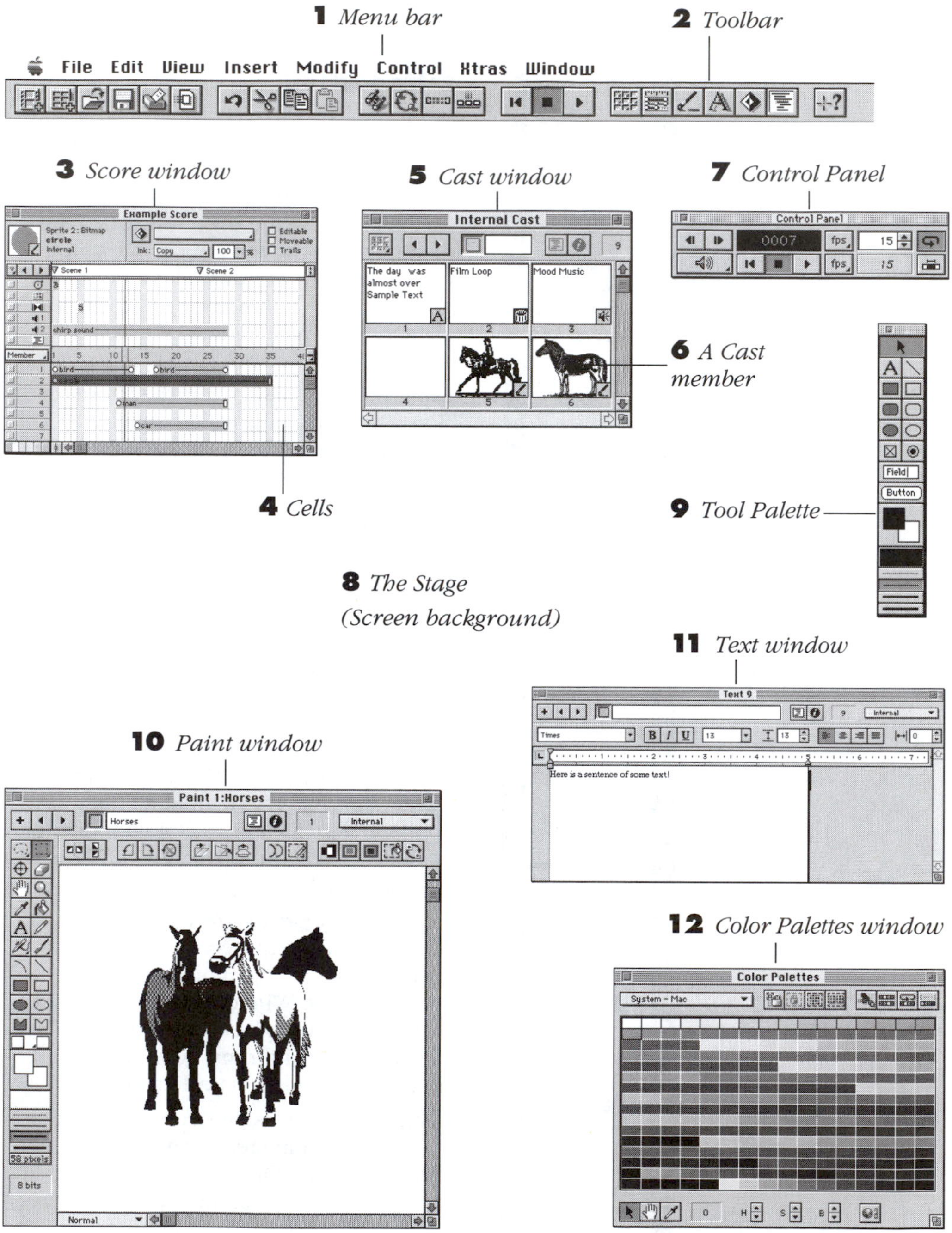

Key to the Director screen and windows

1 *Menu bar*

There are nine standard menu choices available in Director's menu bar—File, Edit, View, Insert, Modify, Control, Xtras, Window, and Help menus.

2 *Toolbar*

The Toolbar provides a convenient way to open frequently used windows such as the score, cast, and paint windows, and to select commonly used commands found under the File, Edit, Modify, and Control menus.

3 *Score window*

The score window is a frame-by-frame record of your Director movie. It is organized into frames and channels, which store all the components of your movie. These components include information such as the positions of each of your sprites during each frame, sound effects, color palette transitions, tempo changes, scene transitions—in short, all details pertaining to your movie.

4 *Cells*

The score is composed of cells, the storage units that hold all the information about your movie. Columns of cells are organized into frames, while rows of cells make up the score channels.

5 *Cast window*

Cast windows are the storage places for cast members in Director. A cast window is arranged into rows and columns of small windows, each of which can hold a unique cast member.

6 *A Cast member*

A cast member is a multimedia component such as a bitmapped image, or a sound effect, that you can incorporate into a Director movie. There are many different cast member types such as sounds, color palettes, text, buttons, bitmapped images, and shapes.

7 *Control Panel*

The control panel provides VCR-type control over the playback of your movie. You can rewind, play, fast forward, stop, and pause your movie from the control panel, as well as set the movie tempo.

8 *The Stage*

The stage is the background on which your movie plays.

9 *Tool Palette*

The Tool Palette allows you to create QuickDraw shapes, text, fields, and buttons on Director's stage.

10 *Paint window*

The paint window is Director's built-in paint program that allows you to edit and create bitmapped cast members. The paint window offers a menubar of effects such as rotate and distort that can be applied to your images.

11 *Text window*

The text window is used to create and edit text cast members.

12 *Color Palettes window*

The color palette displays the current set of colors used to draw your cast members on the stage.

About menus

Director has nine standard menus in its menu bar—File, Edit, View, Insert, Modify, Control, Xtras, Window, and Help. Menu selections in the Edit and View menus change depending on which Director window is active. Selections in the Insert and Xtras menus change when you install additional Xtras into Director.

The File menu

The File menu selections, such as Save, Open, Import, Preferences, and Create Projectors, apply to your Director movie as a whole.

The Edit menu

The Edit menu provides standard editing commands such as cut and paste, which are applied in various windows in Director. The Edit commands vary according to which Director window is currently active. Below, the Edit commands apply to sprites since the score window is the active window.

The Find command is located in the Edit menu, which allows you to search for specific cast members, handlers, and text.

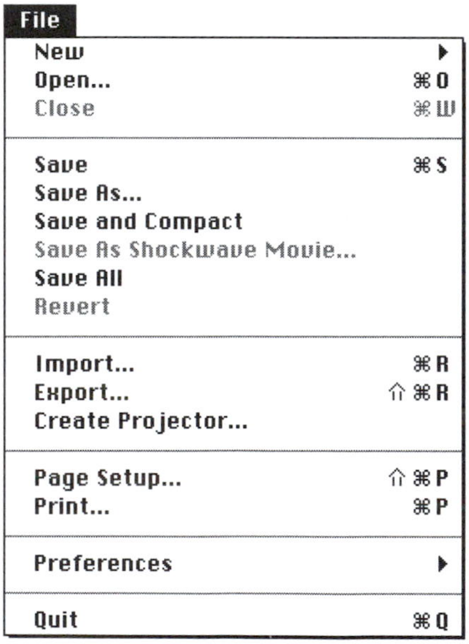

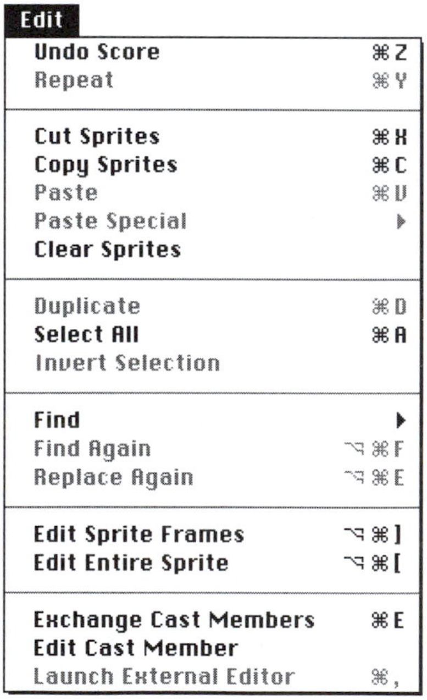

The View menu

The View menu commands generally deal with displaying or hiding certain visual guides and tools such as the stage grid, Onion Skin toolbar, and sprite labels.

The Insert menu

The commands under the Insert menu allow you to insert and remove frames from the score, and insert media elements such as bitmaps and sound into a cast window.

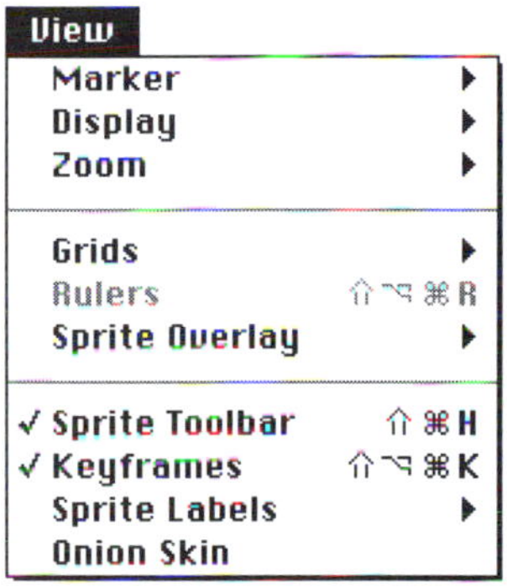

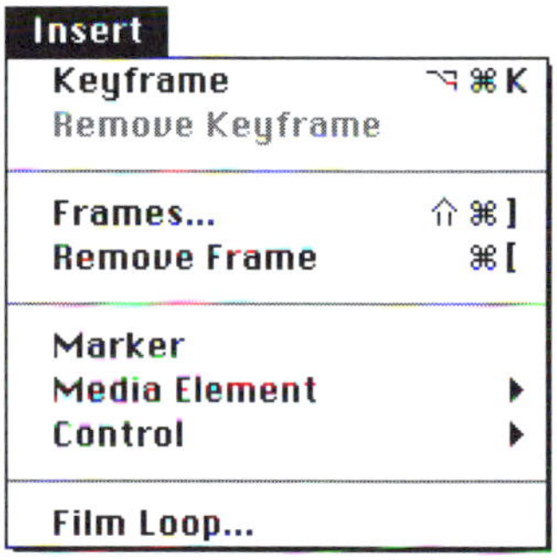

The Modify menu

The Modify menu commands allow you to modify the properties of casts, cast members, sprites, frames, and set parameters that affect your overall movie, such as stage size, and the default color palette. Commands which alter properties of cast members include Font, Transform Bitmap, and Convert Bitmap. Commands which change properties of sprites include Sprite, Align, and Tweak. The Modify menu commands also allow you to change the arrangement of sprites in the score. These include Arrange, Reverse Sequence, and Space to Time. You can also change the arrangement of cast members in a cast window using the Sort command.

The Control menu

The commands in the top half of the Control menu direct the playback of your movie. These include Play, Rewind, and Loop Playback. You can access these same commands using Director's control panel.

The commands in the bottom half of the Control menu deal with debugging Lingo scripts. These include Toggle Breakpoint and Recompile All Scripts.

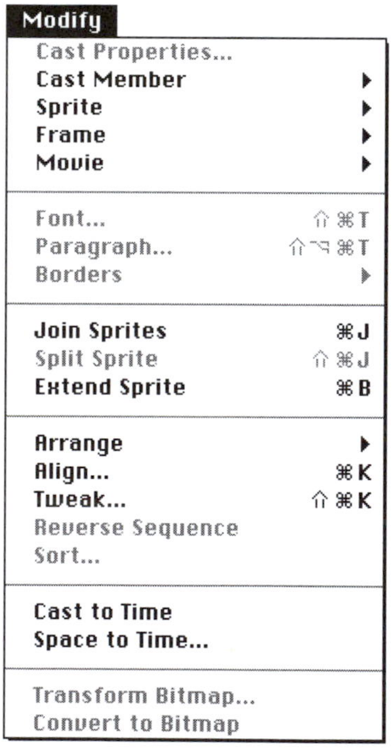

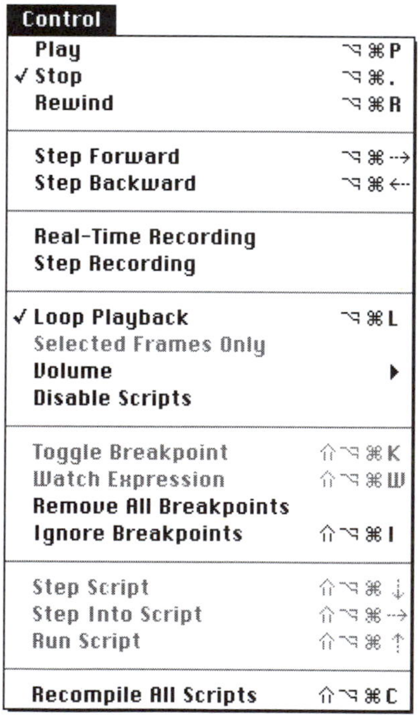

The Xtras menu

The commands in the Xtras menu generally deal with accessing Xtras (third party software modules), which expand the functionality of Director. The Filter Bitmap and Auto Filter commands allow you to apply Photoshop image filters to your bitmapped cast members. Any menu selections at the bottom portion of the Xtras menu are Tool Xtras, which become available when placed in the Xtras folder in the Director application folder. Tool Xtras enhance the authoring environment in Director.

The Update Movies command updates older versions of Director movies, and the Auto Distort command is used to automatically generate a sequence of cast members.

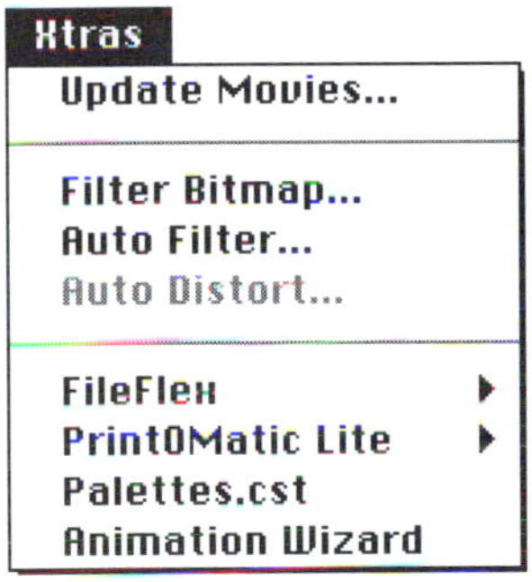

The Window menu

Choosing a selection in the Window menu either opens or closes the corresponding window. Open windows have checkmarks beside their names.

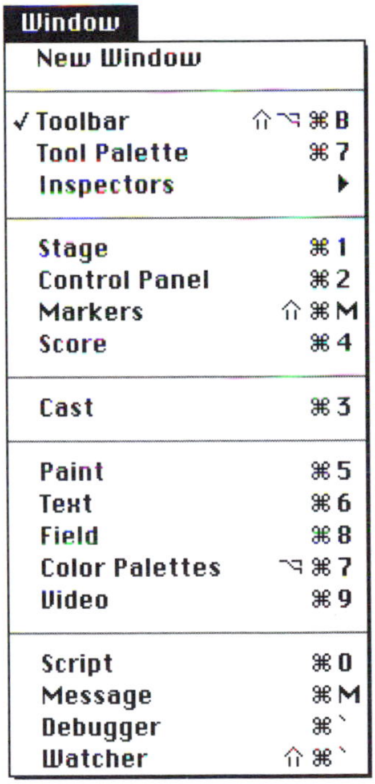

The Help menu

Use the Help menu commands to access online help in Director, and to electronically register Director with Macromedia.

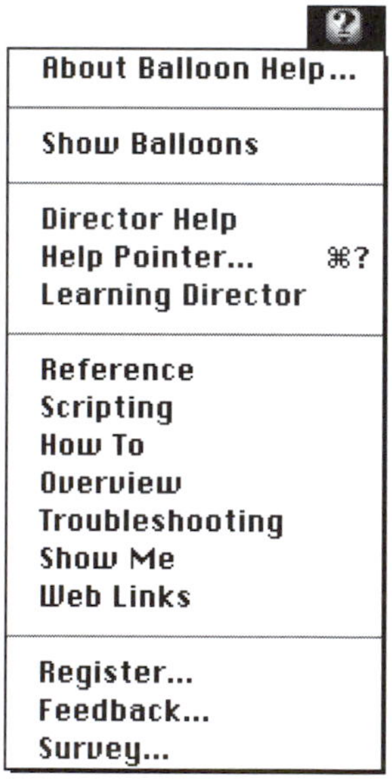

Hardware requirements to create movies

In order to create movies with Director for Macintosh, you need the following minimum hardware:

68040 Macintosh computer with System 7.1 or greater.

8 megabytes RAM, more is advised.

Double-speed CD-ROM drive (quad speed is preferable).

13-inch monitor (640x480 pixels), color definitely preferable.

A second monitor is highly recommended since it makes authoring movies much more convenient.

Hardware requirements to play back projector movies

To play a projector, you need at least a 68020 Macintosh with 4 megabytes of RAM, running System 7 or greater. This is the bare minimum.

If you intend to play Director movies that are extensive productions—that feature 24-bit color, intensive animation, or digital video—you will need a fast 68040 with 8 megabytes of RAM as a minimum for acceptable performance.

Director's Toolbar

You can use the Toolbar **(Figure 1)** as a shortcut to select commonly used commands found under the File, Edit, Modify, and Control menus, and to open frequently used windows such as the score, cast, and paint windows.

Choose Toolbar from the Window menu **(Figure 2)** to either show or hide Director's Toolbar.

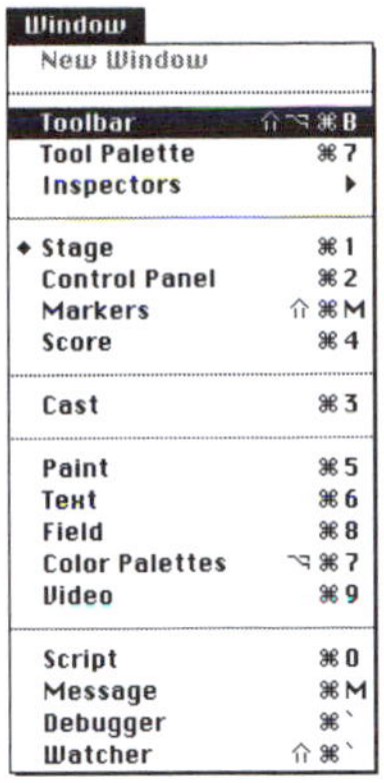

Figure 2. Choose **Toolbar** from the **Window** menu to either show or hide the Toolbar.

Figure 1. The Toolbar.

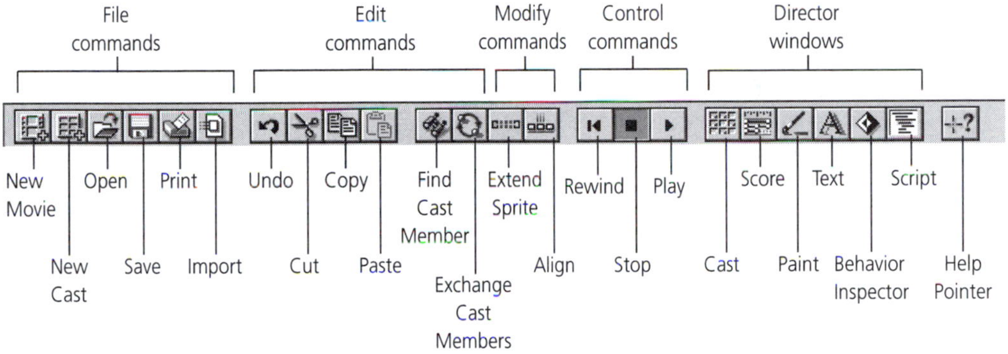

Shortcut menus

Control-click in any Director window or on a sprite to display a shortcut menu of commonly used commands that apply in that window or for that sprite.

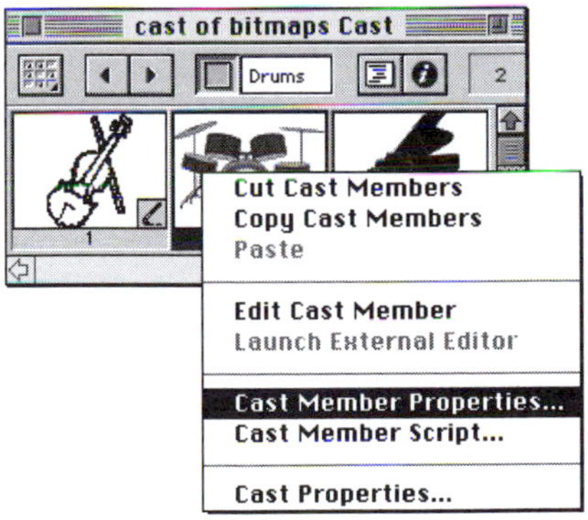

Keyboard shortcuts:

Most Director commands that you choose from the menus have a keyboard equivalent called a keyboard shortcut. To perform a keyboard shortcut, hold down one or more keys such as Command and Shift, and then press and release another key to execute the Director command.

(See Appendix B for a list of keyboard shortcuts)

To choose the Open command using a keyboard shortcut:

1. Hold down the Command key.
2. Press and release the "O" key.
3. Release the Command key.

To start Director:

Open the Director folder that was installed on your hard drive by double-clicking it. Then double-click the Director application icon **(Figure 3)**.

or

Double-click a Director movie icon **(Figure 4)**.

Figure 3. Double-click the Director application icon to start Director.

Figure 4. A Director movie icon.

✔ Tip

- Chances are, your Macintosh will be running System 7 or greater. If so, you can create an alias for Director that allows you to launch the program easily from the Apple menu. Single-click the Director application icon and choose Make Alias from the File menu. Now drag the alias icon into the Apple Menu Items folder in your System Folder.

To create a new movie:

When you start Director, it is ready for you to begin creating a new movie. If at any point you wish to start over from scratch, choose New from the File menu and select Movie from the pop-up menu **(Figure 5)**. You assign a name to a movie when you save it—by choosing Save from the File menu.

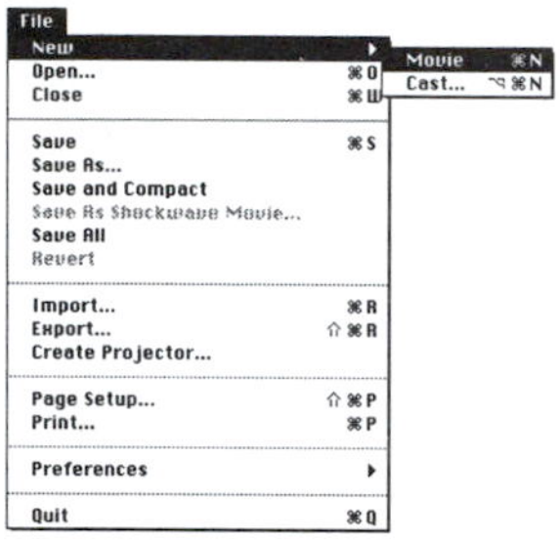

Figure 5. Choose **New** from the **File** menu and select **Movie** from the pop-up menu.

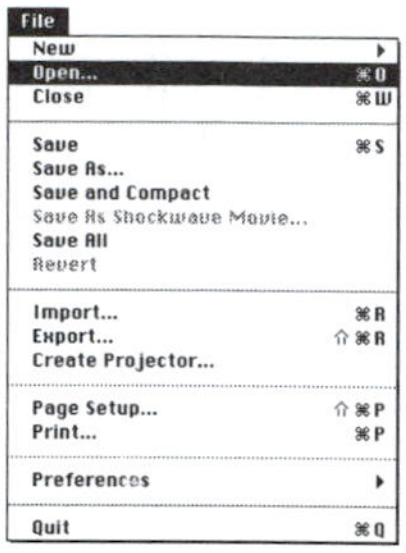

Figure 6. Choose **Open** from the **File** menu to open an existing movie.

To open an existing movie:

Choose Open from the File menu to open a Director movie or an external cast **(Figure 6)**. In the Open dialog box, select the movie's name and click the Open button, or double-click the movie's name **(Figure 7)**. The dialog box displays cast files and the names of Director movies created with the Macintosh version of Director. It also displays movies with a ".DIR" extension that were created with the Windows version of the program.

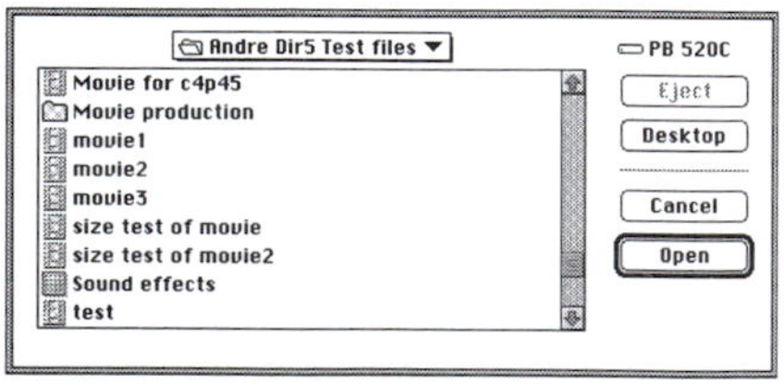

Figure 7. In the **Open** dialog box, select the movie's name from the file directory and click **Open**.

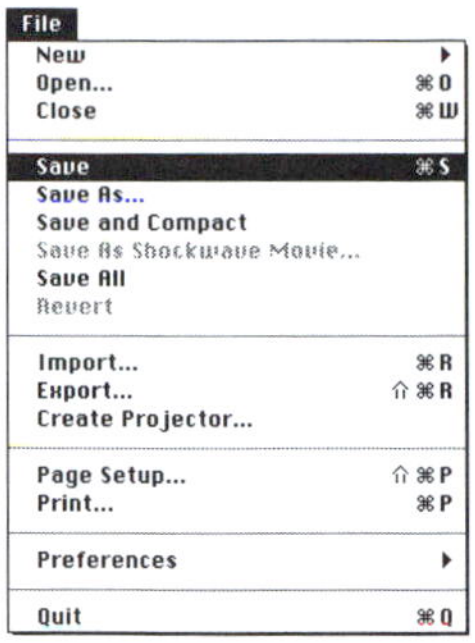

Figure 8. Choose **Save** from the **File** menu to save the current version of your movie.

To save a movie:

Choose Save from the File menu to save the current version of your movie to disk, writing over the movie's previous saved version **(Figure 8)**. You should save often to preserve your most recent work in case Director crashes, or your Macintosh loses power.

When you save a movie for the first time, Director brings you to the Save As dialog box, where you can name your movie and choose the area of your hard disk the movie should be saved to.

To save and compact a movie:

Choose Save and Compact from the File menu to save an optimized version of your movie under its original file name **(Figure 9)**. This takes longer than the Save command since Director reorders the cast, reduces the movie to its minimum size, and eliminates any unused space that might have accumulated in the original file. Use this command to gain optimal playback performance on a CD-ROM.

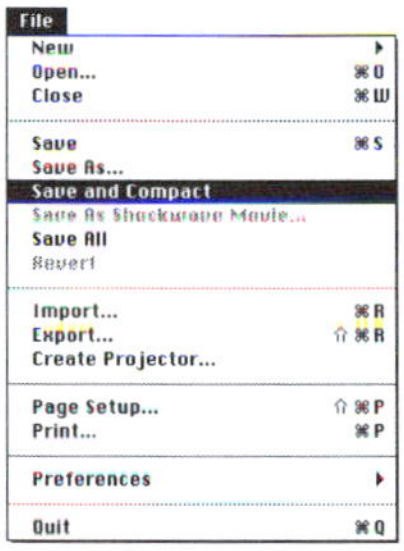

Figure 9. Choose **Save and Compact** from the **File** menu to save an optimized version of your current movie.

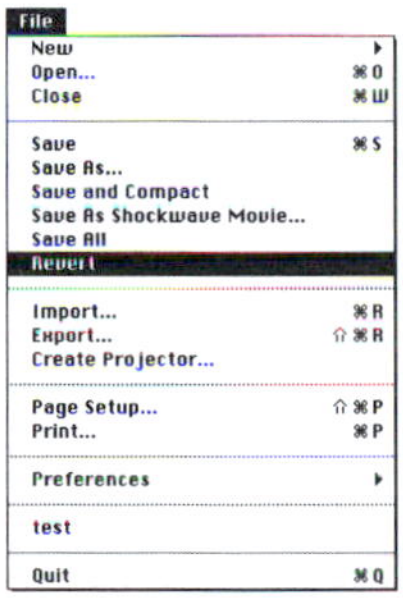

Figure 10. Choose **Revert** from the **File** menu to open the last saved version of your current movie.

Revert

Choose the Revert command from the File menu to open the last saved version of your current movie **(Figure 10)**. This is useful if you have made some undesirable changes to your movie, and wish to quickly go back to the previous saved version.

UPDATE MOVIES

The Update Movies command under the Xtras menu is used for three different purposes:

- Convert Director 4 and 5 movies to the Director 6 file format.
- Protect movies from being opened or edited. *(See page 197 in the Create a Projector chapter)*
- Convert a movie to the Shockwave format.

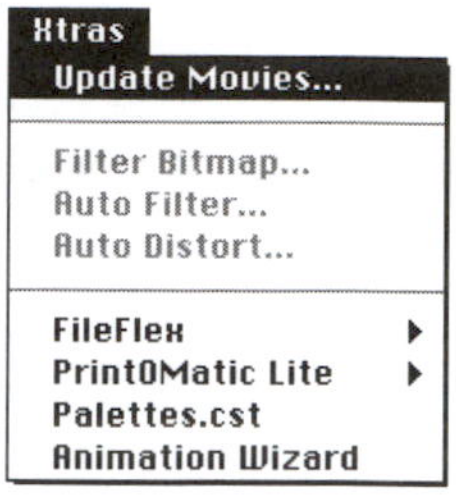

Figure 11. Choose **Update Movies** from the **Xtras** menu.

To update Director movies:

Follow the steps below to update a Director 4 or 5 movie.

If you have a Director 4.x movie that uses a shared cast (a file called shared.dir), you must update that movie before you can use it with Director 6. The shared cast becomes a linked external cast named shared.cst. Make sure that you add the shared.dir file along with the Director 4.x movie file in step 5 below.

Director 4.x movies which don't have a shared cast, and Director 5 movies can be opened in Director 6, but it is still a good idea to update them first since this converts them into the Director 6 file format, and compacts the file by removing any fragmented data.

1. Choose Update Movies from the Xtras menu **(Figure 11)**.
2. Click the Update button **(Figure 12)**.

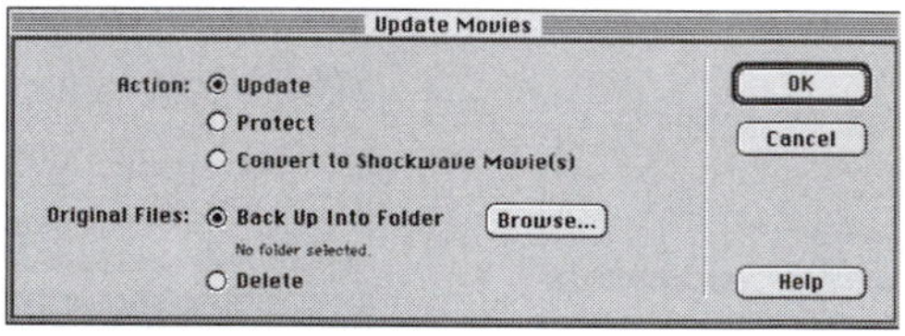

Figure 12. Click the **Update** radio button in the **Update Movies Options** dialog box.

Update Movies

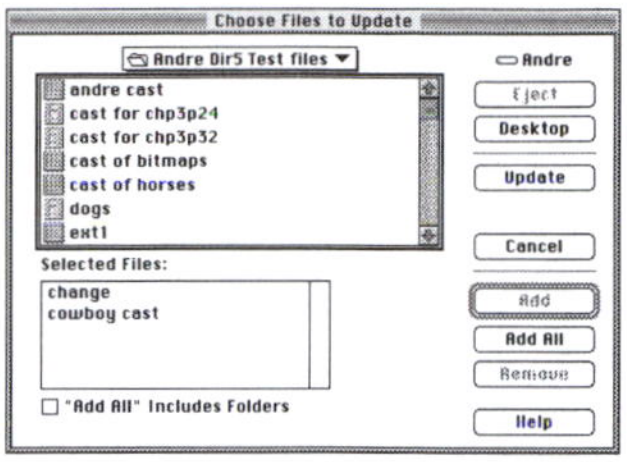

Figure 13. Add the files that you wish to update in the **Choose Files to Update** dialog box.

3. Click the Back Up into Folder radio button if you wish to place the original files into a specified folder. Click the Browse button to select the folder in which to place these original files.

or

3. Click the Delete button if you want the new updated files to overwrite the originals. Make sure that you have backed up the original files since you cannot undo this conversion.
4. Click OK
5. In the Choose Files to Update dialog box, select a Director 4 or 5 movie file that you wish to update. Click Add **(Figure 13)**. Repeat this step to add all the files you wish to update to the list at the bottom of the dialog box. Click Add All to add all the files in the current folder to the list of files to update.
6. Click Update.

THE HELP WINDOW

To open Director's Help window, choose Director Help from the Help menu.

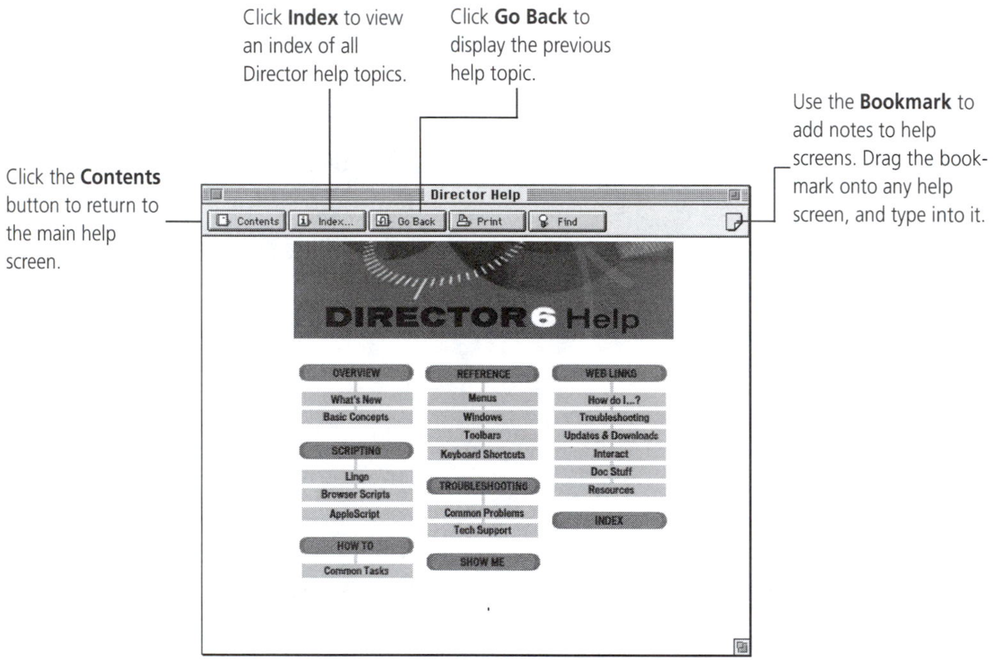

✔ Tip

- Choose Help Pointer from the Help menu, or click the Help Pointer button in the Toolbar to get context-sensitive help. The mouse pointer turns into a question mark, and when you choose a command or click in a window, an appropriate help screen is displayed.

GENERAL PREFERENCES

Use the General Preferences dialog box if you wish to change properties of Director's stage and user interface. Choose Preferences from the File menu and select General from the pop-up menu to open this dialog box. You don't need to change any of the default settings to start creating a Director movie.

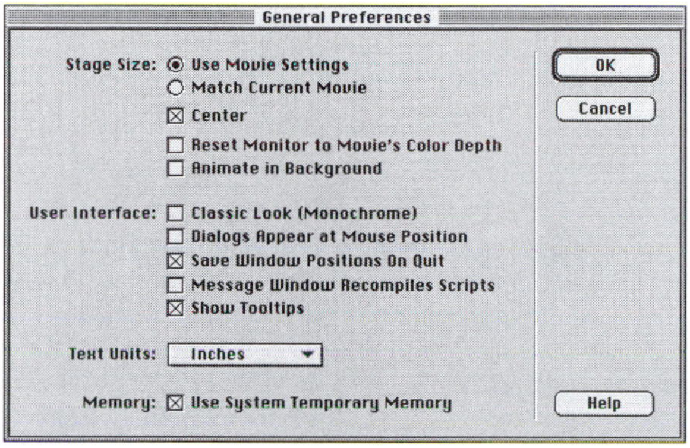

Stage Size

Use Movie Settings

Select this option for the stage size to take on the dimensions of any new movie that is opened.

Match Current Movie

When set, the stage dimensions of the current movie are used for any movie that is opened.

Center

The stage is automatically centered on the screen (this comes in handy when the stage is smaller than the full screen dimensions). If not checked, the position of the stage is determined by the movie that is opened.

Reset Monitor to Movie's Color Depth

When checked, your monitor's color depth changes to match the color depth of any movie that is opened.

Animate in Background

When checked, your movie can run in the background. This allows you to work in other applications while your movie plays on the stage behind the application windows.

Memory

When checked, Director will use available system memory when its own memory partition becomes full. If virtual memory is turned on, this option is disabled.

User Interface

Classic Look (Monochrome)

When checked, Director displays the user interface in black and white. This improves performance since Director doesn't need to update any colors in the user interface when the current color palette is switched.

Dialogs Appear at Mouse Position

When checked, dialog boxes are displayed at the position of the mouse pointer. If this option is not selected, the dialog boxes will be centered on the monitor.

Save Window Positions On Quit

Saves the positions of all Director windows each time you quit.

Message Window Recompiles Scripts

This is checked by default. If not checked, your scripts should be manually recompiled using the Recompile All Scripts command under the Control menu before any Lingo is entered in the Message window.

Show Tooltips

When checked, definitions appear when the mouse pointer is positioned over tools. This is checked by default.

Text Units

Use the Text Units pop-up menu to select which units of measure are displayed on the text and field windows' ruler.

MOVIE PROPERTIES

Use the Movie Properties dialog box to set a number of properties that affect the current movie, such as the default palette and stage location. You don't need to change the default settings to start creating a Director movie. Choose Movie from the Modify menu and select Properties from the pop-up menu to open the Movie Properties dialog box.

Stage Location

Centered

The stage appears in the center of your monitor.

Upper Left

The stage is placed starting from the top left corner of the screen.

Other

Allows you to enter values into the Left and Top fields to indicate by how many pixels the stage should be offset from the top left corner of the screen.

Stage Size

You can change the size of the stage by choosing a monitor size from the pop-up menu, or by entering values into the Width and Height fields. This is useful when you wish to display movies on a smaller or larger monitor.

Stage Color

Sets the color of the stage. Click the color chip to select a new stage color from the pop-up color palette.

Default Palette

The Default Palette pop-up menu allows you to set the default color palette for your movie. This palette remains in effect until Director encounters a different palette setting in the palette channel.

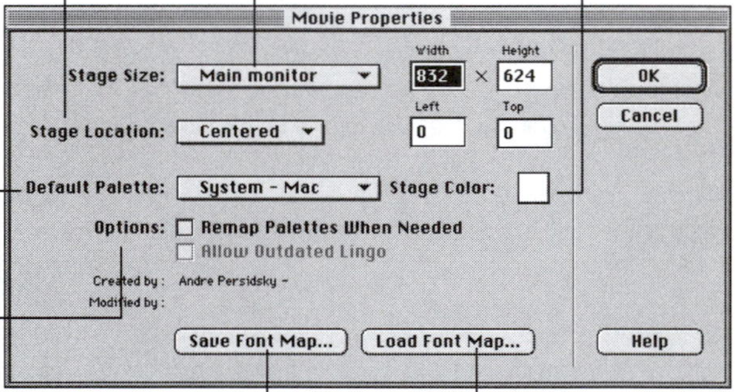

Options

Remap Palettes When Needed

If this box is checked, all cast members displayed on the stage that have a color palette different from the currently active palette are remapped to a common palette that Director creates. This is a useful feature to enable when you have many cast members that use many different palettes.

Allow Outdated Lingo

Allows you to include Lingo commands from Director 5 that have been eliminated in Director 6.

Save Font Map

Click to save current font map settings in a specified text file.

Load Font Map

Click to load font map settings.

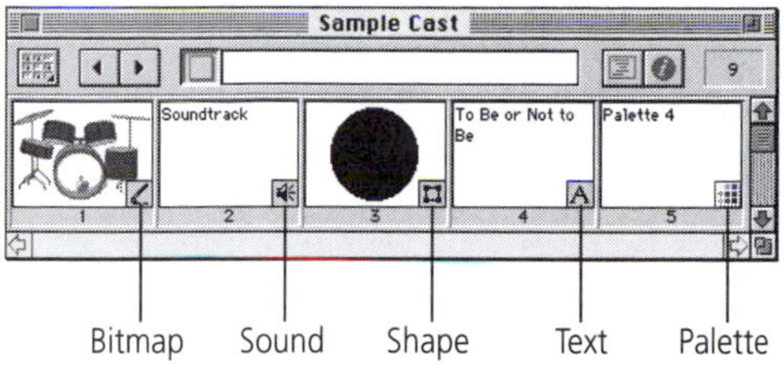

Figure 1. Cast members are stored in Director's **Cast** windows. Each cast member occupies a small numbered window, and its type is indicated by a small icon in the lower right corner.

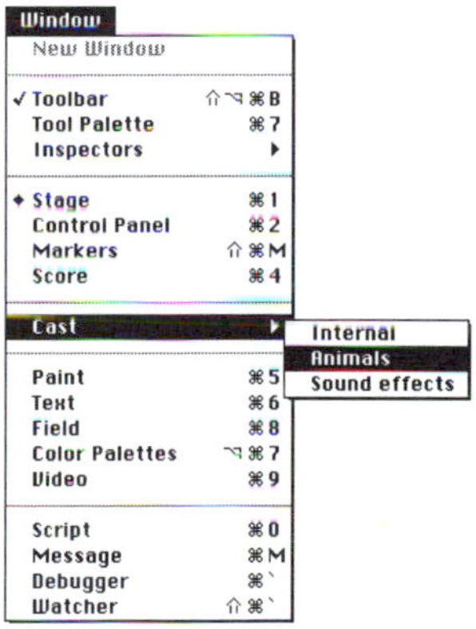

Figure 2. Choose **Cast** from the **Window** menu. If multiple casts are being used, select the cast you wish to view from the pop-up menu.

CREATING MOVIES

The steps involved in creating a Director movie mirror many of the ideas behind traditional Hollywood film production. You start by assembling a group of **Cast members**, which in Director are the multimedia elements that comprise your movies. Cast members can include graphics, sounds, text, buttons, digital videos, and color palettes, among others.

You create a movie by assigning cast members to various parts of the score. The **Score** is a detailed record that tells Director what your cast members should do on a frame-by-frame basis, very much like a script *(see page 20)*.

Your movie plays out on Director's **Stage**, which is the background upon which graphical cast members are animated.

Cast window

Your cast members are stored in a **Cast window**, which is a kind of multimedia database **(Figure 1)**. Cast members are numbered in the small windows they occupy, and their type is indicated by a small icon in the lower right corner. You can organize your cast members into separate casts, where each cast is viewed in its own cast window. *(See the Cast Windows chapter on page 25 for more details)*

To open a cast window:

1. Choose Cast from the Window menu **(Figure 2)**. If multiple casts are present, choose the cast you wish to view from the pop-up menu.

Creating cast members

Director has its own set of in-house tools for producing cast members. These tools include the paint window, Tool Palette, text and field windows, and the Sound command used to record sounds. For high end production, you may prefer to create your cast members using applications such as Photoshop or SoundEdit Pro, which offer more advanced tools. Director allows you to import externally generated cast members. *(See page 28)*

The **Paint window** in Director is actually quite extensive and can be used to create fairly elaborate bitmap cast members **(Figure 3)**. The paint window includes a variety of tools in its tool palette **(Figure 4)** such as the Air Brush, Shape, and Text tools. The paint window also offers a menu bar of special effect commands, such as Rotate and Warp, which can be applied to your bitmap cast members. *(See the Paint Window chapter on page 95 for more details)*

To create a cast member using the paint window:

1. Choose New from the File menu and select Movie from the pop-up menu **(Figure 5)**.
2. Choose Paint from the Window menu to open the paint window **(Figure 6)**.
3. Click the Filled Ellipse tool in the tool palette **(Figure 4)** (in this example we create a shaded ellipse).
4. Select a foreground color by clicking and holding the Foreground color chip **(Figure 3)**. Choose a color from the pop-up color palette that appears.
5. Drag in the paint window to size and draw your ellipse.
6. When you close the paint window, your drawing automatically becomes a bitmap cast member. It is placed into the first available slot in the current cast window.

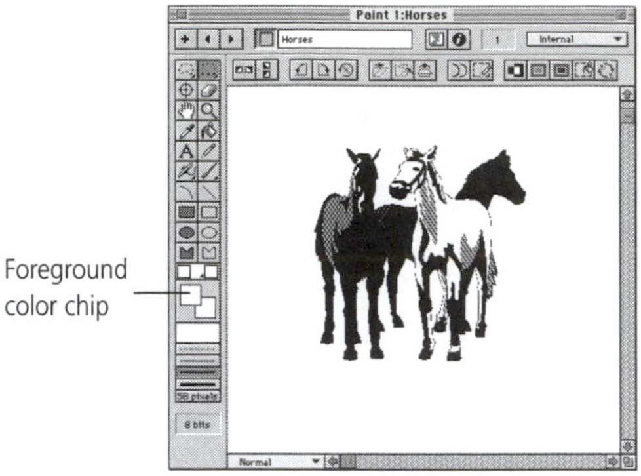

Figure 3. The paint window is used to create and edit bitmap cast members.

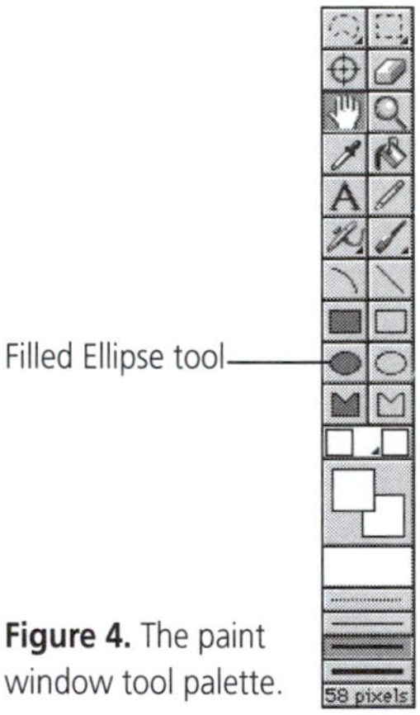

Figure 4. The paint window tool palette.

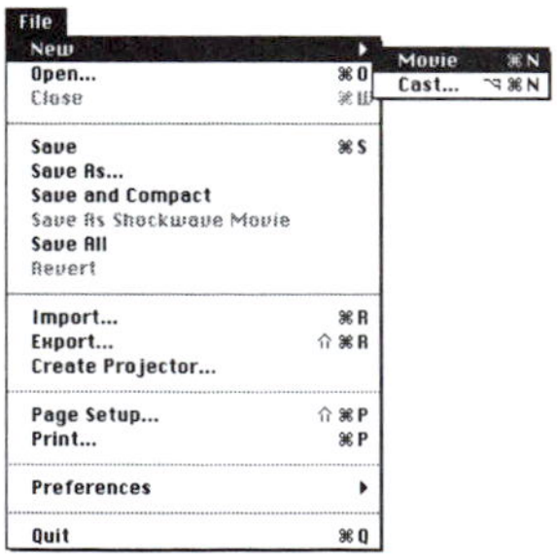

Figure 5. Choose **New** from the **File** menu and select **Movie** from the pop-up menu to open a new untitled movie.

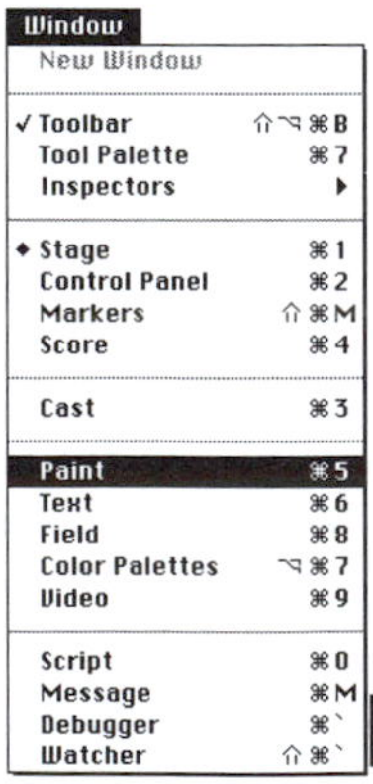

Figure 6. Choose **Paint** from the **Window** menu.

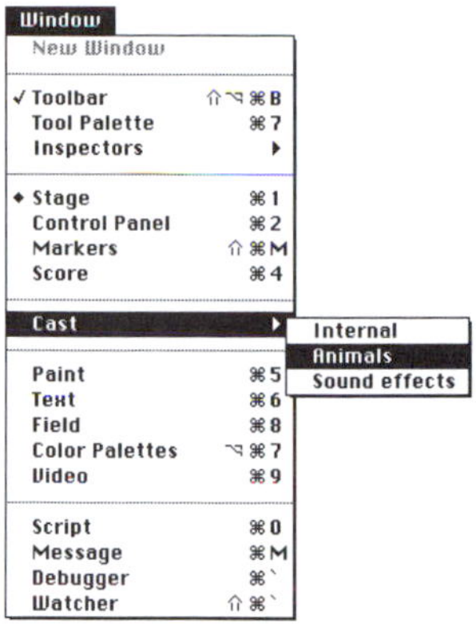

Figure 7. Choose **Cast** from the **Window** menu. If multiple casts are being used, select the cast you wish to view from the pop-up menu.

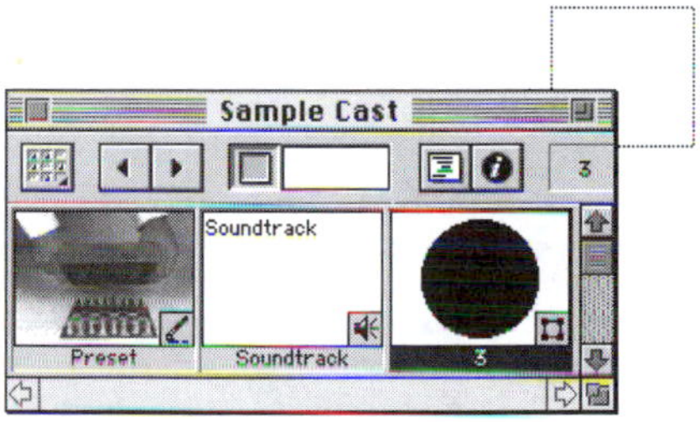

Figure 8. Dragging a cast member from a cast window onto the stage automatically places it in a single frame of the score. The dotted outline here represents a cast member being dragged.

Optional

7. Choose Cast from the Window menu. The cast window appears and you should now see your ellipse in the first cast member position. Notice that the cast member type is a bitmap as indicated by the small icon.

✔ **Tip**

- Double-click a bitmap cast member in a cast window to open it in the paint window.

To place a cast member onto the stage:

Once you have assembled your cast members in a cast window, you will want to start building your movie. You incorporate cast members into your movie by placing them into the score, or by dragging them onto the stage—the background upon which they are animated.

1. Choose Cast from the Window menu to open a cast window **(Figure 7)**.

2. Drag a cast member onto the stage, that is, onto any area of the screen not occupied by an open window **(Figure 8)**. This action places the cast member into your movie and automatically records it in a range of frames in the score. If the cast member is a graphical type, its location on the stage is also recorded in the score.

Frames

A Director movie, like any movie, is broken down into a series of frames. A **Frame** is a snapshot of your movie that holds all the information about what's happening in a particular time segment. Each frame can include information such as the positions of each of your cast members on the stage, and what sound effects are being played at that instant.

Score window

Director's score window is a frame-by-frame record of your movie **(Figure 9)**. It contains all the information about what your cast members are doing on the stage at any given instant. Consequently, building a Director movie is largely a process of placing cast members into the score, through various ranges of frames where they will be active.

Cast members in the score are represented by objects called sprites **(Figure 9)**. A **sprite** consists of a cast member, and a set of properties and behaviors which direct when, where, and how the cast member appears in your movie.

The score is composed of **cells**, which are its individual storage units that hold information about your sprites. Cells are organized into rows and columns **(Figure 10)**, where columns form the frames of your movie, and rows form the score channels. Frames are numbered in the center of the score window.

Score channels store the specific types of media information that comprise each frame **(Figure 10)**. For instance, when you wish to incorporate a graphical cast member in a certain frame, you place it into one of the sprite channels. Likewise, sounds are placed and stored in one of the two sound channels. There are 126 score channels in all, five of which are called effects channels (tempo, palette, transition, sound 1 & 2), one script channel, and 120 sprite channels *(see the Score and Sprite Basics chapter on page 43 for more details)*. The effects channels are used to create effects such as color palette transitions and tempo changes in the scenes of your movie.

The position of the **Playback head** in the score indicates which frame of the movie is currently displayed on the stage **(Figure 10)**. You can drag the playback head to display any single frame of your movie on the stage.

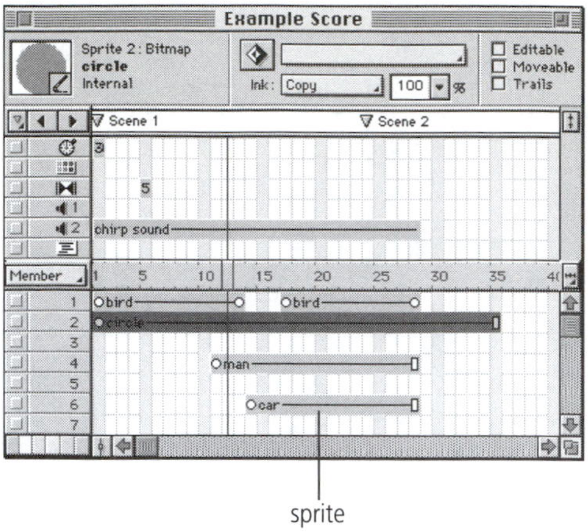

Figure 9. The score window is a frame-by-frame record of your Director movie. Cast members in the score are represented by objects called sprites.

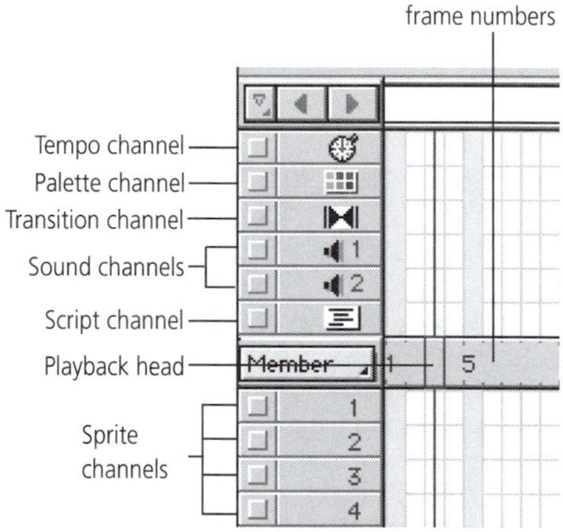

Figure 10. The cells in the score are organized into rows and columns, where columns form the frames of your movie, and rows form the score channels.

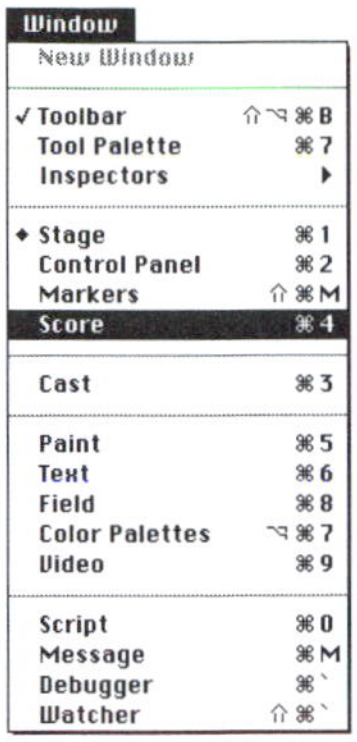

Figure 11. Choose **Score** from the **Window** menu.

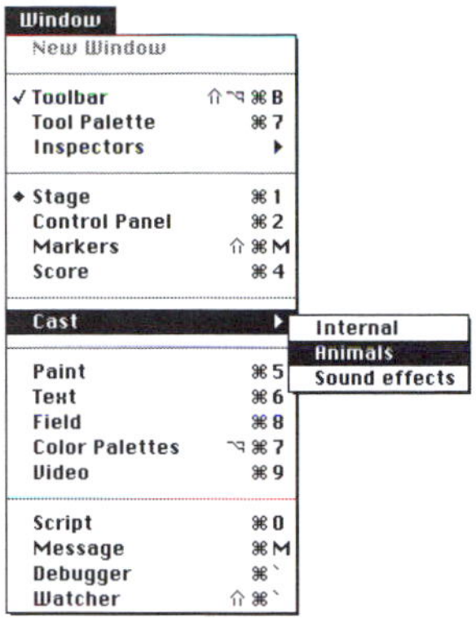

Figure 12. Choose **Cast** from the **Window** menu. If multiple casts are being used, select the cast you wish to view from the pop-up menu.

To place a cast member into the score:

You can enter a cast member into the score (and therefore into your movie) by dragging it from a cast window and placing it into a specific range of frames in a channel. If the cast member is a graphical type (bitmap, shape, or PICT) it automatically appears centered on the stage in the frame you place it in.

1. Choose Score from the Window menu to open the score **(Figure 11)**.
2. Choose Cast from the Window menu to open a cast window **(Figure 12)**.
3. In this example, drag a graphical cast member from a cast window into the first sprite channel, starting in the first frame of the score **(Figure 13)**. The cast member is recorded into the score and appears centered on the stage.

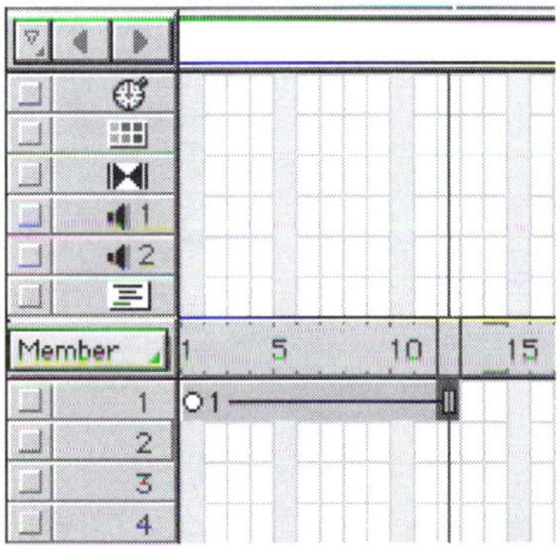

Figure 13. Drag a graphical cast member from a cast window into the first sprite channel starting in the first frame of the score window.

Figure 14. Director can automatically generate a series of frames that lie between two key frames through tweening.

Animation

An animation is created by positioning one or more graphical cast members on the stage, and then slightly changing the positions of these sprites in the successive frames of your movie. When the frames are played back at a high speed, animation is achieved. Director provides several techniques to expedite the process of animating your sprites. These include tweening and Real-time recording.

The idea of tweening is based on setting up key frames. A **key frame** is a frame in which a property of a sprite changes, such as its size or stage position. You can use tweening to automatically fill in all the intermediary frames between key frames, sparing you from a lot of repetitive work **(Figure 14)**.

Director's **Real-time recording** feature lets you record the path of mouse movements and then substitute a cast member to follow this recorded path to produce animation. *(See the Animating Sprites chapter on page 69 for more details)*

Control Panel

Director's control panel offers you VCR-type control over the playback of your movie. You can rewind, play, jump forward to any frame, and even change the tempo setting of your movie by using the control panel **(Figure 15)**.

Figure 15. Director's control panel offers VCR-type control over the playback of your movie.

A simple movie example:

The following steps result in a simple movie animation. Before proceeding, follow the steps on page 18 to create the bitmap cast member of an ellipse that's used in this example:

1. Open the cast and score windows by choosing them from the Window menu.
2. Drag the ellipse from the cast window into frame 1, starting in sprite channel 1 in the score **(Figure 16)**. The ellipse appears in the center of the stage.
3. Click the last frame of the sprite in the score to select it **(Figure 17)** (this is the end frame indicated by a square).
4. Choose Keyframe from the Insert menu to insert a new key frame at the end of the sprite **(Figure 18)**.
5. Click the first frame of the sprite in the score to select it **(Figure 19)** (this is a key frame which is indicated by a circle).
6. Drag the ellipse from the center of the stage to the left hand side.
7. Click the last frame of the sprite in the score to select it (now a key frame indicated by a circle).
8. Drag the ellipse from the center of the stage to the right hand side.
9. Click the sprite in the score to select it. Be sure not to click either of its key frames; click anywhere between them to select the entire sprite.

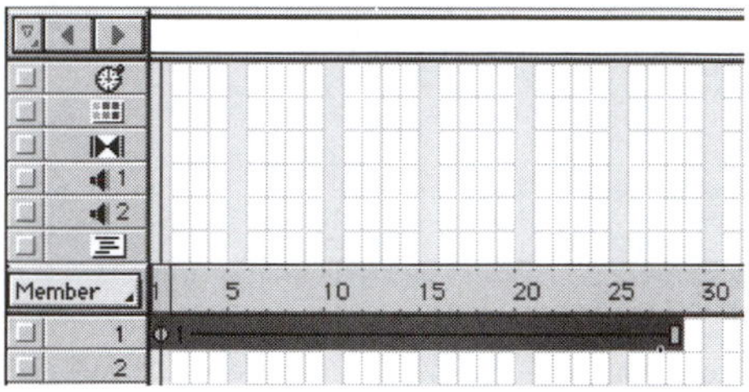

Figure 16. Drag the ellipse from the cast window into sprite channel 1, starting in frame 1 in the score.

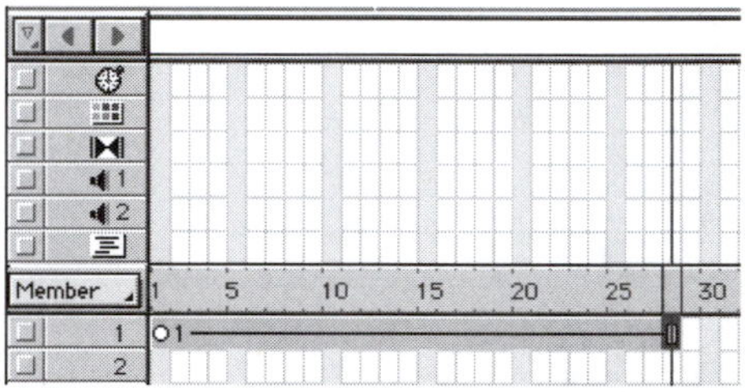

Figure 17. Click the last frame of the sprite in the score to select it.

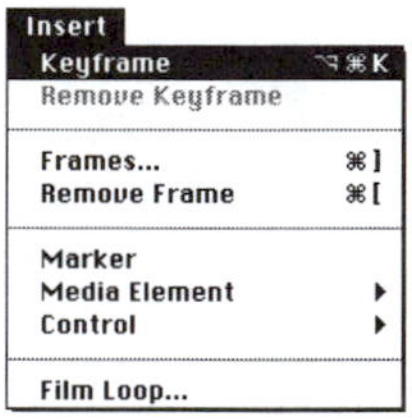

Figure 18. Choose **Keyframe** from the **Insert** menu.

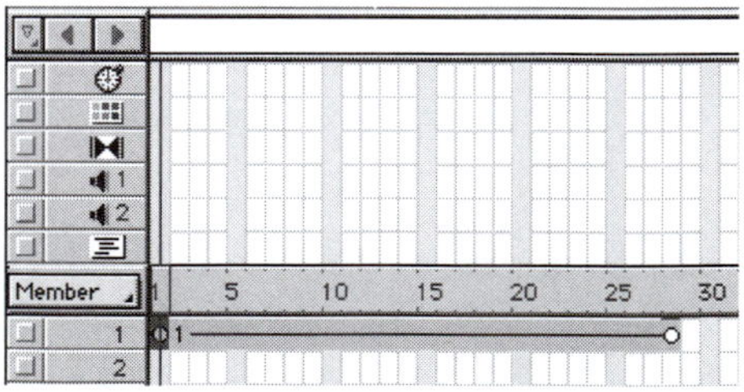

Figure 19. Click the first frame of the sprite in the score to select it. This frame is a key frame.

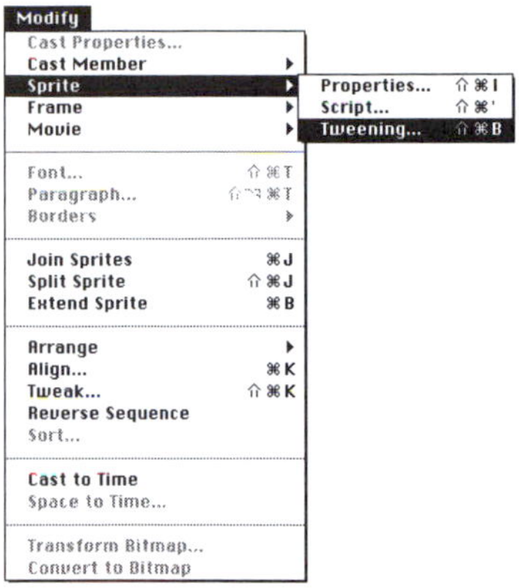

Figure 20. Choose **Sprite** from the **Modify** menu and select **Tweening** from the pop-up menu.

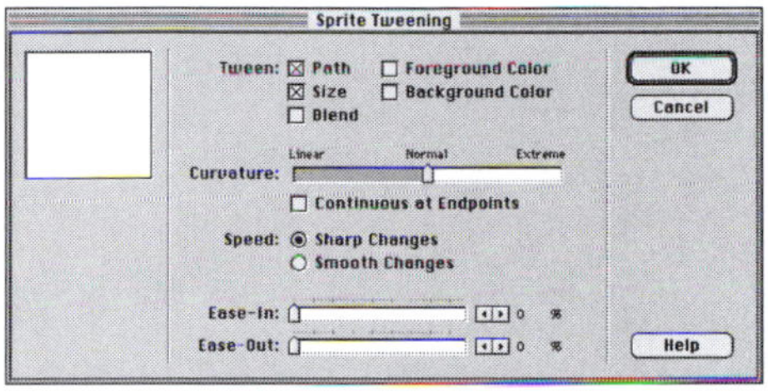

Figure 21. Click the **Path** option in the **Sprite Tweening** dialog box.

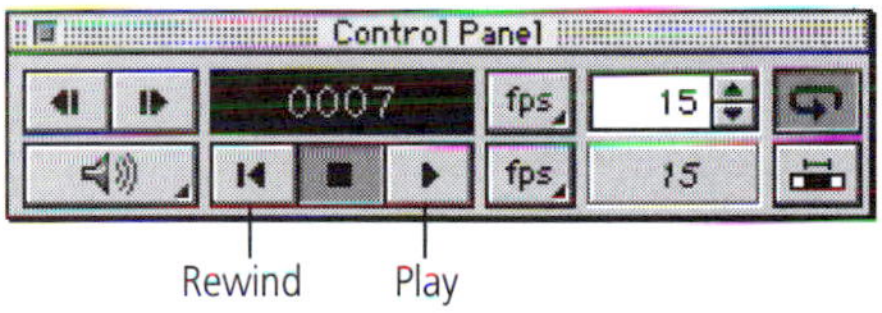

Figure 22. The control panel.

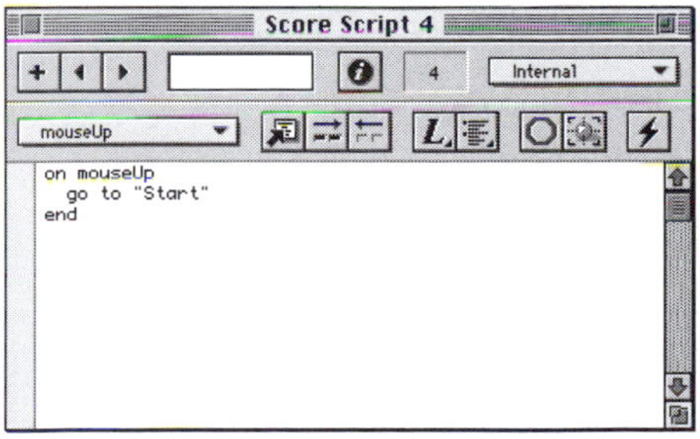

Figure 23. The script window.

10. Choose Sprite from the Modify menu and select Tweening from the pop-up menu **(Figure 20)**.

11. Click the Path option in the Sprite Tweening dialog box **(Figure 21)**.

12. Choose Control Panel from the Window menu to open the control panel **(Figure 22)**.

13. Click the Rewind button to set the playback head to frame 1.

14. Click Play to watch your movie. The ellipse moves across the stage from left to right.

Lingo and interactivity

Director movies, unlike traditional animation or video, can incorporate interactive features, which allow your viewers to become active participants. They can change the course of your movie in many different ways, using mouse and keyboard input. Such interactivity is created by using Lingo—Director's scripting language.

Lingo scripts are instructions written in the script window **(Figure 23)** that tell Director how your movie should respond to user input, and to other changing conditions. For example, you can write a script that creates interactive buttons, which allow your viewers to navigate through the scenes of your movie at will. This is very common in an information kiosk setup. *(See the Interactivity through Lingo chapter on page 201 for an introduction to script writing)*

If you want to avoid learning about writing Lingo scripts, but still wish to incorporate basic interactivity in your movies, you can do so by using a new feature in Director 6 called drag and drop behaviors. *(See page 227 in the Drag and Drop Behaviors chapter)*

CAST WINDOWS 3

Cast window

Choose Cast from the Window menu to open a cast window, or press Command-3. If multiple casts are being used, select the cast you wish to view from the pop-up menu **(Figure 1)**.

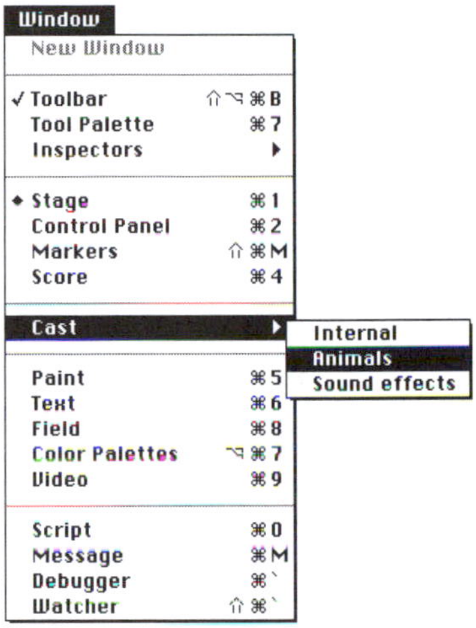

Figure 1. Choose **Cast** from the **Window** menu. If multiple casts are being used, select the cast you wish to view from the pop-up menu.

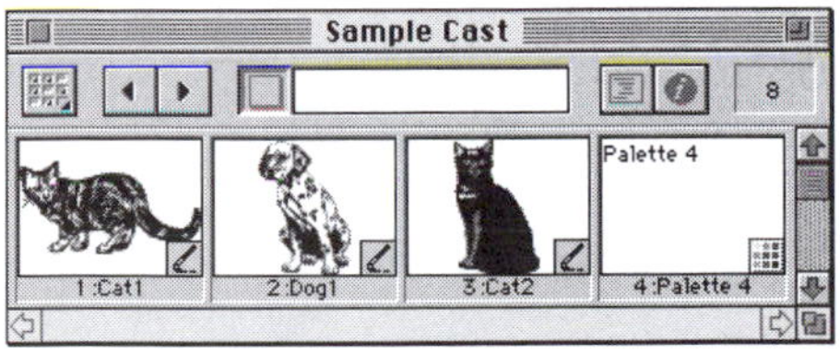

Figure 2. A cast window showing four cast members.

Director's **Cast windows** act as the viewing and storage areas for the cast members used in your movie (remember that cast members include pictures, sounds, strings of text, color palettes, digital videos, film loop animation, and Lingo scripts, among others). When you're ready to incorporate a cast member into your movie, simply drag it from a cast window onto Director's stage or right into its score window. *(See the Score and Sprite Basics chapter on page 43 for more about incorporating cast members into the score)*

Director 6 allows you to create and work with multiple independent casts within a single movie. Each cast is displayed in its own window. Casts are either internal or external. (*See page 31 for more about internal and external casts*)

In order for a cast member to become available for your movie, it must first be placed in a cast window **(Figure 2)**. If the cast member has already been created and saved by some other program (such as a background created in Fractal Design Painter, or a sound effect mixed with SoundEdit Pro), the cast member must first be imported into a cast window before it can be incorporated into your movie (*see page 28 for importing cast members*). However, if you're creating a cast member within Director itself (for instance, by using Director's paint window, or its Sound command feature), **the cast member is automatically added to the cast window**.

A cast window can contain up to 32,000 cast members available for use in your movie. Each cast member is represented by a thumbnail image, and identified by a number that corresponds to the position it occupies.

Cast member types

Each cast member in a cast window has a small icon in its lower-right corner that identifies its type **(Figure 3)**.

Cast Selector

Use the Cast Selector **(Figure 4)** to choose which cast is displayed in the current cast window, or to create a new cast. You can choose from all internal casts, and external casts that have been linked to the current movie. These casts are displayed in the pop-up menu. (*See page 31 for more about internal and external casts*)

Previous, Next Arrows

Click the Previous or Next arrow to select the previous or next cast member (in relation to whatever cast member is currently selected) in the cast window **(Figure 4)**. The key combination Command-Left Arrow selects the previous cast member, and Command-Right Arrow moves to the next cast member.

Place button

The Place button is useful when you wish to move some cast members to a new position in a cast window, where the new position is beyond the visible range of the selected cast members. First click the cast member in the cast window you wish to move **(Figure 4)**. You may Shift-click to select more than one cast member at a time and move them together. Now scroll through the cast window to the position to which you wish to move the selected cast member(s). Drag the Place button to the new position in the cast window. Release the mouse button to move the selected cast member(s) **(Figure 5)**.

✔ Tip

- Hold the Option key while dragging the Place button to copy selected cast members to their new position.

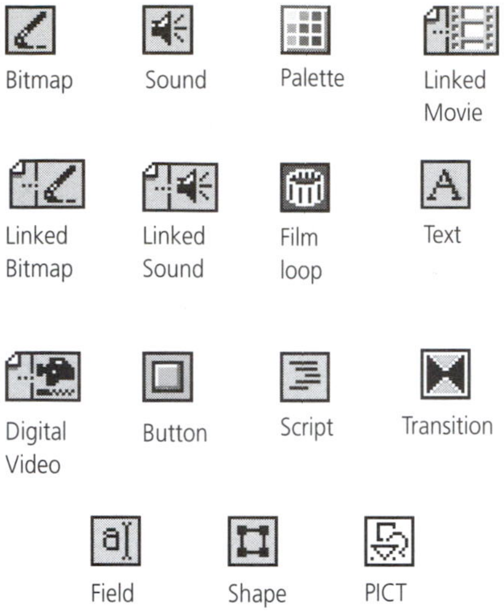

Figure 3. Cast member types are indicated by a small icon in the lower-right corner of each cast member.

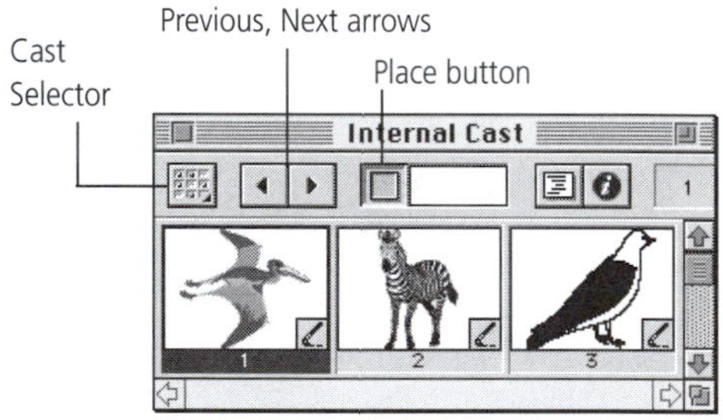

Figure 4. The **Place** button is used to move selected cast members to new positions in the cast window. Click the cast member you wish to move, such as cast member 1 depicted here.

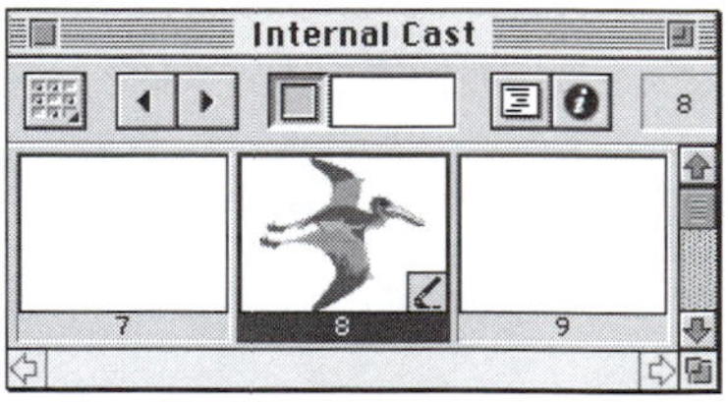

Figure 5. Drag the **Place** button to the new position in the cast window. Release the mouse button to move the selected cast member.

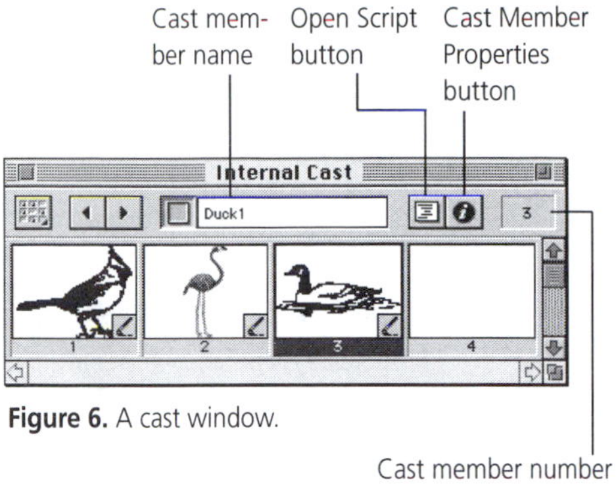

Figure 6. A cast window.

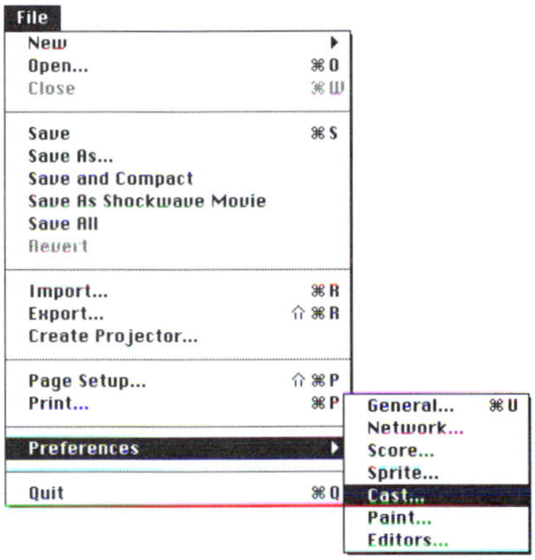

Figure 7. Choose **Preferences** from the **File** menu, and select **Cast** from the pop-up menu.

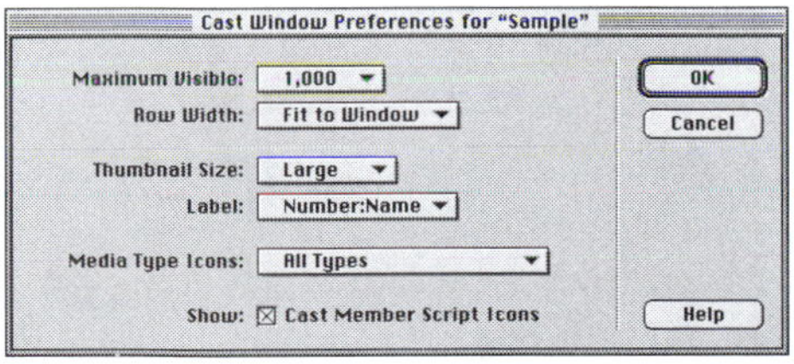

Figure 8. Use the pop-up menus in the **Cast Window Preferences** dialog box to change the appearance of a cast window.

Cast member name

Displays the name of the selected cast member assuming you have opted to assign one **(Figure 6)**. *(See page 39 for more about Cast member names)*

Open Script button

Click the Open Script button to open a script window for the currently selected cast member. *(See the Interactivity through Lingo chapter on page 202 for more about scripts)*

Cast Member Properties button

Click the Cast Member Properties button to display the Cast Member Properties dialog box for the currently selected cast member (you can also press Command-I). *(See page 34 for more about the Cast Member Properties dialog box)*

Cast member number

Displays the numerical position that the currently selected cast member occupies in the cast window. Positions are numbered left to right, and row by row in the window.

To change cast window preferences:

Director allows you to control how cast windows are displayed. You can change characteristics such as row width, thumbnail size, how labels are displayed, and which media type icons are visible.

1. Activate the cast window whose preferences you wish to change by clicking it.
2. Choose Preferences from the File menu, and select Cast from the pop-up menu **(Figure 7)**.
3. Use the pop-up menus in the Cast Window Preferences dialog box to make the desired changes **(Figure 8)**.

IMPORTING CAST MEMBERS

If you want your Director movie to incorporate graphics or sounds that have already been created in some other application (for instance, a background created in Photoshop, or a set of sound effects compiled in SoundEdit Pro), you'll first have to import those elements into a cast window.

You can import the following graphics formats into a cast: BMP, GIF, JPEG, LRG (xRes), Photoshop 3.0, MacPaint, PNG, TIF, PICT, PICS, and Scrapbook formats (the last two are multiple image formats). You can also import sounds saved in the AIFF, AIFC, or System 7 formats, Apple QuickTime movies, Director casts, color palettes, text saved as plain text or in the rich text (RTF) format, and other Director movies.

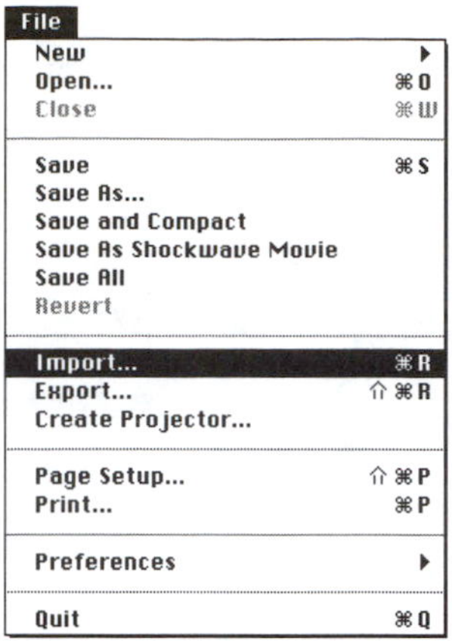

Figure 9. Choose **Import** from Director's **File** menu.

To import a cast member:

1. Choose Import from Director's File menu (or press Command-R on the keyboard) **(Figure 9).**
2. In the Import dialog box, use the Show pop-up menu to indicate what kind of cast member you'd like to import **(Figures 10–11).** Only files in this selected format are displayed in the dialog box.
3. Use the Folders pop-up menu to navigate through your hard drive's file folders, and open the folder that contains the cast member you wish to import.
4. Click the desired cast member file, and then click the Add button to add it to the list of cast members you wish to import. Click the Add All button to add all the displayed cast member files to the list. Click the Import button to bring the added cast member(s) into the currently selected cast window.

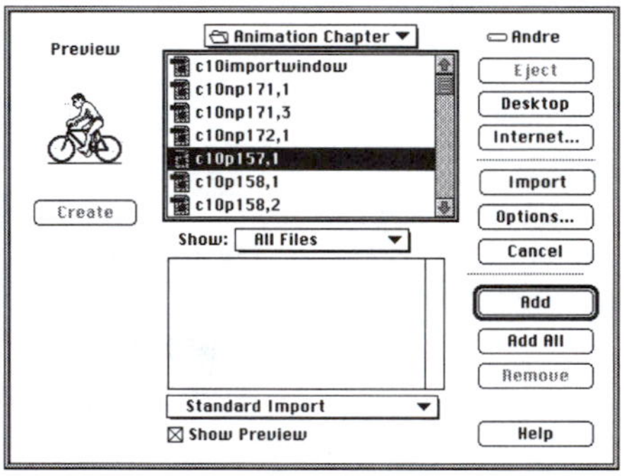

Figure 10. The **Import** dialog box.

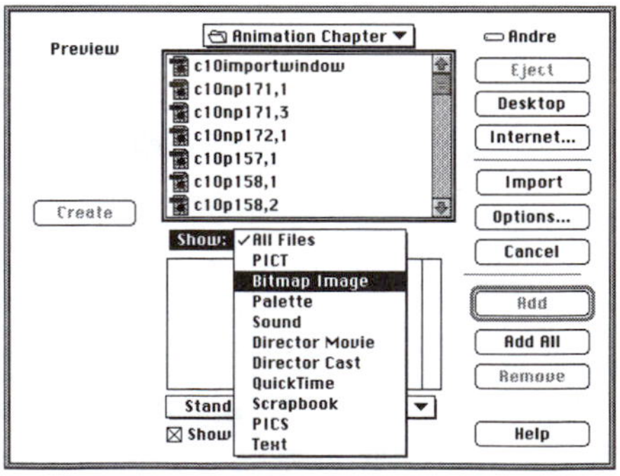

Figure 11. Use the **Show** pop-up menu to select a cast member type.

Importing Scrapbook or PICS files:

When importing Scrapbook or PICS files, Director allows you to set several options in the Import Options dialog box **(Figure 12)**. Open this box by clicking the Options button in the Import dialog box. The Range option allows you to control which frames comprising your PICS or Scrapbook file are imported. Click All Frames to import every frame in the file (each frame becomes a separate cast member) or select a specific range of frames to be imported. Checking the "Contract White Space" checkbox causes the images to be imported without any surrounding white space. The Scrapbook option lets you set whether Scrapbook images are imported in their original position, or centered in relation to other artwork in the sequence.

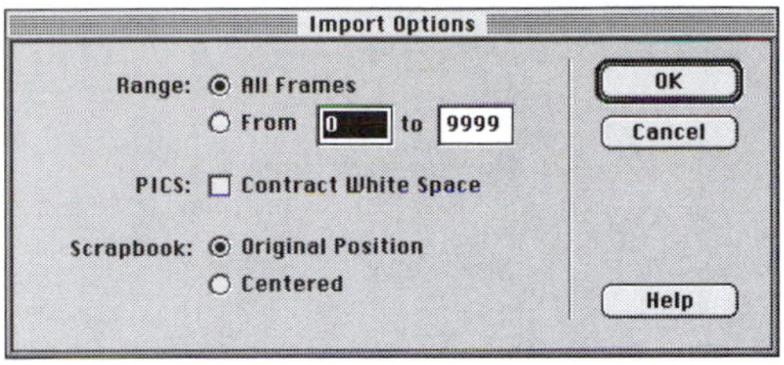

Figure 12. When importing a Scrapbook or PICS file, Director allows you to set several options in the **Import Options** dialog box.

Image options for bitmap cast members:

When you import a bitmap cast member with a color depth or palette different than the current movie's, an Image Options dialog box appears, which allows you to set color depth and palette attributes **(Figure 13)**.

The Color Depth option sets the desired color depth for the cast member. If you wish to import the image at its original color depth, click the Image option. Click the Stage option to import the image at the movie's color depth. (*See page 140 in the Color in Director chapter for details on movie color depth*)

The Palette option allows you to either import the image's original color palette (where it becomes installed as a cast member), or to remap the image to one of the currently available palettes in Director. By installing the cast member's palette into the cast window, you can ensure that the cast member will maintain its original colors when its palette is active.

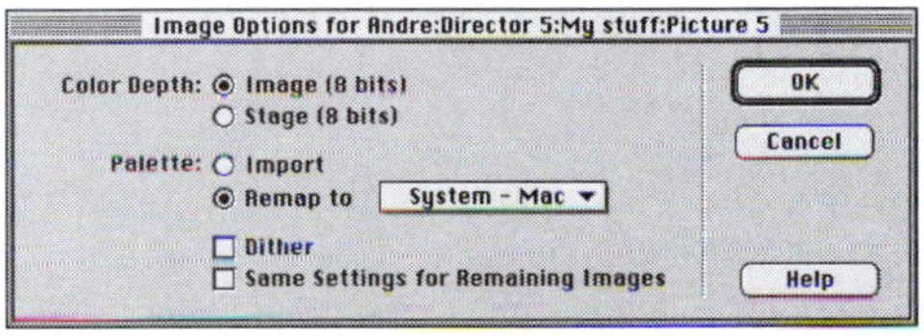

Figure 13. The **Image Options** dialog box allows you to set color depth and palette attributes for imported graphical cast members.

"Remap to" causes Director to replace the image's colors with the most similar colors from the palette you select in the pop-up menu.

Set the "Same Settings for Remaining Images" option if you wish to apply the same settings to all the files you have selected for importing.

Linking to a file:

When you import a cast member file, Director actually copies the contents of that file into your movie, thus increasing its size. You can avoid this when you import PICT, sound, or Director movie files by linking to those files. Do so by choosing the Link to External File option in the pop-up menu at the bottom of the Import dialog box **(Figure 14)**. Not only does this approach keep your movie from bloating up in size, but it also means that if you ever change that linked cast member (for instance, if you use SoundEdit Pro to alter a sound file after it's been imported), Director will automatically reflect that change, and the updated cast member won't have to be imported again. Also different movies can share the same linked files.

The drawback to linking to cast member files is that those files must always be on hand when you play your movie. If Director cannot find a linked file, it will ask you to locate any missing files before going on.

Note: Director always links to QuickTime files (digital videos) when they are imported.

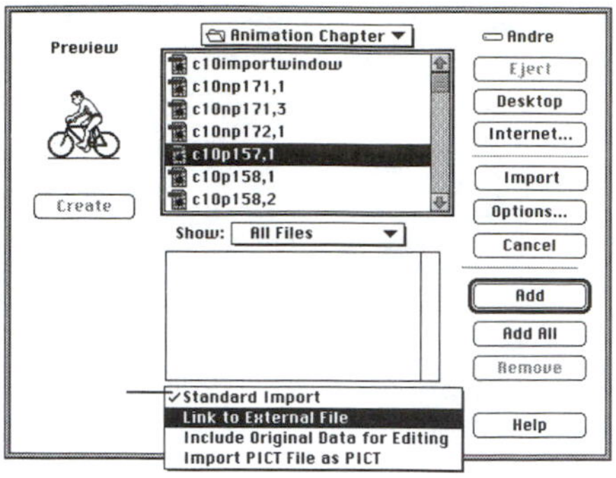

Figure 14. Choose **Link to External File** from the pop-up menu in the **Import** dialog box.

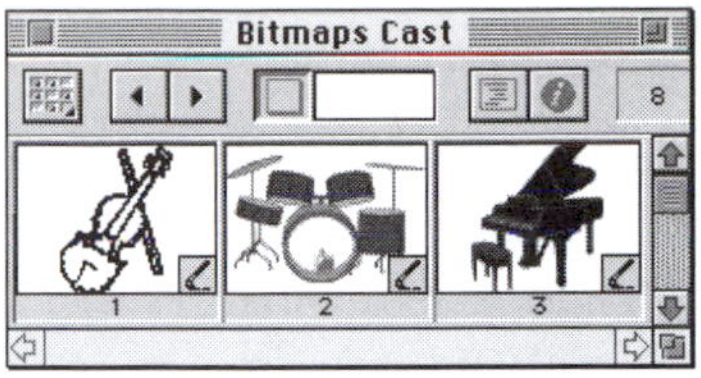

Figure 15. A cast window, organized to hold bitmaps.

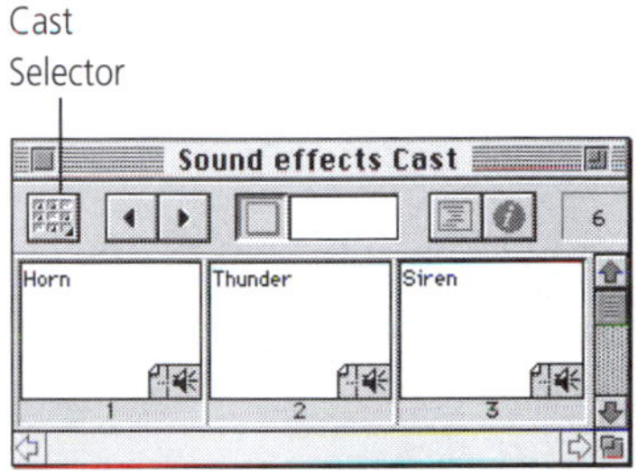

Figure 16. A cast window, organized to hold sounds.

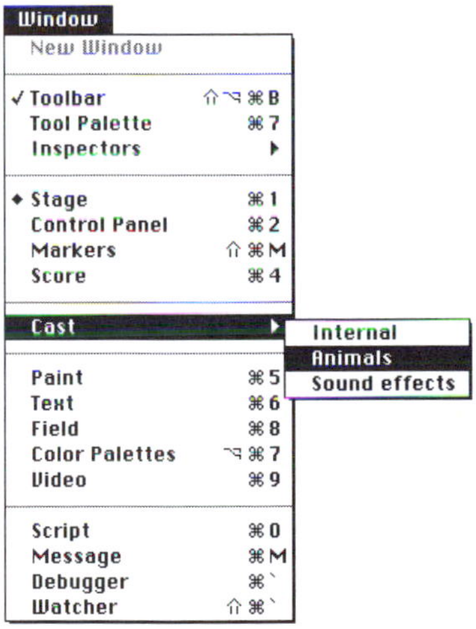

Figure 17. Choose **Cast** from the **Window** menu. If multiple casts are being used, select the cast you wish to view from the pop-up menu.

MULTIPLE CASTS

Director 6 supports the use of multiple casts in your movies. If your movie involves a large number of cast members, it is helpful from an organizational standpoint to group together related cast members into separate casts. For example, you may choose to create two casts, one for storing bitmaps, and the other for sounds. Each cast is viewed in its own separate cast window **(Figures 15–16)**.

To open a specific cast window:

1. Choose Cast from the Window menu, and select the cast you wish to view from the pop-up menu **(Figure 17)**.

✔ Tip

■ You can also use the Cast Selector **(Figure 16)** to choose which cast is displayed in the current cast window.

Internal and External Casts

Casts in Director 6 are either internal or external. You can add as many internal or external casts as you wish to your movie. Director 6 automatically creates an **internal** cast for a new movie. Internal casts cannot be shared between Director movies. When you save your movie, all internal casts are automatically saved in the movie file. Internal casts are also stored directly in Projector files.

The advantage of using **external** casts is that they can be shared between Director movies. External casts are stored in separate files outside of the movie file. In order to incorporate cast members from an external cast in your movie, the external cast must first be linked to the movie (*see page 30*). After you link an external cast to the current movie, Director automatically opens that cast whenever you open that movie.

To create a new cast:

You can add as many internal or external casts as you wish to your movie.

1. Choose New from the File menu, and select Cast from the pop-up menu **(Figure 18)**.
2. In the New Cast dialog box, choose internal or external for the cast storage type by clicking the appropriate radio button **(Figure 19)**. If the cast is external, check the "Use in Current Movie" checkbox if you want the cast linked to the current movie.
3. Type a name for the cast in the text box.
4. Click the Create button.

✓ **Tip**

- You can also create a new cast by clicking the Cast Selector in a cast window, and selecting New Cast from the pop-up menu.

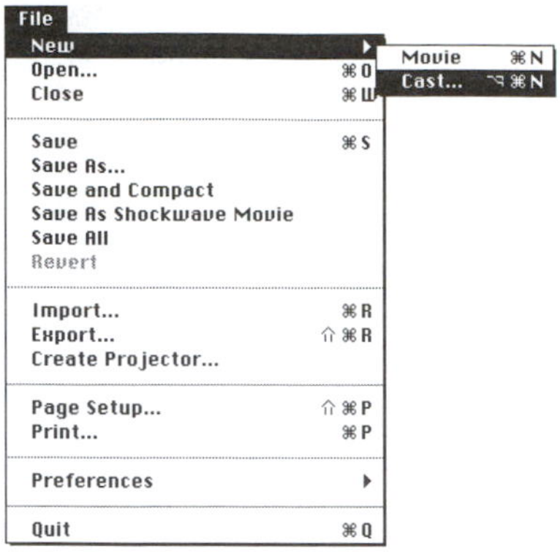

Figure 18. Choose **New** from the **File** menu, and select **Cast** from the pop-up menu.

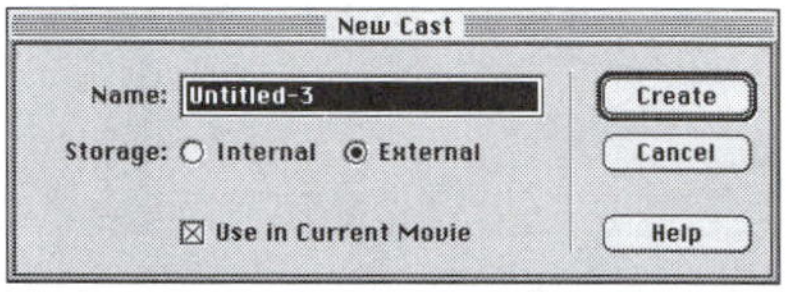

Figure 19. In the **New Cast** dialog box, choose internal or external for the cast storage type, and enter a name for the new cast.

To open an external cast:

External casts which are not linked to the current movie must be opened separately to access their cast members.

1. Choose Open from the File menu.
2. Select the external cast file you wish to open.
3. Click Open. The external cast is placed in its own cast window.

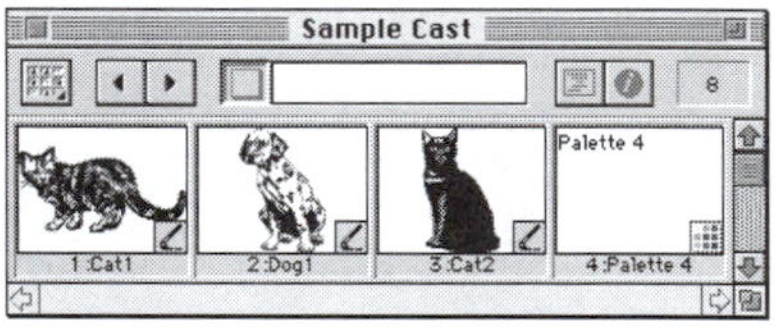

Figure 20. Activate the external cast that you wish to save by clicking its window.

To save an external cast:

1. Activate the external cast that you wish to save by clicking its window **(Figure 20)**.
2. Choose Save As from the File menu **(Figure 21)**.
3. Type a file name for the external cast and click Save.

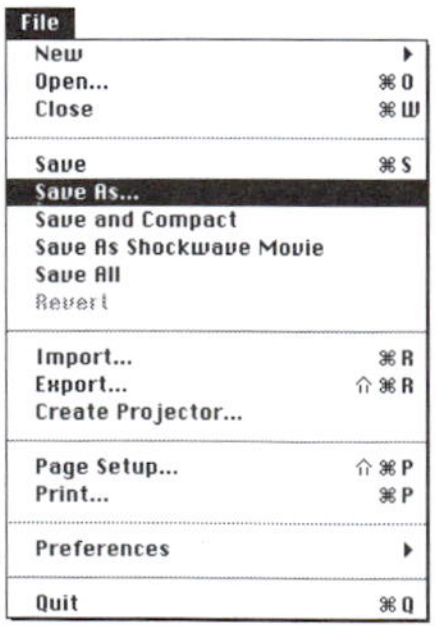

Figure 21. Choose **Save As** from Director's **File** menu.

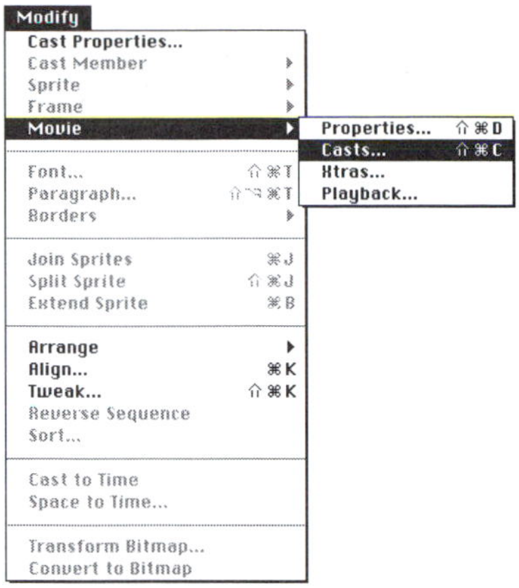

Figure 22. Choose **Movie** from the **Modify** menu, and select **Casts** from the pop-up menu.

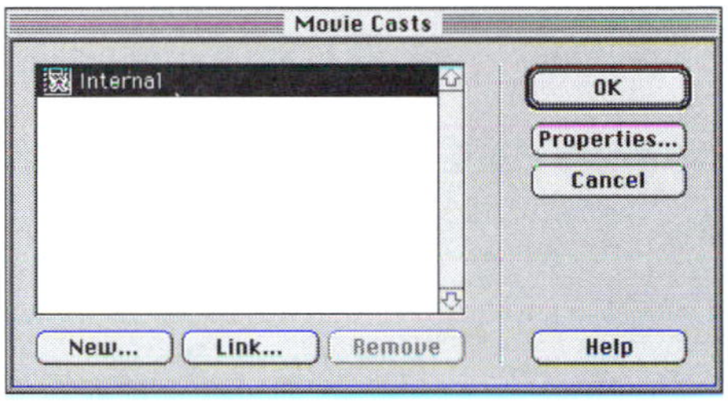

Figure 23. Click the **Link** button in the **Movie Casts** dialog box and select the external cast you wish to link to the current movie.

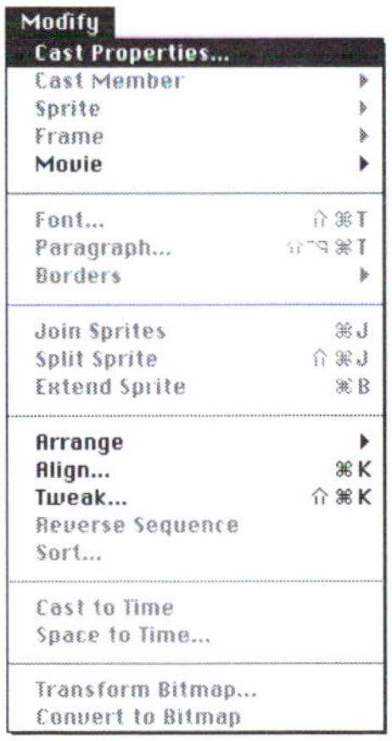

Figure 24. Choose **Cast Properties** from the **Modify** menu.

To link an external cast to the current movie:

1. Choose Movie from the Modify menu, and select Casts from the pop-up menu **(Figure 22)**.
2. Click the Link button in the Movie Casts dialog box **(Figure 23)**.
3. Select the External cast file you wish to link to the current movie.
4. Click OK.

To change and view properties of a cast:

Use the Cast Properties command to view and change settings for the currently selected cast. These settings include name, storage type (whether the cast is internal or external), size in kilobytes, and Preload (which determines when the cast is loaded into memory).

1. Activate the cast whose properties you wish to view or change by clicking in its window.
2. Choose Cast Properties from the Modify menu **(Figure 24)** to open the Cast Properties dialog box **(Figure 25)**.

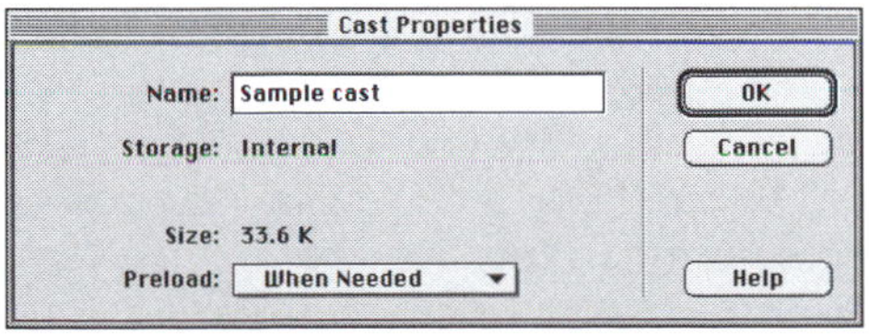

Figure 25. Use the **Cast Properties** dialog box to view and change settings for the currently selected cast.

MANAGING CAST MEMBERS

To get (and set) Cast Member Properties:

The Cast Member Properties command provides a variety of information regarding each cast member in your movie. For instance, you can use the Cast Member Properties command to find out how much memory a sound effect requires or what color palette is assigned to a cast member. Cast Member Properties also allows you to control a variety of cast member settings. You can turn on or off an accompanying sound in a film loop cast member or a linked movie. For a digital video cast member (which is a QuickTime movie), you can specify the frame rate at which the video plays. You can also use the Cast Member Properties command to determine how Director will manage all your cast members within the memory limitations of your Macintosh.

1. From a cast window, select the cast member whose properties you wish to see.
2. Choose Cast Member from the Modify menu and select Properties from the pop-up menu **(Figure 26)**. You can also click the Cast Member Properties button in a cast window.
3. The Cast Member Properties dialog box appears. The dialog box differs depending on the type of cast member you've selected—for instance, a bitmap graphic, a sound effect, a color palette, or a QuickTime movie **(Figures 27–28)**. This dialog box offers key information about the selected cast member, and lets you specify a variety of settings that control the cast member's behavior.
4. Click OK to save any settings you may have made to the cast member.

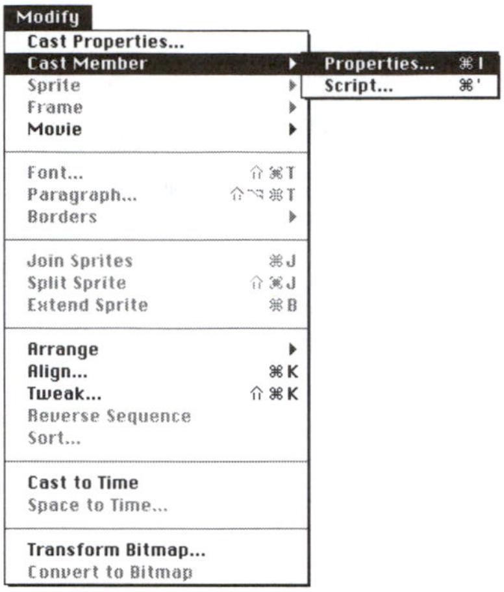

Figure 26. Choose **Cast Member** from the **Modify** menu and select **Properties** from the pop-up menu.

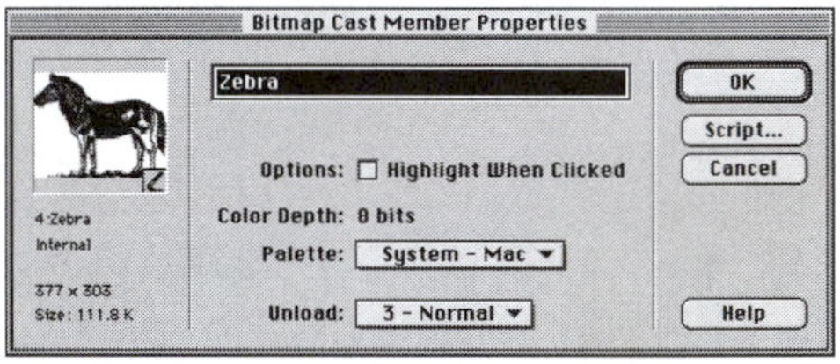

Figure 27. Cast Member Properties dialog box for a bitmap cast member.

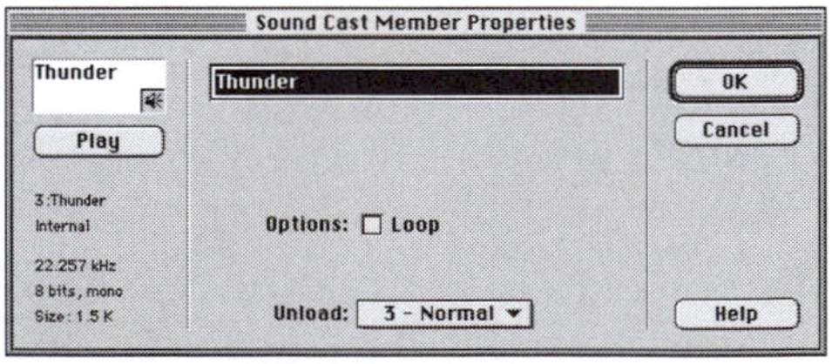

Figure 28. Cast Member Properties dialog box for a sound.

Unload setting

Director allows you to set the following Unload values in the Cast Member Properties dialog box:

3 (Normal) Cast member is purged from memory as necessary.

2 (Next) Cast member is among the next group to be purged from memory.

1 (Last) Cast member is among the last group to be purged from memory.

0 (Never) Cast member is never purged from memory.

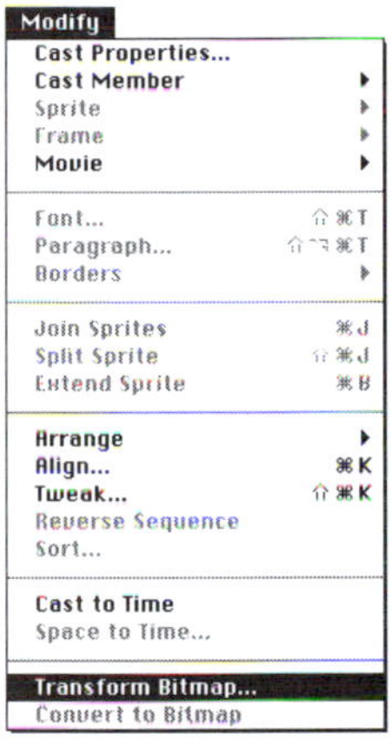

Figure 29. Choose **Transform Bitmap** from the **Modify** menu.

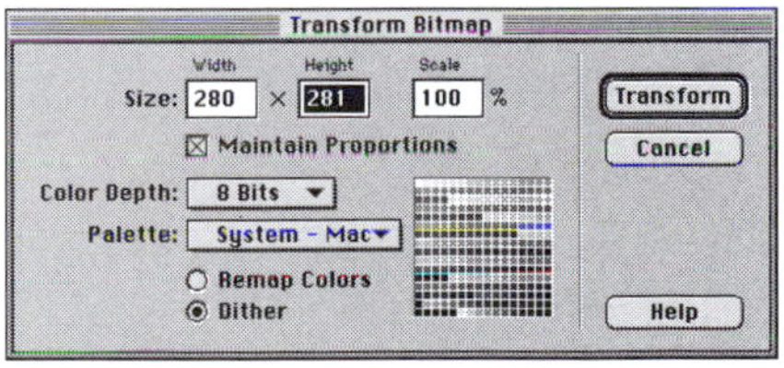

Figure 30. Change a cast member's size by entering new Width and Height dimensions, or a Scale percentage in the **Transform Bitmap** dialog box.

Note: The Cast Member Properties dialog box allows you to set the **Unload value** for the selected cast member. If your Macintosh begins to run low on memory while playing your movie, Director tries to purge certain cast members from RAM to free more memory. If a purged cast member is required again, Director must load it back into memory from your hard disk, which can delay your movie's playback for a moment. For this reason, you can manually set the Unload value for individual cast members, telling Director which cast members are least important to your movie and can be purged first in case memory is low, and which are really key and should not be purged at all.

To change a bitmap cast member's size:

1. From a cast window, select the bitmap cast member whose size you wish to change.
2. Choose Transform Bitmap from the Modify menu **(Figure 29)**.
3. In the Transform Bitmap dialog box, click the Width and Height fields and type in new values **(Figure 30)**. Check the Maintain Proportions option to maintain the cast member's original proportions, or enter a value in the Scale box to proportionately size your cast member.

Note: You cannot undo any changes made to a cast member using the Transform Bitmap command. Make sure you have a duplicate of the original cast member before making any changes.

Note: The Transform Bitmap command is also used to change a cast member's color depth, and the color palette it uses to display its colors. *(See the Color in Director chapter on page 139 for details on color depth and color palettes)*

To duplicate a cast member in a cast window:

Being able to duplicate a cast member is useful for a couple of reasons: If you wish to create a number of cast members that make up an animation sequence, you can base each distinctive frame on duplicates of one or more cast members, making minor changes to each duplicate. Also, if you wish to make changes to a cast member's color palette, it's a good idea to try your ideas on a duplicate. If you don't like the results, you can always go back to the original version.

1. From a cast window, click the cast member that you wish to duplicate **(Figure 31)**.
2. Choose Duplicate from the Edit menu **(Figure 32)**. Director places a copy of the selected cast member in the next available position in the cast window.

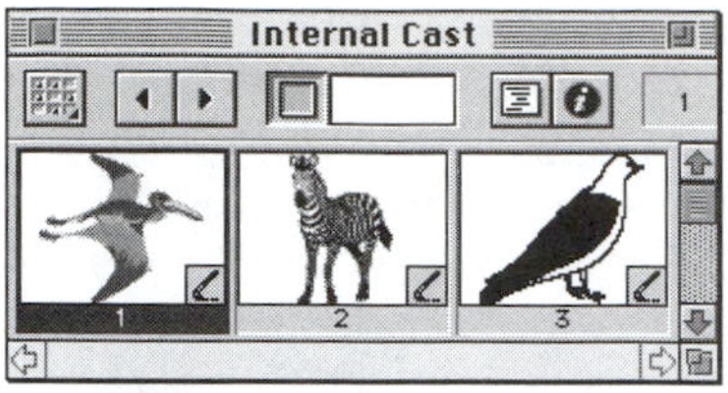

Figure 31. Click the cast member you wish to duplicate.

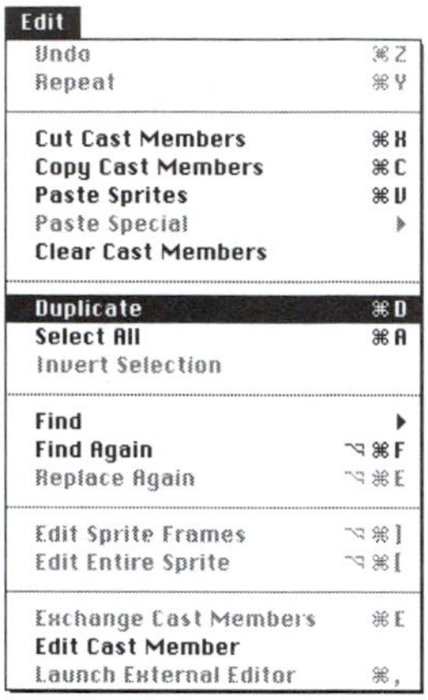

Figure 32. Choose **Duplicate** from the **Edit** menu.

✓ Tip

- You can also create a duplicate cast member by using the Copy and Paste commands under the Edit menu, and also by dragging a cast member in a cast window to a new location while holding the Option key.

To delete a cast member from a cast window:

1. In a cast window, click the cast member you wish to delete. Shift-click to select a range of cast members or hold down Command and click to select multiple non-adjacent cast members.
2. Choose Clear Cast Members from Director's Edit menu to remove the cast member(s) **(Figure 33)**. Even if the cast member has already been assigned to the score, it will no longer appear when you play your movie.

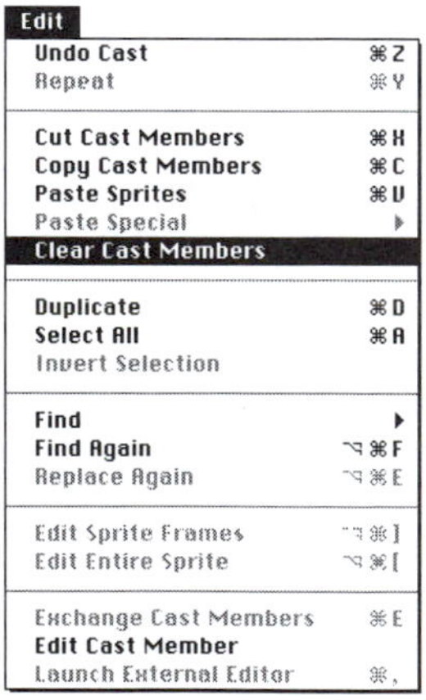

Figure 33. Choose **Clear Cast Members** from the **Edit** menu.

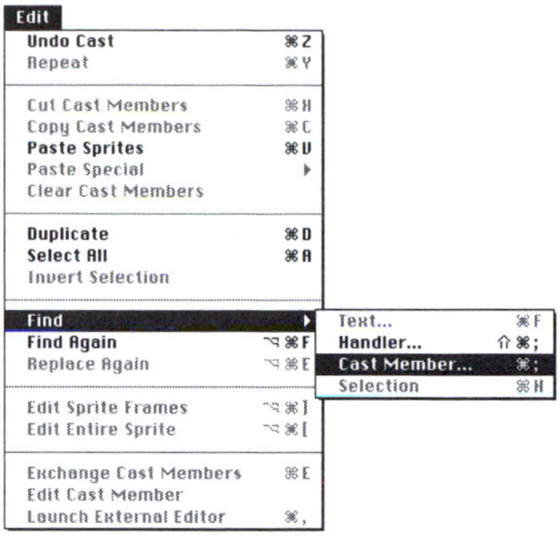

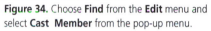

Figure 34. Choose **Find** from the **Edit** menu and select **Cast Member** from the pop-up menu.

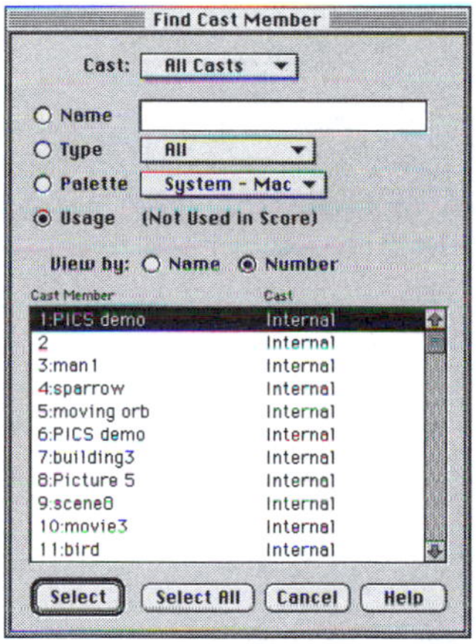

Figure 35. Click the fourth radio button in the **Find Cast Member** dialog box to find cast members not used in the score.

To delete cast members not used in the score:

You may find that you've imported a number of cast members into your movie that you never ended up using and want to delete. Director can find and delete them for you. Deleting unused cast members is wise since it frees memory.

1. Choose Find from Director's Edit menu and select Cast Member from the pop-up menu **(Figure 34)**.
2. Use the Cast pop-up menu in the Find Cast Member dialog box to select the cast whose unused cast members you wish to delete **(Figure 35)**.
3. Click the radio button labeled Usage **(Figure 35)**.
4. Click the Select All button and Director finds and selects all unused cast members in the selected cast. You may first need to click in the list to make the buttons selectable.
5. Choose Clear Cast Members from the Edit menu.

Note: Cast members may be incorporated into your movie by way of Lingo scripts, in which case certain cast members would not necessarily appear in the score. So before deleting the cast members that Director finds, make sure that they are not used in any scripts.

✔ Tip

- Once you've deleted a series of cast members, save your movie by using the Save and Compact command under the File menu. This operation reorders the cast and produces a more compact movie file as well as optimizing movie playback.

To reposition cast members in a cast window:

In some cases it's preferable to place all related cast members together in a cast window. For instance, suppose that you are building an animation sequence of a trotting horse. If you place the first frame of the animation in position 1 of a cast window, you'll want to place the next frame in position 2, the next in position 3, and so on **(Figure 36)**. Placing related cast members together is not only efficient from an organizational standpoint, but also helpful for creating film loop cast members.

Director makes it easy to reorder cast members within a cast window by dragging them from one position to another.

1. From a cast window, click to select the cast member you wish to reposition **(Figure 37).** You can Shift-click to choose multiple adjacent cast members or hold the Command key to select multiple non-adjacent cast members.
2. Drag the selected cast member (or one cast member in a multiple selection) to a new position in the cast window **(Figure 38)**.
3. Release the mouse button to place the cast member in its new location. If you were dragging multiple cast members, they will be positioned sequentially from that point.

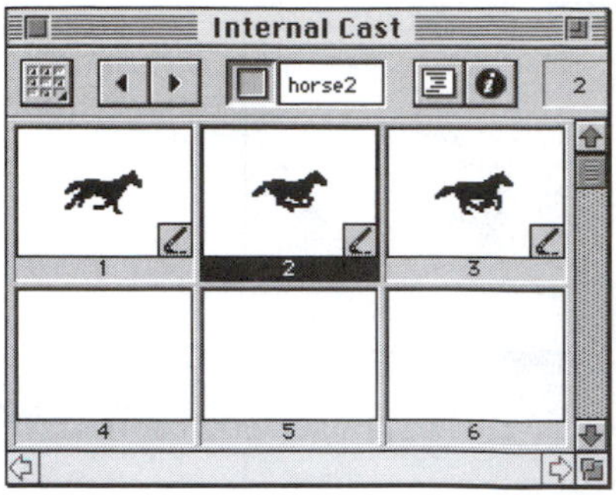

Figure 36. Related cast members, such as multiple frames in an animation, should be placed side by side in a cast window.

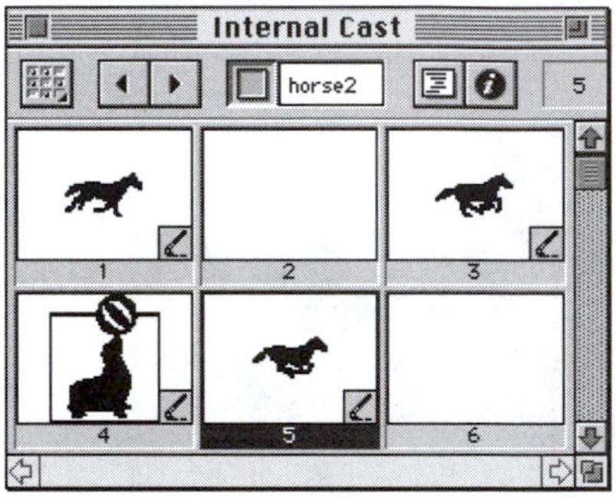

Figure 37. Click the cast member, such as the horse in position 5.

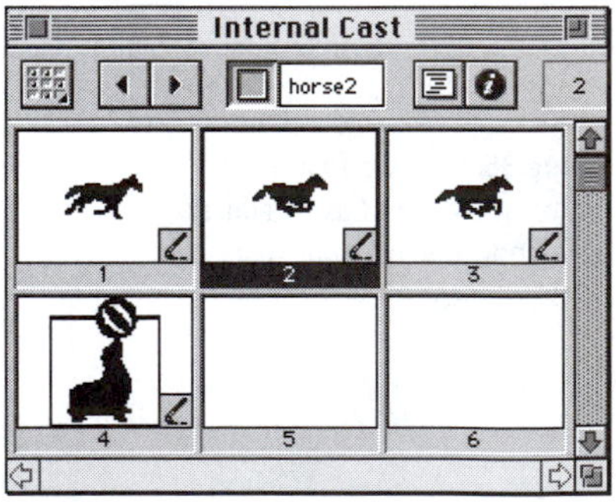

Figure 38. Drag the selected cast member to its new location and release the mouse button.

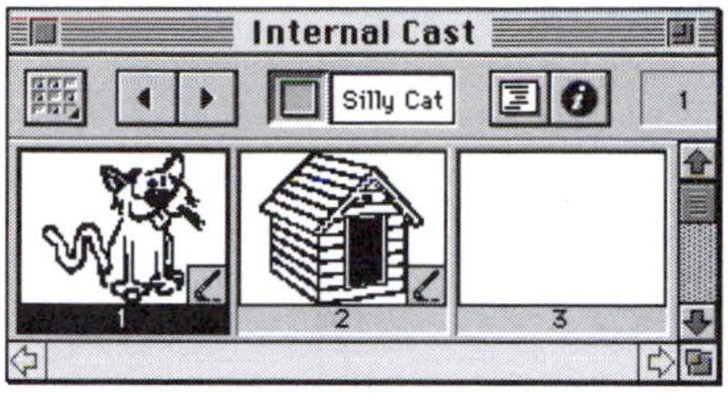

Figure 39. Select the cast member you wish to name.

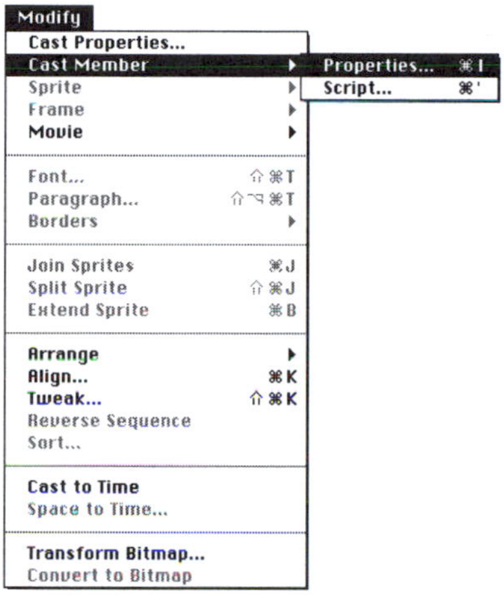

Figure 40. Choose **Cast Member** from the **Modify** menu and select **Properties** from the pop-up menu.

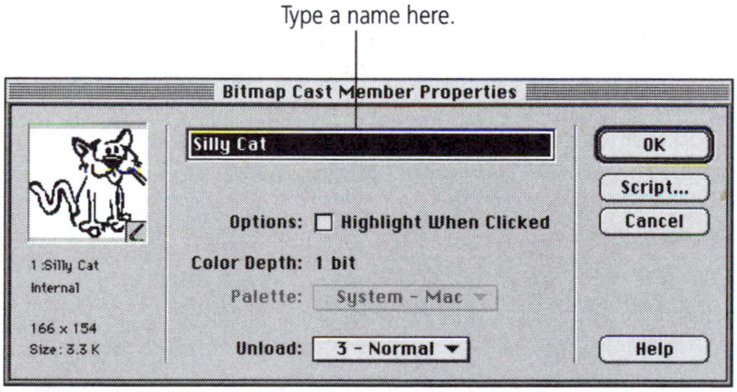

Figure 41. Enter a name in the **Cast Member Properties** dialog box.

To name a cast member in the cast window:

You can give cast members descriptive names (such as Sunset, Bird, Man 1, and Man 2) so that they're easier to find and manage in the cast window and throughout your entire movie.

1. In a cast window, click to select the cast member that you wish to name **(Figure 39)**.
2. Choose Cast Member from the Modify menu and choose Properties from the pop-up menu **(Figure 40)**.
3. In the Cast Member Properties dialog box, type the name you wish to assign the selected cast member **(Figure 41)**.
4. Click OK.

✔ **Tip**

- You can also enter a name for a selected cast member directly at the top of its cast window.

To find a cast member by its name:

If your movie contains a large number of cast members, it can become tedious to search through the casts to find one cast member out of potentially hundreds. If you've named your cast member, however, Director can find it for you automatically. It can also find a range of cast members that share common elements in their names, such as Man 1, Man 2, and Man 3.

1. Choose Find from Director's Edit menu and select Cast Member from the pop-up menu **(Figure 42)**.
2. In the Find Cast Member dialog box **(Figure 43)**, select which cast you wish to search from the Cast pop-up menu.
3. In the Find Cast Member dialog box, click the first radio button labeled "Name".
4. In the adjacent text box, type the name of the cast member(s) you'd like to find. You may type the name partially to find multiple cast members with similar names. For instance, you'd type "Man" to find cast members Man 1, Man 2, and so on.
5. Click Select and Director finds and selects the first cast member with a matching name in the specified cast. Click Select All if you wish to select all cast members with matching names. If the Select and Select All buttons are unselectable for some reason, click a cast member in the Find Cast Member dialog box list to make them selectable.

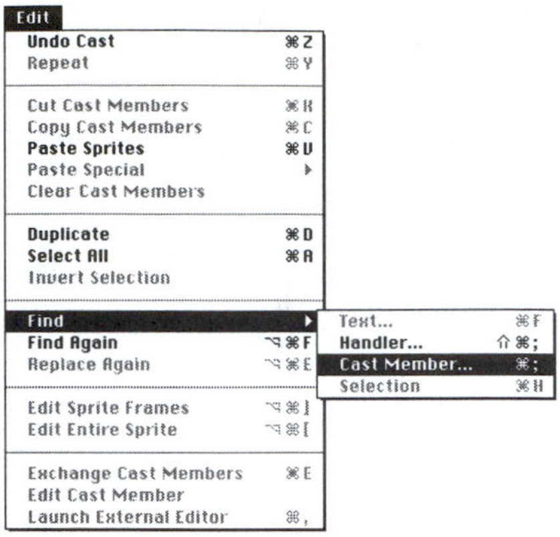

Figure 42. Choose **Find** from the **Edit** menu and select **Cast Member** from the pop-up menu.

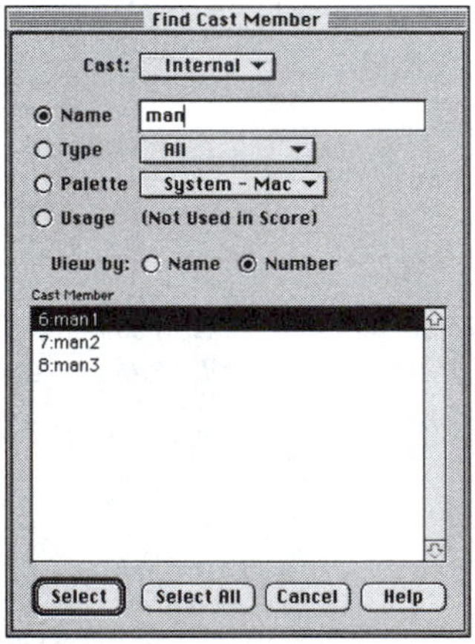

Figure 43. In the **Find Cast Member** dialog box, click the **Name** radio button and type a cast member name in the adjacent text box for the cast member you want to find.

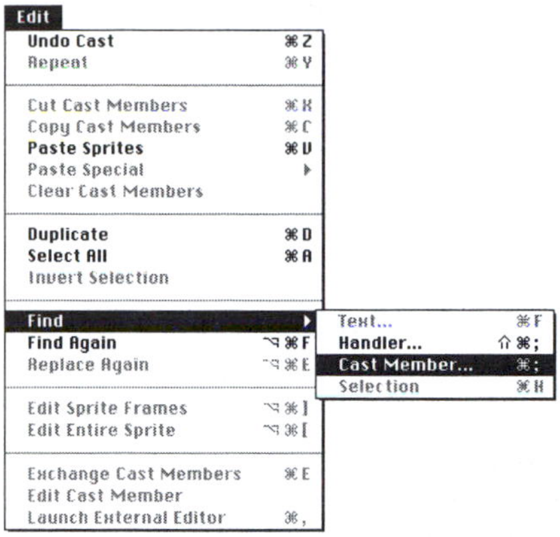

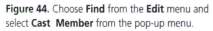

Figure 44. Choose **Find** from the **Edit** menu and select **Cast Member** from the pop-up menu.

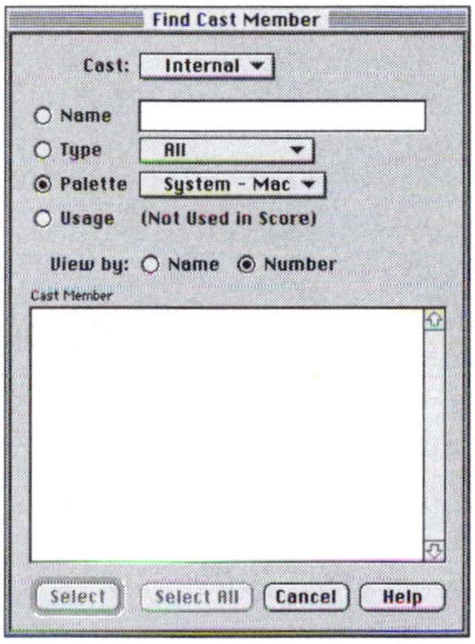

Figure 45. In the **Find Cast Member** dialog box, click the third option and choose a palette to search by from the pop-up menu.

To find a cast member by its color palette:

You can search and find cast members in your casts by the color palette they use. This is useful if you have a number of cast members that are mapped to one particular color palette, but must eventually be remapped to another one.

1. Choose Find from Director's Edit menu and choose Cast Member from the pop-up menu **(Figure 44)**.
2. In the Find Cast Member dialog box, select which cast you wish to search from the Cast pop-up menu.
3. In the Find Cast Member dialog box, click the third radio button and use the adjacent pop-up menu to select the palette used by the cast members you wish to find **(Figure 45)**.
4. Click the Select All button and Director finds and selects all the appropriate cast members in the specified cast. If the Select and Select All buttons are unselectable for some reason, click a cast member in the Find Cast Member dialog box list to make them selectable.

To sort cast members in a cast window:

Director can sort cast members by name, type, size, and the order in which they appear in your score. Being able to sort cast members is a great way to keep a large, unwieldy cast well organized. When Director sorts cast members, it also removes gaps in the cast window where you have cut or relocated earlier cast members.

1. Activate the cast window that you wish to sort.
2. Choose Select All from Director's Edit menu **(Figure 46)**.
3. Choose Sort from the Modify menu **(Figure 47)**.
4. In the Sort dialog box, select the method of sorting you wish to use **(Figure 48)**.
5. Click Sort.

✔ **Tip**

- When you sort a cast window, most or all cast members will be reassigned position numbers based on their new location in the window. However, if you have created Lingo scripts that refer to those cast members by number, rather than name, your scripts will no longer be able to find the proper cast members. To avoid this, refer to cast members by name in your scripts.

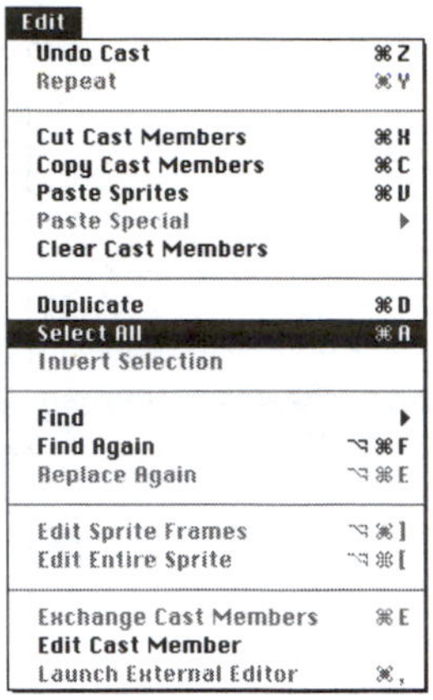

Figure 46. Choose **Select All** from the **Edit** menu.

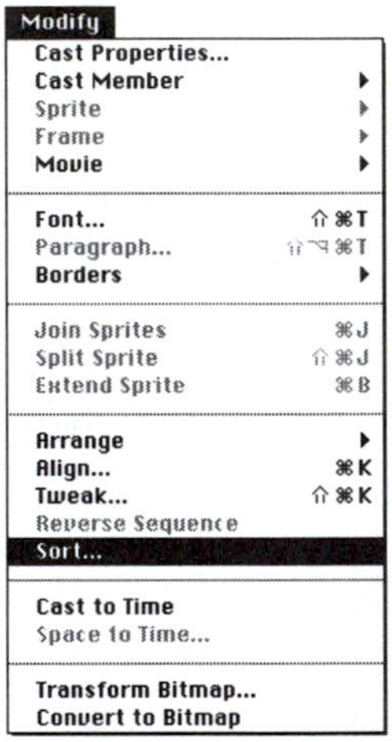

Figure 47. Choose **Sort** from the **Modify** menu.

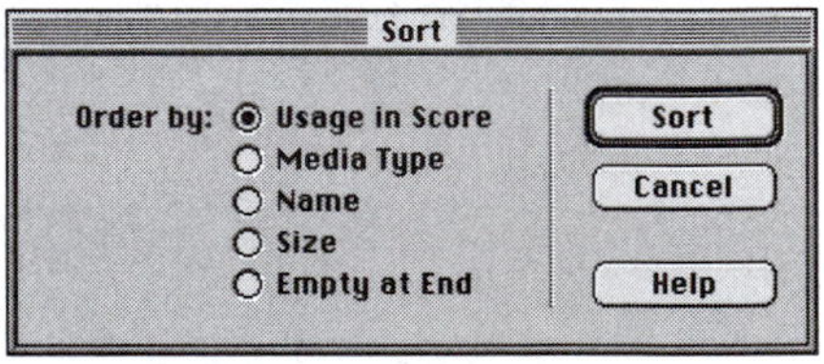

Figure 48. Select the method of sorting you wish to use.

4 SCORE AND SPRITE BASICS

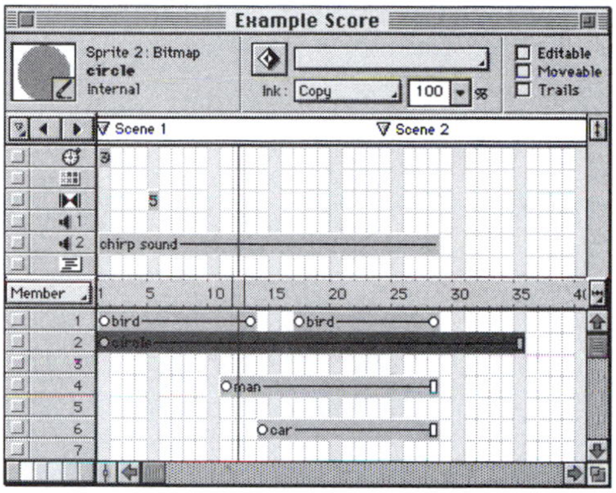

Figure 1. The score window provides a frame-by-frame record of all the components that form your Director movie.

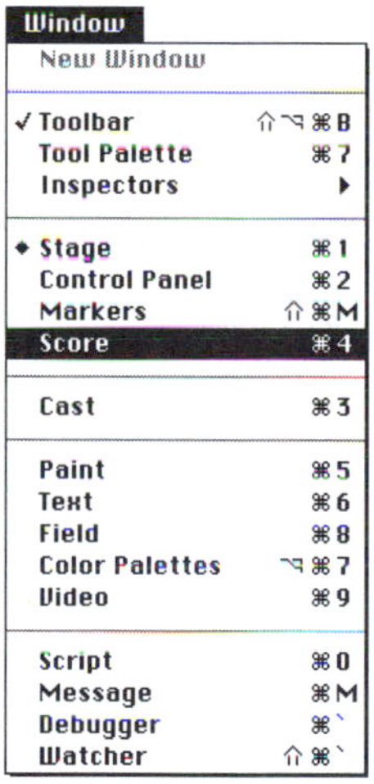

Figure 2. Choose **Score** from the **Window** menu.

Director's score **(Figure 1)** is similar to the script of a Hollywood movie. It describes what your cast members should do and when they should do it on the stage which is where your movie plays out. It usually takes up the full dimensions of your Macintosh's screen, and it can be seen in the background behind Director's cast, score, and other windows.

A Director movie is assembled by placing cast members (such as graphics and sounds) and events (such as visual transitions and tempo changes) into various frames of the score, which represent various segments of time in your Director movie.

Cast members placed into the score are represented by objects called sprites. A **sprite** consists of a cast member and a set of properties and behaviors that direct how, when, and where the cast member appears in your movie. *(See page 46 for more details on sprites)*

You open the score window by choosing Score from the Window menu, or by pressing Command-4 **(Figure 2)**.

This chapter explains the basics of working with sprites in the score—knowledge that is essential for building a Director movie. You will learn how to create sprites, edit their properties, and manipulate them in the score and on the stage. You will also learn about the various score window viewing features (such as zooming, viewing multiple scores, and displaying and changing the contents of sprite labels).

Frames

The first thing to know about the score is that it is divided into small segments of time called **frames**. Each frame forms a column of cells, and the frames are arranged horizontally across the score in sequential order **(Figure 3)**. Frames are numbered in the center of the score window. There's no limit to the number of frames you can have in a movie.

Frames in Director are just like the frames you find on a strip of celluloid film—each provides the opportunity to change or continue the action taking place in the movie. For instance, a sound effect may begin playing at frame 1 but stop playing at frame 15. In an animation sequence, frame 1 might feature a cast member graphic on the left-most side of the stage. In frame 2, however, that cast member might move a little toward the right. It will appear to move even farther in frame 3, and so on. When a sequence of frames is played in rapid succession, **animation** occurs. How quickly Director plays the frames of a movie is known as **tempo**, which you can set in frames per second. *(See page 189 in the Movie Tempo chp)*

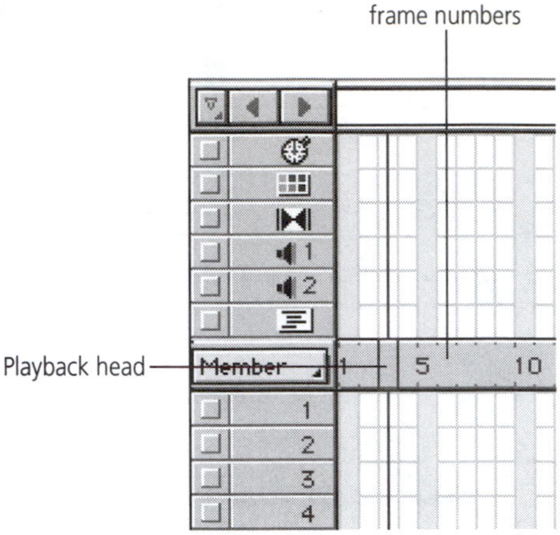

Figure 3. Each frame forms a column of cells, and the frames are arranged horizontally across the score window in sequential order.

Playback head

The position of the **playback head** in the score indicates which frame is currently displayed on the stage **(Figure 3)**. You can move the playback head by dragging it to any frame in the score, or by just clicking in a frame.

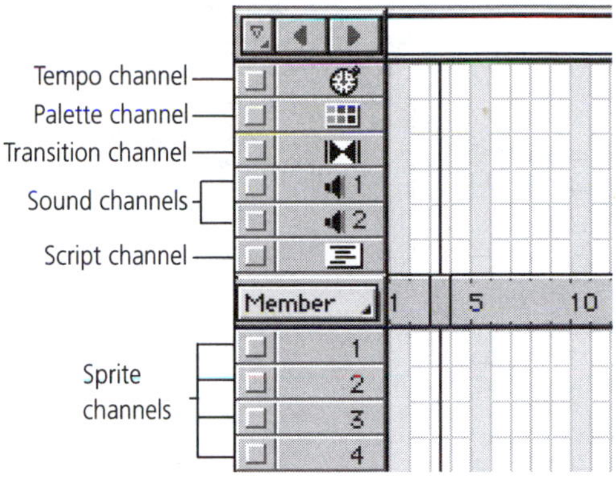

Figure 4. Score channels run vertically along the left side of the score window. Each channel forms a row of cells.

Score channels

A large number of events can occur in any frame of Director's score. For instance, several cast member graphics can appear, a sound effect or two can play, and a transition to a new color palette can begin. You manage and direct these elements and events by placing each of them into a **channel** of the score.

Director's channels run vertically along the left side of the score **(Figure 4)**. Each channel forms its own row of cells extending through the frames. The first five channels at the top of the score are called the **effects channels** (tempo, palette, transition, and sound 1 & 2).

The following is a description of all of the channels available in the score:

- The tempo channel allows you to set the speed at which Director plays your entire movie, or just a sequence of frames *(see page 189 in the Movie Tempo chapter)*.
- The palette channel allows you to set the color palette used to display your movie *(see page 145 in the Color in Director chapter)*.
- The transition channel allows you to set video transition effects between scenes such as dissolves or wipes *(see page 187 in the Setting Scene Transitions chapter)*.
- Two sound channels allow you to incorporate sound effects, musical scores, and voice tracks *(see page 179 in the Sound in Director chapter)*.
- The script channel allows you to incorporate Lingo scripts, which are used to add interactive features to your movie *(see page 214 in the Lingo and Interactivity chapter)*.
- 120 sprite channels are used to animate your cast member graphics.

SPRITE BASICS

A **sprite** is an object which consists of a cast member and a set of properties and behaviors. These properties and behaviors determine how, where, and when a cast member appears in your movie.

You work with sprites in two main environments: the score and the stage. In the score, each sprite is represented by a **sprite span (Figure 5)** that you place over a range of frames to indicate when the sprite appears during your movie. On the stage, a sprite is represented by the image of its cast member graphic, which you can position and resize **(Figure 6)** to indicate how and where the sprite should appear in the frames of your movie.

You animate a sprite by changing its properties (such as position, size, or blend percentage) on a frame-by-frame basis *(these techniques are covered in the Animating Sprites chapter on page 69)*. Doing so does not alter the cast member on which the sprite is based **(Figure 7)**. You can create many sprites in your movie based on the same cast member.

Behaviors are special cast members which can be assigned to sprites to add interactive features *(see page 227 for details on Behaviors)*.

The term *sprite* usually refers to a graphical cast member in the score but can refer to any other type of cast member placed into the score, such as a sound or a transition **(Figure 8)**. In the latter case, the sprite does not have a graphic counterpart on the stage. Throughout the rest of this chapter, *sprites* refer to graphical cast members placed into the score.

The first frame of a sprite is a keyframe **(Figure 5)** which is indicated by a circle. A **keyframe** is where a tweenable property of a sprite changes *(see page 69 for an explanation of tweening)*. The end frame of a sprite is indicated by a square.

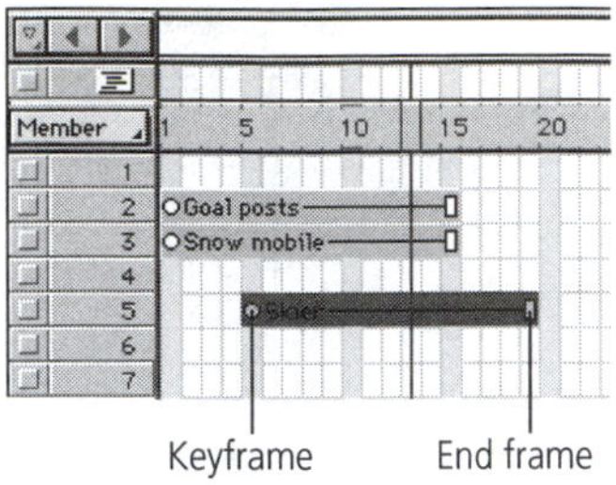

Figure 5. In the score, each sprite is represented by a sprite span.

Figure 6. On the stage, a sprite is represented by the image of its cast member graphic, which you can position and resize.

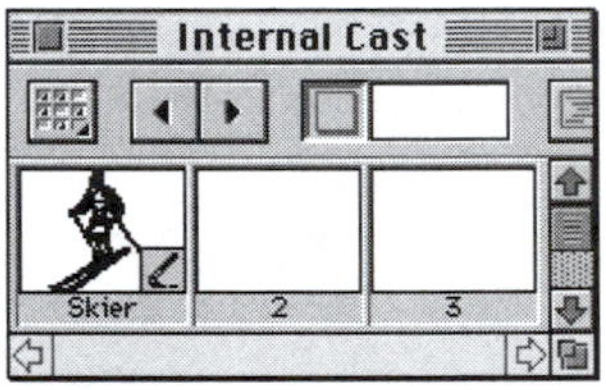

Figure 7. Changing the properties of a sprite does not alter the original cast member on which the sprite is based.

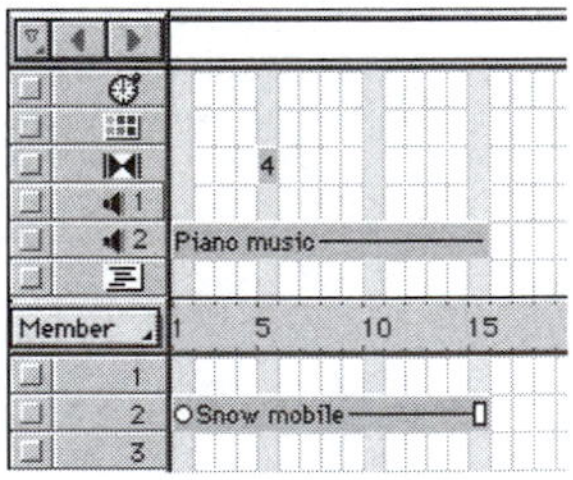

Figure 8. Sprites usually are graphical cast members placed in the sprite channels in the score, but the term can refer to any other type of cast member placed in the score, such as a sound or transition.

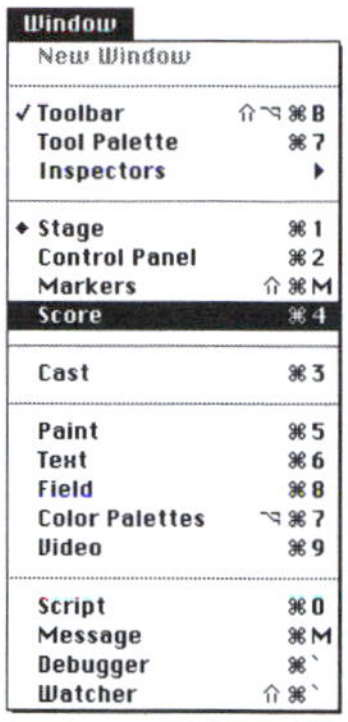

Figure 9. Choose **Score** from the **Window** menu.

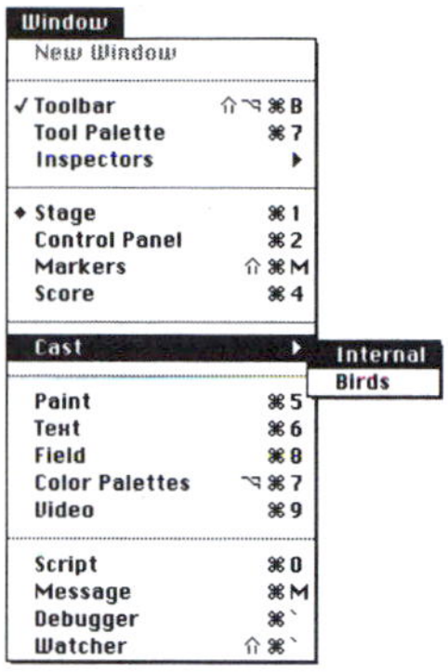

Figure 10. Choose **Cast** from the **Window** menu.

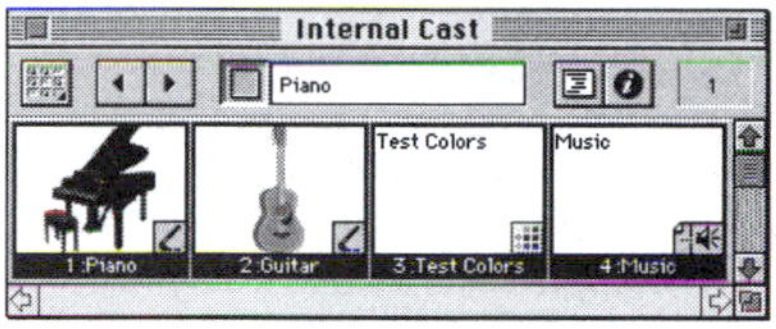

Figure 11. In a cast window, select the cast member(s) you wish to place in the score. Cast members 1–4 are selected here.

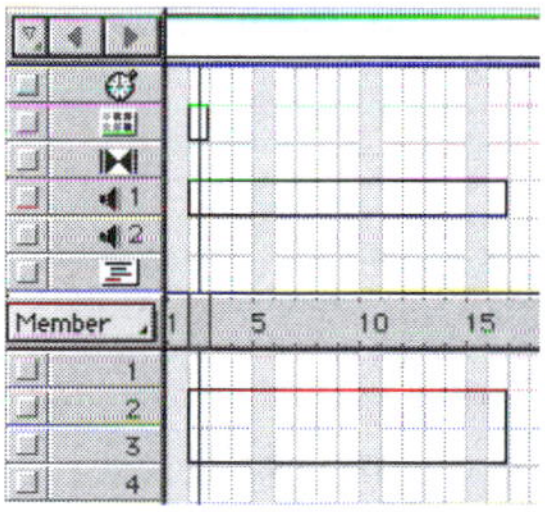

Figure 12. As you drag a cast member selection into the score, Director outlines the range of cells where sprites will be created.

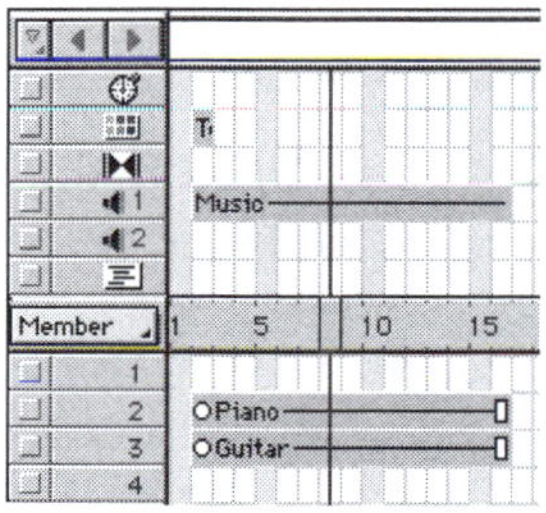

Figure 13. Drag your cast member selection to the stage. Your new sprites appear in the score.

To create a sprite:

You create a sprite as soon as you place a cast member into the score. You can do this by dragging it from a cast window to particular cells in the score window, or from a cast window to Director's stage. This is a key step in creating any Director movie.

1. Open the score by choosing Score from the Window menu **(Figure 9)**.
2. Open a cast window by choosing Cast from the Window menu and selecting the appropriate cast from the pop-up menu **(Figure 10)**.
3. In the cast window, click the cast member that you wish to place into the score. If you wish to place multiple cast members, select them together by Shift-clicking **(Figure 11)**. Command-click to select multiple discontinuous cast members.
4. Drag your cast member selection from the cast window to a cell in the score. As you drag, Director outlines the range of cells where sprites will be created **(Figure 12)**. Director outlines only cells that will accommodate your cast members (for instance, sounds can be dragged only to cells in the sound channels). When you release the mouse button, any graphical cast members which are part of your cast member selection appear in the center of the stage as sprites.

or

4. In the score window, click the location where you wish to create and place your sprites.
5. Drag your cast member selection from the cast window to the stage. Your new sprites appear in the score window **(Figure 13)**. Graphical cast members that are part of your selection also appear on the stage as sprites at the location to which they were dragged.

To change the default sprite span duration:

Each new sprite you create has a default duration of 28 frames, called the **span duration**. You can change this duration as follows:

1. Choose Preferences from the File menu and select Sprite from the pop-up menu **(Figure 14)**.
2. In the Sprite Preferences dialog box, enter a value for the Span Duration option **(Figure 15)**. If you want new sprites to span the width of the score, click the Width of Score Window radio button. Click the Terminate at Markers option if you want new sprites to end two frames before the next marker.

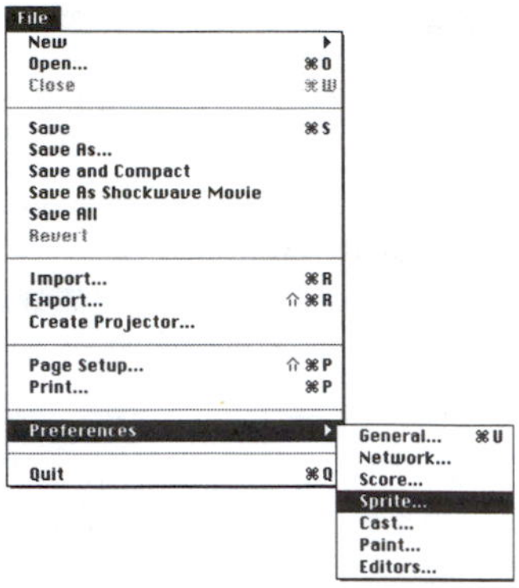

Figure 14. Choose **Preferences** from the **File** menu and select **Sprite** from the pop-up menu.

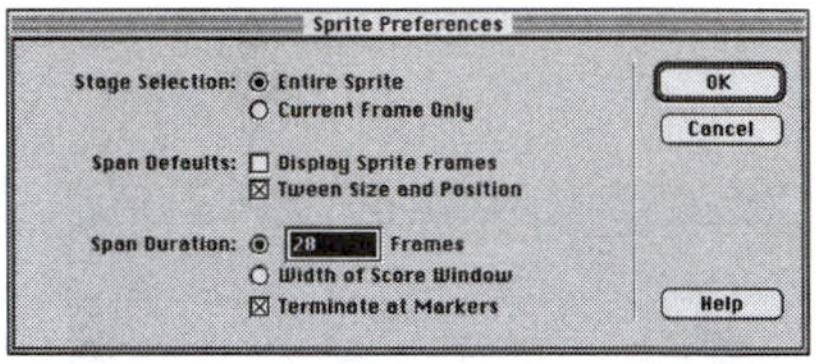

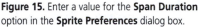

Figure 15. Enter a value for the **Span Duration** option in the **Sprite Preferences** dialog box.

Selecting a sprite

There are several different ways of selecting a sprite in the score. When you wish to select an entire sprite **(Figure 16)**, click the horizontal line within its span to select all of its frames (don't click a keyframe or the end frame). You can also select the entire sprite by clicking the sprite on the stage. When an entire sprite is selected, any changes you make to its properties affect all of its frames.

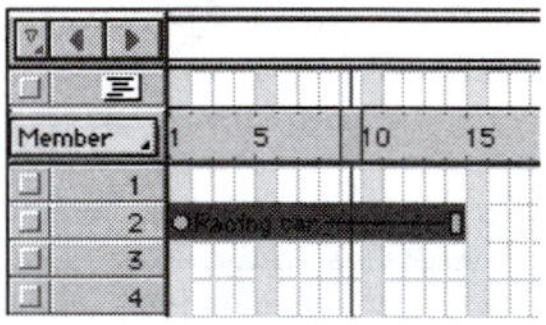

Figure 16. Click the horizontal line within a sprite span to select the entire sprite.

You can select an individual frame within a sprite by Option-clicking a frame in its span **(Figure 17)**, or by Option-clicking the sprite on the stage *(see page 51 for more details on editing sprite frames)*. If the single frame you wish to select is a keyframe or end frame, simply click that frame in the score without Option-clicking. You can select multiple discontinuous frames in a sprite by Command-Option clicking. Shift-Option click to select a continuous range of frames.

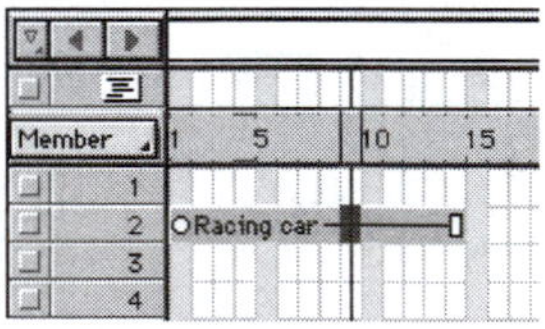

Figure 17. Select an individual frame within a sprite by Option-clicking the desired frame.

✔ Tip

- You can select a continuous range of sprites in the score by clicking the first sprite, then Shift-clicking the last sprite **(Figure 18)**. Command-click to select multiple discontinuous sprites.

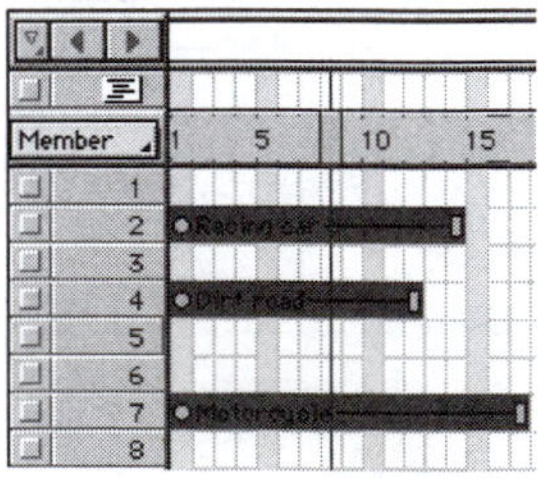

Figure 18. Shift-click to select a continuous range of sprites in the score. Command-click to select multiple discontinuous sprites.

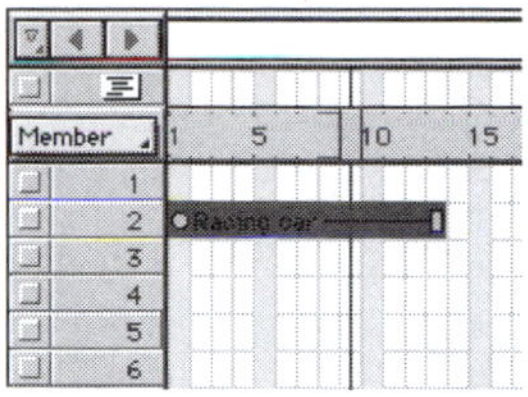

Figure 19. Select the sprite you wish to move by clicking within its span.

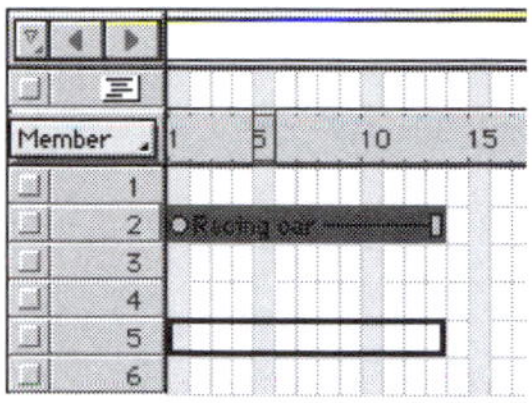

Figure 20. Drag the selected sprite to a new frame and/or channel in the score to reposition it.

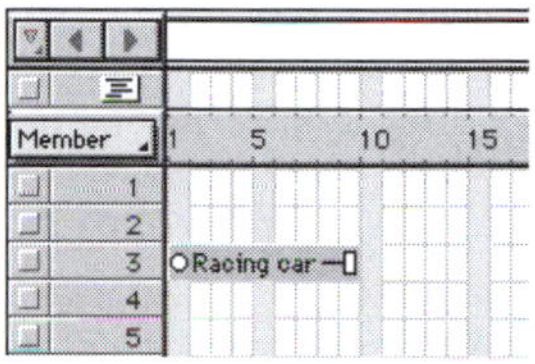

Figure 21. You can drag either the start or end frame to shorten or lengthen a sprite.

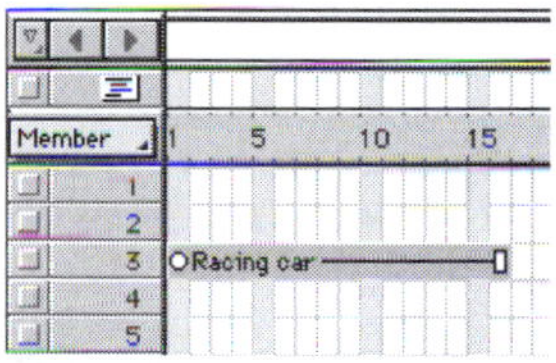

Figure 22. The end frame has been dragged here to lengthen the sprite.

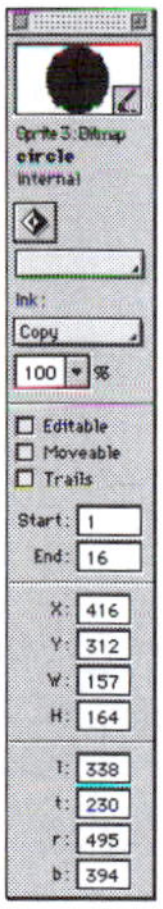

Figure 23. You can change a sprite's span duration by entering values into the **Start** and **End** fields in the **Sprite Inspector** window.

To reposition a sprite on the stage:

1. Choose Score from the window menu to open the score.
2. In the score, click the appropriate sprite that you wish to reposition on stage. The sprite span in the score darkens, and your sprite is highlighted on stage.
3. Drag the sprite to its new position on the stage. The sprite is repositioned to this new location throughout its entire span in the score *(see page 51 to select the individual frames of a sprite)*.

To move a sprite to a new location in the score:

1. In the score, click the sprite that you wish to move **(Figure 19)**. The mouse pointer becomes a hand.
2. Drag the selected sprite to a new frame and/or channel in the score window. Director outlines the new range of frames the sprite will occupy **(Figure 20)**.

To shorten or lengthen a sprite's span duration:

You can shorten or lengthen the span of a sprite so that it occupies any number of frames in the score.

1. Open the score window.
2. Drag either the start frame (a keyframe indicated by a circle) or the end frame (represented by a square) of a sprite to the desired frame **(Figures 21–22)**.

✔ Tip

- You can also change a sprite's span by entering the appropriate values into the Start and End fields in the Sprite Inspector window **(Figure 23)**. Open this window by choosing Inspectors from the Window menu, and Sprite from the pop-up menu.

To extend a sprite:

The Extend command under the Modify menu provides another way of altering a sprite's span duration.

1. Select the sprite in the score that you wish to extend **(Figure 24)**.
2. While the sprite is selected, click within the frame channel to indicate the frame to which you wish to extend the sprite **(Figure 25)**. The playback head is repositioned to this frame.
3. Choose Extend Sprite from the Modify menu **(Figure 26)**. If the playback head is to the right of the end frame, the sprite is extended to the right **(Figure 27)**. If the playback head is positioned in the body of the sprite, the sprite is shortened to this point. If the playback head is to the left of the sprite's start frame, the sprite is extended to the left in the score.

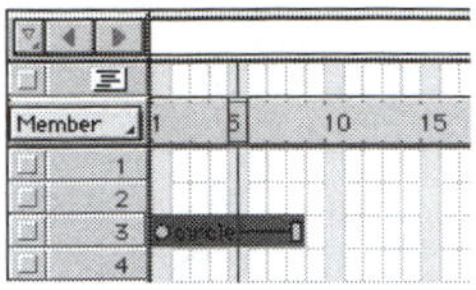

Figure 24. Select the sprite you wish to extend.

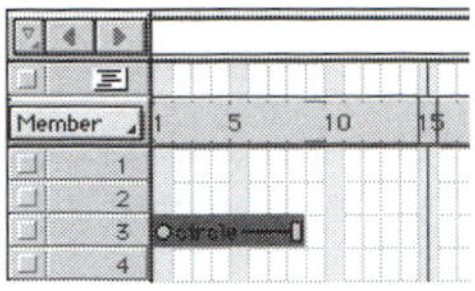

Figure 25. Click the frame within the frame channel to where you wish to extend your sprite.

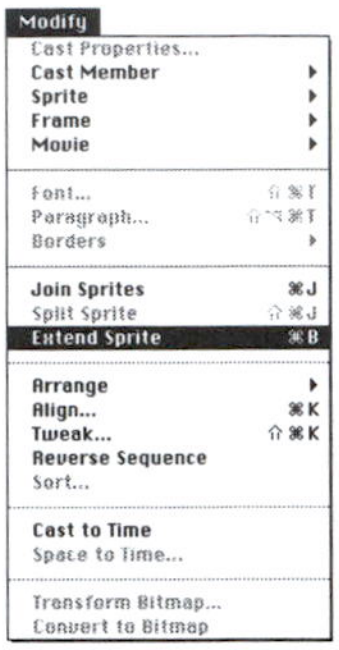

Figure 26. Choose **Extend Sprite** from the **Modify** menu.

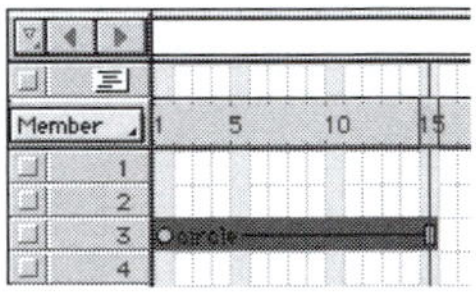

Figure 27. The sprite has been extended to the position of the playback head.

To cut and paste sprites in the score:

1. In the score, select the sprite or range of sprites you wish to cut, copy, or clear. Select a range of sprites by dragging in the score to encompass them (start from an empty cell). Select multiple discontinuous sprites by Command-clicking them.
2. Choose Cut or Copy Sprites from the Edit menu **(Figure 28)**. If you wish to delete them, choose Clear Sprites.
3. Click the cell in the score where you wish to paste your sprite selection.
4. Choose Paste Sprites from the Edit menu. If the placement of this sprite selection threatens to overwrite any existing sprites, the Paste Options dialog box appears **(Figure 30)**.

✔ **Tip**

- You can paste your sprite selection in a way that inserts it into the score rather than overwriting any data. To do this, choose Paste Special from the Edit menu and select Insert from the pop-up menu **(Figure 29)**.

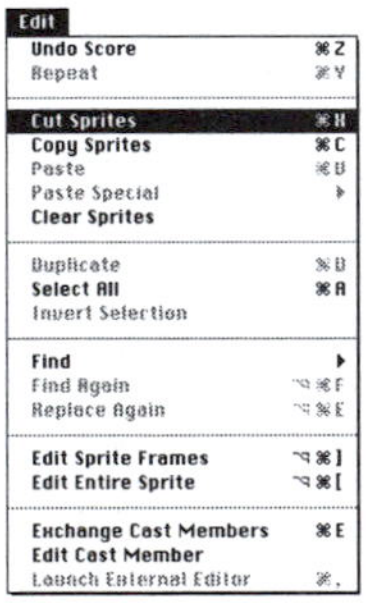

Figure 28. Choose **Cut**, **Copy**, or **Clear Sprites** from the **Edit** menu.

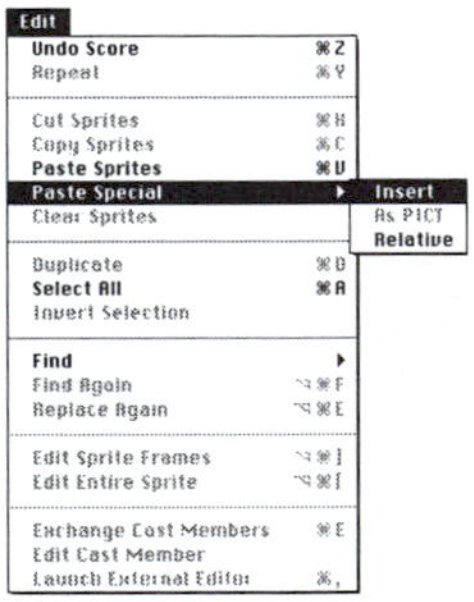

Figure 29. Choose **Paste Special** from the **Edit** menu and select **Insert** from the pop-up menu.

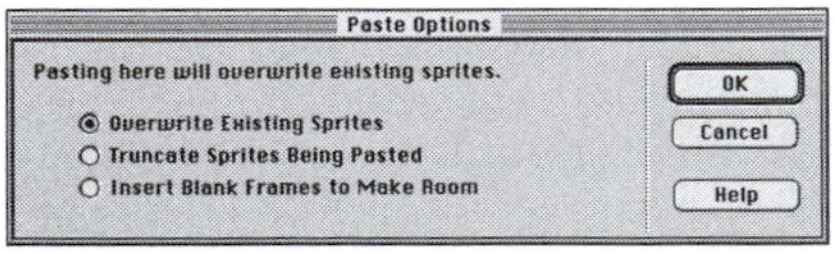

Figure 30. The **Paste Options** dialog box.

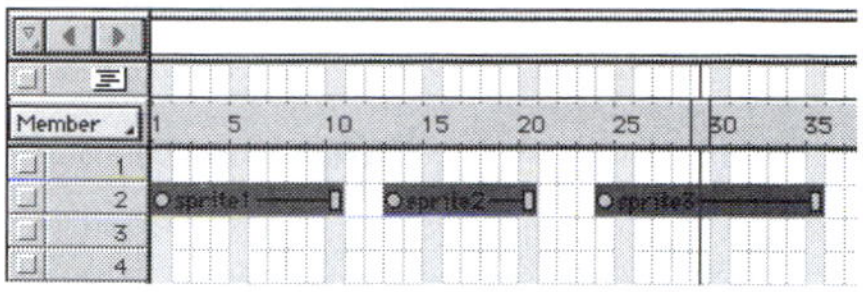

Figure 31. Select the sprites that you wish to join.

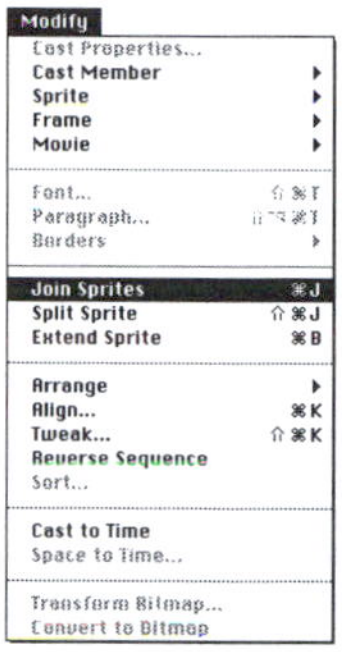

Figure 32. Choose **Join Sprites** from the **Modify** menu.

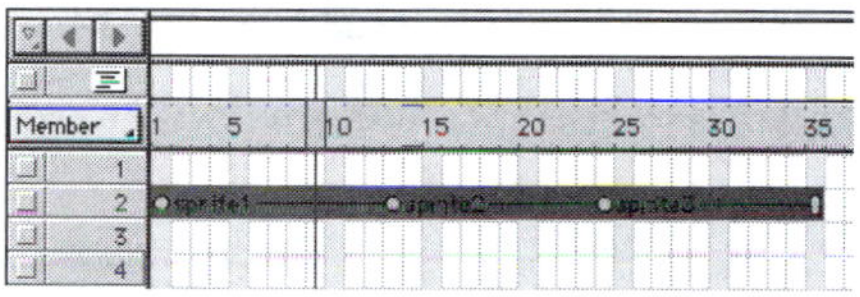

Figure 33. The sprites are joined into one sprite.

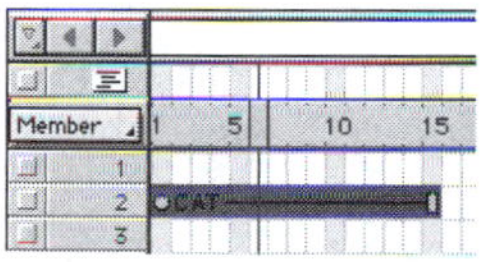

Figure 34. Click the frame within a sprite where you want a split to occur.

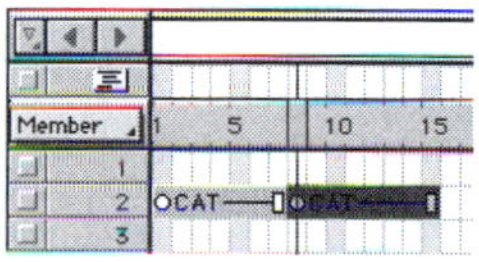

Figure 35. The sprite is divided into two sprites at the playback head location.

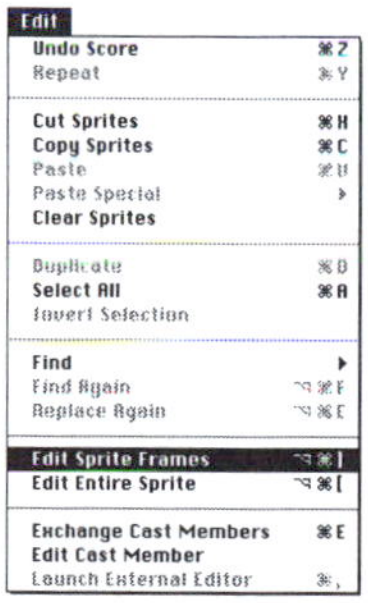

Figure 36. Choose **Edit Sprite Frames** from the **Edit** menu.

Figure 37. Choose **Edit Entire Sprite** from the **Edit** menu.

To join sprites:

Sometimes you may find that you need to combine two or more sprites into one. Joining sprites is useful, for example, when you have created a series of animation sequences as separate sprites, and you wish to consolidate them into one sprite.

1. Select the sprites in the score that you wish to join together. They can have gaps between them, but they must all occupy the same channel **(Figure 31)**.
2. Choose Join Sprites from the Modify menu **(Figure 32)**.

To split a sprite:

1. In the score window, click a frame within a sprite where you want a split to occur **(Figure 34)**.
2. Choose Split Sprite from the Modify menu. The sprite is divided into two new sprites at the location of the playback head **(Figure 35)**.

To edit individual sprite frames:

Normally, clicking a sprite in the score or on stage selects the entire sprite. As already discussed in this chapter *(see page 48)*, you can Option-click to select a sprite's individual frames. If you plan on frequently adjusting a sprite's properties on a frame-by-frame basis (a process which is typical when creating an animation), use the Edit Sprite Frames command under the Edit menu.

1. In the score, click to select the sprite whose individual frames you wish to edit.
2. Choose Edit Sprite Frames from the Edit menu **(Figure 36)**. Now when you click a frame within this sprite, only that single frame will be selected. Turn this feature off by selecting any frame in the sprite and choosing Edit Entire Sprite from the Edit menu **(Figure 37)**.

To insert frames in the score:

1. Click the frame in the score where you wish to insert one or more frames.
2. Choose Frames from the Insert menu **(Figure 38)**.
3. Enter the number of frames you wish to insert in the Insert Frames dialog box **(Figure 39)**. If sprites are present in the frame you selected, they are extended to the right.

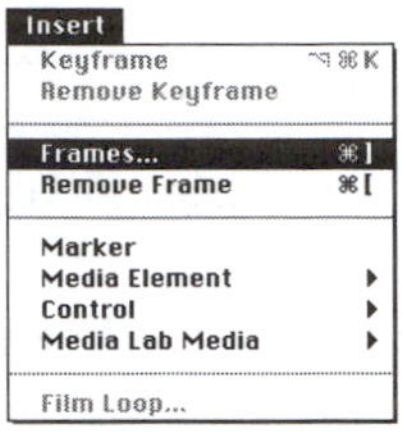

Figure 38. Choose **Frames** from the **Insert** menu.

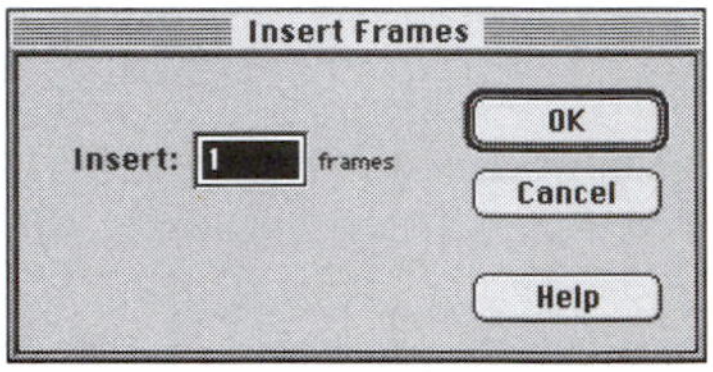

Figure 39. Enter the number of frames you wish to insert in the **Insert Frames** box.

To remove a frame from the score:

1. Click the frame you wish to remove.
2. Choose Remove Frame from the Insert menu **(Figure 40)**.

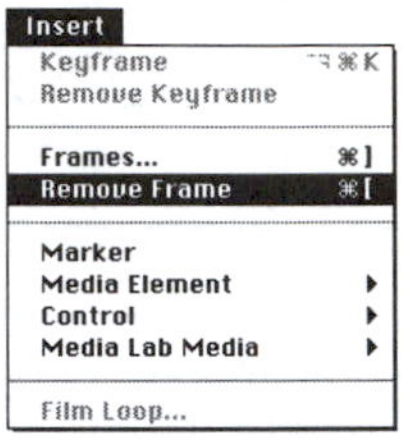

Figure 40. Choose **Remove Frame** from the **Insert** menu.

Foreground and background order of sprites

When sprites overlap on the stage, their order in the sprite channels determines which sprites appear in the foreground. Basically, sprites in higher numbered channels always appear in front of sprites in lower numbered channels (for instance, a sprite in channel 2 will appear in the background when overlapped by a sprite in channel 15). In animating a character walking down a street, for example, the character may appear to walk in front of buildings **(Figure 41)** but behind parked cars, street lamps, and signposts.

Figure 41. A sprite's foreground/background priority is determined by its order in the 120 sprite channels. Here, the sprite of the person is in the foreground, while the city sprite is in the background.

To change the foreground and background order of sprites:

1. In the score, select the sprite that you wish to move forward or backward on stage **(Figure 42)**.
2. Choose Arrange from the Modify menu and select the appropriate command from the pop-up menu. Bring to Front places the selected sprite on top of all other sprites, while Move Forward moves the sprite one step closer to the foreground. The Reverse commands accomplish the opposite.

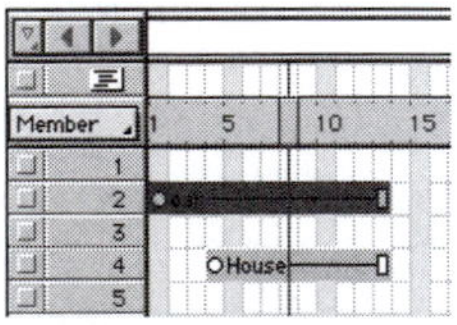

Figure 42. Select the sprite you wish to move forward or backward.

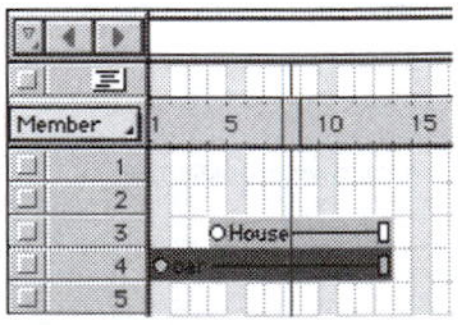

Figure 43. The selected sprite here has been placed in front of the other sprites.

Figure 44. The **Sprite Inspector**.

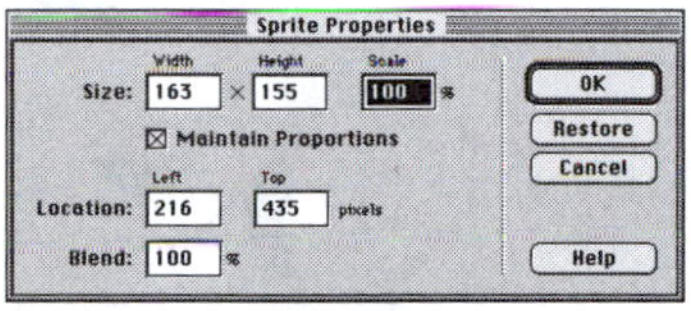

Figure 45. The **Sprite Properties** box.

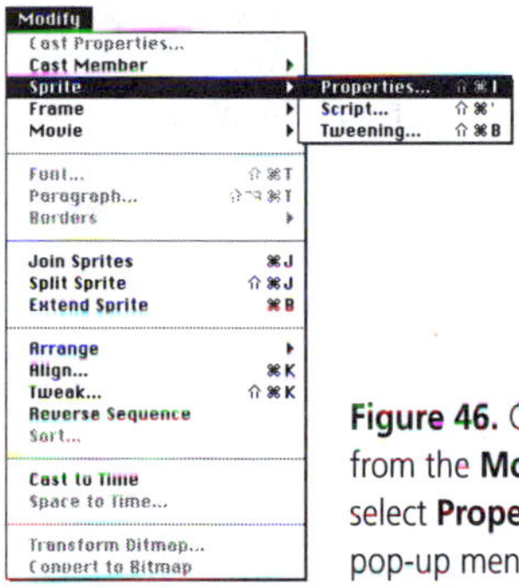

Figure 46. Choose **Sprite** from the **Modify** menu and select **Properties** from the pop-up menu.

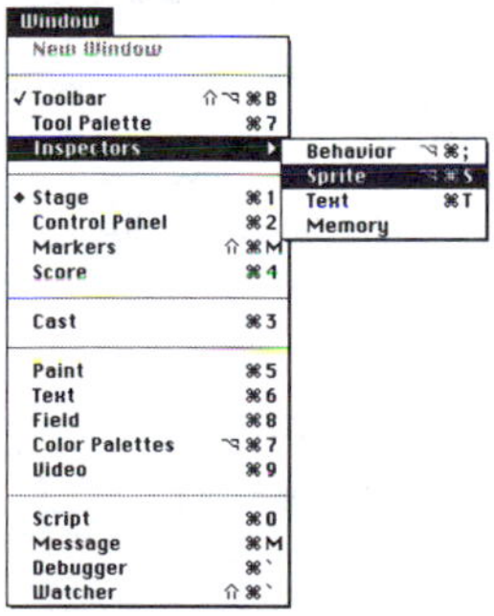

Figure 47. Choose **Inspectors** from the **Window** menu and select **Sprite** from the sub-menu.

Figure 48. Choose **Sprite Toolbar** from the **View** menu to display the sprite toolbar at the top of the score.

CHANGING SPRITE PROPERTIES

Each sprite possesses a set of properties that describe how the sprite appears in your Director movie. These properties include a sprite's stage coordinates, size, blend percentage, ink effect, and start and end frames, as well as Moveable, Editable, and Trails options. These properties can vary on a frame-by-frame basis within a sprite. For example, you can set a sprite's stage coordinates to change in each frame to make the sprite move across the stage in an animation sequence *(see the next chapter)*.

Some sprite properties, such as size and stage coordinates, can be changed by directly moving or resizing a sprite on the stage. These as well as other sprite properties can be changed by using the **Sprite Inspector (Figure 44)**, and the **Sprite Properties** dialog box **(Figure 45)**.

To open the Sprite Properties dialog box:

1. In the score, select the sprite whose properties you wish to change.
2. Choose Sprite from the Modify menu and select Properties from the pop-up menu **(Figure 46)**.

To open the Sprite Inspector window:

1. In the score, select the sprite whose properties you wish to change.
2. Choose Inspectors from the Window menu and select Sprite from the pop-up menu **(Figure 47)**.

✔ Tip

- The information in the Sprite Inspector is also visible at the top of the score when the **Sprite Toolbar** option is selected under the View menu **(Figure 48)**. You can change your sprites' properties using either interface.

To view sprite properties on the stage:

You can view the most significant sprite properties on the stage by using the Sprite Overlay command.

1. Choose Sprite Overlay from the View menu and select Show Info from the pop-up menu **(Figure 49)**. Sprite properties are displayed in a small rectangular panel **(Figure 50)** beneath a sprite.

2. You can change for which sprites the sprite overlay is displayed by choosing Sprite Overlay from the View menu and selecting Settings from the pop-up menu **(Figure 51)**. Click the Roll Over option in the Overlay Settings dialog box **(Figure 52)** for sprite properties to be displayed when the pointer rolls over a sprite on the stage. Click the Selection option for properties to be displayed for selected sprites. Or click the All Sprites option for properties to be displayed for all sprites on the stage.

✓ **Tip**

- Click the small icons on the left side of a Sprite Overlay panel to edit the sprite properties **(Figure 50)**. Click the first icon to open the Cast Member Properties dialog box. Click the second icon to open the Sprite Properties dialog box, and the last one to open the Behavior Inspector window.

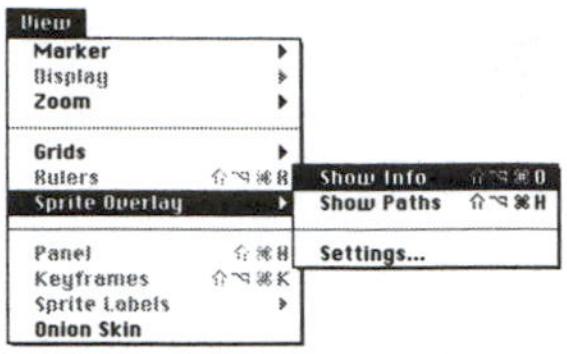

Figure 49. Choose **Sprite Overlay** from the **View** menu and select **Show Info** from the pop-up menu.

Figure 50. When you use the Sprite Overlay, sprite properties are displayed in a small rectangular panel beneath a sprite.

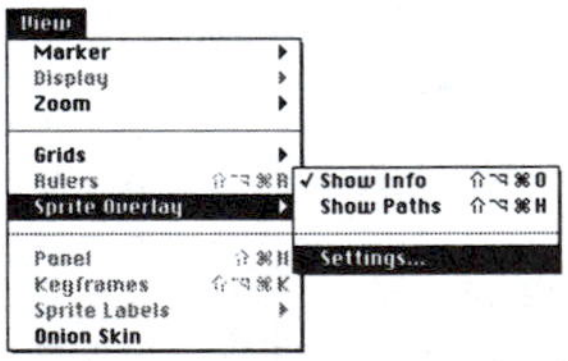

Figure 51. Choose **Sprite Overlay** from the **View** menu and select **Settings** from the pop-up menu.

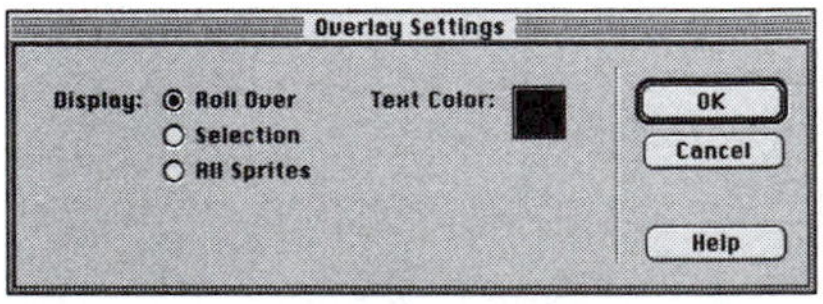

Figure 52. The **Overlay Settings** dialog box.

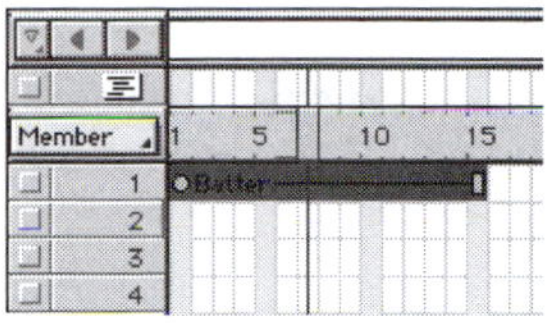

Figure 53. Select the sprite you wish to resize in the score.

Figure 54. A rectangular outline surrounds the selected sprite on the stage.

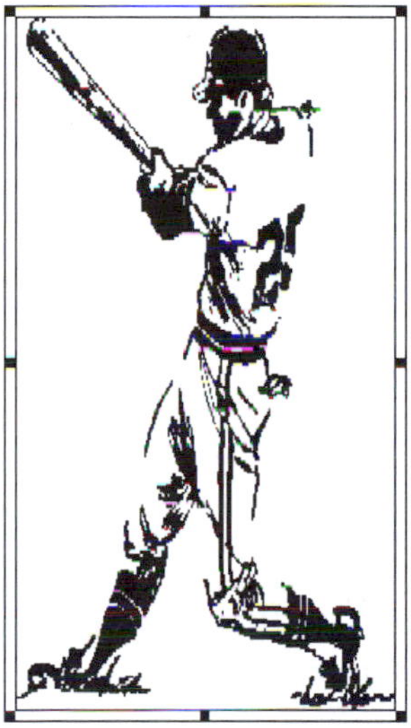

Figure 55. Drag any of the selected sprite's resize handles to stretch or squeeze it.

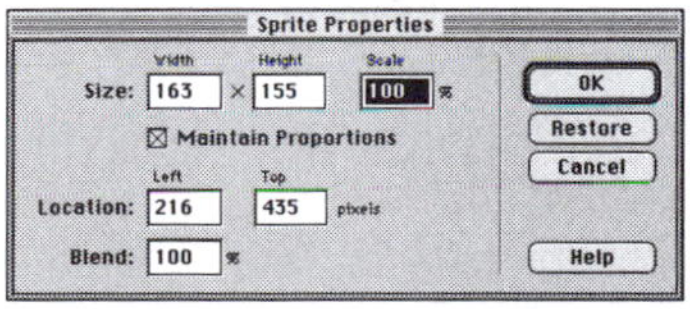

Figure 56. You can resize a sprite by entering width and height dimensions in the **Sprite Properties** dialog box.

To resize a sprite:

You can change the size and look of a sprite by stretching or squeezing it along either axis. Again, the change only affects the selected sprite; the original cast member in the cast window is not changed by this operation *(see page 35 to change a cast member's actual size)*.

Resizing sprites can lead to some interesting effects, especially when combined with Director's tweening capabilities *(see page 76 in the Animating Sprites chapter)*, which allow you to gradually change the size of sprites over multiple frames.

1. In the score, select the sprite you wish to resize **(Figure 53)**. A rectangular outline with resize handles surrounds the sprite on the stage **(Figure 54)**.
2. Drag any of the selected sprite's resize handles to stretch or squeeze it **(Figure 55)**.

✔ Tips

- You can resize multiple sprites at once by selecting them together in the score, and then resizing one of the selected sprites on the stage. All of the selected sprites will be resized in the same way.
- You can also resize a sprite by entering width and height dimensions in the Sprite Properties dialog box **(Figure 56)**. First select the sprite in the score that you wish to resize, then open the Sprite Properties dialog box by choosing Sprite from the Modify menu and Properties from the pop-up menu. Check the Maintain Proportions option to maintain the sprite's original proportions while changing width and height values, or enter a value in the Scale box to proportionately resize your sprite.

To set the blend percentage of a sprite:

The blend percentage of a sprite controls its transparency level. A 100% blend is completely opaque, while a 0% blend makes a sprite totally transparent to other sprites behind it.

1. Select a sprite or range of sprites whose blend setting you wish to change.
2. Choose Sprite from the Modify menu and select Properties from the pop-up menu **(Figure 57).**
3. Enter a new value in the Blend box in the Sprite Properties dialog box to set a new blend percentage **(Figure 58).**

✔ Tip

■ You can fade sprites in or out while animating by using the Blend setting in the Sprite Tweening dialog box *(see page 77 in the Animating Sprites chapter).*

To set a sprite's trails property:

Setting a sprite's Trails property makes a moving sprite leave a trail of images on the stage **(Figure 59)**. This feature is wonderful for creating an animated handwriting effect (where a trace is left wherever a sprite happens to move, as if someone were writing with a pencil).

1. In the score window, select the sprite or sprites whose trails option you wish to set **(Figure 60)**.
2. Choose Inspectors from the Window menu and select Sprite from the pop-up menu.
3. Click the Trails option in the Sprite Inspector window **(Figure 61)**.

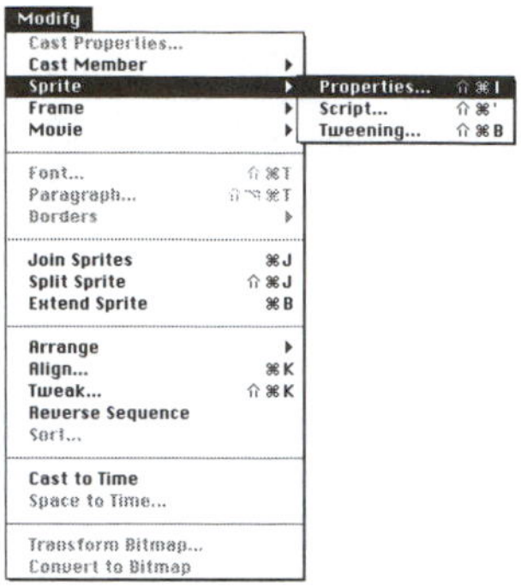

Figure 57. Choose **Sprite** from the **Modify** menu and select **Properties** from the pop-up menu.

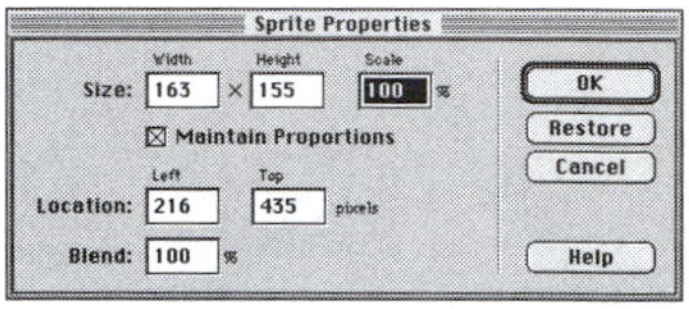

Figure 58. Enter a new value in the **Blend** box in the the **Sprite Properties** dialog box.

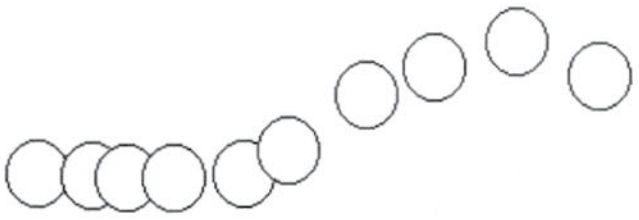

Figure 59. You can set a sprite to leave behind a trail of images as it's moved around by selecting the **Trails** option in the **Sprite Inspector** window.

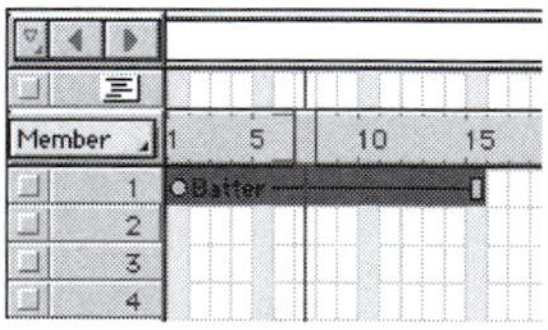

Figure 60. Select the sprite whose **Trails** option you wish to set.

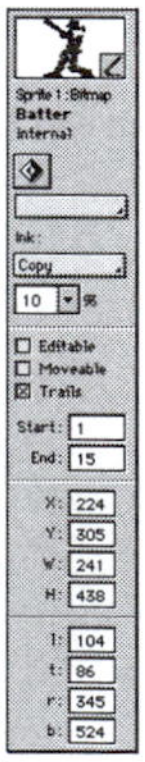

Figure 61. Click the **Trails** option in the **Sprite Inspector** window.

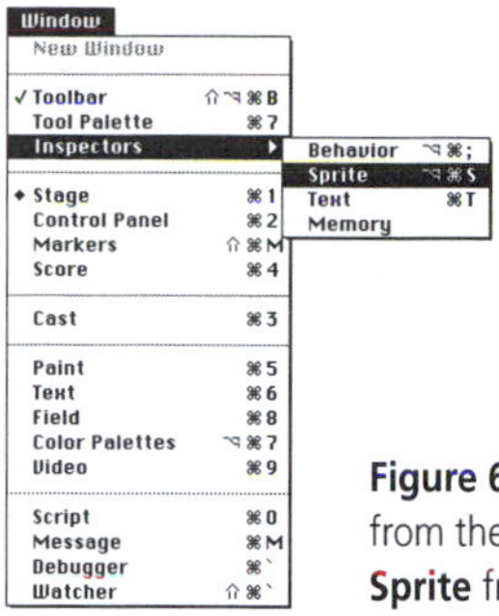

Figure 62. Choose **Inspectors** from the **Window** menu and select **Sprite** from the pop-up menu.

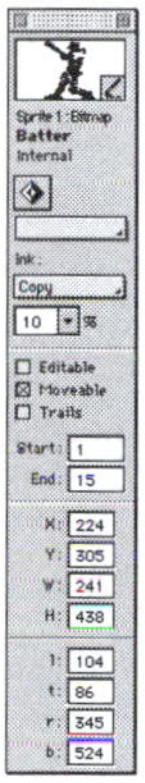

Figure 63. Click the **Moveable** option in the **Sprite Inspector** window.

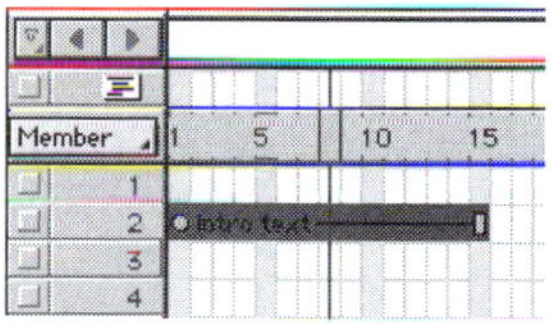

Figure 64. Select the field sprite whose **Editable** option you wish to set.

Figure 65. Click the **Editable** option in the **Sprite Inspector** window.

To make sprites moveable during movie playback:

Setting the Moveable property of a sprite allows you to drag the sprite on the stage while your movie is playing. This feature could be useful in an educational game, for example, where children can rearrange a variety of items on the screen.

1. In the score, select the sprite or range of sprites whose moveable property you wish to set.
2. Choose Inspectors from the Window menu and select Sprite from the pop-up menu **(Figure 62)**.
3. Click the Moveable checkbox in the Sprite Inspector window **(Figure 63)**. Remember that the sprites will be moveable only when Director is currently playing through the frames that contain the sprites you selected in step 1.
4. If you wish to cancel the moveable effect, simply select the sprites that have been rendered moveable, and deselect the Moveable checkbox.

To make field sprites editable during movie playback:

Director allows you to select and edit the text of field sprites on the stage while the movie is actually playing *(see page 177 in the Creating Text in Director chapter for details on field cast members)*.

1. In the score, select the field sprite or range of field sprites that you wish to render editable by the user during movie playback **(Figure 64)**.
2. Choose Inspectors from the Window menu and select Sprite from the pop-up menu **(Figure 62)**.
3. Click the Editable checkbox in the Sprite Inspector window **(Figure 65)**.
4. If you wish to cancel the editable effect, simply select the sprites you've rendered editable, and deselect the Editable checkbox.

To set an ink effect for a sprite in the score:

Director features a variety of ink effects that can be applied to sprites to change the way they appear on the stage, especially when they overlap one another. For example, you can use ink effects to make sprites appear transparent, or to darken or lighten them.

1. In the score, select the sprite or range of sprites to which you wish to apply a new ink effect **(Figure 66)**.
2. Choose Inspectors from the Window menu and select Sprite from the pop-up menu.
3. Use the Ink pop-up menu in the Sprite Inspector window to select the desired ink effect **(Figure 67)**.

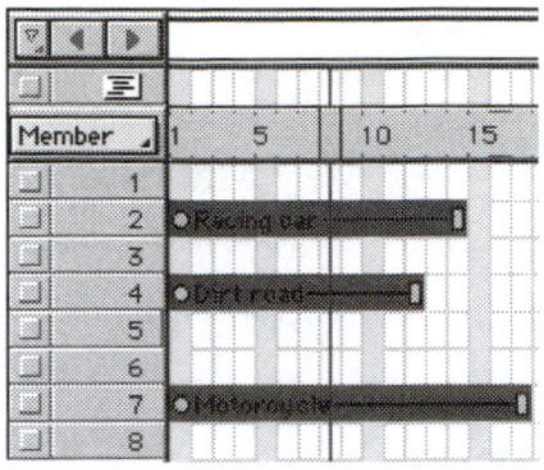

Figure 66. Select the sprite or range of sprites to which you wish to apply a new ink effect.

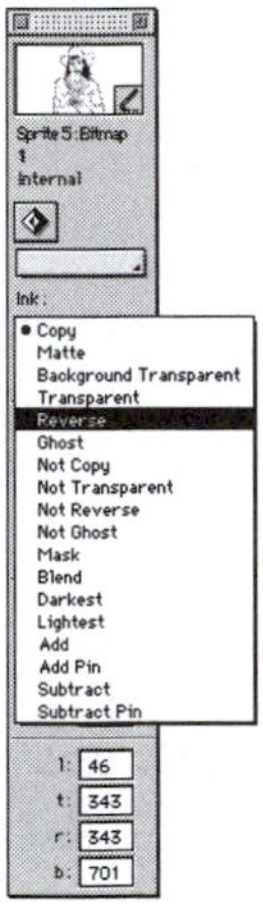

Figure 67. Select the desired ink effect from the **Ink** pop-up menu in the **Sprite Inspector** window.

The following list describes the effects that various inks have on your sprites. Although these explanations will help you determine the differences from one effect to another, the best way to understand them is through trial and error.

Copy This is the default ink effect. Sprites painted with this ink are surrounded by a rectangular bounding box. This box appears invisible on a white stage, but when the sprite is on a colored stage, or passes in front of another sprite, the bounding box is visible. Director animates sprites painted in the Copy ink more quickly than those using any other ink.

Matte Sprites appear without the white bounding box associated with the Copy ink effect, but use more memory, and animate less quickly, than those using the Copy ink.

Bkgnd Trans — Pixels in the sprite that were painted in the background colors are transparent, so you can see the background through them.

Transparent — Makes all colors transparent so that you can see any artwork behind them.

Reverse — White pixels in the sprite become transparent, so the background shows through.

Ghost — When two sprites overlap, any black pixels in the foreground sprite turn the pixels beneath the sprite white. Any white pixels in the foreground sprite become transparent.

Not Copy
Not Transp.
Not Reverse
Not Ghost

These inks act like the standard Copy, Matte, Transparent, and Ghost effects, except that they first reverse the foreground colors of a sprite.

Mask — Allows you to specify which parts of a sprite should be transparent and which opaque. For Mask ink to work, you need to design a special 1-bit mask cast member, which you place in the cast window in the position immediately following the cast member you wish to mask *(see page 129 for more on creating masks)*.

Blend — The colors of a sprite painted in this ink will blend with the colors of the background sprite it passes over. Because this blend is created on the fly, this option can significantly reduce Director's animation performance. Director creates the blend based on the percentage specified in the Sprite Properties dialog box.

Darkest — With this ink effect, Director compares the pixel colors of foreground and background sprites, and uses whichever pixels of the two are darker to color the foreground sprite. In other words, the darker colors of two overlapping sprites are made visible.

Lightest — Works like the Darkest ink effect, except that the lighter pixels of two overlapping sprites are visible.

Add When two sprites overlap, Director repaints that area in a new color that is created by adding the colors of the overlapping pixels together. If the value of the new color is greater than the maximum color value, then Director wraps the new color value around to the beginning of the color palette.

Add Pin Works the same way as the Add ink effect, except the new color value can't exceed the maximum color value.

Subtract Works the same way as the Add ink effect, except the new color for overlapping sprites is created by subtracting the foreground sprite's color value from the background sprite's color value. If the value of the new color is less than the minimum color value, Director wraps the new color value around to the top of the color palette.

Subtract Pin Works the same way as the Subtract ink effect, except the new color value can't be less than the current palette's minimum color value, and no wrap occurs.

✔ **Tip**

- Remember that using ink effects other than the default Copy ink can slow down your movie's animation performance. Try to use ink effects in strategic places, rather than across the board, if speedy animation is desired.

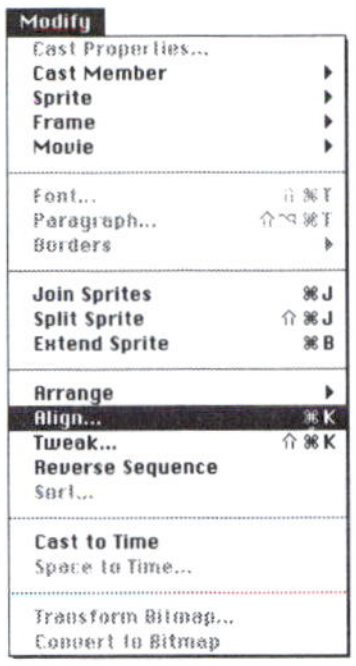

Figure 68. Choose **Align** from the **Modify** menu.

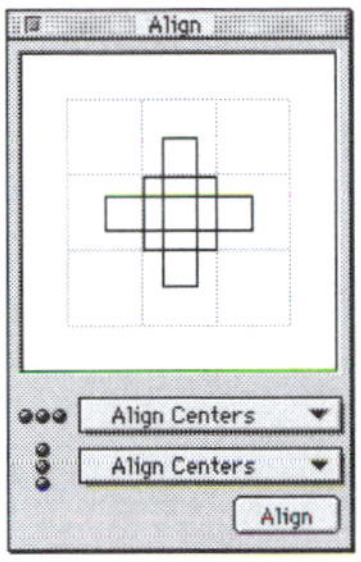

Figure 69. Use the **Align** dialog box to align the positions of selected sprites on the stage.

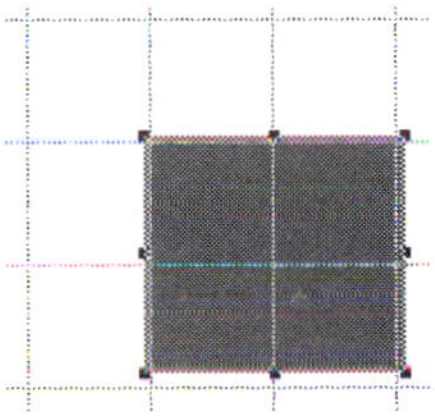

Figure 70. Use the grid to align sprites on the stage.

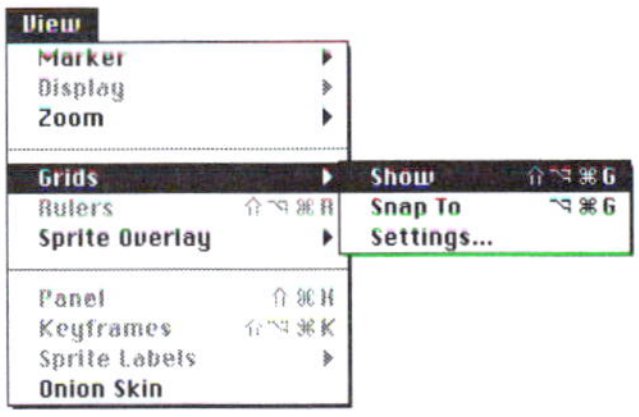

Figure 71. Choose **Grids** from the **View** menu and select **Show** from the pop-up menu.

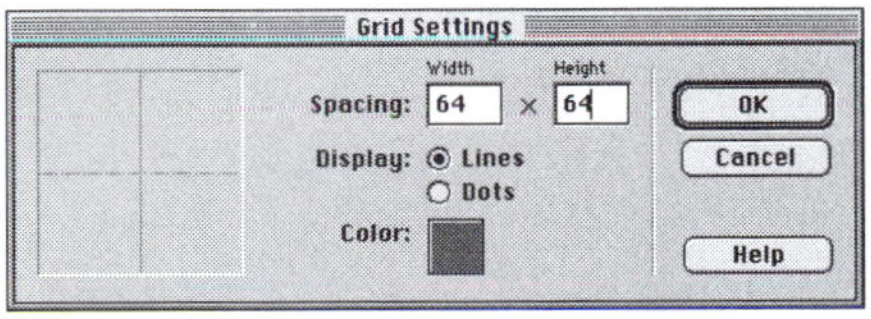

Figure 72. Use the **Grid Settings** dialog box to adjust the spacing and color of grid lines.

To align sprites:

Sometimes you may need to align the positions of sprites on the stage so that they are all registered with respect to some reference point. This alignment is often necessary when building an animation to ensure that the sprites don't appear to shift from one frame to the next.

You can align sprites on the stage by using the Align command under the Modify menu. Sprites can be aligned with respect to their centers, registration points (*see "To set a new cast member registration point" on page 102*), or to any of the eight points around the bounding box that encompasses each sprite. Aligning sprites does not change their cast members' registration points.

1. Choose Score from the Window menu.
2. Select the sprites that you wish to align.
3. Choose Align from the Modify menu **(Figure 68)**.
4. In the Align dialog box **(Figure 69)**, choose how you wish to align the sprites from the pop-up menus, and click Align. The sprites are aligned with respect to the first sprite you selected in step 2 above.

To align sprites to the grid:

You can use the grid in Director to align sprites on the stage **(Figure 70)**.

1. Choose Grids from the View menu, and select Show from the pop-up menu **(Figure 71)**. The grid appears.
2. If you wish your sprites to snap to the nearest grid line, choose Grids from the View menu, and select Snap To from the pop-up menu.
3. You can adjust the spacing and color of the grid lines in the Grid Settings dialog box **(Figure 72)**. To open this box, choose Grids from the View menu and select Settings from the pop-up menu.

To tweak sprites:

You can use the Tweak window to move sprites a precise number of pixels in the X and Y directions on the stage.

1. Select the sprite(s) you wish to tweak on the stage or in the score. Shift-click to select multiple sprites.
2. Choose Tweak from the Modify menu **(Figure 73)**.
3. Drag in the left side of the Tweak window to specify visually the offset by which to move the selected sprites **(Figure 74)**. You can also click the up and down arrows to specify the X and Y offsets.
4. Click Tweak to move the sprites.

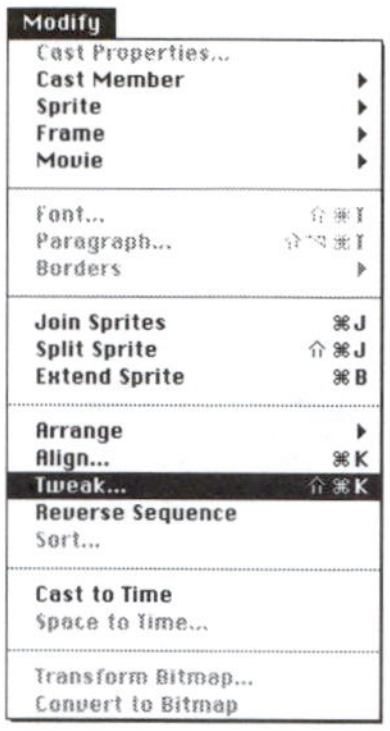

Figure 73. Choose **Tweak** from the **Modify** menu.

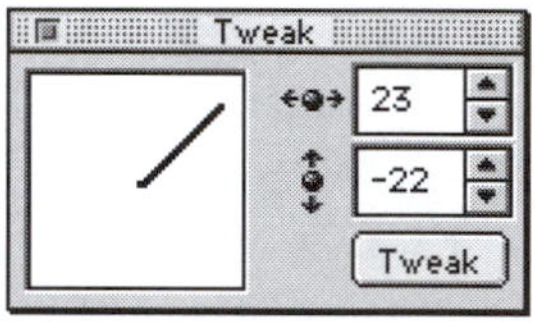

Figure 74. Use the Tweak window to move selected sprites by a precise number of pixels.

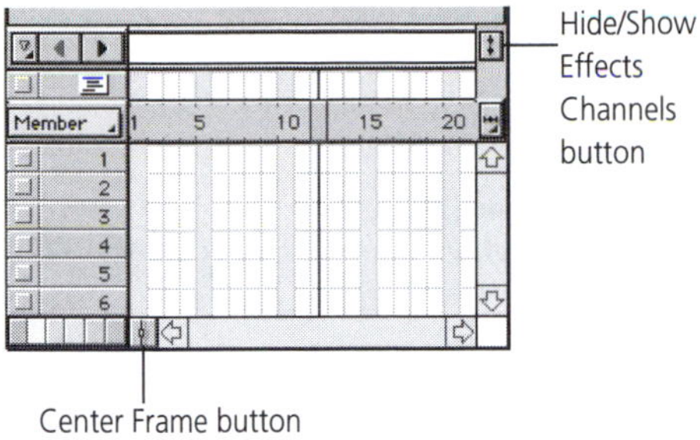

Figure 75. The score window.

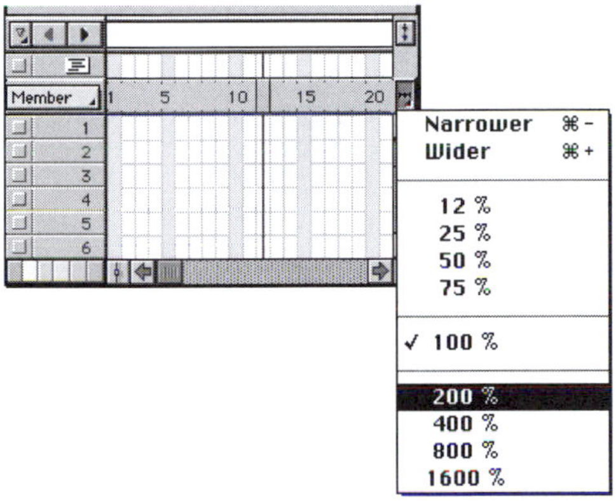

Figure 76. Click the **Zoom Menu** button and select a zoom setting from the pop-up menu.

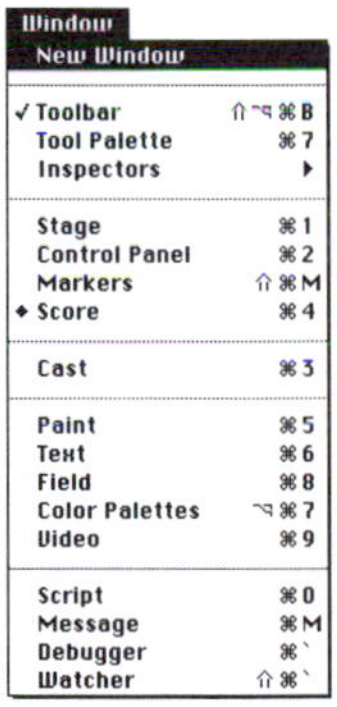

Figure 77. Choose **New Window** from the **Window** menu.

SCORE WINDOW VIEWING FEATURES

Scroll bars

Use the scroll bar at the bottom of the score to move to any frame in your movie. Use the scroll bar at the right side of the score to scroll through channels.

Center Frame button

Click the Center Frame button so that the frame where the playback head is located becomes the center frame in the score window **(Figure 75)**.

Hide/Show Effects Channels

Click the Hide/Show Effects Channels button to hide or show the effects channels at the top of the score window.

Zooming

Click the Zoom Menu button and select from the pop-up menu **(Figure 76)** to enlarge or decrease the size of frames in the score. Zooming in allows you to see more data in each frame. Zooming out makes it easier to select and edit large portions of score data.

To view multiple score windows:

You can view and edit different parts of the score on the screen at the same time by opening additional score windows. This way you can more easily drag data between different parts of the score without having to scroll the frames constantly.

1. Choose Score from the Window menu to open the score.
2. Choose New Window from the Window menu to open an additional score window **(Figure 77)**. Use the scroll bars to move to the appropriate frame and channel in the new window. You can open as many additional score windows as you need.

To show or hide keyframes in the score:

1. Choose Keyframes from the View menu **(Figure 78)** to toggle between viewing or hiding keyframe indicators within the sprite bars in the score.

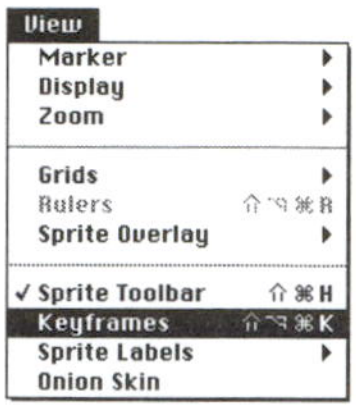

Figure 78. Choose **Keyframes** from the **View** menu.

To view sprite labels in the score:

Sprite labels are the information that is visible within the sprite bars in the score window. Sprite labels make it much easier to work with sprites and edit your movie by providing key information, such as the name and number of the cast member on which a sprite is based **(Figure 79)**.

1. Open the score window.
2. Choose Sprite Labels from the View menu and select the option from the pop-up menu **(Figure 80)** that determines at what points in a sprite bar the sprite label information is displayed.

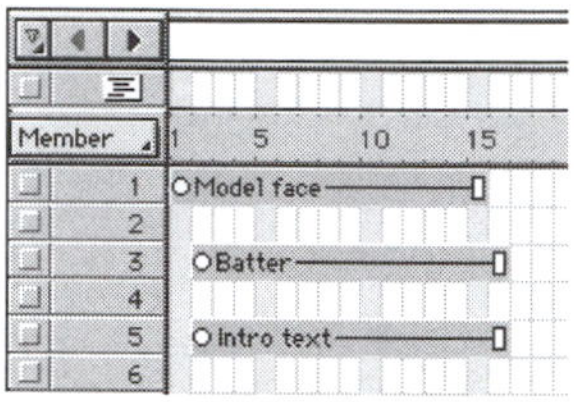

Figure 79. Sprite labels, which are visible within sprite bars, provide key information about your sprites.

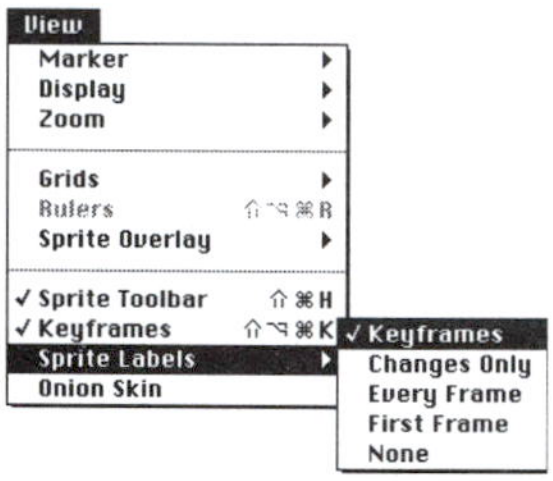

Figure 80. Choose **Sprite Labels** from the **View** menu and select from the pop-up menu.

To change the display option for sprite labels:

You can change the type of information that appears in sprite labels by setting the appropriate display option in the Display pop-up menu in the score window **(Figure 81)**, or by choosing the Display command from the View pop-up menu and selecting the appropriate display option.

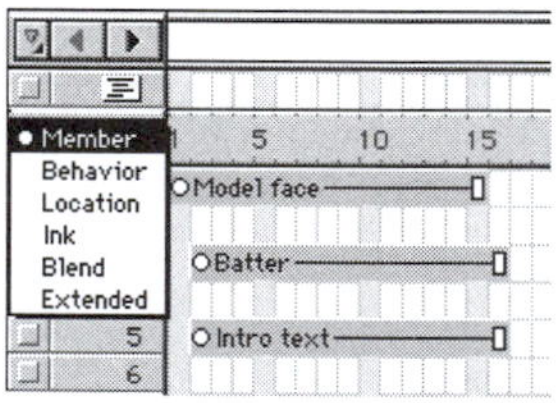

Figure 81. Use the **Display** pop-up menu in the score to select what info is displayed by sprite labels.

The **Member** display option displays the name and number of each sprite's cast member. The **Behavior** option displays the behavior assigned to each sprite. The **Location** option displays the coordinates of each sprite's registration point. The **Ink** option displays the ink effect applied to sprites. The **Blend** option shows each sprite's blend percentage. And the **Extended** option allows you to view any combination of display options specified in the Score Window Preferences dialog box **(Figure 82)**.

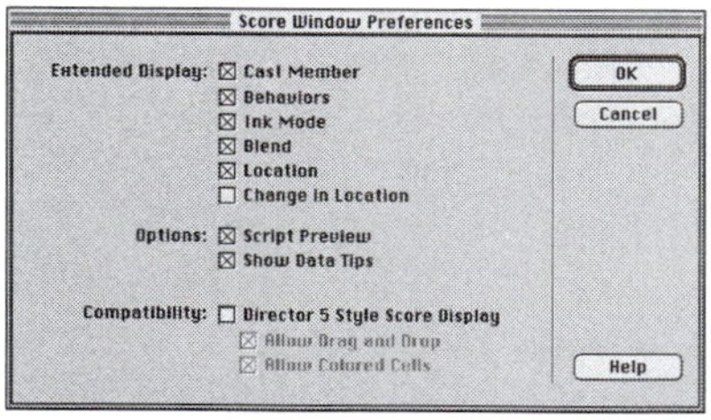

Figure 82. Choose **Preferences** from the **File** menu and select **Score** from the pop-up menu to open the **Score Window Preferences** dialog box, where you can specify a combination of display options.

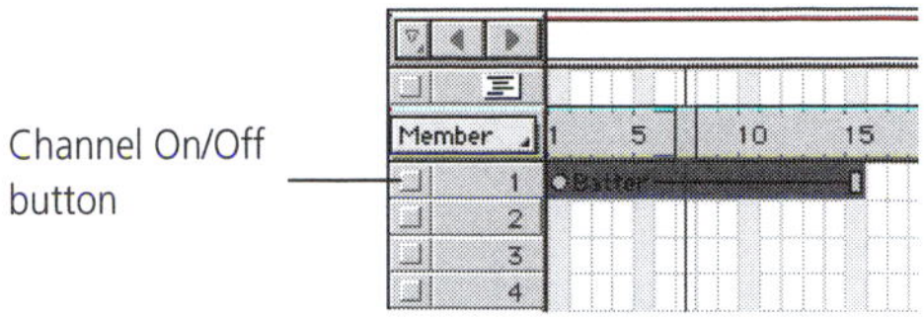

Figure 83. Click the button at the left side of a channel to turn the channel on/off during movie playback.

To turn a channel on or off:

By default, all channels are turned on. Click the button at the left side of a channel to turn the channel off during movie playback **(Figure 83)**. Doing so causes Director to ignore all information in that channel, including any sprites; this can improve playback performance. Turning the script channel off causes Director to ignore all scripts during playback. To turn a channel back on, click the button again.

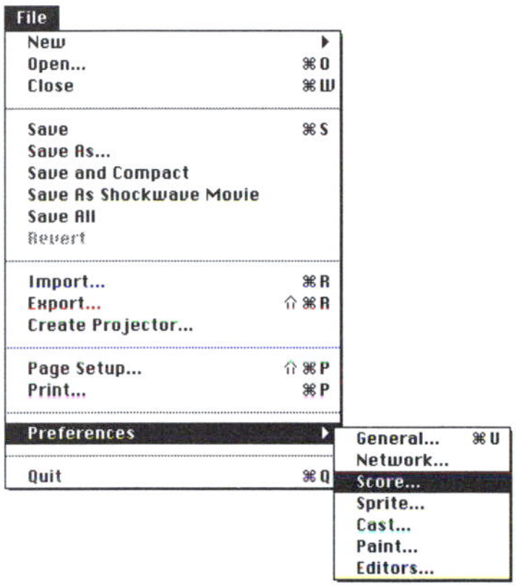

Figure 84. Choose **Preferences** from the **File** menu and select **Score** from the pop-up menu.

To use the Director 5 style score display:

The score window in Director 6 features many improvements compared to its counterpart in Director 5, most notably in the way that sprites are displayed. In some cases, you may still prefer to view the score using the old format, for example, when you are editing a Director 5 movie.

1. Choose Score from the Window menu to open the score.
2. Choose Preferences from the File menu and select Score from the pop-up menu **(Figure 84)**.
3. In the Score Window Preferences dialog box, select the Director 5 Style Score Display option **(Figure 85)**.

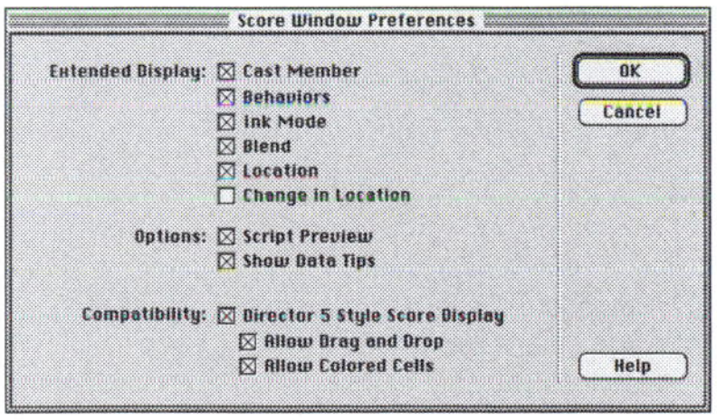

Figure 85. In the **Score Window Preferences** dialog box, select the **Director 5 Style Score Display** option.

MARKERS

One helpful way to manage a movie composed of many frames is to use markers to label important sections. These markers are placed into the Marker channel in the score window **(Figure 86)** above a specific frame.

Lingo scripts that navigate through your movie almost always refer to marker names rather than to changeable frame numbers *(see the Interactivity Through Lingo chapter on page 202 for details on scripts)*.

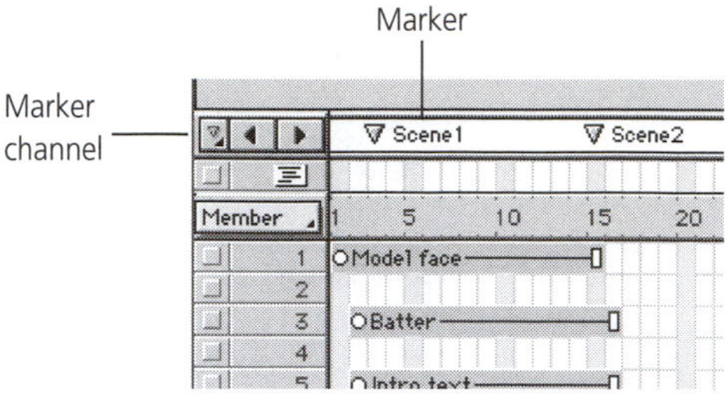

Figure 86. Markers are placed above specific frames in the **Marker** channel in the score window to label sections of your movie.

To create a marker:

1. In the score, click a frame in the marker channel **(Figure 86)** where you wish to insert a new marker.
2. Type the name for your marker and press Return.

To reposition a marker:

1. Simply drag the marker left or right to a new frame.

To delete a marker:

1. Drag the marker you wish to delete out of the Marker channel.

✔ Tip

- You can jump to the previous or next marker in the score by clicking the Previous Marker or Next Marker button in the score **(Figure 87)**. To jump to a specific marker, click the Markers Menu button and select the appropriate marker from the pop-up menu **(Figure 87)**.

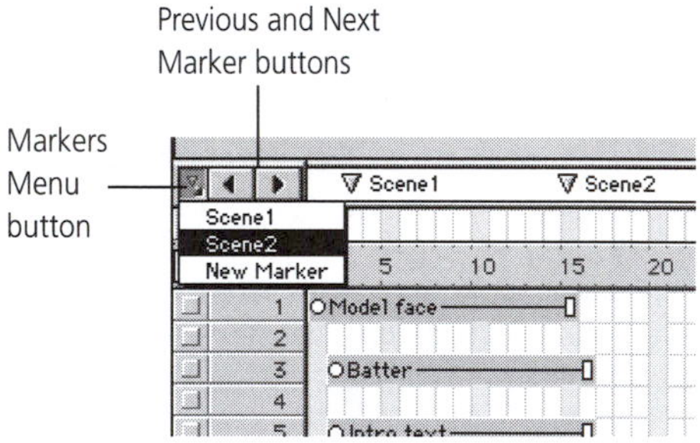

Figure 87. Click the **Previous Marker** or **Next Marker** button to jump to the previous or next marker in the score. Jump to a specific marker by clicking the **Markers Menu** button and selecting the appropriate marker from the pop-up menu.

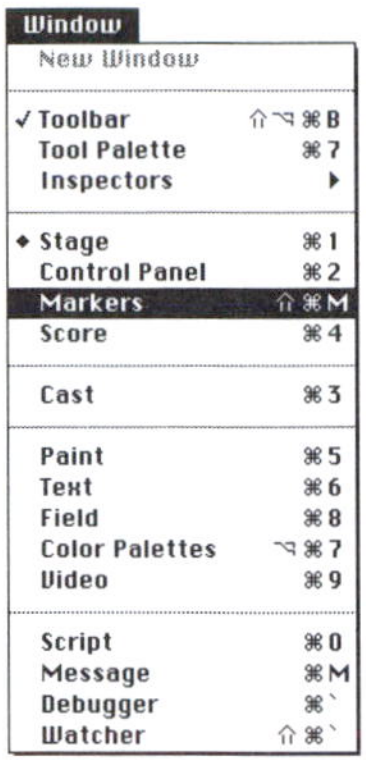

Figure 88. With the score window open, choose **Markers** from the **Window** menu.

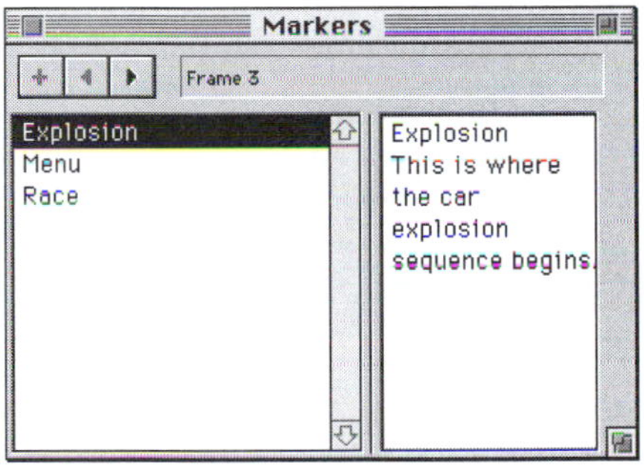

Figure 89. In the **Markers** window, click the name of the marker that you wish to annotate. Add commentary on the right side of the **Markers** window.

To annotate markers in the Markers window:

Director features a Markers window that allows you to add descriptive comments to markers—for instance, scene descriptions, or any other notes that might help someone understand what role the marked frames play in your movie.

1. With the score open, choose Markers from the Window menu **(Figure 88)**.
2. In the Markers window, click the name of the marker that you wish to annotate **(Figure 89)**. In the score, Director immediately moves the playback head to the frame that contains the selected marker.
3. If you wish to add commentary to the selected marker, click the right half of the Markers window first to unselect the marker name that's repeated there. Make sure you then press Return after the marker name before typing any commentary.

ANIMATING SPRITES 5

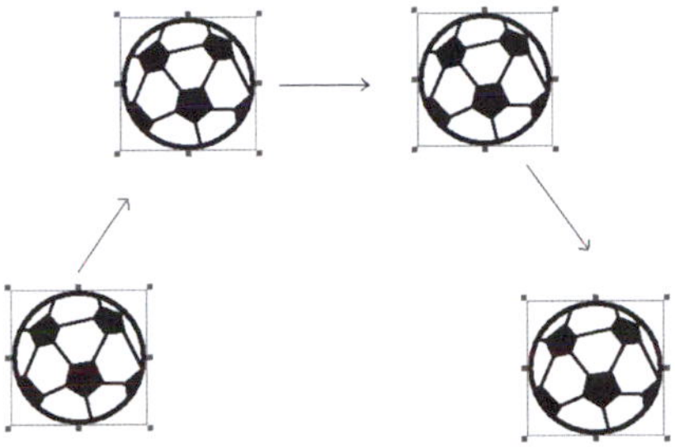

Figure 1. A sprite can be animated by changing its position on the stage over successive frames.

There are two basic ways of animating a sprite in Director. The first is by changing its position on the stage over successive frames to create motion **(Figure 1)**. The second is by altering its image over successive frames.

A sprite's image can be changed in several ways: First, you can gradually alter the image by changing one of its properties, such as size **(Figure 2)** or color, over a series of frames. Second, you can exchange a sprite's image altogether with another cast member graphic. This technique allows you to create an **animated sequence**, which is a series of related cast members **(Figure 3)** appearing in an alternating fashion on the stage.

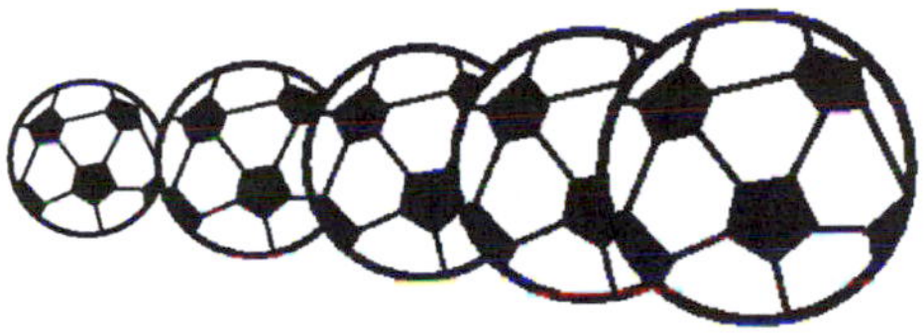

Figure 2. A sprite can also be animated by changing its image over successive frames, such as making it appear to grow.

It is very common to combine both the motion of a sprite and the changing of its image into a single animation. An example of this would be the images of the dog in Figure 3 alternating through their sequence while moving across the stage.

This chapter covers all the basic techniques of moving and changing the images of sprites to create animation. These techniques include tweening, step recording, real-time recording, and the Cast to Time, Space to Time, and Paste Relative commands. Film loops are covered at the end of the chapter.

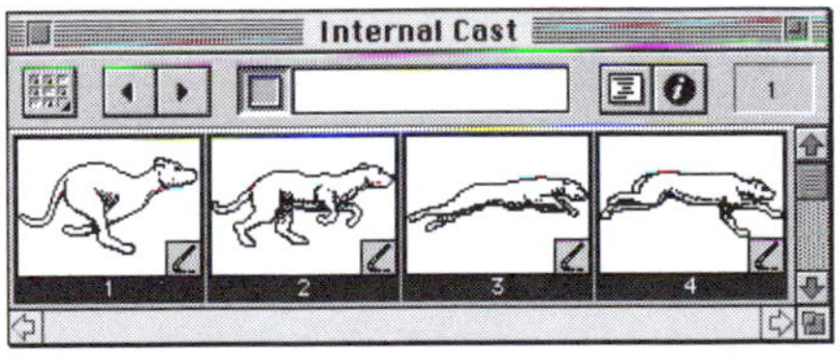

Figure 3. An animated sequence is a series of related cast members appearing in an alternating fashion on the stage.

TWEENING

Tweening offers one of the most practical and convenient ways of animating a sprite, because the tweening feature automatically creates frames for you. All you need to do is set up keyframes within a sprite, and Director can then automatically generate all the in-between frames.

A keyframe is a frame where any tweenable property of a sprite changes (sprite properties that can be tweened are position, size, foreground and background color, and blend percentage). Tweening occurs between two keyframes: the first specifies the initial state of a property and the next specifies the desired target state that the property should reach. For example, you can create a keyframe wherein the sprite is positioned on the left side of the stage. In the next keyframe, the sprite could be positioned on the right side **(Figure 4)**. Director can then generate all the frames between these keyframes to create an animation of the sprite gradually moving from left to right **(Figure 5)**.

Figure 4. These images represent two keyframes in which the sprite is positioned at opposite ends of the stage.

Figure 5. Director can automatically generate all the frames between keyframes to create animation. Ten separate frames are shown here all at once.

In the score, a keyframe is represented by a circle within a sprite **(Figure 6)**. The first frame of every sprite is always a keyframe; you can create as many additional keyframes within a sprite as there are frames in its span. The end frame of a sprite (represented by a square) is not a keyframe, but you can place one there.

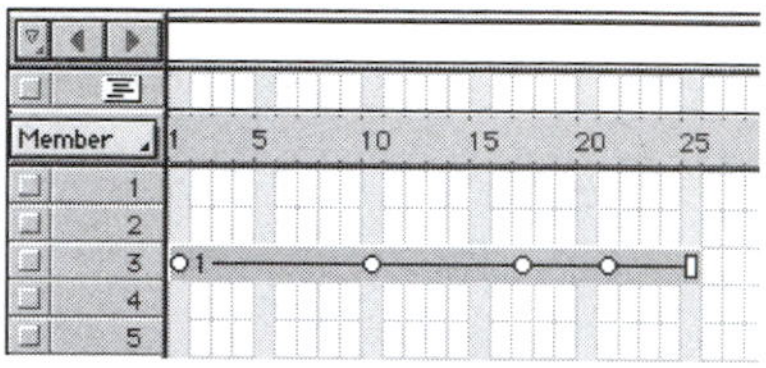

Figure 6. In the score, a keyframe is represented by a circle within a sprite.

The more frames that separate your keyframes, the more gradual will be the change in the tweened property. For example, if two keyframes are separated by 100 frames, and the sprite is positioned at opposite ends of the stage in these frames, the resulting tween will produce fairly smooth motion. On the other hand, if only five frames separate the keyframes, the sprite will appear to move in a very jerky and sudden fashion.

To create a keyframe within a sprite:

1. Select a sprite in the score.

2. Click the frame within the frame channel to indicate where you wish to create a keyframe **(Figure 7)**.

3. Choose Keyframe from the Insert menu to create it **(Figures 8–9)**.

Figure 7. Click the frame in the frame channel where you wish to create a keyframe.

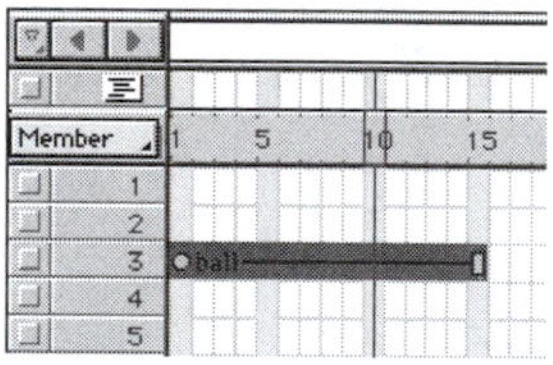

Figure 8. Choose **Keyframe** from the **Insert** menu.

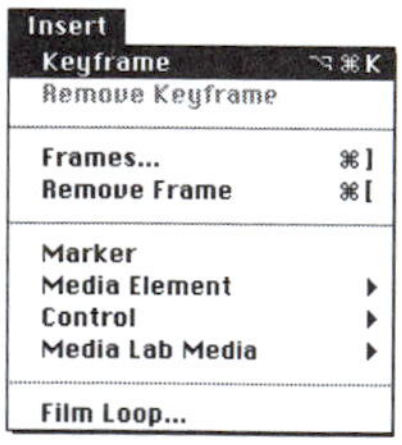

Figure 9. A keyframe is created at the selected frame.

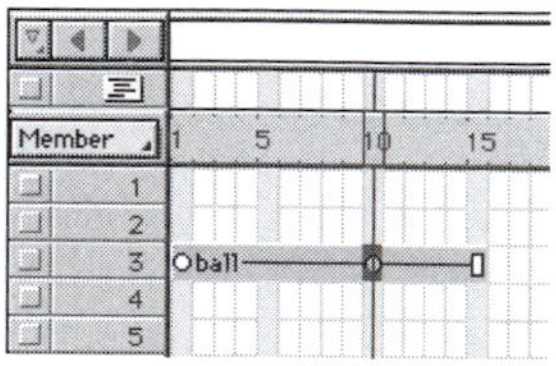

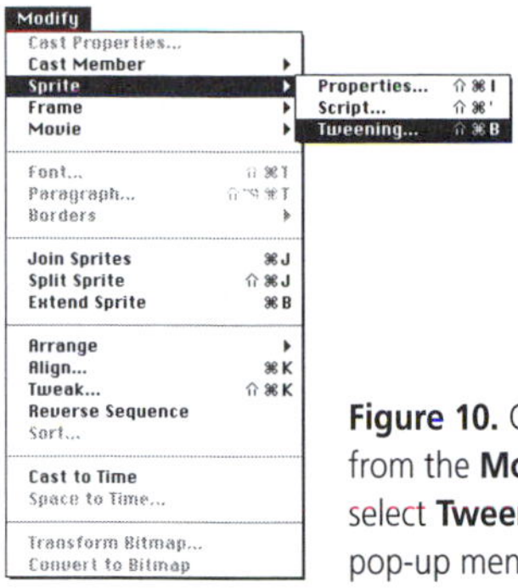

Figure 10. Choose **Sprite** from the **Modify** menu and select **Tweening** from the pop-up menu.

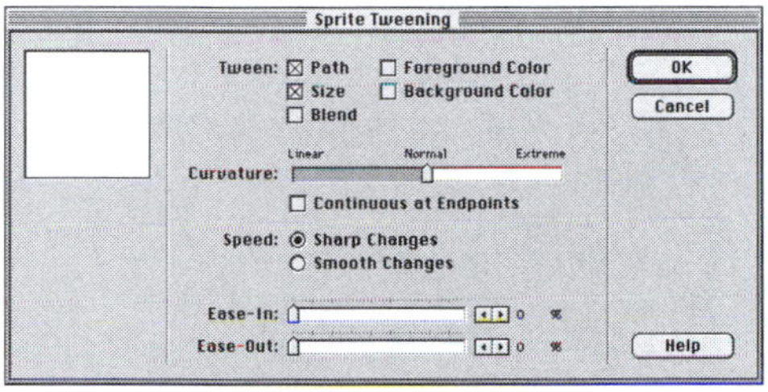

Figure 11. Click the **Path** option in the **Sprite Tweening** dialog box.

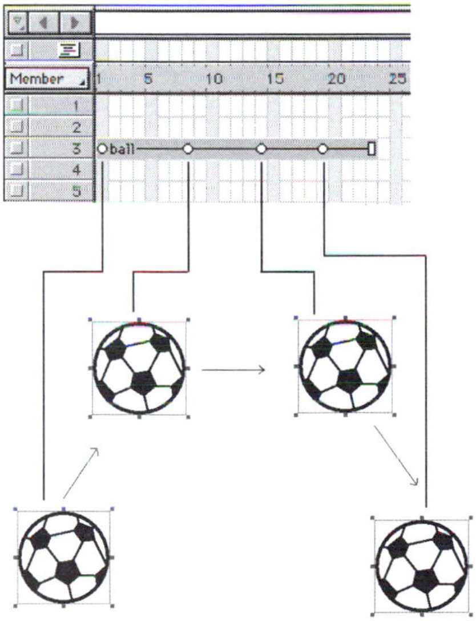

Figure 12. Create keyframes within a sprite that feature it at different positions on the stage. Director can then tween the path of the sprite to generate all the in-between frames.

To tween the path of a sprite:

The most common use of tweening is to create a path for a sprite to follow. You do this by creating keyframes that feature the sprite at different positions on the stage. Director can then tween the path between these keyframes.

1. Place a cast member into the score to create a sprite whose path you wish to tween.
2. With the sprite selected in the score, choose Sprite from the Modify menu and select Tweening from the pop-up menu **(Figure 10)**.
3. Click the Path checkbox in the Sprite Tweening dialog box **(Figure 11)** to activate tweening for the position property of the sprite, and click OK.
4. In the score, click the first frame of the sprite (which is a keyframe).
5. On stage, drag the sprite to the starting location of its animation path.
6. In the score, click a frame within the sprite to indicate where you wish to create a new keyframe.
7. Choose Keyframe from the Insert menu.
8. On stage, drag the sprite to the location where you want it to stop moving or change direction.
9. Repeat steps 6–8 to create as many keyframes as necessary **(Figure 12)**. You can create very complex paths.
10. Rewind and play back the movie to see how the sprite moves.

✔ Tip

- You can adjust the path of a sprite by selecting one of its keyframes in the score, then dragging the sprite to a new position on the stage. Remember that when you select an entire sprite in the score and then drag it on stage, you move the entire sprite throughout all of its frames to the new position (as opposed to adjusting the position in a single keyframe).

✔ Tips

- You can make a sprite end its path at the same point that it began by selecting the sprite and checking the Continuous at Endpoints option **(Figure 13)** in the Sprite Tweening dialog box. (Open this box by choosing Sprite from the Modify menu and Tweening from the pop-up menu.) The sprite will loop back to its starting point between the last keyframe and the end frame. You can use this option to create a circular path *(see page 74)*.
- You can make Director automatically tween the size and position property of sprites by setting the Tween Size and Position option in the Sprite Preferences dialog box **(Figure 14)** (you then no longer need to set these options explicitly in the Sprite Tweening dialog box). Open the Sprite Preferences dialog box by choosing Preferences from the File menu and selecting Sprite from the pop-up menu.
- A shortcut to creating a keyframe is to Option-click a frame within a sprite (this selects a single frame) and then change one of the sprite's tweenable properties, such as position, size, or blend percentage. In order for a keyframe to be created, the property you are changing must be enabled for tweening in either the Sprite Tweening dialog box or the Sprite Preferences dialog box.
- If you plan on creating many keyframes within a sprite, a more convenient approach than Option-clicking is to enable the Edit Sprite Frames command under the Edit menu *(see page 51 in the Score and Sprite Basics chapter)*. You can then create a keyframe by clicking within a sprite to select a single frame, and then altering a tweenable property of the sprite which is enabled for tweening.

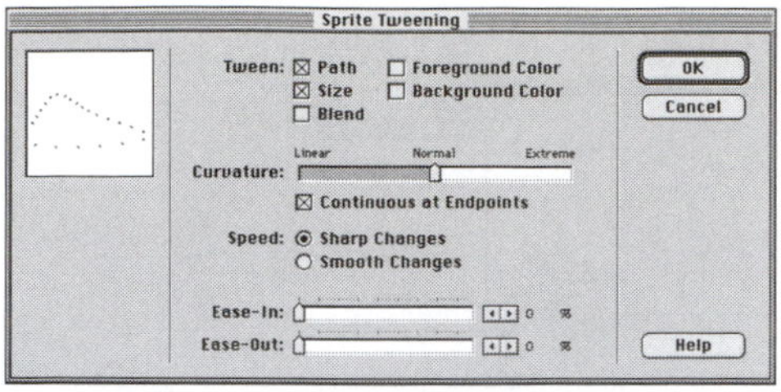

Figure 13. Select the **Continuous at Endpoints** option in the **Sprite Tweening** dialog box.

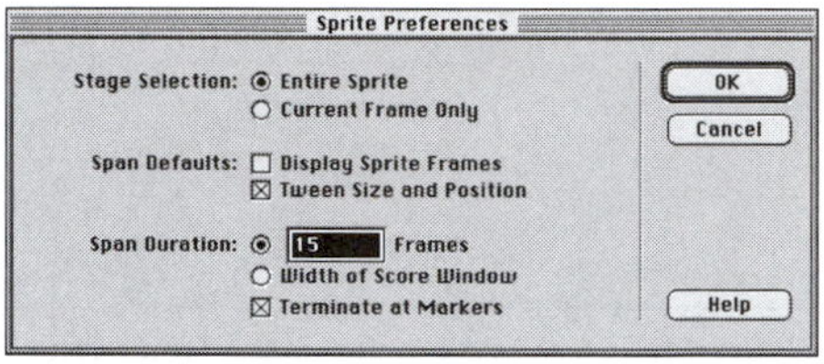

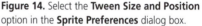

Figure 14. Select the **Tween Size and Position** option in the **Sprite Preferences** dialog box.

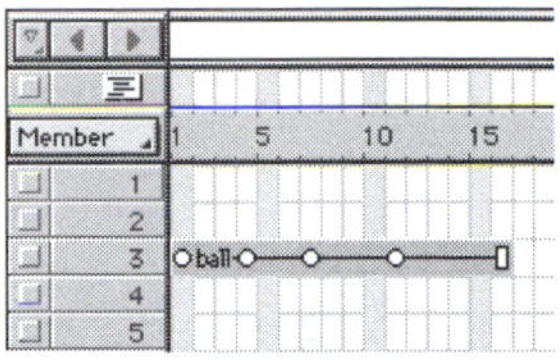

Figure 15. A sprite before being extended.

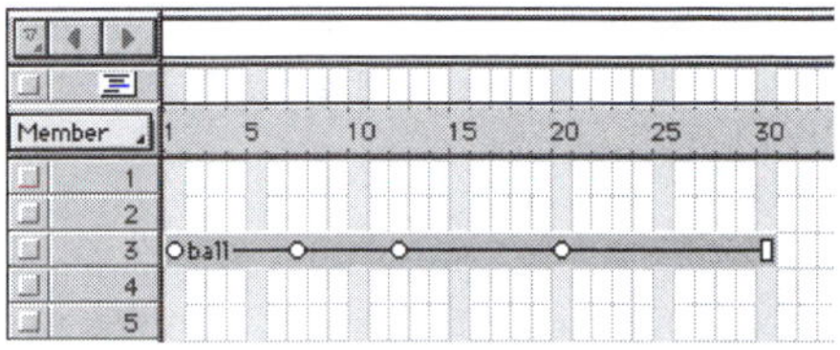

Figure 16. When a sprite is extended, its keyframes grow proportionately farther apart.

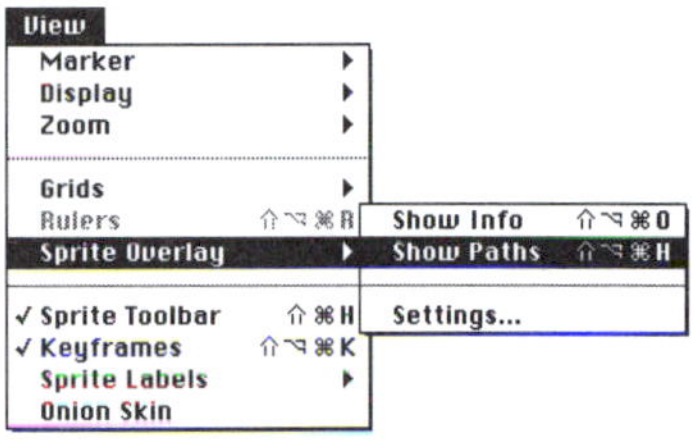

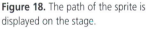

Figure 17. Choose **Sprite Overlay** from the **View** menu and **Show Paths** from the pop-up menu.

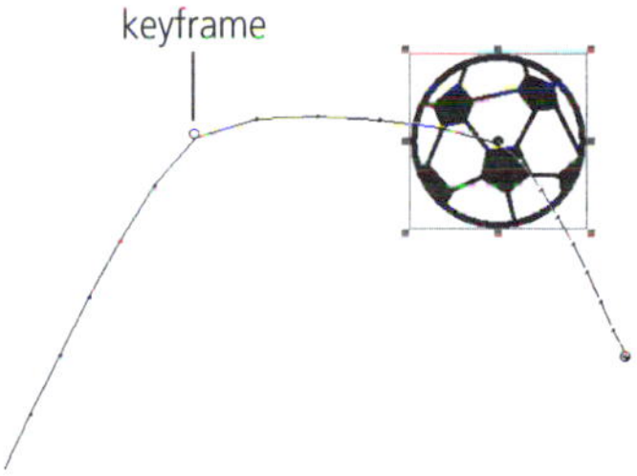

Figure 18. The path of the sprite is displayed on the stage.

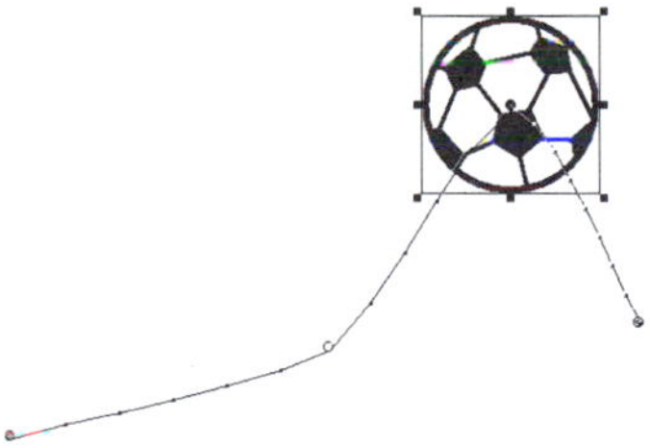

Figure 19. You can adjust the path by dragging any keyframe.

To reposition keyframes in the score:

You can change the position of any keyframe within a sprite by dragging the keyframe in the score to the desired new frame. By changing the number of frames between keyframes, you can control how smooth tweening is.

When you drag either the start or end frame of a sprite to shorten or lengthen its span duration, all keyframes within the sprite grow proportionately closer or farther apart **(Figures 15–16)**.

✔ Tips

- Hold the Command key while dragging the end frame of a sprite to extend it without moving its keyframes.
- You can duplicate a keyframe by Option-dragging it in the score to a new frame.

To view and adjust the path of a sprite on the stage:

The quickest and most convenient way to adjust the path of a sprite is to use the Sprite Overlay command, which allows you to view the complete path of the sprite on the stage.

1. In the score, select the sprite whose path you wish to view or adjust.
2. Choose Sprite Overlay from the View menu and select Show Paths from the pop-up menu **(Figure 17)**. The complete path of the sprite is displayed on stage **(Figure 18)**. Keyframes within the path are represented by small circles, and regular frames are represented by small dots.
3. You can adjust the path of the sprite by dragging any keyframe within the overlay to a new position on the stage **(Figure 19)**. You don't need to use the score. The sprite's path is adjusted immediately.

To add curvature to a sprite's tweened path:

You can add curvature to the tweened path of a sprite when the sprite uses three or more keyframes. **Curvature** refers to how the sprite moves between keyframes (for example, in straight lines, or by curving between them).

1. In the score, select the sprite whose path you wish to adjust.
2. Choose Sprite from the Modify menu and select Tweening from the pop-up menu.
3. In the Sprite Tweening dialog box, drag the Curvature slider bar to adjust how much curvature there is in the sprite's path. Drag to the Linear setting if you want the sprite to move in straight lines between keyframes **(Figures 20–21)**. Drag to Normal to give the sprite moderate curvature. Drag to Extreme for maximum curvature in the path between keyframes **(Figures 22–23)**. You can preview the adjusted path at the left side of the Sprite Tweening dialog box.

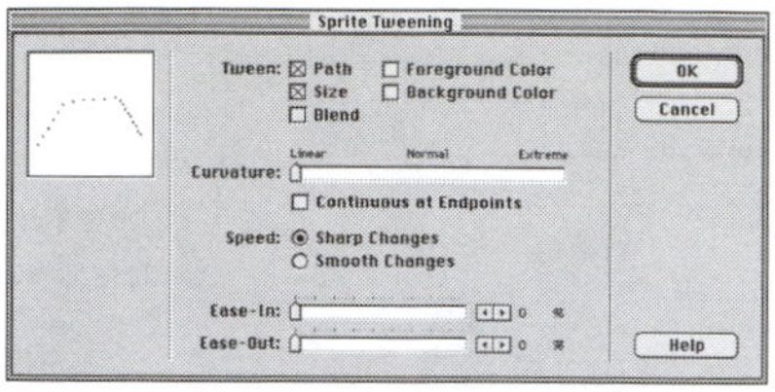

Figure 20. Drag to Linear for a sprite to move in straight lines between keyframes.

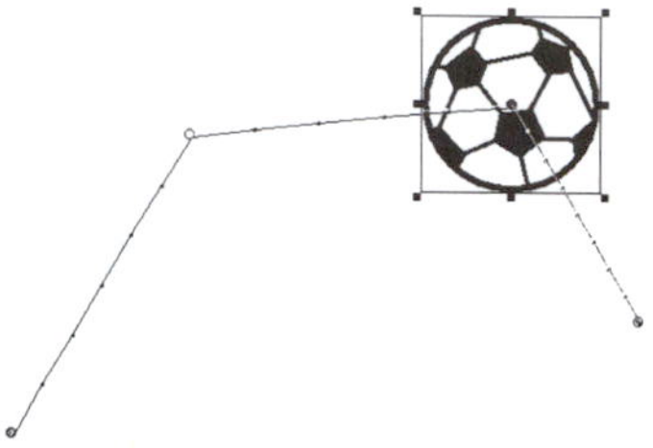

Figure 21. A sprite path with curvature set at Linear.

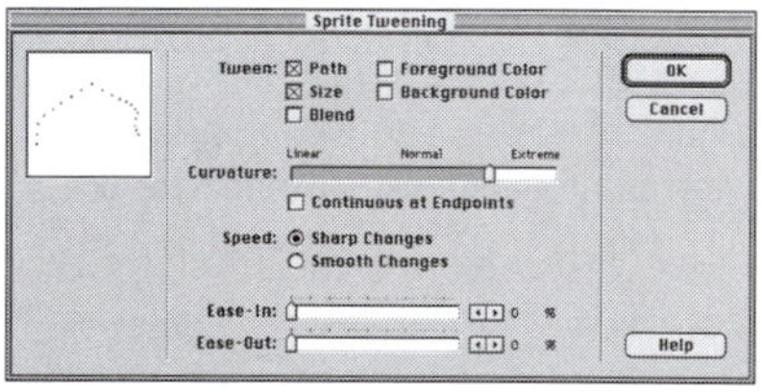

Figure 22. Drag to Extreme for a sprite to move with maximum curvature between keyframes.

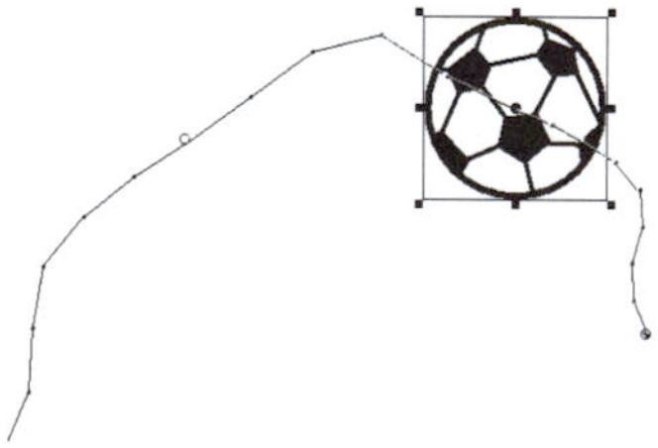

Figure 23. A sprite path with curvature set at Extreme.

To create a circular path for a sprite:

1. Place a cast member into the score to create a sprite.
2. Create a total of three keyframes within the sprite **(Figure 24)** (you can use the start frame, but don't create a keyframe at the end frame).
3. Choose Sprite Overlay from the View menu and select Show Paths from the pop-up menu.
4. Position the sprite in the three keyframes so that these positions form a shape similar to an equilateral triangle **(Figure 25)**.
5. Select the sprite in the score and choose Sprite from the Modify menu and Tweening from the pop-up menu.

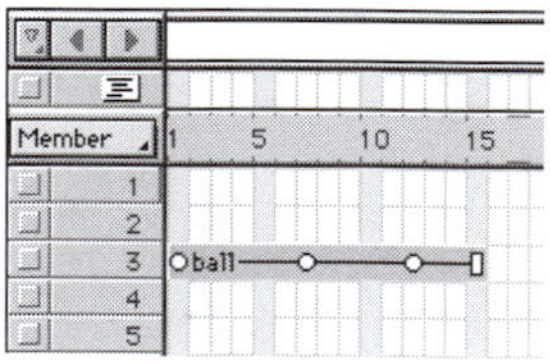

Figure 24. Create a total of three keyframes.

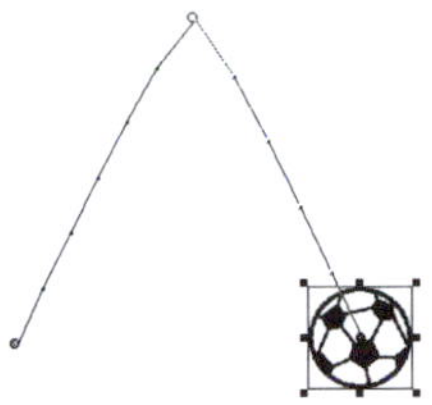

Figure 25. Position the sprite in the keyframes to form a shape similar to an equilateral triangle.

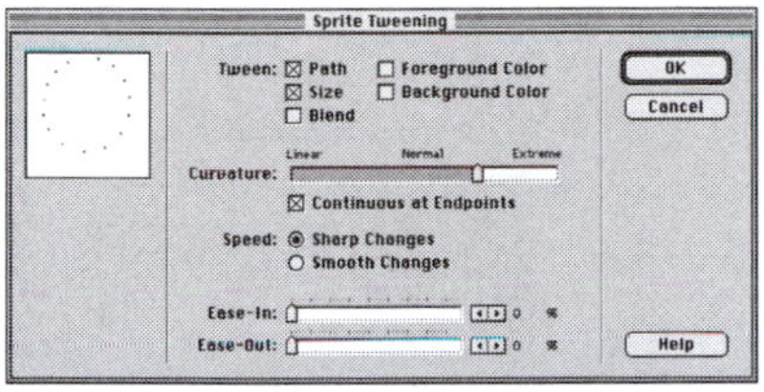

Figure 26. Click the **Continuous at Endpoints** option in the **Sprite Tweening** dialog box and drag the Curvature slider bar to the right.

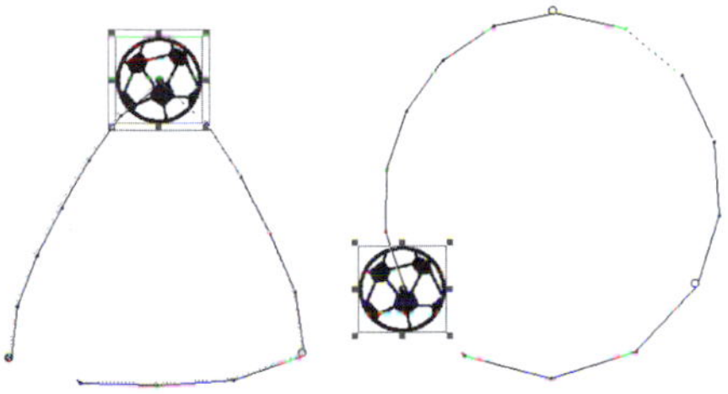

Figures 27–28. Drag the Curvature bar in the **Sprite Tweening** dialog box to the right to make the path of your sprite more circular.

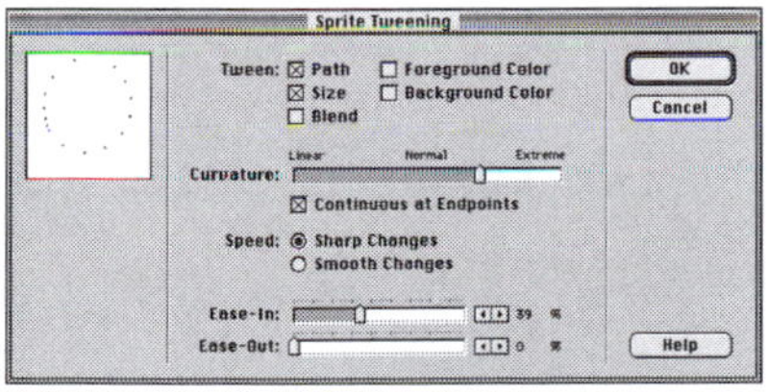

Figure 29. Drag the Ease-In and Ease-Out slider bars in the **Sprite Tweening** dialog box to control a sprite's acceleration and deceleration.

6. Click the Continuous at Endpoints option in the Sprite Tweening dialog box **(Figure 26)**.
7. Drag the Curvature slider bar to the right to make the sprite's path closer resemble a circle **(Figures 26–28)**. A preview of the path is displayed at the left side of the Sprite Tweening box.
8. Click OK.
9. To fine tune the circular path, drag the keyframes within the Sprite Overlay on the stage (represented by circles) **(Figure 28)**.

To accelerate or decelerate a sprite along its path:

When you tween a sprite along any type of path, you can make it appear to accelerate at the beginning of its path, or decelerate at the end. This adds a touch of realism to how your sprite appears to move.

1. Set up the keyframes and tween your sprite along a path *(as described on page 71)*.
2. Select the sprite in the score.
3. Choose Sprite from the Modify menu and select Tweening from the pop-up menu.
4. In the Sprite Tweening dialog box, drag the **Ease-In** and **Ease-Out** slider bars to control the sprite's acceleration at the beginning of the animation, and the deceleration at the end of the animation **(Figure 29)**.

To smooth out the speed changes of a moving sprite:

When a sprite follows a tweened path, it may appear to move smoothly and slowly between certain keyframes, but then suddenly speed up and move abruptly between other keyframes. These abrupt speed changes occur when not enough frames lie between keyframes. Director normally calculates separately how to move a sprite between each pair of keyframes, and it does not smooth out sudden jumps. Smooth out abrupt speed changes through the following steps:

1. Select the sprite whose speed changes you wish to smooth out.
2. Choose Sprite from the Modify menu and select Tweening from the pop-up menu.
3. In the Sprite Tweening dialog box, click the Smooth Changes speed option **(Figure 30)** (the Sharp Changes option is the default).

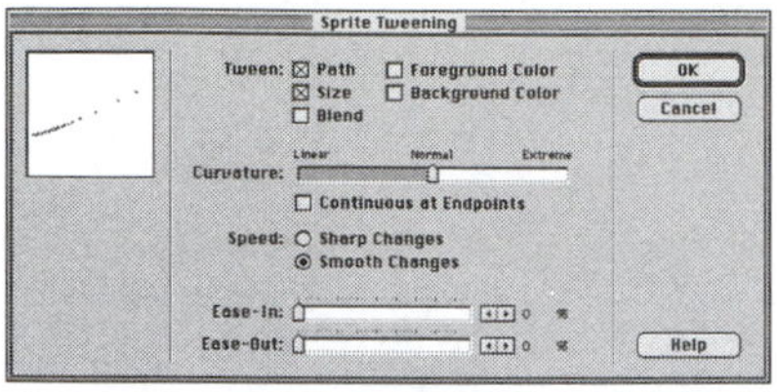

Figure 30. Click the **Smooth Changes** option in the **Sprite Tweening** dialog box.

To tween the size of a sprite:

1. In the score, select or create a keyframe within a sprite to indicate where you wish to start tweening the size **(Figure 31)**.
2. Choose Sprite from the Modify menu and select Tweening from the pop-up menu.
3. Check the Size option in the Sprite Tweening dialog box **(Figure 30)**.
4. Click OK.
5. If you wish to change the initial size of the sprite for this tween, drag any of its resize handles on the stage to resize it **(Figure 32)**.
6. In the score, click or create another keyframe within the sprite to indicate where the size tween should end **(Figure 33)**. To create a new keyframe, first select the desired frame within the sprite and then choose Keyframe from the Insert menu.

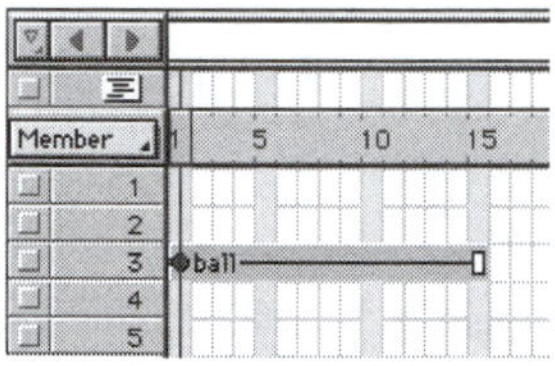

Figure 31. Select or create a keyframe where you wish to start tweening the size of your sprite.

Figure 32. Drag the resize handles to change the size of the sprite in the initial keyframe.

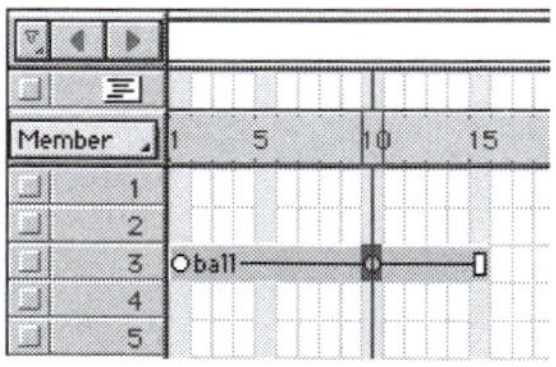

Figure 33. Select or create another keyframe where you wish the size tween to end.

Figure 34. Drag the resize handles to change the size of the sprite in the final keyframe.

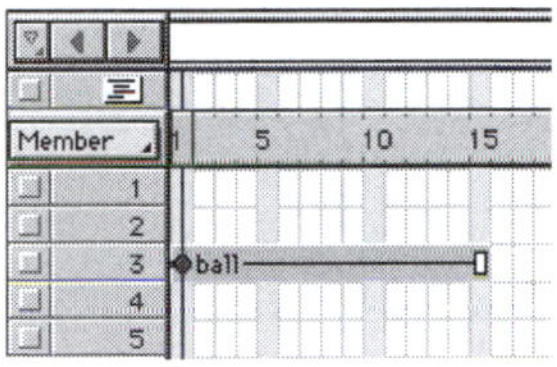

Figure 35. Select or create a keyframe where you wish to start the blend tween for your sprite.

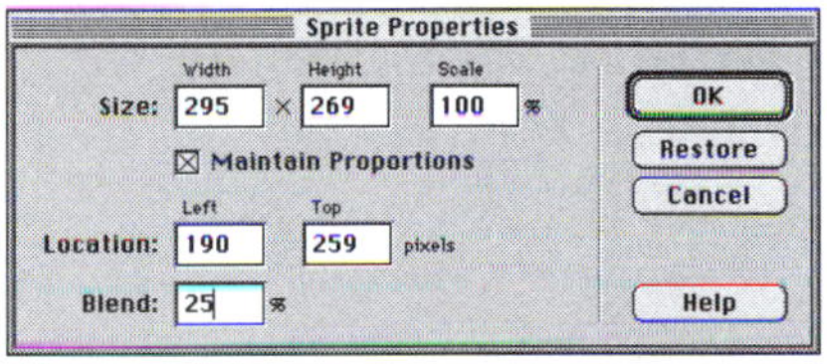

Figure 36. Set the desired initial blend percentage in the **Sprite Properties** dialog box.

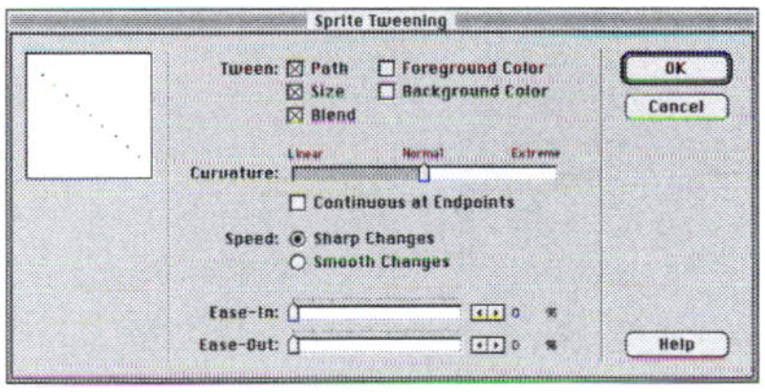

Figure 37. Click the **Blend** option in the **Sprite Tweening** dialog box.

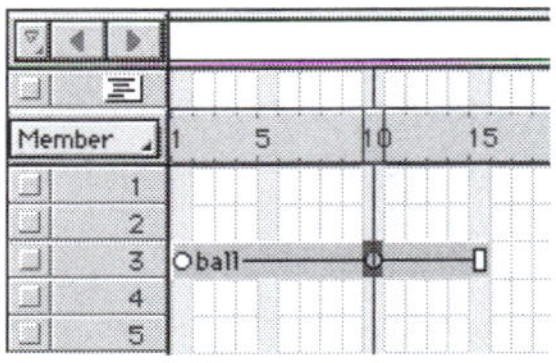

Figure 38. Select or create another keyframe where you wish the blend tween to end.

7. On the stage, drag any of the sprite's resize handles to size it for the final keyframe of the tween **(Figure 34)**.

✔ **Tip**

- You can tween multiple sprite properties at once, such as size and position, by selecting multiple tweening options in the Sprite Tweening dialog box.

To tween the blend property of a sprite:

You can make a sprite appear to fade in or out by tweening its blend property.

1. In the score, select or create a keyframe within a sprite where you wish the fade-in or fade-out tween to start **(Figure 35)**.
2. Choose Sprite from the Modify menu and select Properties from the pop-up menu.
3. In the Sprite Properties dialog box, set the desired initial blend percentage **(Figure 36)** and click OK. This value should be low if you're fading in, and high if you're fading out.
4. Choose Sprite from the Modify menu and select Tweening from the pop-up menu.
5. Click the Blend checkbox in the Sprite Tweening dialog box to enable tweening for the sprites's blend property **(Figure 37)** and click OK.
6. In the score, click or create another keyframe within the sprite to indicate where the fade-in or fade-out should end **(Figure 38)**. To create a new keyframe within the sprite, first select the desired frame and then choose Keyframe from the Insert menu.
7. Choose Sprite from the Modify menu and Properties from the pop-up menu.
8. In the Sprite Properties dialog box, set the desired blend percentage for this second keyframe. This value should be high if you're fading in, and low if you're fading out.

To tween the foreground or background color of a sprite:

1. In the score, select or create a keyframe in a sprite where you want to start the color tween **(Figure 39)**.
2. Choose Tool Palette from the Window menu **(Figure 40)**.
3. Choose the foreground and background colors for your first keyframe by clicking the color chips in the Tool Palette **(Figure 41)**. These are the starting colors for your color tween.
4. Choose Sprite from the Modify menu and select Tweening from the pop-up menu.
5. Check the Foreground or Background options in the Sprite Tweening box to indicate which color you are tweening **(Figure 42)**. You can tween both colors at the same time. Click OK.
6. In the score, click or create another keyframe within the sprite to indicate where the color tween should end **(Figure 43)**. To create a new keyframe within the sprite, first select the desired frame and then choose Keyframe from the Insert menu.
7. Choose the foreground and background colors for your second keyframe by clicking the color chips in the Tool Palette **(Figure 42)**. These are the ending colors for your tween.

Note: Director generates colors for a color tween by referencing the current color palette. The tweened colors correspond to the colors in the palette that lie between the starting and ending colors. If the palette colors between your keyframe colors don't form a gradient, you will find that the color tween isn't very effective because the color transition is not gradual. So for best results, choose starting and ending colors where the colors between them are gradually changing from the first to the second *(see page 159 on creating a blend of colors in a palette)*.

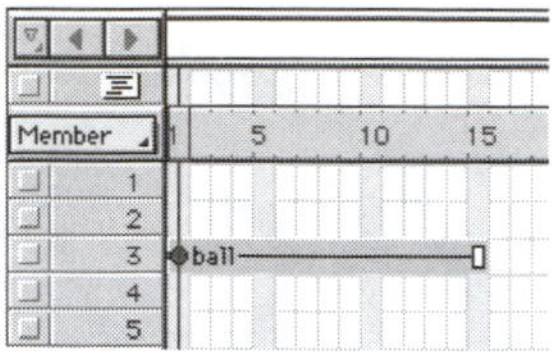

Figure 39. Select or create a keyframe where you wish to start the color tween for your sprite.

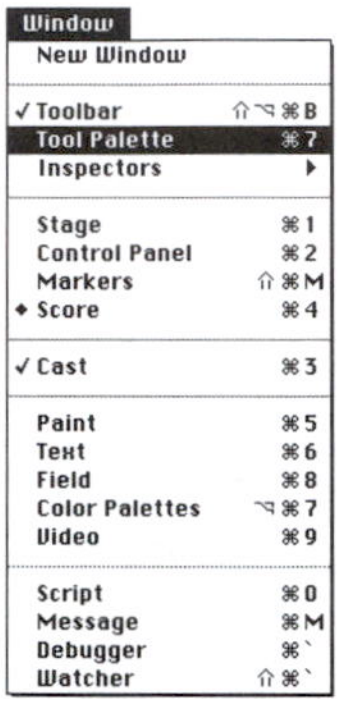

Figure 40. Choose **Tool Palette** from the **Window** menu.

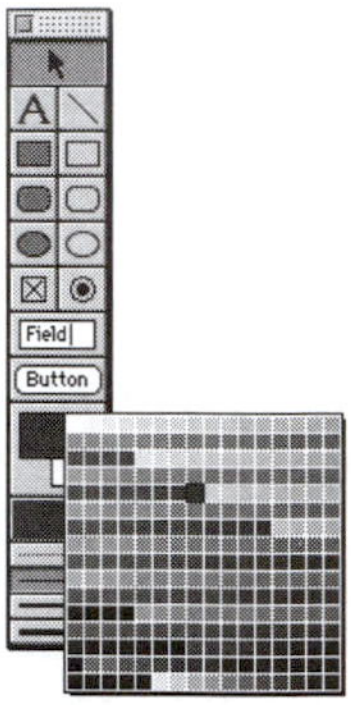

Figure 41. Choose the foreground and background colors for your first keyframe.

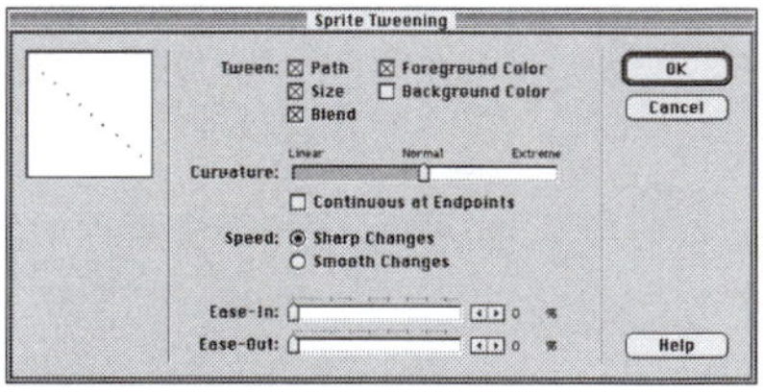

Figure 42. Select the **Foreground** or **Background** options (or both) in the **Sprite Tweening** dialog box.

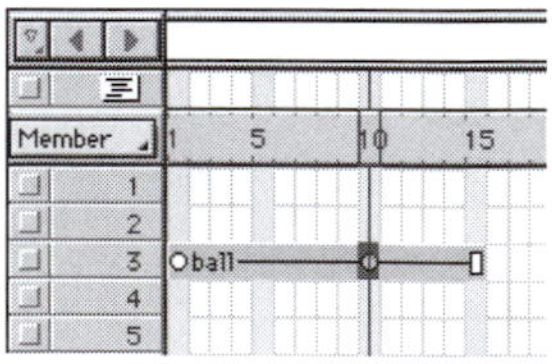

Figure 43. Select or create another keyframe where you wish the color tween to end.

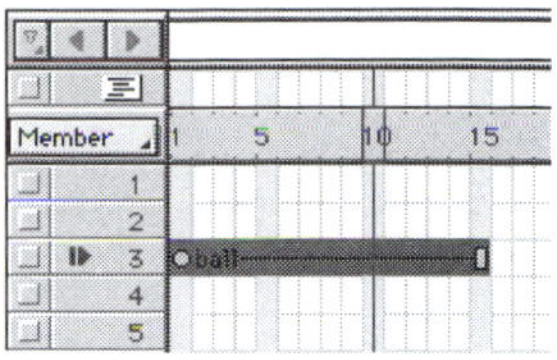

Figure 44. Select the sprite that you want to step record and click the frame in the frame channel where you wish to start.

Figure 45. Choose **Step Recording** from the **Control** menu.

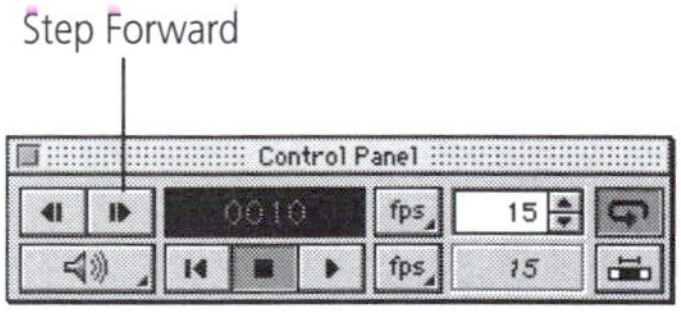

Figure 46. Click the Step Forward button in the control panel to record a frame to the score.

STEP RECORDING

Step recording is a technique of animating a sprite one frame at a time. The idea is that you manually adjust the properties of a sprite, such as position, on a frame-by-frame basis to create an animation. This technique gives you very precise control but is much more labor intensive than tweening, where the frames between keyframes are automatically filled in.

Step recording is useful when you need to create a very precise path that a sprite should follow.

To step record:

1. In the score window, select the sprite(s) that you will be step recording **(Figure 44)**.
2. Click the frame in the frame channel where step recording will start.
3. Choose Step Recording from the Control menu **(Figure 45)**. An indicator appears **(Figure 44)** in each channel that contains a selected sprite.
4. Choose Control Panel from the Window menu.
5. Arrange the selected sprites on the stage as they should appear in the first frame of your step recording.
6. Click the Step Forward button in the control panel **(Figure 46)** to record the frame to the score.
7. Arrange the selected sprites on the stage in the next frame of your step recording.
8. Click Step Forward to record and advance to the next frame. If you step past a sprite's last frame, the sprite is extended into the next frame.
9. Repeat steps 6–7 to step record as many frames as you wish. You can cancel step recording for any particular sprite by selecting the sprite and disabling the Step Recording command under the Control menu.

REAL-TIME RECORDING

One of the most direct ways to animate sprites in Director is to use real-time recording. With real-time recording, you drag a sprite around the stage, and Director automatically records its movement to the score. This is especially useful if you want to animate a sprite along a natural, free-flowing path, with many changes in direction.

The drawback to this approach is that the motion generated by your hand is often considerably less smooth than you might like. After you record a sprite's motion in real-time, however, you can go back and adjust individual frames in the score.

1. Select the sprite in the score that you wish to real-time record.
2. Arrange the sprite on the stage as it should appear in the initial frame of your animation.
3. With the sprite still selected, click in the frame channel within the sprite's range of frames to indicate the starting frame for your real-time recording **(Figure 47)**.
4. Choose Real-Time Recording from the Control menu **(Figure 48)**. A real-time recording indicator appears in the channel which contains the selected sprite **(Figure 47)**.
5. Drag the selected sprite on the stage to start real-time recording.
6. Release the mouse button to end your real-time recording session. If you record beyond the last frame of a sprite, the sprite is extended through the score until you stop recording **(Figure 49)**, or until the start of another sprite is reached in the same channel (in this case, recording is automatically stopped since real-time recording will not overwrite other sprites).

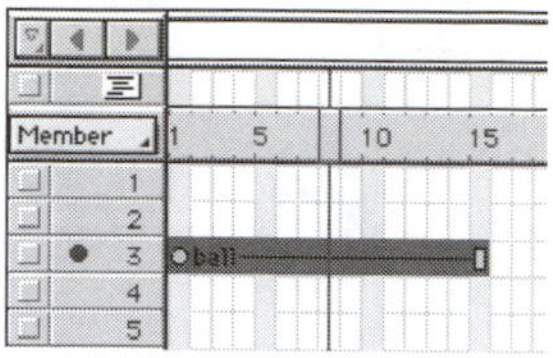

Figure 47. Select a sprite and click in the frame channel to indicate where to start real-time recording.

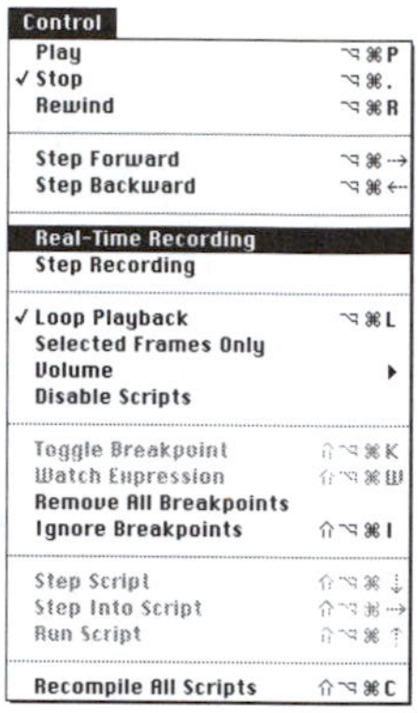

Figure 48. Choose **Real-Time Recording** from the **Control** menu.

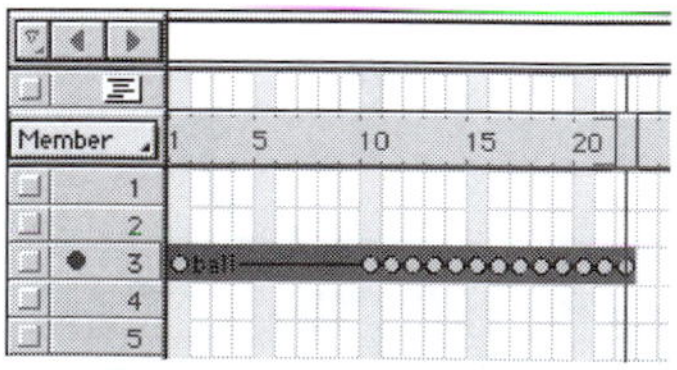

Figure 49. If you record beyond a sprite's end frame, the sprite is extended through the score until you stop recording.

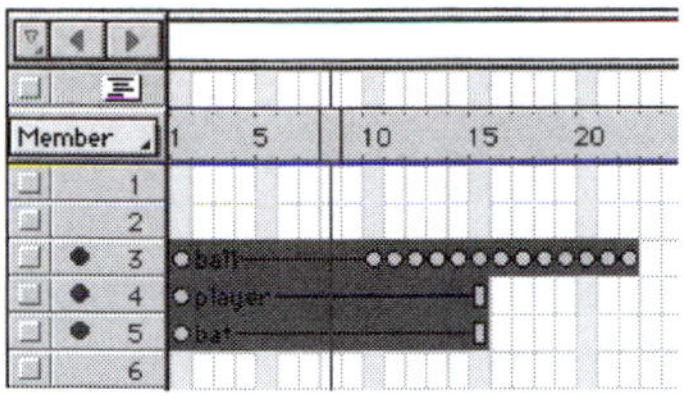

Figure 50. You can real-time record multiple sprites by selecting them together and enabling the Real-Time Recording command.

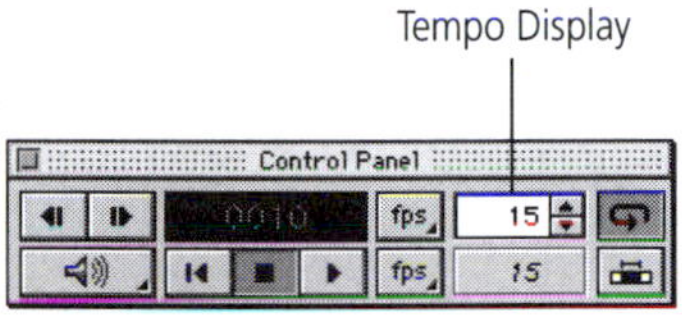

Figure 51. You can slow down the tempo at which Director real-time records by entering a new value in the Tempo Display in the control panel.

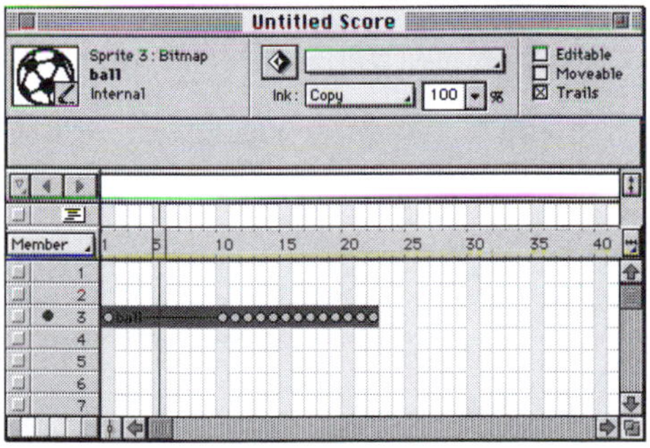

Figure 52. Select your real-time recorded sprite and click the **Trails** option in the score to create a hand-writing-type effect as the sprite moves on the stage.

✔ Tips

- You can real-time record multiple sprites simultaneously by selecting them together and enabling the Real-Time Recording command **(Figure 50)**. The real-time recording indicator appears in each sprite channel that is involved. You start recording as soon as you begin dragging any one of the enabled sprites on the stage.
- If real-time recording seems too sensitive to your mouse movements, you can make it less so by slowing down the tempo at which Director records. To do this, set a new tempo in the control panel window by entering a new value (in frames per second) in the Tempo display **(Figure 51)**. When you're finished recording, you can reset the tempo value to its higher rate to play back your animation.
- You can create a handwriting-type effect by selecting your real-time recorded sprite, and clicking the Trails checkbox in the score **(Figure 52)**. As your sprite moves across the stage, it leaves behind a trail.

CREATING ANIMATED SEQUENCES

An animated sequence in Director refers to a series of related cast members **(Figure 53)**, which appear in an alternating fashion on the stage.

Up to now, you have worked with sprites that consist of only one cast member. But a single sprite can consist of multiple cast members, and this greatly simplifies the process of creating and working with animated sequences in your movie. For example, a sprite can display cast member 1 between frames 1–10 and cast member 2 between frames 11–20.

This section explores the various ways of animating with a series of cast members.

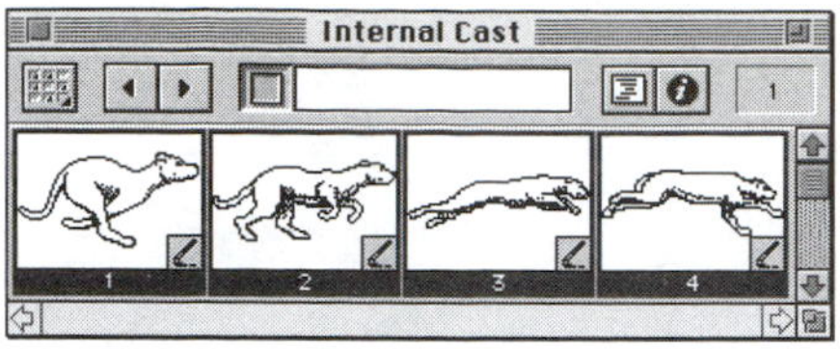

Figure 53. An animated sequence is a series of related cast members appearing in an alternating fashion on the stage.

To exchange a cast member within a sprite:

You can exchange the cast member that a sprite is based on for either the entire sprite, or for a range of frames. The path of the original sprite (if any) is preserved in the exchange.

1. Create a sprite by dragging a single cast member to the stage or score.
2. If you wish to exchange the cast member throughout the entire sprite, select the entire sprite in the score.

or

2. Option-click a frame **(Figure 54)** if you wish to exchange the cast member in that single frame within the sprite. If you wish to exchange the cast member in a range of frames, then Option-click the first frame and Shift-Option click the last frame in the range.
3. In the cast window, select the new cast member.
4. Choose Exchange Cast Members from the Edit menu **(Figure 55)**.

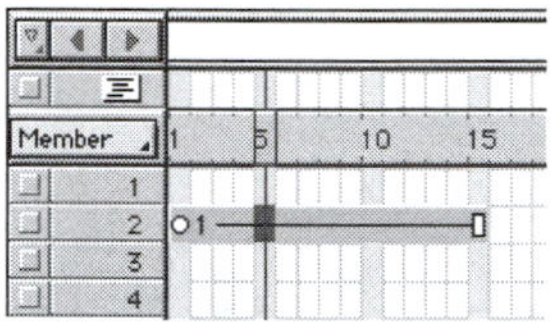

Figure 54. Option-click the frame in which you wish to exchange the cast member.

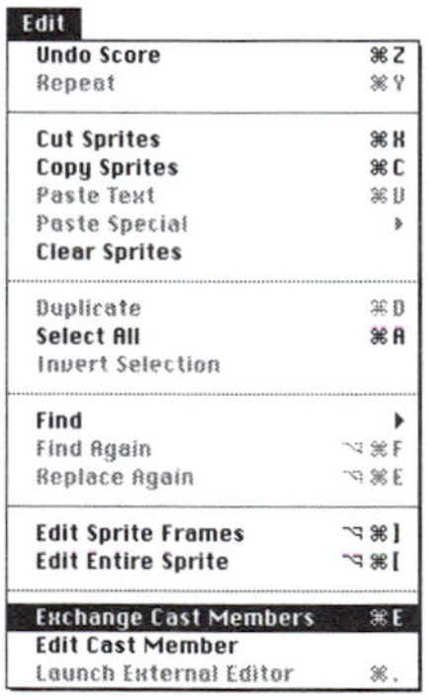

Figure 55. Choose **Exchange Cast Members** from the **Edit** menu.

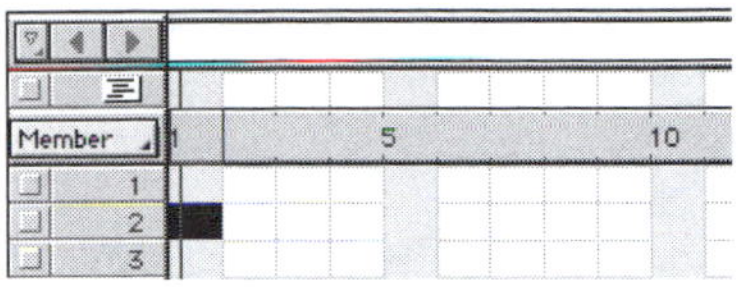

Figure 56. Click a cell to indicate where your cast members should be placed.

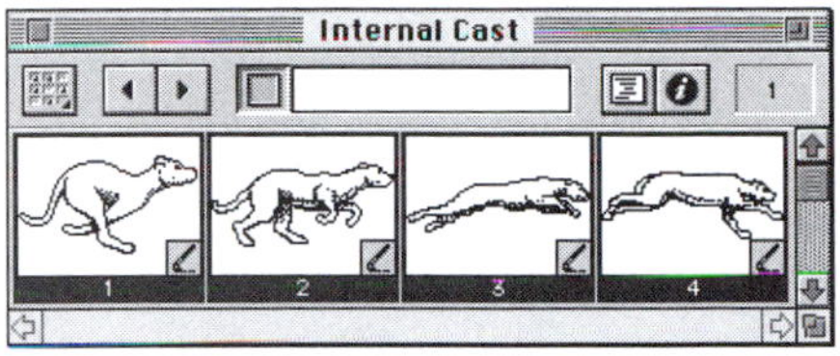

Figure 57. Select the sequence of cast members that you wish to move into the score.

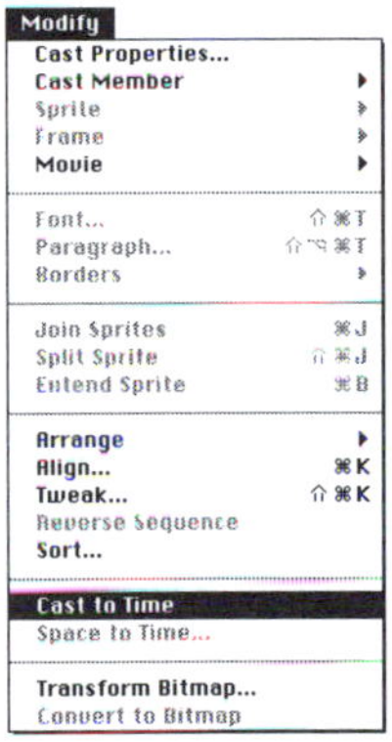

Figure 58. Choose **Cast to Time** from the **Modify** menu.

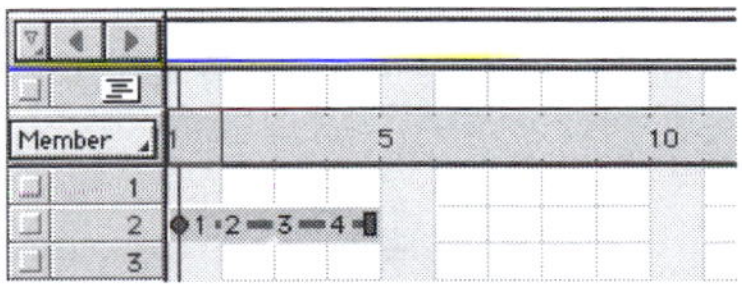

Figure 59. Director creates a single sprite which consists of the cast members you selected.

To place cast members into sequential frames using Cast to Time:

The Cast to Time command offers a convenient way to create an animated sequence by moving a series of cast members from a cast window into sequential frames in the score, forming a single sprite.

1. In the score window, click a cell to indicate the starting point where your cast members should be placed **(Figure 56)**.
2. In the cast window, select the sequence of cast members that you want to move into the score window **(Figure 57)**.
3. With the cast window still active, choose Cast to Time from the Modify menu **(Figure 58)**. Director creates a sprite which consists of as many frames as there are cast members in your sequence, with each frame containing one of the cast members. **(Figure 59)**.
4. Rewind and play back your movie to watch the animated sequence.

✓ Tips

- As a shortcut for Cast to Time, you can place selected cast members across frames in the score by holding the Option key while dragging them from the cast window into the score.
- Before using Cast to Time, make sure that the order of cast members in your selected sequence corresponds to the order that the cast members should appear in your frames.
- Sometimes a sequence of cast members placed in the score may appear to jump or shift as your movie plays. This could be because their registration points are not properly aligned *(see page 102 in the Paint Window chapter on aligning cast member registration points)*.

Space to Time

When you create an animated sequence, you may find it convenient to initially place your series of cast members into a single frame in the score, so that you can view all of them at once on the stage for proper positioning. After positioning, you can then use the Space to Time command to transfer these sprites into a single sprite within a single channel to form an animated sequence.

1. Select a cell in the score where you wish to create your animated sequence.
2. Drag the cast members that comprise your animated sequence one by one from the cast window onto the stage area, and arrange their positions as they should appear in the animated sequence. Be sure to drag them in the order in which your animated sequence takes place. Director automatically places these cast members into sequential channels in the score, creating separate sprites **(Figure 60)**.
3. Select all the sprites you just created in the score.
4. Make all of the sprites' span duration just one frame long. Do so by entering the same value for the Start frame and End frame at the top of the score window **(Figure 61)** or in the Sprite Inspector window.
5. Choose Space to Time from the Modify menu to rearrange your sprites into a single sprite in a single channel **(Figure 62)**.
6. In the Space to Time dialog box, enter the Separation value that indicates how many frames apart the sprites should be placed **(Figure 63)** within your new sprite **(Figure 64)**.

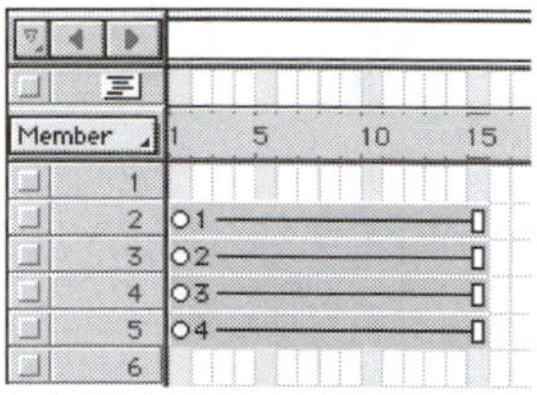

Figure 60. Director places the cast members into sequential channels in the score.

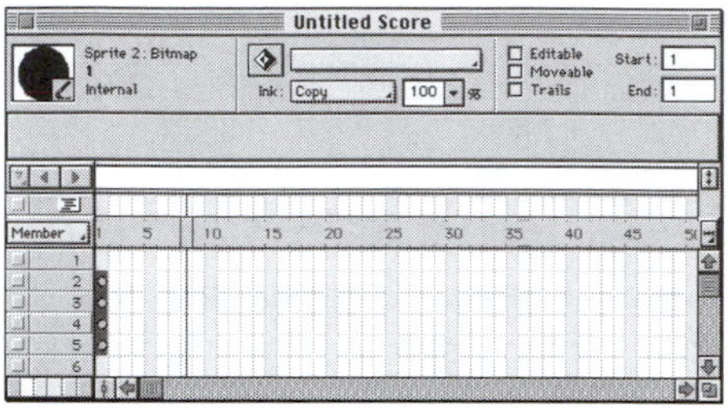

Figure 61. Enter the same value for the **Start** and **End** frame in the score to make your sprites one frame long.

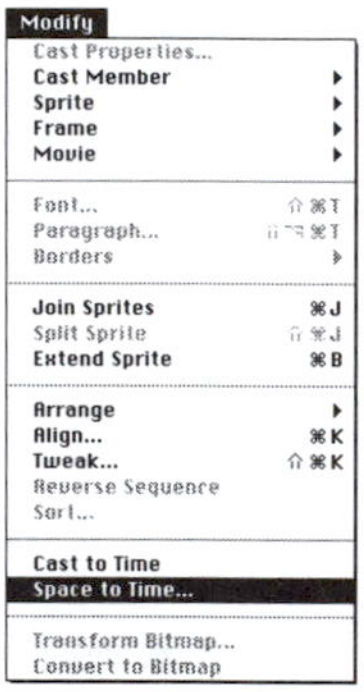

Figure 62. Choose **Space to Time** from the **Modify** menu.

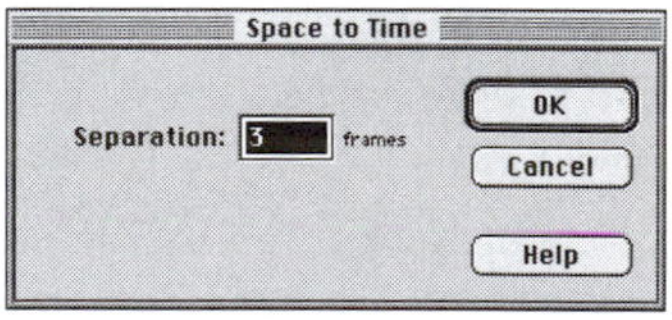

Figure 63. Enter the **Separation** value in the **Space to Time** dialog box.

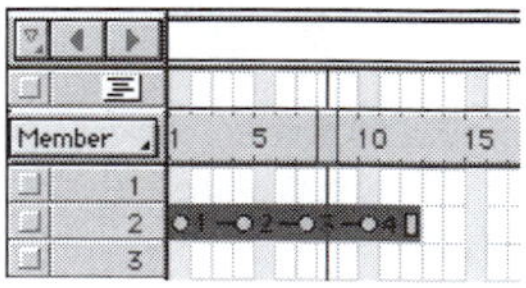

Figure 64. The sprites are combined into a single sprite.

Figure 65. You can use the **Paste Relative** command to align the end frame of a sprite with the start frame of the next sprite. This is a great way to link together a series of animated sequences.

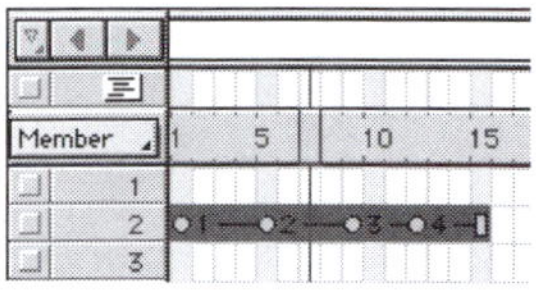

Figure 66. Select the sprite which you wish to paste relative to another sprite.

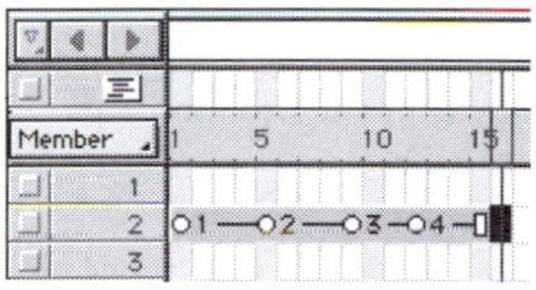

Figure 67. Select the cell immediately following the last cell of your sprite.

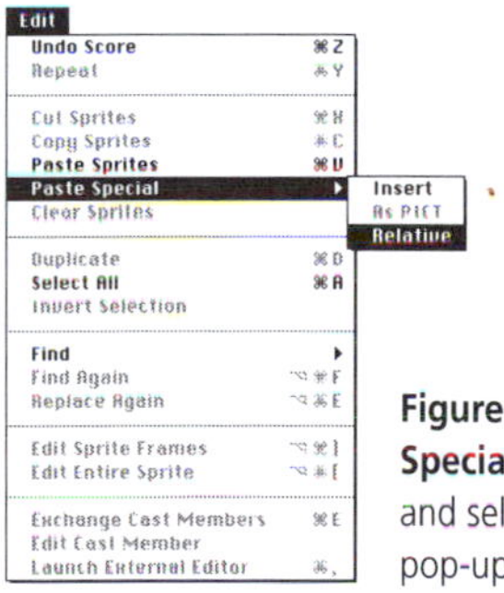

Figure 68. Choose **Paste Special** from the **Edit** menu and select **Relative** from the pop-up menu.

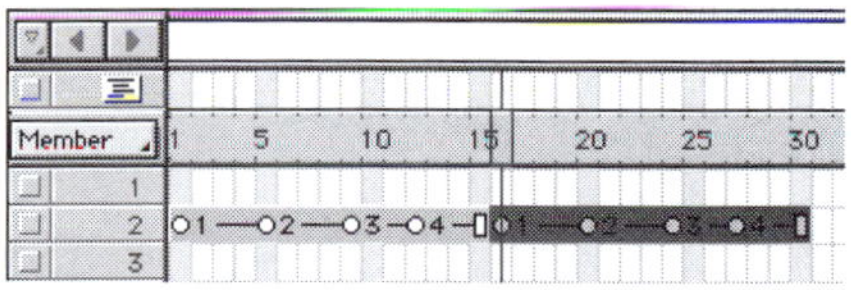

Figure 69. Using **Paste Relative**, a copy of an animated sequence is placed into the score and onto the stage exactly where the previous sequence ends.

To link an animated sequence with Paste Relative:

You can use the Paste Relative command to align the end frame of one sprite with the start frame of the next sprite. This is very useful when you have an animated sequence that you wish to extend across the stage **(Figure 65)**.

1. In the score, select the sprite which contains your animated sequence **(Figure 66)**.
2. Choose Copy Sprites from the Edit menu.
3. Select the cell in the score window immediately following the last cell of your sprite **(Figure 67)**.
4. Choose Paste Special from the Edit menu and select Relative from the pop-up menu **(Figure 68)**. A copy of your animated sequence is placed onto the stage beginning exactly where the previous sequence ends **(Figure 69)**.

To reverse a sequence:

You can reverse the order of cast members in a sprite using the Reverse Sequence command.

1. In the score, select the sprite whose sequence of cast members you wish to reverse.
2. Choose Reverse Sequence from the Modify menu. The order of the cast members **(Figure 70)** in the sprite is reversed.

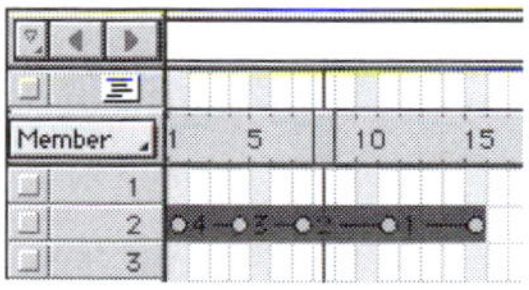

Figure 70. The order of cast members in the sprite is reversed.

FILM LOOPS

Think of a film loop as an animated cast member. Instead of consisting of just one image, it's actually composed of a range of score data. For example, suppose you have five sprites in five separate channels and each in a separate range of frames **(Figure 71)**. You can consolidate all this information into a single film loop cast member. When this cast member is placed into the score, a single sprite is created which consists of all the sprite data which was placed into the film loop **(Figure 72)**. Film loops can even include data from the Sound channels.

Film loops make it much easier to work with large complex animations. They also make it easier to work with animated sequences. Suppose, for example, that you have a sprite which consists of the four cast members shown in **Figure 73**, forming an animated sequence. If you create a film loop cast member out of that sprite, you can then place that film loop into the score to create a sprite with the same animated sequence, but simplified since all of its frames consist of the same cast member, namely the film loop.

Film loops can be used with Director's tweening feature and Real-Time Recording command to create complex animations. For instance, the film loop of a bird flapping its wings can be tweened to move from one side of the screen to another.

Like conventional cast members, a film loop is kept in a cast window. It is identified by the film loop icon **(Figure 74)**.

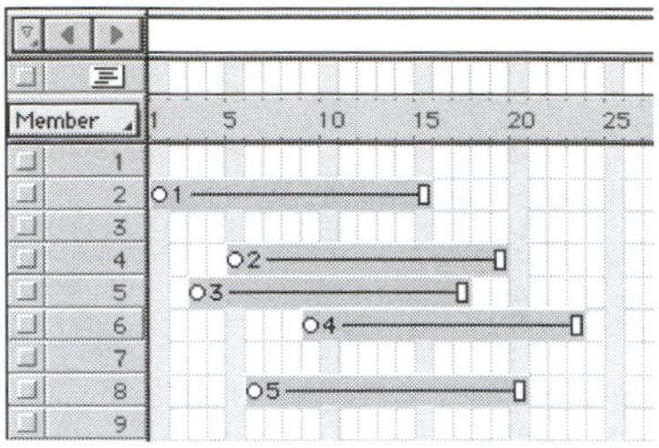

Figure 71. You can consolidate all this sprite data into a single film loop cast member.

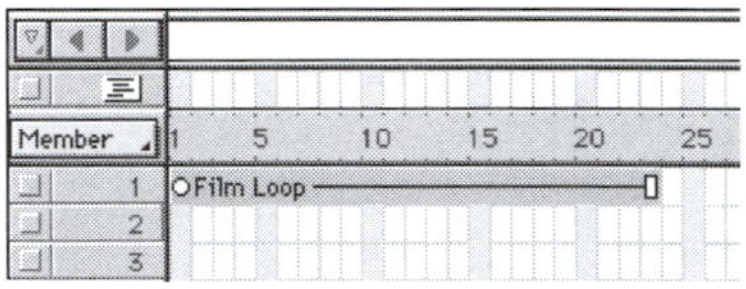

Figure 72. This single film loop replaces all the score data in **Figure 71**.

Figure 73. A sprite is shown, which consists of these four cast members.

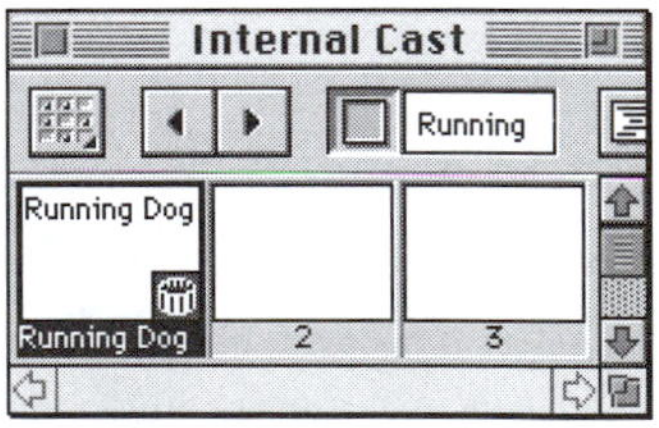

Figure 74. A film loop cast member in a cast window.

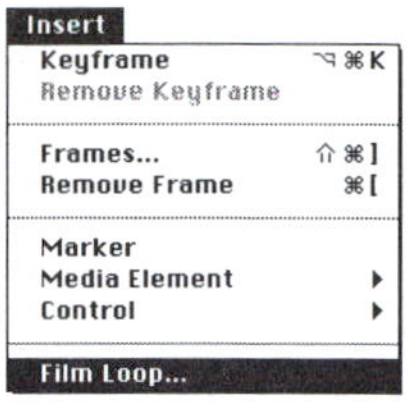

Figure 75. Choose **Film Loop** from the **Insert** menu.

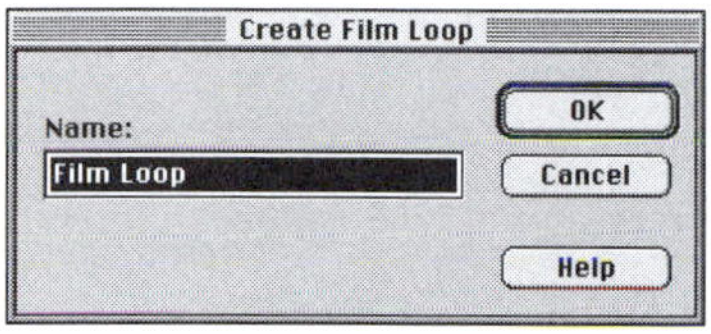

Figure 76. Enter a name for the film loop in the **Create Film Loop** dialog box.

To create a film loop:

1. In the score, select all of the sprites that you wish to turn into a film loop. Command-click to select non-adjacent sprites. You can include sprites in either of the two sound channels.
2. Choose Film Loop from the Insert menu **(Figure 75)**.
3. Type in a name for the film loop in the Create Film Loop dialog box **(Figure 76)**. The film loop is inserted into the next available position in the cast window.

Note: A film loop cast member is inserted into your movie like any other graphical cast member—by dragging it to the stage or into cells in the score. A film loop cast member must occupy enough continuous cells in the score in order for all of its frames to have a chance to play. For example, if a film loop consists of four frames, the film loop cast member should be placed through at least four continuous frames in the score, so that during playback, all of its frames are displayed.

Note: Even though you've placed a film loop into your movie, it will not appear to animate if you step through its frames using the control panel, or if you drag Director's playback head across the frames in the score. Film loops animate only when you play your movie.

Note: You cannot apply score ink effects to film loops. These effects must first be applied to the individual sprites that make up a film loop.

✓ Tips

- As a shortcut, you can create a film loop by dragging a selection of frames from the score into a cast window.
- A film loop itself can be composed of other film loops. For example, suppose you have two film loops placed in the score, one of a walking man, and the other of a running dog. You can create a single film loop which includes both of these loops.

To Real-time record with a film loop:

You can use real-time recording to record a path for a film loop cast member to follow across the stage (very similar to real-time recording with a non-film loop cast member described earlier in this chapter). As your film loop cast member cycles through its frames during playback, it will also move across the stage. This is a great technique to use to set up animations such as birds flapping their wings across the stage.

1. Select the film loop sprite in the score that you wish to real-time record **(Figure 77)**.
2. Arrange the sprite on the stage as it should appear in the initial frame of your animation.
3. With the sprite still selected, click in the frame channel within the sprite's range of frames to indicate the starting frame for your real-time recording.
4. Choose Real-Time Recording from the Control menu **(Figure 78)**.
5. Drag the selected sprite on the stage to start real-time recording.
6. Release the mouse button to end your real-time recording session.

Tweening with a film loop:

Making use of the tweening feature with a film loop cast member creates a powerful animation effect. For example, you can animate a film loop cast member of a racing dog, having it travel across the stage in any variety of predetermined paths, while its frames alternate. You can specify a straight, or curved path, just as you can with a sprite based on a regular bitmap cast member. Follow the same steps on page 71, but simply use a film loop cast member.

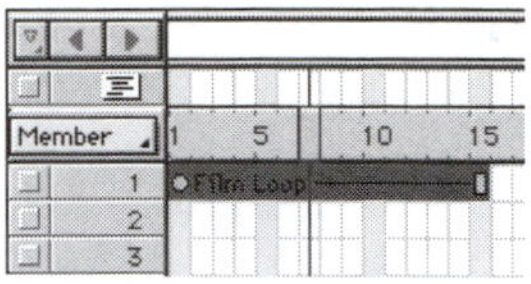

Figure 77. Select the film loop sprite that you wish to real-time record.

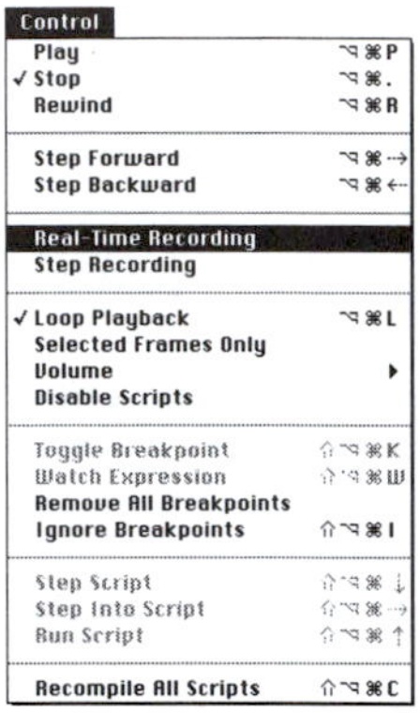

Figure 78. Choose **Real-Time Recording** from the **Control** menu.

CONTROL PANEL 6

Director's Control Panel is used to control the playback of your movie **(Figure 1)**. Much like the controls on a VCR, you can play, rewind, step forward, or step backward through the frames of your movie. The Control Panel also allows you to adjust volume, and set loop playback. Open the Control Panel by choosing Control Panel from the Window menu **(Figure 2)** or by pressing Command-2.

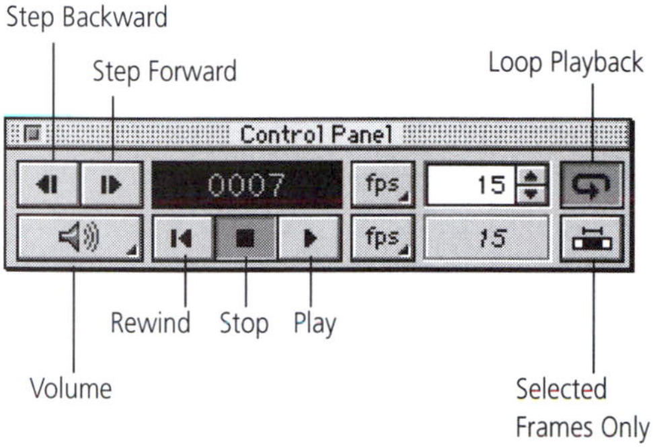

Figure 1. The Control Panel.

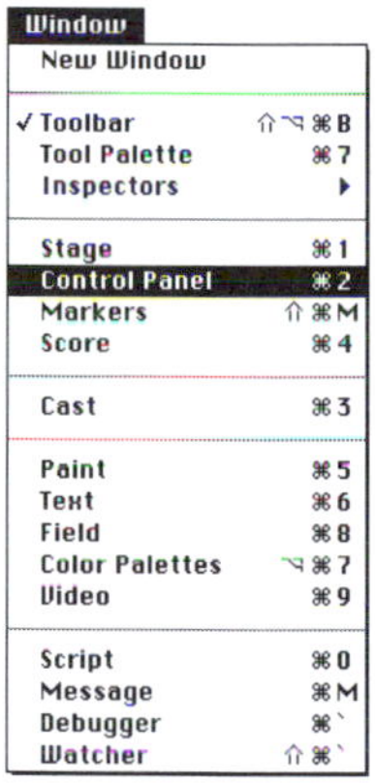

Figure 2. Choose **Control Panel** from the **Window** menu.

CONTROL PANEL BUTTONS

Rewind

Click the Rewind button (Command-Option-R) to reset the movie to frame 1 **(Figure 3)**. Doing so during playback automatically stops the movie and rewinds to frame 1.

Figure 3. The **Rewind** button.

Step Backward

Step Backward (Command-Option-Left Arrow) steps the movie back one frame at a time **(Figure 4)**. Holding down this button steps backward continuously.

Figure 4. The **Step Backward** button.

Stop

Stop (Command-.) stops the movie **(Figure 5)**.

Figure 5. The **Stop** button.

Step Forward

Step Forward (Command-Option-Right Arrow) steps the movie forward one frame at a time **(Figure 6)**. Hold down this button to step forward continuously.

When a Score channel is in Step Recording mode, click Step Forward to copy the contents of the current frame to the next frame. *(See page 79 in the Animating Sprites chapter on Step Recording)*

Figure 6. The **Step Forward** button.

Play

Play (Command-Option-P) starts the movie **(Figure 7)**. Press Command-1 to hide all open windows and the menu bar.

Figure 7. The **Play** button.

Volume

(Figure 8) *(See page 182 in the Sound chapter)*

Figure 8. The **Volume** button.

Loop Playback

Loop Playback (Command-Option-L) controls whether your movie will repeat over and over **(Figure 9)**. If this button is selected, your movie will automatically start over from frame 1 each time it reaches the last frame. Loop is on by default.

Loop enabled (default) | Loop disabled

Figure 9.

Selected Frames Only

Selected Frames Only **(Figure 10)** allows you to play a portion of the current movie. First, open the score and select the frames you wish to play back. Then click the Selected Frames Only button. A green bar appears in the score above the selected frames. Now when you click the Play button, only these marked frames will play. Click the Selected Frames Only button again to remove the green bar and turn off the selection.

Selected Frames Only enabled | Selected Frames Only disabled

Figure 10.

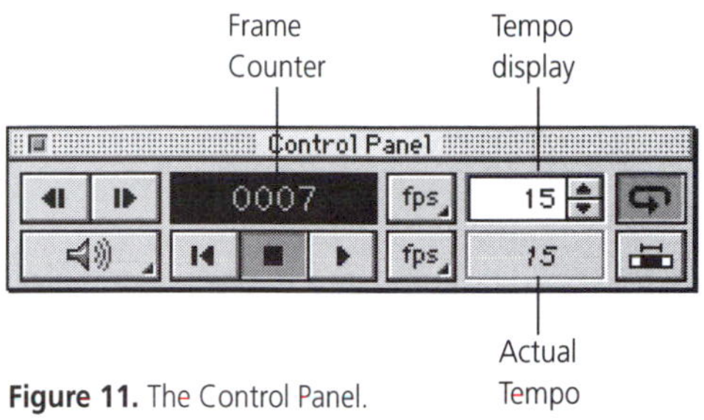

Figure 11. The Control Panel.

Figure 12. The Frame Counter.

Figure 13. The Tempo display.

CONTROL PANEL INDICATORS

Frame Counter

The Frame Counter indicates which frame of your movie is currently displayed on the stage **(Figures 11–12)**. This corresponds to the Playback head indicator in the score window *(see page 44)*. You can enter a frame number to jump to by double-clicking the displayed frame number and typing a value.

Tempo display

The Tempo display indicates the preset tempo that the current frame should play at, in frames per second **(Figure 13)**. Director will never play a given frame faster than this tempo, but may play slower because of performance limitations of your computer *(see the "Actual Tempo" section on page 92)*. You can change this target tempo setting for each frame by clicking the up or down arrows, or by double-clicking the displayed tempo number and typing a value. If a tempo setting has been entered in the tempo channel of the score at a certain frame, that setting takes precedence, and will be indicated here *(see page 189 in the Movie Tempo chapter for details on the Tempo channel)*. If no such tempo setting has been made, the Tempo display field displays a default value.

Actual Tempo

The Actual Tempo display **(Figure 14)** indicates the *actual* duration of the current frame in frames-per-second. The actual tempo of your frames can fall behind the set or desired tempo shown in the Tempo display, due to speed limitations of your computer.

Figure 14. The Actual Tempo display.

To compare the set tempo to the actual tempo:

You can step through a movie frame-by-frame and compare the set tempo in the Tempo display to the Actual Tempo. Since Macintosh computers can vary in speed performance, some of them may not keep up with your set tempo. If you plan to run your movie on a wide range of Macintoshes, comparing the set tempo to the actual tempo on a slower Macintosh allows you to set appropriate tempo values for the frames, so that the actual tempo never falls below the set tempo. *(See the Movie Tempo chapter on page 192 for more details)*

1. Open the Control Panel by choosing Control Panel from the Window menu **(Figure 15)**.
2. Click Rewind to reset the movie to the first frame.
3. Click the Step Forward button and compare the number shown in the Tempo display to the number in the Actual Tempo display **(Figure 16)**.
4. Use the arrows in the Tempo display to set new tempo values for the frames.

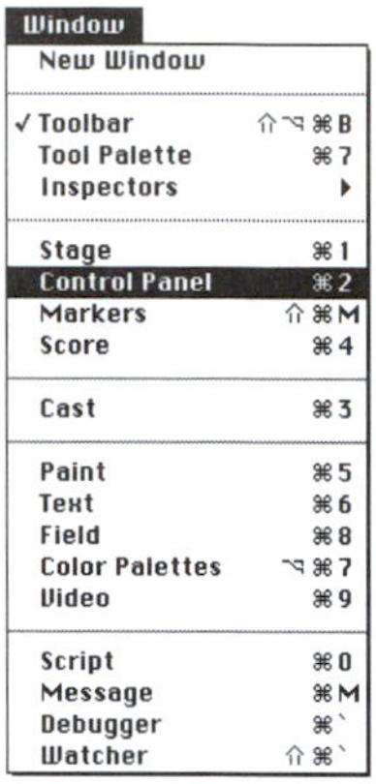

Figure 15. Choose **Control Panel** from the **Window** menu.

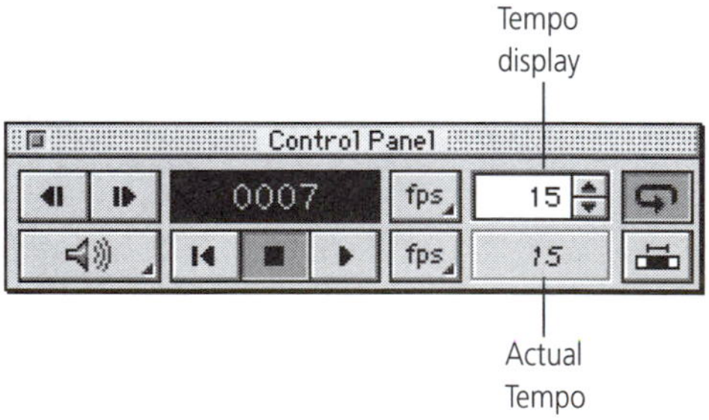

Figure 16. In the Control Panel, compare the set tempo value of each frame, shown in the Tempo display, to the Actual Tempo of each frame.

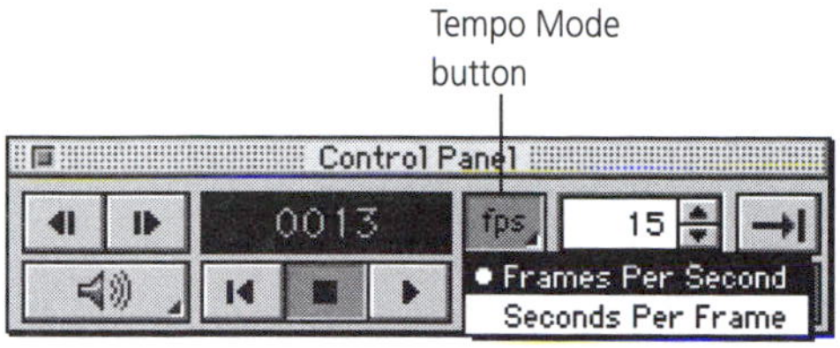

Figure 17. Use the **Tempo Mode** button to choose whether the Tempo display is shown in frames per second or seconds per frame.

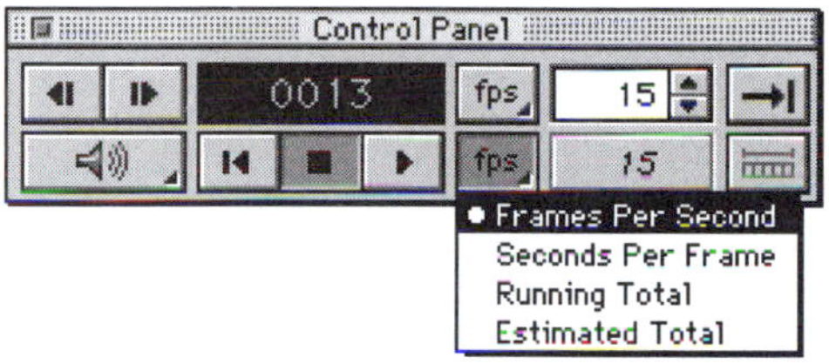

Figure 18. Click and hold the **Actual Tempo** mode button to display a pop-up menu which determines how the Actual Tempo is displayed.

Tempo Mode button:

Use the Tempo Mode button to choose whether the Tempo display value in the Control Panel is displayed in frames per second (FPS) or seconds per frame (SPF). Click and hold the Tempo Mode button and choose from the the pop-up menu **(Figure 17)**.

Actual Tempo Mode button:

Click and hold the Actual Tempo mode button **(Figure 18)** to display a pop-up menu of choices which determine how the Actual Tempo value is displayed. Your choices are Frames per Second, Seconds per Frame, Running Total, and Estimated Total. Running Total indicates the total elapsed time in seconds from the start of your movie to the current frame. Estimated Total is similar to Running Total, but is more accurate since it includes palette changes and transitions in its calculation of the frame durations.

✔ Tip

- Don't leave your Actual Tempo display in Estimated Total mode while playing back your movie, since this mode can lower playback speed due to its more intensive calculations.

PAINT WINDOW 7

Paint Window

The paint window is used throughout this chapter. Choose Paint from the Window menu to open it **(Figure 1)** or press Command-5.

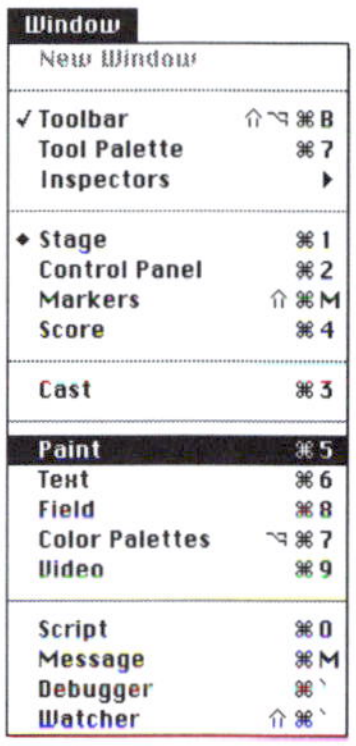

Figure 1. Choose **Paint** from the **Window** menu.

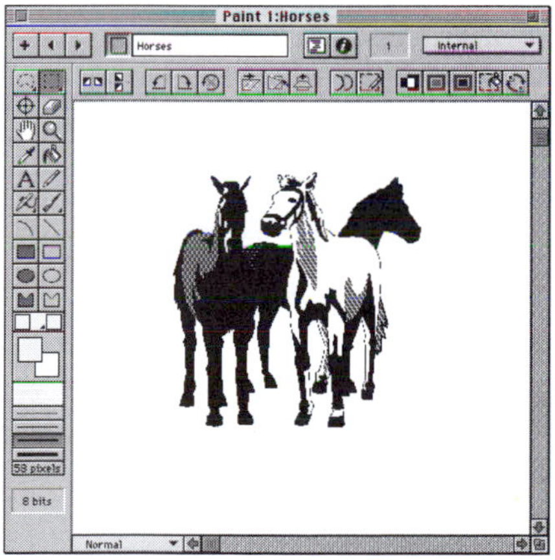

Figure 2. The paint window.

Director's paint window provides numerous tools such as the Air Brush, Paint Bucket, and Lasso for creating and editing bitmap cast member graphics **(Figure 2)**. While these tools aren't as elaborate as the Adobe Photoshop or MacDraw Pro tools, they are robust enough to create many of the cast members you're likely to showcase in your movies.

The paint window also offers an **Effects** toolbar, which contains numerous special-effects commands that can be applied to your artwork, such as Rotate, Warp, Skew, and Perspective.

Director 6 provides a feature called Onion Skinning, which allows you to create a cast member in the paint window while viewing one or more reference cast members that appear dimmed in the background. This technique is very useful for creating animated sequences. *(See page 131)*

Director 6 allows you to use image filters from Photoshop or Premiere to modify bitmap cast member graphics in the paint window. *(See page 133)*

Shape or PICT cast members cannot be edited in the paint window. If you wish to create a shape cast member, use Director's Tool Palette. *(See page 135 in the Tool Palette chapter for details)*

This chapter covers the use of all tools and effects in the paint window. Ink masks, the Onion Skinning feature, and using image filters are covered in the last three sections of the chapter.

THE PAINT WINDOW

The link between the paint and cast windows

It's important to know that when you create a graphic in Director's paint window, that graphic also becomes a cast member in a cast window **(Figures 3–4)**.

In fact, the paint window shares a dynamic link with the cast window. From a cast window, you can double-click a bitmap cast member and it automatically opens in the paint window. And from the paint window, you can access all the bitmap cast members in a cast window by clicking the Previous and Next buttons in the paint window's upper left corner **(Figure 3)**. You specify which cast to work with by using the Cast selector pop-up menu in the upper right corner of the paint window.

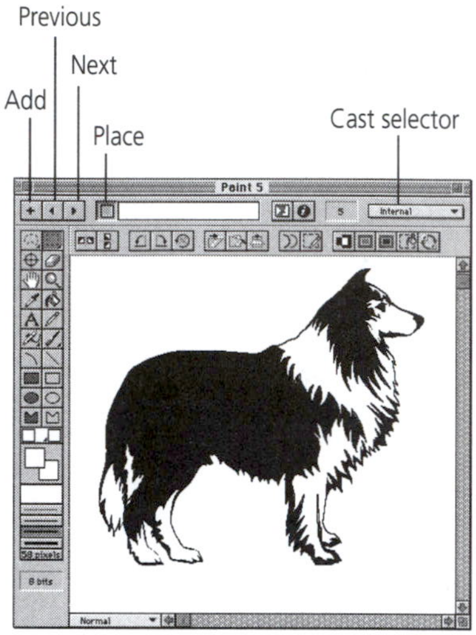

Figure 3. Objects drawn in the paint window automatically become new cast members, as shown below in the cast window.

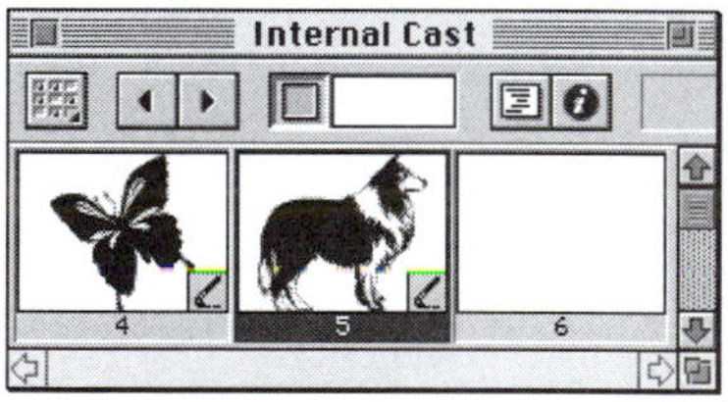

Figure 4. The cast window.

To add a new cast member while using the paint window:

1. Click the Add button to create a new cast member **(Figure 3)**. Director displays an empty paint window and the image you draw becomes a cast member in the first available position in the cast window as soon as you close the paint window.

To place a graphic onto the stage from the paint window:

1. Drag the Place button onto the stage and Director places the image from the paint window onto the stage and into the score.

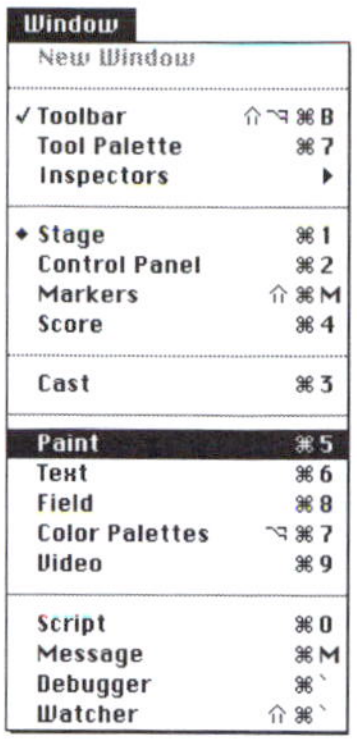

Figure 5. Choose **Paint** from the **Window** menu.

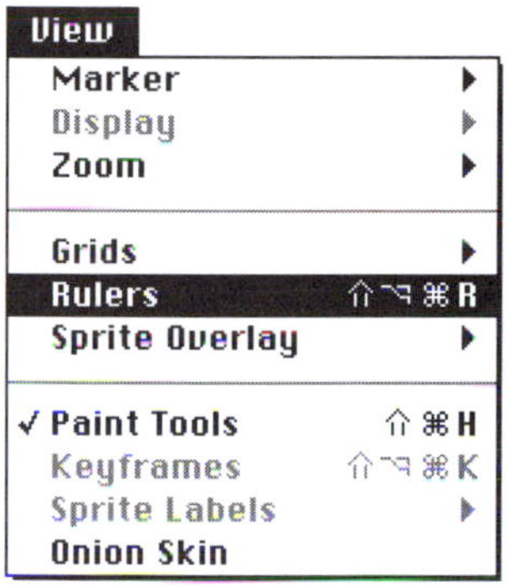

Figure 6. Choose **Rulers** from the **View** menu.

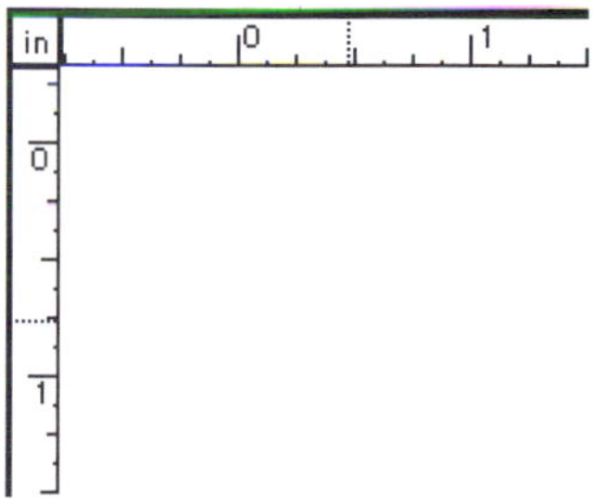

Figure 7. To change the ruler's units of measurement, click the upper-left corner of the ruler.

To show or hide rulers in the paint window:

You can display a set of horizontal and vertical rulers in the paint window to help you align and measure your artwork. The rulers can display their measurement values in either inches, centimeters, or pixels.

1. Choose Paint from the Window menu **(Figure 5)**.
2. Choose Ruler from the View menu. To hide the Ruler, choose it again **(Figure 6)**.

✓ Tips

- You can set a ruler's zero point by clicking the ruler and dragging to the point where you'd like the new zero point to be.
- To display the ruler's measurements in a new unit (inches, centimeters, etc.), click the upper-left corner where the horizontal and vertical rulers meet **(Figure 7)**.

To show or hide the paint tool palette:

If you need more space to work with in the paint window, you can hide the paint tool palette. Make sure to select the paint tool you wish to use first.

1. With the paint window open, choose Paint Tools from the View menu to show or hide the paint tool palette.

PAINT TOOL PALETTE

Director provides an assortment of painting tools used to create and modify bitmap cast members. These tools are located in the paint tool palette, which is found on the left side of the paint window **(Figure 8)**.

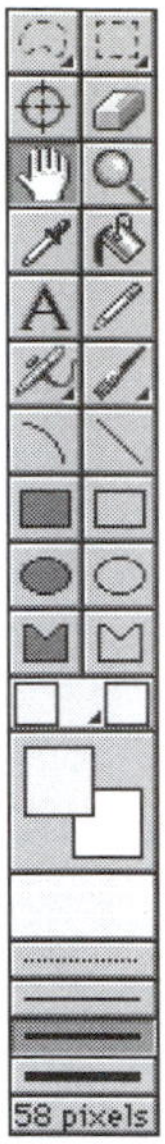

Figure 8. The paint tool palette is found on the left side of the paint window.

Lasso and Marquee tools

Like most Macintosh paint programs, Director's paint window features a selection rectangle (called the Marquee), and a Lasso that allow you to select all or just parts of cast member artwork. Once artwork has been selected, you can use the other tools in the paint window to modify the selection—for instance, drag it to another region of the paint window, cut or copy it, rotate it, change its colors, warp it, and so on.

While the two tools work similarly, there is one important difference between them: The Marquee allows you to select rectangular regions of artwork, while the Lasso selects any region you "draw" with, giving you much greater flexibility in making artwork selections. Another difference is that some of Director's paint features work only with artwork selected by the Marquee, not by the Lasso (or vice versa). These instances are identified later in the chapter.

Figure 9. The Marquee tool.

To select artwork with the Marquee:

1. Click the Marquee tool in the paint tool palette **(Figure 9)**.
2. The mouse pointer becomes a crosshair. Position the crosshair wherever you want to begin your selection.
3. Drag the pointer up or down and to one side to outline a rectangular selection around your artwork **(Figure 10)**.

Figure 10. Drag the pointer to outline a rectangular selection or "marquee" around your artwork.

Figure 11. To stretch or compress an artwork selection, hold the Command key, click anywhere in the selection, and drag.

Figure 12. Click and hold the Marquee tool until the **Options** pop-up menu appears.

You'll see a dotted line called a "marquee" encase your artwork selection.

4. Release the mouse button to select the artwork within the marquee.

✔ **Tips**

- You can reposition your artwork selection by moving the mouse to the selection marquee (the crosshair becomes a pointer again) and dragging the artwork to a new area.
- Hold down the Option key while dragging an artwork selection to drag a copy of it, leaving the original in place.
- To stretch or compress an artwork selection, hold down the Command key, click anywhere in the selection and drag **(Figure 11)**. To stretch or compress while keeping the image's original proportions, hold down the Command and Shift keys while dragging.
- To erase a selection, press the Backspace or Delete key.
- Double-click the Marquee tool to select the entire visible portion of the paint window.

To choose Marquee tool options:

You can control how the Marquee behaves when selecting artwork.

1. Click the Marquee tool in the paint tool palette. Hold the mouse button down until the Options pop-up menu appears **(Figure 12)**.
2. Drag to select one of the four options in the menu. Your choices are Shrink, No Shrink, Lasso, and See Thru Lasso.

Shrink makes the selection marquee tighten around whatever object you've selected, although the selection still keeps its rectangular shape. Director identifies an object's border by looking for color differences between pixels.

No Shrink selects all the artwork that you encased with the selection marquee.

Lasso makes the selection marquee tighten around whatever object you've selected but allows the selection area to take on an irregular shape, as if you had actually used the Lasso tool.

See Thru Lasso is similar to the Lasso option, but it makes all white pixels in your selection become transparent.

To select artwork with the Lasso tool:

1. Click the Lasso tool in the paint tool palette **(Figure 13)**.
2. The mouse pointer turns into a lasso when you move it inside the paint window. Position the Lasso wherever you want to begin your selection.
3. Drag the Lasso to draw a line around the art you wish to select **(Figure 14)**. Try to end your selection at the point where you started it.
4. Release the mouse button and Director highlights the selected area with the marquee. If you did not entirely encase your selection, Director automatically connects its starting and ending points.

Figure 13. The Lasso tool.

Figure 14. Drag the Lasso to draw a line around the artwork you wish to select.

✔ **Tips**

- You can use the Lasso tool to select a polygonal shape. Hold the Option key while dragging the Lasso to create an anchor point and draw a straight selection line. Repeat this step to encase your artwork with such lines. Double-click to end your selection.
- You can reposition your artwork selection by positioning the Lasso within the selection (the Lasso becomes a mouse pointer again), and dragging the artwork to a new location. If you hold down the Option key, you drag a copy of the artwork, leaving the original in place.

Figure 15. Click and hold the Lasso tool to display the **Options** pop-up menu.

To choose Lasso options:

You can control how the Lasso behaves when selecting artwork.

1. Click the Lasso tool in the paint tool palette. Hold the mouse button down until the Options pop-up menu appears **(Figure 15)**.
2. Drag to select one of the three options in the menu. Your choices are No Shrink, Lasso, and See Thru Lasso.

No Shrink selects all the artwork that you encase with the Lasso and does not fine-tune the selection.

Lasso makes the selection marquee tighten around whatever object you've selected. Director tries to identify an objects border by looking for color differences between pixels. The idea is to "fine-tune" the selection you made by hand.

See Thru Lasso makes all the white pixels in your selection become transparent.

Registration Points

A registration point is a fixed point of reference in a bitmap image. Every bitmap cast member in your movie has a default registration point, which is placed directly at its center **(Figure 16)**

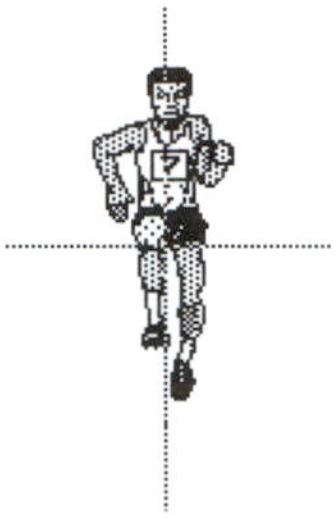

Figure 16. A cast member with its registration point shown in the paint window.

When you create cast members for an animation sequence, there's a chance that they may appear to jump and shift from one frame to the next when animated. To avoid this problem, you can adjust their registration points. For instance, if you were animating several frames of an athlete running, you could set a registration point where the character's feet touch the ground for each cast member in the sequence. This would ensure that the runner's feet never hit above or below ground level. *(Also see "To align Sprites" on page 61)*

You can view your cast member's registration point by opening the cast member in the paint window and clicking the Registration Point tool **(Figure 17)**.

Figure 17. The Registration Point tool.

To set a new cast member registration point:

1. Open a cast member in Director's paint window.
2. Click the Registration Point tool in the paint tool palette to select it **(Figure 17)**. The current registration point assigned to the cast member appears at the intersection of the dotted lines.
3. Move the crosshair pointer to a new location in the paint window, and click to place the registration mark in this new location **(Figure 18)**.

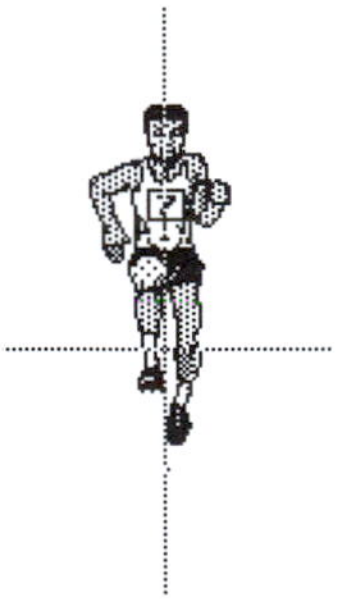

Figure 18. The registration point here has been moved downward.

✔ Tip

- If you ever want to reset a registration point to its default position (that is, directly at the center of the cast member), double-click the Registration Point tool in the paint tool palette.

Figure 19. The Eraser tool.

Eraser tool

Erase a portion of an image by dragging the Eraser tool **(Figure 19)** across it. Double-click the Eraser tool to clear the entire image in the paint window.

Figure 20. The Hand tool.

Hand tool

The Hand tool is used to move an image around in the paint window **(Figure 20)**. Click the Hand tool then drag the image in the paint window to move it in any direction. Press the Spacebar in the paint window as a shortcut for selecting the Hand tool.

Figure 21. The Magnifying glass tool.

Magnifying glass tool

Select the Magnifying glass tool, and then click with it in the paint window to zoom in on your artwork **(Figure 21)**. Shift-click to zoom out.

Figure 22. The Eyedropper tool.

Eyedropper tool

The Eyedropper tool is used to "pick up" and match colors **(Figure 22)**. Click the Eyedropper anywhere in the paint window, and the color it is positioned on becomes the new foreground color. *(See page 111 on switching colors with the Eyedropper)*

Figure 23. The Paint Bucket tool.

Paint Bucket tool

Position the Paint Bucket **(Figure 23)** over empty space in your artwork and click to fill the space with the selected foreground color.

Figure 24. The Pencil tool.

Pencil tool

Drag the Pencil tool **(Figure 24)** to draw single pixels in the selected foreground color. Drawing over existing pixels in the foreground color will change the pixels to the selected background color.

Text tool

The Text tool allows you to enter bitmap text anywhere within the paint window **(Figure 25)**. Simply click the Text tool icon and then click the desired location in the paint window where text should be entered. A blinking cursor box appears. The text's font, size, and style can be modified in the Font dialog box, which is opened by choosing Font from the Modify menu, or by double-clicking the Text tool *(see the Creating Text in Director chapter on page 170)*. Once the bitmap text has been entered, there is no way of changing the font, size, or style of the text. Any effects or color changes can be applied to bitmap text just like to a regular bitmap image.

Figure 25. The Text tool.

Air Brush tool

Drag the Air Brush **(Figure 26)** to "spray" paint in the selected foreground color, and pattern if any. A variety of air brush settings allow you to specify the size and density of the Air Brush's spray. *(See page 123)*

Figure 26. The Air Brush tool.

Paint Brush tool

The Paint Brush tool **(Figure 27)** allows you to paint in the selected foreground color and pattern by dragging the mouse across the paint window. You can choose from a variety of brush shapes and design your own as well. *(See page 120)*

Figure 27. The Paint Brush tool.

Arc tool

The Arc tool **(Figure 28)** draws one quarter of an ellipse. Drag to preview the length and angle of your arc, and release the mouse button to draw it. Hold the Shift key while dragging to draw 45 degree arcs, and hold the Option key while dragging to draw an arc in the currently selected pattern.

Figure 28. The Arc tool.

Line tool

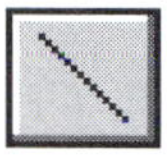

Figure 29. The Line tool.

The Line tool **(Figure 29)** is used to draw straight lines. Drag to set any angle for your line. Hold the Shift key while dragging to draw 45 degree lines, and hold the Option key while dragging to draw lines in the currently selected pattern. Use the Line Width Selector in the paint tool palette to change the thickness of the line.

Filled Rectangle tool

Figure 30. The Filled Rectangle tool.

Select the Filled Rectangle tool **(Figure 30)**, then drag the pointer to draw a solid rectangular shape in the selected foreground color, and pattern if any. The thickness of the border of the rectangle (visible only when a pattern is used) is set by the Line Width Selector located at the bottom of the paint tool palette. Hold down the Shift key while dragging to constrain the rectangle to a perfect square.

Rectangle tool

Figure 31. The Rectangle tool.

Select the Rectangle tool **(Figure 31)** then drag the pointer to outline a hollow rectangular shape of any size in the current foreground color.

Filled Ellipse tool

Figure 32. The Filled Ellipse tool.

Select the Filled Ellipse tool **(Figure 32)**, then drag to size the ellipse's solid shape. Hold down the Shift key while dragging to draw a circle. When you release the mouse button, the ellipse is drawn in the selected foreground color, and pattern if any.

Ellipse tool

Figure 33. The Ellipse tool.

Select the Ellipse tool **(Figure 33)** then drag the pointer to outline a hollow elliptical shape of any size in the current foreground color.

Filled Polygon tool

Select the Filled Polygon tool **(Figure 34)**, then click the mouse to draw straight lines that make up a polygon. Each mouse click draws a new line in the polygon, starting from the last line's ending point, and ending where the mouse pointer is positioned. Double-click to draw the polygon's final line segment that connects the first and last lines together. When the final segment of the polygon is drawn, its shape is filled with the selected foreground color, and pattern if any.

Figure 34. The Filled Polygon tool.

Polygon tool

Works just like the Filled Polygon tool, except the shape is hollow **(Figure 35)**.

Figure 35. The Polygon tool.

To set the width of a line or border:

You can change the width of a line or border drawn by the paint window's Line, Rectangle, Arc, Ellipse, and Polygon tools.

1. In the paint tool palette, click a line style in the Line Width Selector **(Figure 36)**. Click the dotted line item in the selector to draw filled shapes with no border. The bottom selection lets you use a custom line thickness. *(See Tip below)*
2. In the paint tool palette, select one of Director's shape tools (either the Line, Rectangle, Arc, Ellipse, or Polygon tool). When you draw with the tool, it will use the line thickness you just selected.

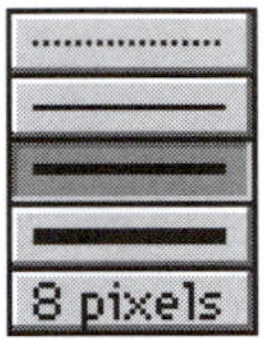

Figure 36. The Line Width Selector.

✔ Tip

- To create a custom line width, choose Preferences from the File menu, and select Paint from the pop-up menu. Use the scroll bar at the center of the dialog box to set the line thickness **(Figures 37–38)**. This value will be used when you choose the custom selection in the Line Width Selector.

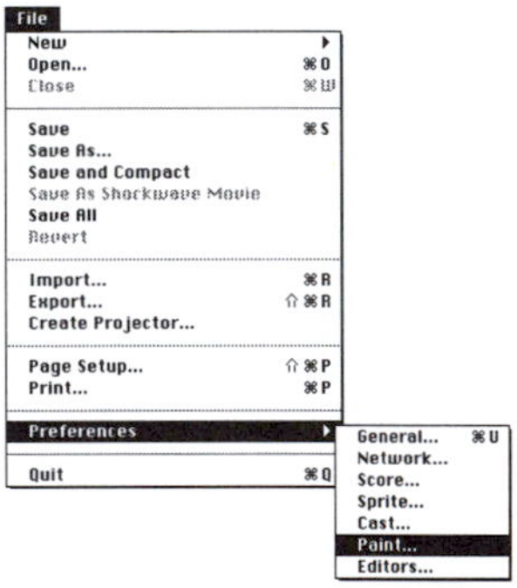

Figure 37. Choose **Preferences** from the **File** menu and select **Paint** from the pop-up menu.

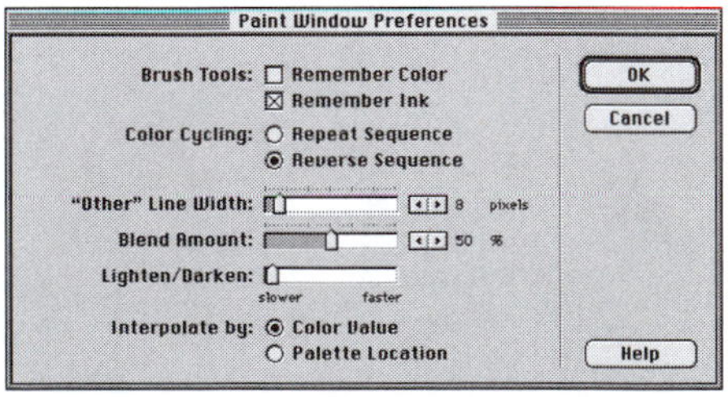

Figure 38. In the **Paint Window Preferences** dialog box, use the scroll bar at the center to set the custom line width.

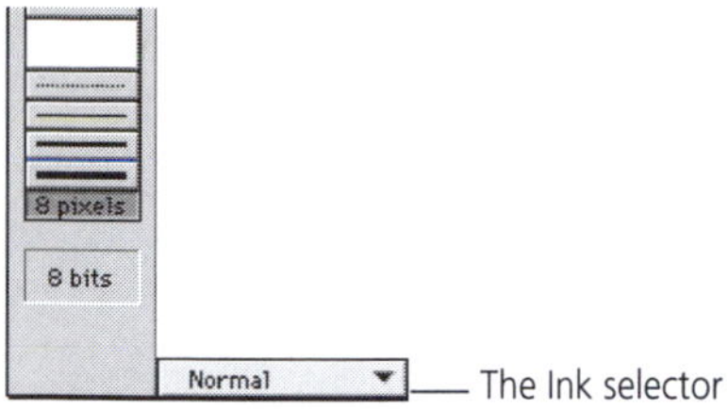

Figure 39. The Ink selector is located at the bottom-left side of the paint window.

Figure 40. Click and hold the Ink selector to display the **Ink** pop-up menu.

INK EFFECTS

Director features a wide variety of **Ink effects** that can be applied to the artwork you create in the paint window (some of the effects include Reverse, Transparent, Smooth, Smear, Darken, and Lighten). These effects are applied with a specific paint tool (such as the Paint Bucket or Paint Brush). Director remembers which Ink effect you select for a specific tool to paint with.

To choose an Ink effect:

1. In Director's paint window, select the tool in the paint tool palette that you wish to apply an Ink effect with (for instance, the Paint Brush or Air Brush).
2. Click and hold the Ink selector at the bottom-left side of the paint window. The Ink pop-up menu appears **(Figures 39–40)**.
3. From the pop-up menu, choose the Ink effect that you wish to use with the selected paint tool and release the mouse button. *(See the following pages for a description of the various Ink effects available)*

Note: You can apply Ink effects to sprites via the score window. This is different from using Ink effects in the paint window, where you are actually modifying the original cast members. Applying Ink effects through the score only affects the cast members' sprites, and can create a very different visual effect. *(See pages 58–60 about using Ink effects in the score window)*

Normal
Normal is the default ink setting. This ink is simply the current foreground color, and any selected pattern.

Transparent
Transparent ink makes the background color used in patterns transparent. When you paint with Transparent ink, you can see any artwork behind the pattern.

Reverse
Any color that you paint over using Reverse ink changes to its "mirror" color at the opposite end of the color palette. For example, a color ten spaces from the top of the palette changes to the color ten spaces from the bottom of the palette.

Ghost
Ghost ink paints with the current background color.

Gradient
Gradient allows you to paint with a blend of colors, ranging from the current foreground color to the current gradient destination color. The gradient options are set in the Gradient Settings dialog box.

Reveal
Reveal ink makes use of the previous cast member. As you paint with reveal ink, you uncover the previous cast member in its original foreground color.

Cycle
As you paint with Cycle ink, the color cycles through all the colors in the color palette between the current foreground color and destination color. Choose black and white for the foreground and Gradient destination colors to cycle through the entire color palette.

Switch
As you paint with Switch ink, any pixels in the current foreground color that you paint over are changed into the Gradient destination color.

Blend
Blend is a transparent ink. As you paint over your artwork, it will still be visible, but its colors are blended with the current foreground color. You can set the percentage of blend in the Paint Window Preferences dialog box.

Darkest
As you paint over an image with Darkest ink, Director compares the level of darkness of the foreground color to the pixels that you are painting over. If the foreground color is darker, the pixels of the image are replaced with its color.

Lightest
As you paint over an image with Lightest ink, Director replaces the pixels with the foreground color where the foreground color is lighter than the pixels of the image.

Darken
Darken ink reduces the brightness of artwork as you paint over it. You can set the rate of this Ink effect in the Paint Window Preferences dialog box.

Lighten
Lighten ink increases the brightness of artwork as you paint over it.

Smooth
Smooth ink blurs artwork as you paint over it. It is useful for smoothing out jagged edges. It only has an effect on existing artwork.

Smear

Smear ink causes the paint of your artwork to spread or smear as you drag the Paint Brush across it. The smear occurs in the direction you drag the Paint Brush.

Smudge

Similar to Smear ink, except the colors fade faster as they are smudged.

Spread

Spread ink works with the Paint Brush. As you drag the brush across your artwork, whatever image is originally under the brush is picked up and becomes the new shape for the Paint Brush.

Clipboard

Uses the contents of the clipboard as the pattern for your brush.

COLORS, PATTERNS, AND GRADIENTS

Color Basics

There are three color specifications that you can set in the paint window which are used in coloring your cast member artwork. **Foreground** color is Director's primary color specification: Whatever color is selected as your foreground color will be used to color all the artwork you create with Director's paint tools (for instance, the Paint Brush, the Air Brush, and the Pencil). The foreground color is also used to color solid patterns, and used as the primary color in multicolored patterns. Director's **Background** color, on the other hand, is used as the secondary color in multicolored patterns. Finally, the **Gradient destination** color is used in conjunction with the foreground color to create a blended color spectrum.

The current foreground color, background and gradient destination colors, and the pattern selector are all displayed in the paint tool palette **(Figure 41)**.

Note: The colors available to you in the paint window depend on the color depth setting of your movie, and the current color palette. *(See the Color in Director chapter on pages 140-142 for details on color depth and the current palette)*

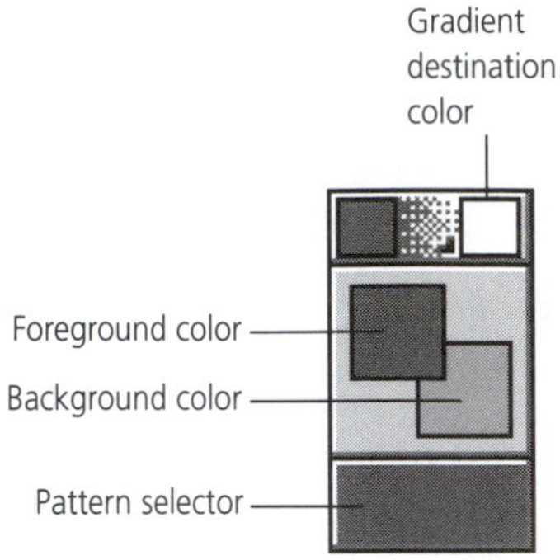

Figure 41. The three color specifications and the Pattern selector are displayed in the paint tool palette.

To choose the foreground color:

1. Click and hold the Foreground color chip in the paint tool palette. A pop-up color palette appears **(Figure 42)**.
2. Drag to the desired color and release the mouse button. The highlighted color becomes the new foreground color.

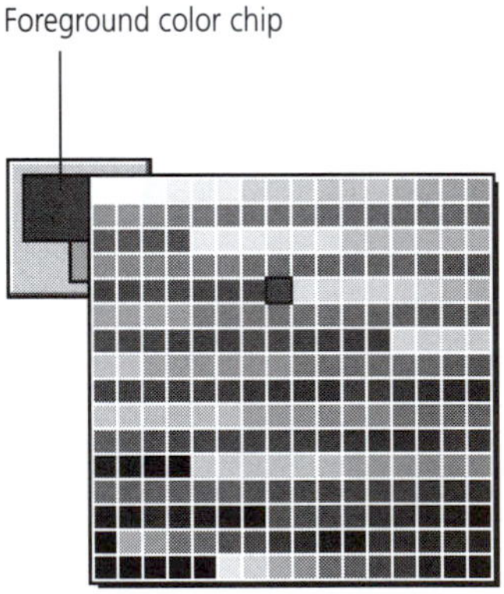

Figure 42. Click and hold the Foreground color chip until the pop-up color palette appears.

✔ **Tip**

- Double-click the Foreground or Background color chip to open the Color Palettes window.

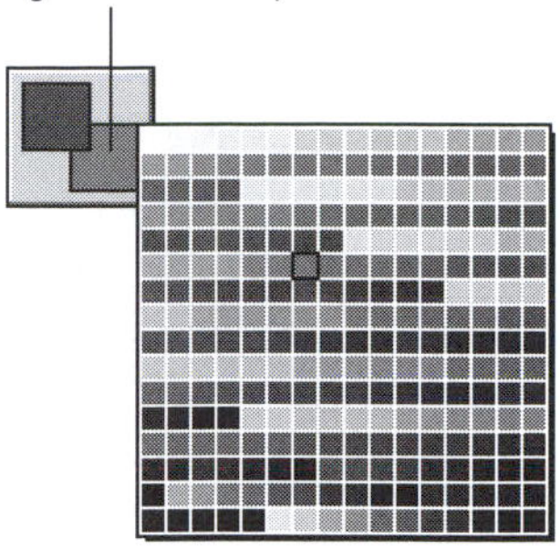

Figure 43. Click and hold the Background color chip until the pop-up color palette appears.

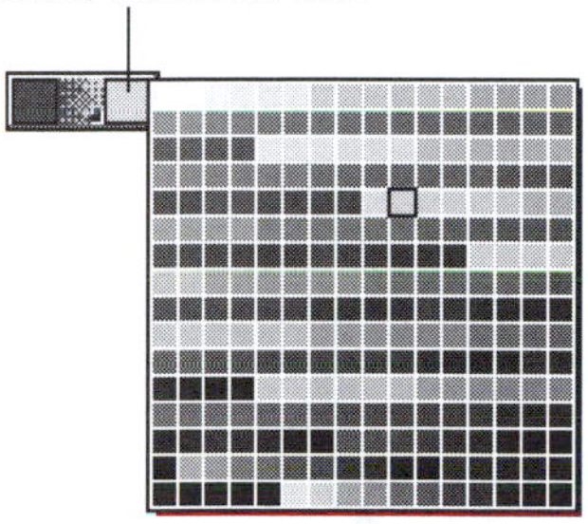

Figure 44. Click and hold the Gradient destination color until a pop-up color palette appears.

Figure 45. The Eyedropper tool

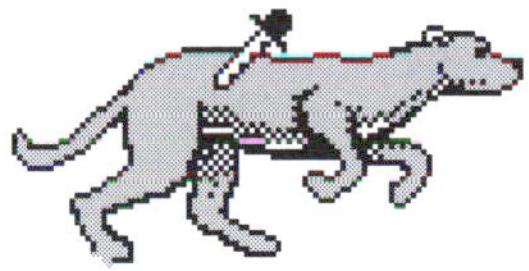

Figure 46. Place the Eyedropper over the particular color that you wish to switch and click the mouse.

Figure 47. Click the **Switch Colors** button in the Effects toolbar in the paint window.

To choose the background color:

1. Click and hold the Background color chip in the paint tool palette. A pop-up color palette appears **(Figure 43)**.
2. Drag to the desired color and release the mouse button.

To choose the Gradient destination color:

1. In the paint tool palette, click and hold the Gradient destination color. A pop-up color palette appears **(Figure 44)**.
2. Drag to the desired color and release the mouse button.

To switch a particular color in a cast member:

Director makes it easy to isolate a particular color in a cast member and then switch that color with any color of your choice.

1. Make sure that your cast member is displayed in Director's paint window.
2. Click the Eyedropper in the tool palette **(Figure 45)**.
3. Move the Eyedropper over the particular color in your cast member that you wish to switch and click the mouse **(Figure 46)**. The color the Eyedropper "picks up" becomes the new foreground color.
4. In the paint tool palette, click and hold the Gradient destination color. A pop-up color palette appears.
5. Drag the pointer to the new color you wish to switch to.
6. Use the Marquee or Lasso tool to select the portion of your image where the color switch should take place.
7. Click the Switch Colors button in the Effects toolbar **(Figure 47)**.

To choose a pattern:

You can use some of Director's paint tools (such as the Paint Bucket, Paint Brush, and Air Brush) to paint with a specific pattern instead of with a solid color.

1. Click and hold the Pattern chip in the paint tool palette. A pop-up pattern palette appears **(Figure 48)**.
2. Drag to the desired pattern and release the mouse button.

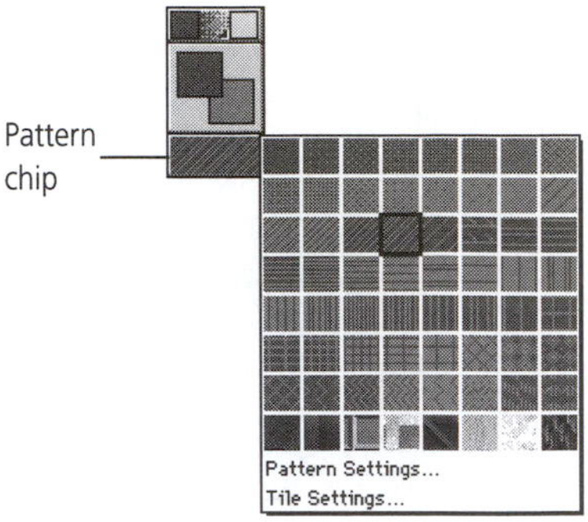

Figure 48. Click and hold the Pattern chip to display the pop-up **Pattern** palette.

✔ Tip

- Double-click the Pattern chip to open the Pattern Settings dialog box, where you can edit patterns or select a different pattern palette to work with. There are four different pattern palettes you can choose from.

To edit or create a pattern:

1. With Director's paint window open, click and hold the Pattern chip and select Pattern Settings at the bottom of the pop-up palette.
2. In the Pattern Settings dialog box, click the pop-up menu and select the Custom menu item **(Figure 49)**. Director features four sets of patterns: The custom set can be edited, while the other three sets—Grays, Standard, and QuickDraw—are always available to you and cannot be changed.
3. Click a custom pattern that you wish to edit. An enlarged version of the selected pattern appears in the pattern edit box **(Figure 50)**.
4. In the pattern edit box, click any open space to place a black pixel in the pattern. Click an existing pixel to make it white.
5. Click the directional arrows to move the pattern shape up, down, and sideways.
6. When you're happy with your custom pattern, click OK, and Director adds it to its custom pattern library.

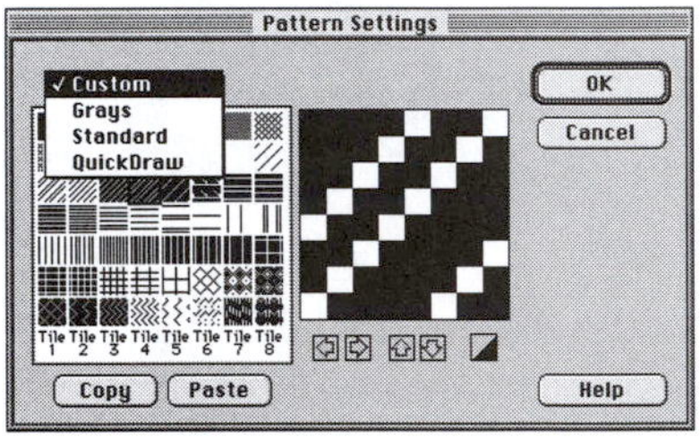

Figure 49. In the **Pattern Settings** dialog box, click the pop-up menu and select the Custom menu item.

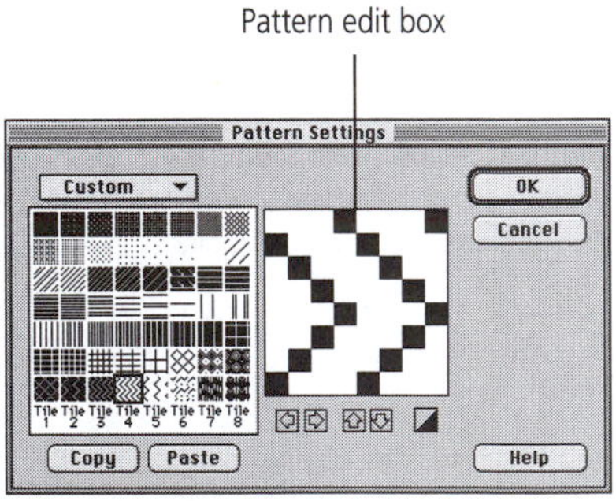

Figure 50. Click the custom pattern that you wish to edit. An enlarged version of the pattern appears in the pattern edit box.

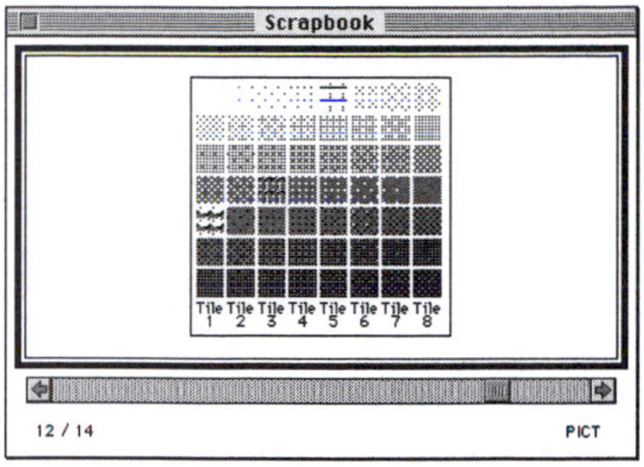

Figure 51. Your custom patterns can be stored in the Macintosh **Scrapbook**.

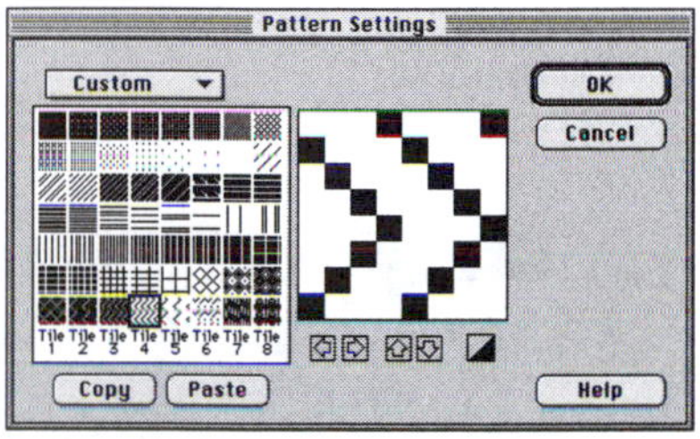

Figure 52. Click the **Copy** button in the **Pattern Settings** dialog box.

To copy your custom pattern library to the Scrapbook:

You can store sets of custom patterns by copying them to and from the Macintosh Scrapbook **(Figure 51)**.

1. Click the Copy button in the Pattern Settings dialog box **(Figure 52)**; this stores the pattern information in the Clipboard.
2. Click Cancel.
3. Open the Scrapbook (choose Scrapbook under the Apple menu).
4. Choose Paste under the Edit menu to store the patterns there.

To reinstall stored patterns from the Scrapbook:

1. Open the Scrapbook and find the Scrapbook entry that contains the desired patterns.
2. Choose Copy from the Edit menu.
3. Return to Director's paint window, open the Pattern Settings dialog box, and click the Paste button to install the copied pattern set.

✔ Tips

- Even though you can't directly edit the patterns contained in Director's Grays, Standards, and QuickDraw patterns, you can copy those predefined patterns into Director's Custom set, and edit them from there. From the Pattern Settings dialog box, use the pattern pop-up menu to select one of Director's noneditable pattern sets, and then click the Copy button. Choose the Custom pattern set from the pattern pop-up menu and click the Paste button.
- Director lets you "pick up" a pattern displayed in its paint window, and edit it in the Pattern Settings dialog box. To do so, open the Pattern Settings dialog box and click on your artwork in the paint window.

To create a gradient:

You can paint your bitmap artwork with a **gradient**, which is a blend of colors that you define. Setting up a gradient is simple: You set the foreground color, which is the color that Director begins the blend with, and choose the Gradient destination color, which is the color that the foreground color will be blended through. Director can then automatically blend the two colors to display a range of colors in between **(Figure 53)**. A good use of a gradient would be to create a sunset, where colors blend from red to yellow.

Figure 53. A sample gradient.

Gradient colors can be used with a number of Director's paint tools, including the Paint Brush, Paint Bucket, Ellipse, Rectangle, and Polygon tools.

1. In Director's paint window, select the painting tool that you wish to apply the gradient color to (for instance, the Paint Brush or Paint Bucket).
2. Click the Foreground color chip in the paint window and select a color from the pop-up color palette **(Figure 54)**. This will be the color that the gradient begins with.

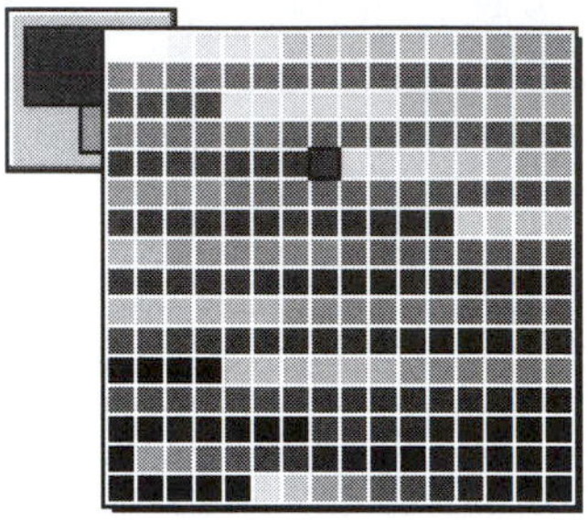

Figure 54. Click the Foreground color chip and select a color to begin the gradient with.

3. Click the Gradient destination color and choose a color from the pop-up color palette. This is the color that your gradient will blend to **(Figure 55)**.

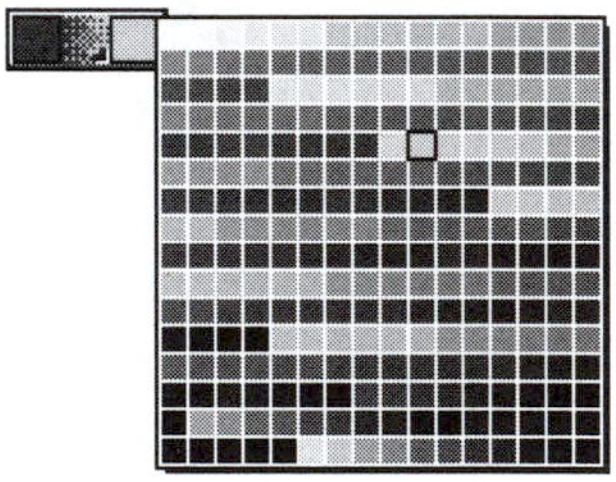

Figure 55. Click the Gradient destination color, and choose the color that your gradient will blend to.

4. Click the Ink selector in the paint window, and choose Gradient from the pop-up menu **(Figure 56)**. The paint tool that you selected in step 1 will now paint with a gradient rather than a solid color.

Figure 56. Click the Ink Selector and choose **Gradient** from the pop-up menu.

✔ Tip

- To stop painting with a gradient, simply choose the Normal Ink effect from the Ink pop-up menu.

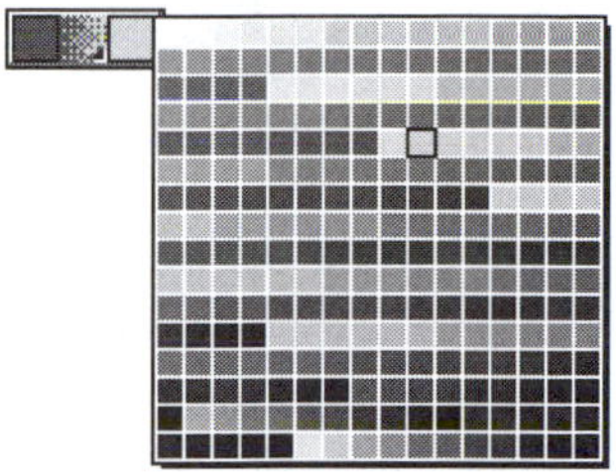

Figure 57. Double-click the Gradient destination color to open the **Gradient Settings** dialog box.

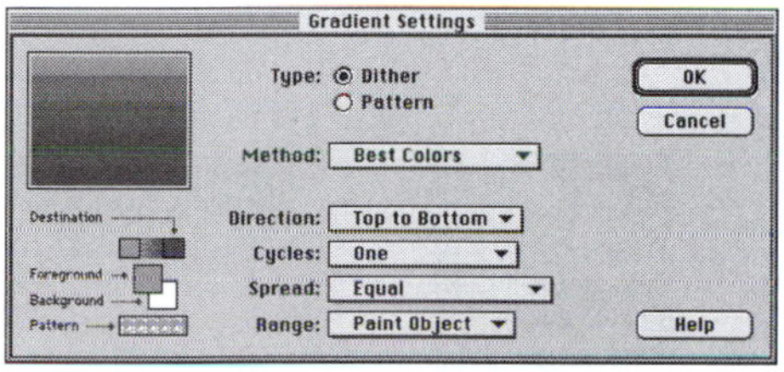

Figure 58. The **Gradient Settings** dialog box.

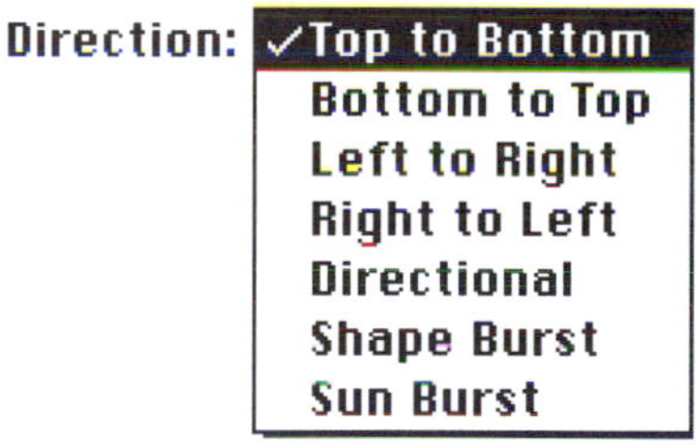

Figure 59. The **Direction** pop-up menu.

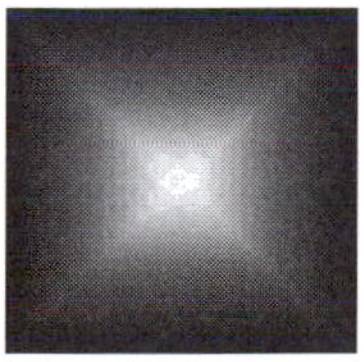

Figure 60. A Shape Burst gradient.

Figure 61. A Sun Burst gradient.

To change gradient settings:

Director allows you to customize a color gradient. For instance, you can control the direction in which the gradient fills a given area (from the top, the bottom, and so on), and the "spread" of the gradient (whether the colors are spread evenly, or concentrated in certain areas).

1. In the paint window, double-click the Gradient destination color to open the Gradient Settings dialog box **(Figure 57)**.
2. In the Gradient Settings dialog box, use the Foreground color chip and Gradient destination color to select the colors used to create your gradient **(Figure 58)**.
3. Use the dialog box's pop-up menus to fine-tune the characteristics of your gradient. Gradient options are described below:

Direction

Use the Direction pop-up menu to control the direction in which your gradient fills a particular area **(Figure 59)**. The directional possibilities include straightforward selections such as **Top to Bottom** and **Bottom to Top**, as well as three unique options: **Directional** allows you to set a custom direction for the gradient with whatever paint tool you are using to apply the gradient. For instance, if you are using the Paint Bucket to fill an area with a gradient, a directional line appears as soon as you click the Paint Bucket in the paint window. Move the directional line in the desired direction, and click to begin your gradient fill. **Shape Burst** creates a gradient that starts at the outer edges of an area, and then fills inward while following the contours of the area **(Figure 60)**.

Sun Burst begins a gradient at the outer edges of an area, and moves toward the center in concentric circles **(Figure 61)**.

Cycles

Use the Cycles pop-up menu to specify how many times a gradient repeats within an area **(Figure 62)**. You can set the gradient to cycle through its color spectrum up to four times in a given area. You also specify whether the gradient is sharp, meaning the gradient cycles from foreground to destination color, and then again from foreground to destination **(Figure 63)**, or smooth **(Figure 64)**, which makes the gradient cycle from foreground to destination color, and then in the next cycle, from the destination color to the foreground color.

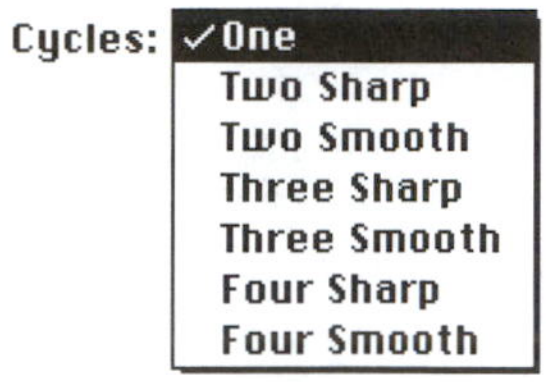

Figure 62. The **Cycles** pop-up menu.

Method

Use the Method pop-up menu together with the Type selector to control how Director blends colors to create its gradient **(Figure 65)**.

Following are the Method selections for the Dither type gradient:

Best Colors ignores the arrangement of colors in the current color palette, and uses only colors that create a continuous blend between your foreground and destination colors, using a dithered pattern.

Adjacent Colors creates the gradient blend by using all the colors in the selected color palette that occur between the foreground and destination colors, even if those in-between colors do not create a smooth blend.

Two Colors blends only the foreground and destination colors with a dithered pattern.

One Color simply fades the foreground color with a dithered pattern.

Standard Colors blends the foreground and destination colors, ignoring the colors between them and adds several blended colors having a dithered pattern.

Multi Colors—similar to Standard Colors, but the dithered pattern is randomized.

Figure 63. A Two Sharp gradient.

Figure 64. A Two Smooth gradient.

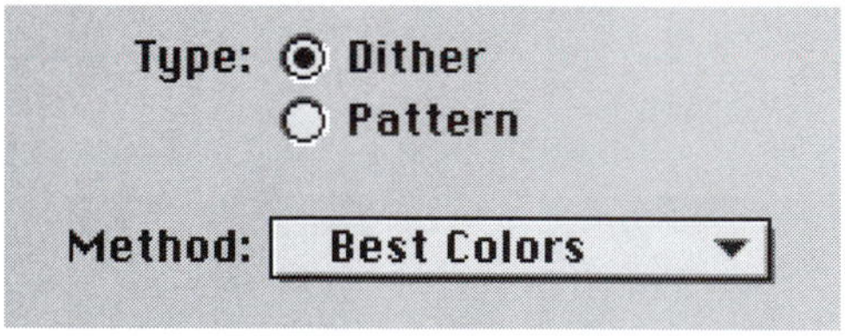

Figure 65. The **Method** pop-up menu and **Type** selector.

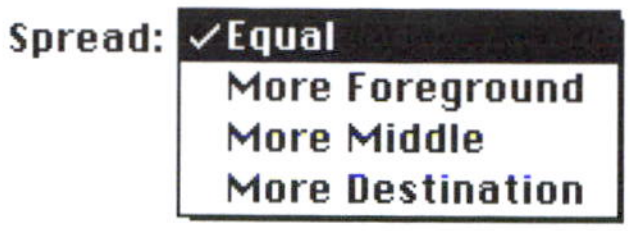

Figure 66. The **Spread** pop-up menu.

Figure 67. A More Foreground gradient.

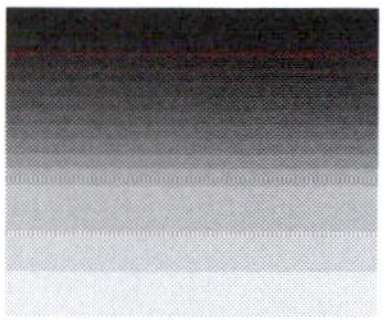

Figure 68. A More Destination gradient.

Figure 69. The **Range** pop-up menu.

Figure 70. A Paint Object gradient.

Figure 71. A Window gradient.

Following are the Method selections for the Pattern type gradient:

Best Colors ignores the arrangement of colors in the palette you're using, and uses only colors that create a continuous blend between your foreground and destination colors. The gradient is drawn with whatever pattern has been selected. The **Transparent** version of this option makes any white pixels in this blend transparent.

Adjacent Colors creates the gradient blend by using all the colors in the selected palette that occur between the gradient's foreground and destination colors, even if those in-between colors do not create a smooth blend. The **Transparent** version of this option makes any white pixels in this blend transparent

Spread

Use the Spread pop-up menu to control how Director distributes the colors of your gradient within an area **(Figure 66)**. **Equal** spaces the gradient's colors evenly throughout an area, while **More Foreground (Figure 67)** or **More Destination (Figure 68)** increases the amount of foreground or destination color in a gradient. **More Middle** devotes more space to the gradient's middle colors.

Range

Use the Range pop-up menu to decide whether the full range of blended colors in your gradient should be applied over a cast member, a paint object, or over the entire paint window **(Figure 69)**. Choosing **Paint Object** ensures that the full range of the gradient's colors will be seen in any sized brush stroke or fill area **(Figure 70)**, while the full range of colors may not be seen with the **Cast Member** or **Window** options **(Figure 71)**.

TILES AND BRUSH SHAPES

Tiles are similar to patterns in that you can apply them as textures or "fillers" to artwork created in Director. The difference between a tile and a pattern is that the tile is created from an existing cast member in your movie. For instance, if you have a cast member of a brick, you can turn it into a tile that can be used to paint a brick wall. Since tiles are based on an existing cast member, they can feature more than the simple foreground/background color combination that limits traditional patterns. A tile features as many colors as the cast member it's based on.

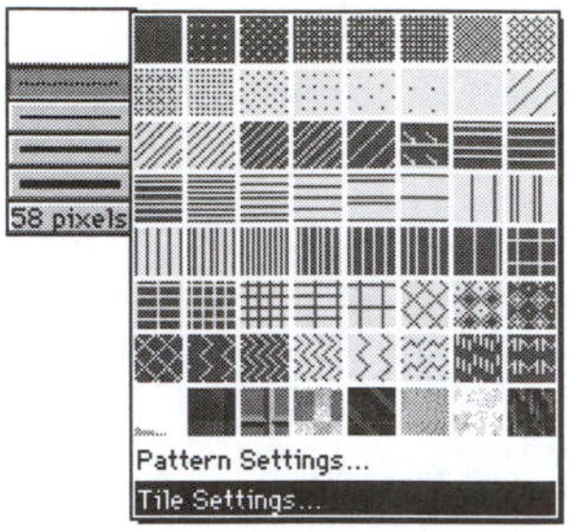

Figure 72. Choose **Tile Settings** from the **Pattern** pop-up menu.

To create a tile from a cast member:

1. Make sure that the cast member you wish to base your tile on has already been placed in a cast window. Creating the tile will have no effect on the cast member.

2. In the paint window, click and hold the Pattern chip. Choose Tile Settings from the Pattern pop-up menu **(Figure 72)**.

3. In the Tile Settings dialog box, click the Cast member radio button to select it **(Figure 73)**. The Cast member radio button will be dimmed if your Director movie has no color cast members. You can also choose from a set of built in tiles by clicking the Built-in radio button. Cast members must be saved in at least two bits of color (four colors total) to be turned into a tile.

4. Click the left and right arrows next to the Cast member radio button to cycle through the cast members and choose the particular cast member you wish to turn into a tile. All the cast members appear in the left side of the Tiles dialog box. The right side of the box displays what the particular cast member will look like in tiled form.

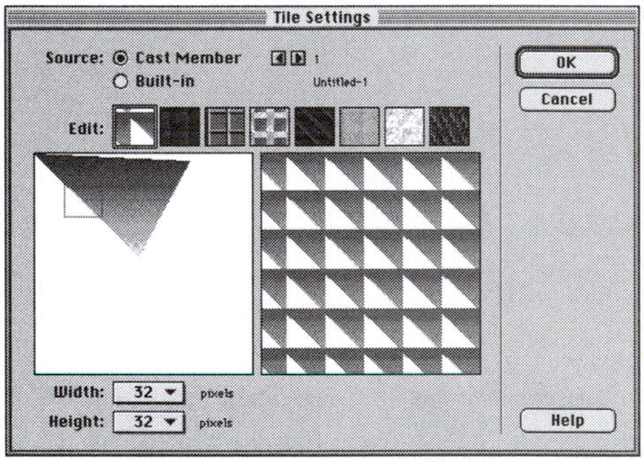

Figure 73. Click the **Cast Member** radio button in the **Tile Settings** dialog box.

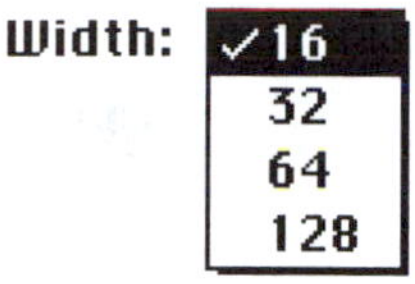

Figure 74. The **Width** pop-up menu.

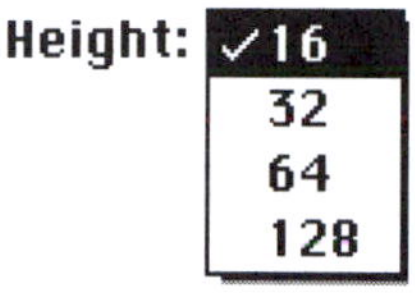

Figure 75. The **Height** pop-up menu.

5. Use the Width and Height pop-up menus to determine the pixel dimensions that the cast member should conform to as a tile **(Figures 74–75)**. The range of dimensions goes from 16 by 16 to 128 by 128 pixels.
6. Drag the dotted border on the left side of the Tile Settings dialog box to encompass the portion of the cast member you wish to turn into a tile.
7. Click OK to create a new tile based on the selected cast member. Your new tile will now be displayed at the bottom of the paint window's Pattern palette, which is displayed by clicking the Pattern selector chip.

To choose a Paint Brush shape:

Director's Paint Brush offers five different shapes—labeled Brush 1 through Brush 5—you can choose from each time you select the brush tool. You can change and customize these brush shapes through Director's Brush Settings dialog box. *(See page 121 for details)*

1. Click the Paint Brush tool in the paint tool palette, and do not release the mouse button. A pop-up menu appears, listing the different brush shapes that you can choose from **(Figure 76)**.

2. Drag to select the brush shape you wish to use. Director will now paint with this particular brush shape.

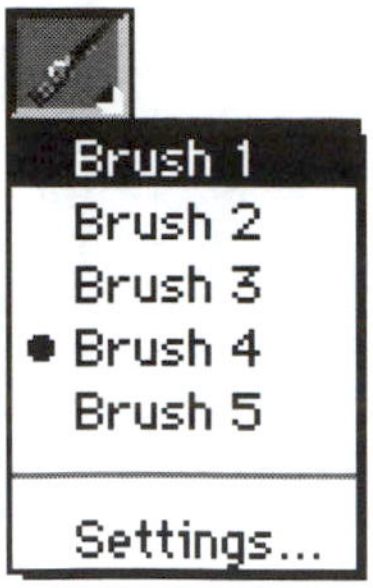

Figure 76. Click and hold the Paint Brush tool in the paint tool palette to display the pop-up menu.

Optional

Only five brush shapes can be selected from the brush's pop-up menu, while Director can actually store a much wider variety of shapes. You can assign different shapes (probably ones that you have customized yourself) to the pop-up menu, replacing the default styles that are initially assigned. To do so, first follow steps 1 and 2 above to select a brush shape that you wish to replace from the pop-up menu.

3. Once you've selected a brush shape (Brush 1 through Brush 5), click the Paint Brush tool and select Settings from the pop-up menu **(Figure 77)**.

4. In the Brush Settings dialog box, select the new brush shape that you wish to substitute **(Figure 78)**.

5. Click OK and Director will remember to use this new brush shape whenever you select the respective brush number (Brush 1 through Brush 5) from the pop-up menu.

Figure 77. Click the Paint Brush tool and select **Settings** from the pop-up menu.

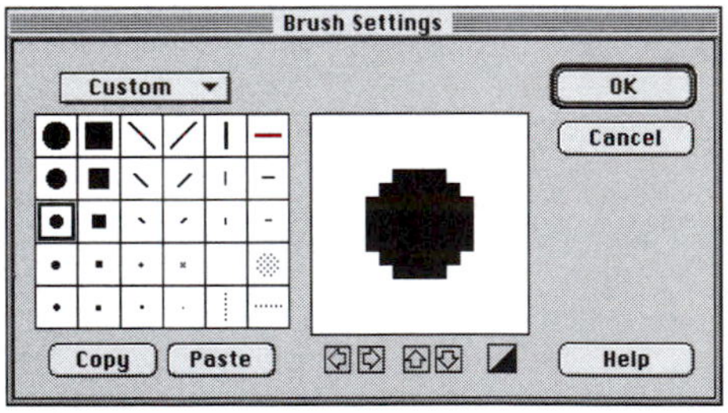

Figure 78. In the **Brush Settings** dialog box, select a new brush shape to use.

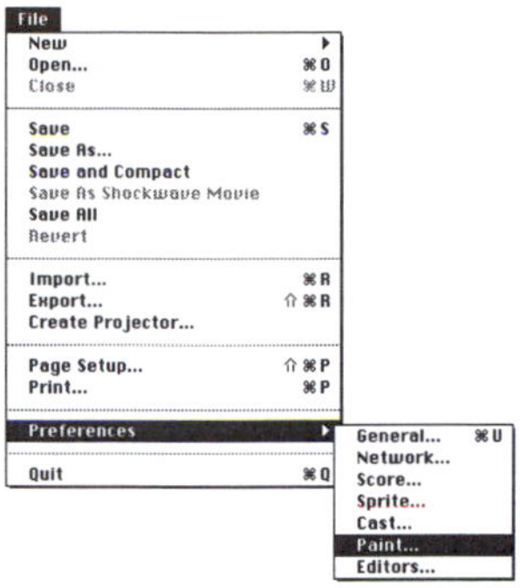

Figure 79. Choose **Preferences** from the **File** menu and select **Paint** from the pop-up menu.

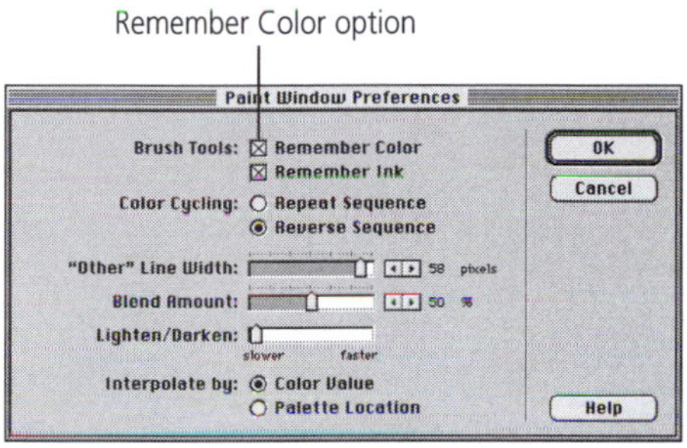

Figure 80. In the **Paint Window Preferences** dialog box, check the **Remember Color** option.

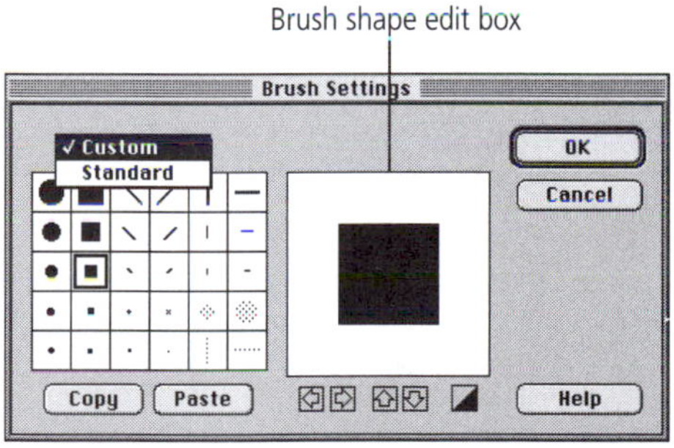

Figure 81. In the **Brush Settings** dialog box, click the pop-up menu and select the Custom menu item.

✔ Tips

- Double-click the Paint Brush tool to open the Brush Settings dialog box.
- You can tell Director to automatically select a particular color when you paint with a particular brush—for instance, red for Brush 1, green for Brush 2, and so on. To make Director remember the particular color settings you've associated with each brush shape, choose Preferences from the File menu, and select Paint from the pop-up menu **(Figure 79)**. In the Paint Window Preferences dialog box, check the Remember Color option **(Figure 80)**.

To edit a Paint Brush shape:

While Director features a variety of existing Paint Brush shapes, you can edit them to form your own custom brush styles. Editing is a matter of rearranging the individual pixels that make up the brush's shape.

1. With Director's paint window open, double-click the Paint Brush tool.
2. In the Brush Settings dialog box, click the pop-up menu and select the Custom menu item **(Figure 81)**. Director recognizes two varieties of brush shapes: Standard shapes, which are always available to you and cannot be changed, and Custom shapes, which you can edit.
3. Click the custom brush shape that you wish to edit. An enlarged version of the selected brush appears in the brush shape edit box.
4. In the brush shape edit box, click any open space to place a new pixel in the brush. Click on a pixel to erase it.

5. Click the directional arrows in the Brush Settings dialog box to move the brush shape up, down, and sideways.
6. When you're happy with your new brush design, click OK, and Director adds the new brush to its custom brush library.

✔ **Tips**

- You can store and retrieve sets of custom brush shapes by copying them to and from the Macintosh Scrapbook **(Figure 82)**. To store your custom brush set, first click the Copy button in the Brush Settings dialog box; this stores the brush information in the Clipboard. Now leave the dialog box (click Cancel), open the Scrapbook (choose Scrapbook under the Apple menu), and choose Paste under the Edit menu to store the brush shapes there. To reinstall these stored brushes, open the Scrapbook, find the Scrapbook entry that contains the desired brush set, and choose Copy from the Edit menu. Return to Director's paint window, open the Brush Settings dialog box, and click the Paste button to install the copied brush set.
- Director lets you "pick up" any pattern displayed in the paint window and use it as a brush shape. To do so, open the Brush Settings dialog box, and click any pattern outside the dialog box to pick it up.

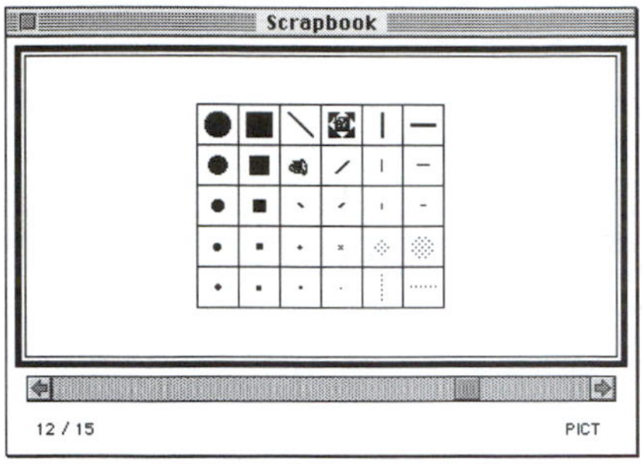

Figure 82. You can store and retrieve your custom brush shapes from the Macintosh **Scrapbook**.

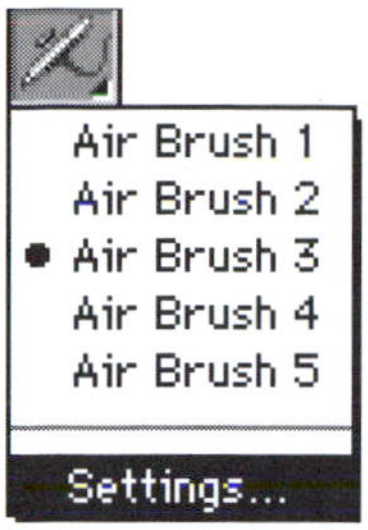

Figure 83. Click and hold the Air Brush tool and select **Settings** from the pop-up menu.

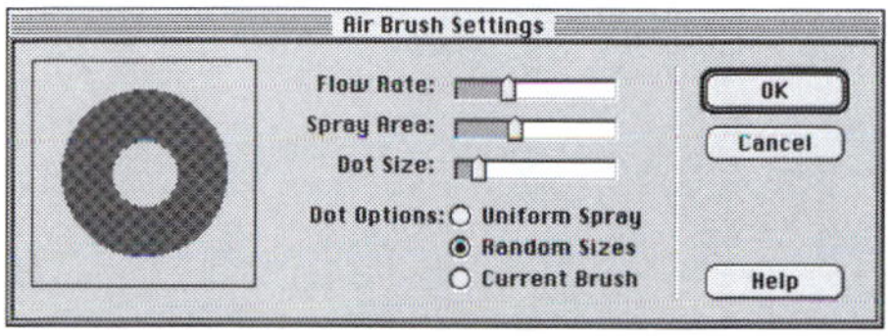

Figure 84. In the **Air Brush Settings** dialog box, drag the Flow Rate, Spray Area, and Dot Size scroll bars to adjust the Air Brush.

Figure 85. The Uniform Spray Air Brush setting.

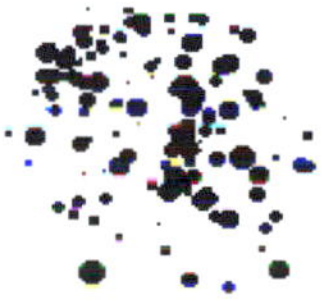

Figure 86. The Random Sizes Air Brush setting.

Figure 87. The Current Brush setting of the Air Brush.

To adjust the Air Brush spray pattern:

Director lets you adjust the size of the Air brush's spray area, the size of the ink dots it sprays into that area, and the speed at which it sprays them.

1. With Director's paint window open, click and hold the Air Brush tool and select Settings from the pop-up menu that appears **(Figure 83)**.
2. In the Air Brush Settings dialog box, drag the Flow Rate, Spray Area, and Dot Size scroll bars to adjust the speed at which it sprays the dots, the size of the Air Brush's spray area, and the size of the dots it sprays into the area **(Figure 84)**. As you adjust the scroll bar values, Director displays a preview of how your new settings will affect the Air Brush tool. The gray circle indicates the current size of the Air Brush's spray area, while the white circle inside represents the size of the dots themselves.
3. Click either the Uniform Spray, Random Sizes, or Current Brush radio buttons to indicate how the Air Brush should spray. With the Uniform Spray setting, your Air Brush sprays dots of identical size, while the Random Sizes setting randomly varies the size of dots sprayed. The Current Brush settings causes the Air Brush to spray in the shape that's currently selected for the Paint Brush tool **(Figures 85–87)**.
4. Click OK so that your new Air Brush settings take effect.

To choose an Air Brush shape:

Director remembers five different Air Brush settings—labeled Air Brush 1 through Air Brush 5—for you to choose from when you select the Air Brush tool. You can change and customize these settings through the Air Brush Settings dialog box.

1. Click and hold the Air Brush tool in the paint tool palette. A pop-up menu appears **(Figure 88)**, listing the different brush settings that you can choose from.

2. Drag to the setting you wish to use, and release the mouse button. Director will now paint with this particular Air Brush setting.

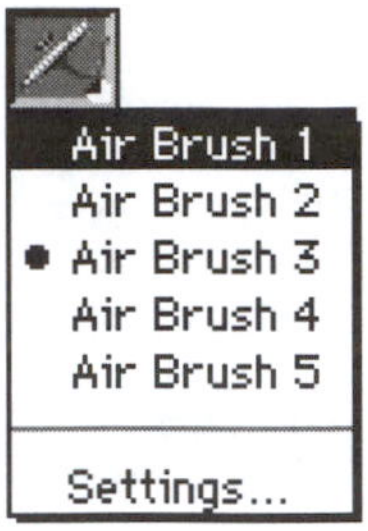

Figure 88. Click and hold the Air Brush tool in the paint tool palette to display the pop-up menu.

Optional

You can replace each of the five Air Brush settings with your own custom ones. To do so, first follow steps 1 and 2 above to select the Air Brush setting that you wish to customize.

3. Double-click the Air Brush tool.

4. In the Air Brush Settings dialog box, change the brush's Flow Rate, Spray Area, and Dot Size settings **(Figure 89)** to the new desired values. *(See page 123 for more about these settings)*

5. Click OK, and Director will remember to use these new settings whenever you select the same brush setting from the Air Brush tool's pop-up menu.

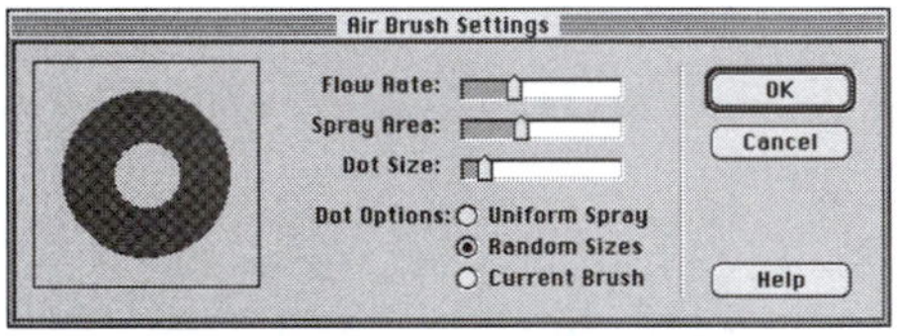

Figure 89. In the **Air Brush Settings** dialog box, drag the Flow Rate, Spray Area, and Dot Size scroll bars to adjust the Air Brush.

Choose an Air Brush Shape

Figure 90. The **Effects** toolbar.

Figure 91. Select the artwork that you wish to rotate with the Marquee tool.

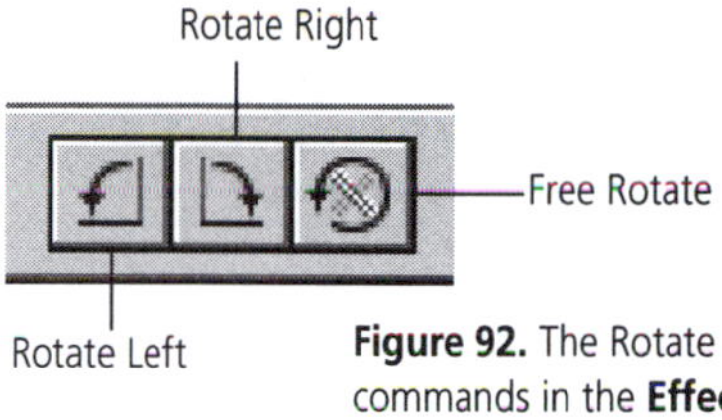

Figure 92. The Rotate commands in the **Effects** toolbar.

Figure 93. The artwork after using **Rotate Right**.

Figure 94. The artwork after using **Rotate Left**.

Figure 95. Using **Free Rotate**, drag one of the handles to rotate your art selection in 1-degree increments.

EFFECTS TOOLBAR

Director's Effects toolbar **(Figure 90)** offers a variety of effects and functions that can be applied to existing artwork. These features include flips and rotations of cast members, edge traces, color switches, and image distortions such as warp and perspective. You can perform an effect on any portion of an image, rather than the whole thing. For most of these effects, you must use Director's Marquee tool, not its Lasso, to make the selection.

To rotate artwork left and right by 90 degrees:

Director lets you rotate entire images or parts of images in 90 degree increments.

1. In Director's paint window, click the Marquee tool and use it to select the artwork that you wish to rotate **(Figure 91)**.
2. Click either Rotate Right or Rotate Left in the Effects toolbar **(Figure 92)** to rotate the selected artwork 90 degrees **(Figures 93–94)**.

To freely rotate artwork in 1-degree increments:

The Free Rotate command lets you rotate artwork in 1-degree increments.

1. In Director's paint window, click the Marquee tool and use it to select the artwork that you wish to rotate.
2. Click Free Rotate in the Effects toolbar. Notice that Director places little "handles" at each corner of your selection.
3. Drag one of the handles to rotate your art selection in 1-degree increments **(Figure 95)**.

To flip artwork horizontally or vertically:

Director lets you "flip" an artwork selection to create a mirror-image **(Figure 96)**.

1. In Director's paint window, click the Marquee tool and use it to select the artwork that you wish to flip.
2. Click either Flip Horizontal or Flip Vertical in Director's Effects toolbar **(Figure 97)**.

Figure 96. You can "flip" an artwork selection to create a mirror-image.

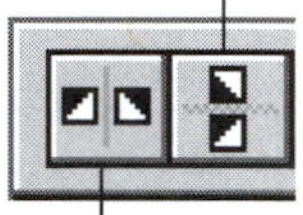

Figure 97. Click either **Flip Horizontal** or **Flip Vertical** in the **Effects** toolbar.

To distort artwork:

You can alter the shape and dimensional appearance of artwork using Director's Skew, Warp, and Perspective commands **(Figures 98–102)**. Skew slants the artwork while maintaining a parallelogram shape; Warp allows you to bend and stretch artwork; and Perspective makes the artwork seem as if it is being viewed from a particular vantage point, with one part of the image appearing to be closer than the other.

1. In the paint window, click the Marquee tool, and use it to select the artwork that you wish to alter.
2. Choose Skew, Warp, or Perspective from Director's Effects toolbar. Notice that Director places little "handles" at each corner of your selection.
3. Drag one of the handles to apply the desired effect to the artwork.

✔ **Tip**

■ You may want to make a copy of your artwork before distorting it. To do so, select the image with the Marquee tool, move the mouse pointer within the selection marquee, hold down the Option key, and drag to copy the artwork to a new location.

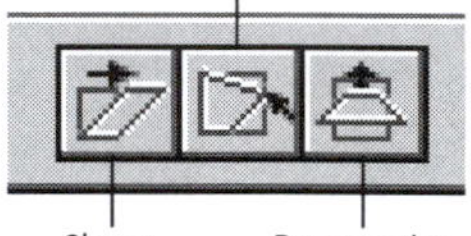

Figure 98. Skew, Warp, and **Perspective** in the **Effects** toolbar.

Figure 99. Unaltered artwork.

Figure 100. The Skew effect.

Figure 101. The Warp effect.

Figure 102. The Perspective effect.

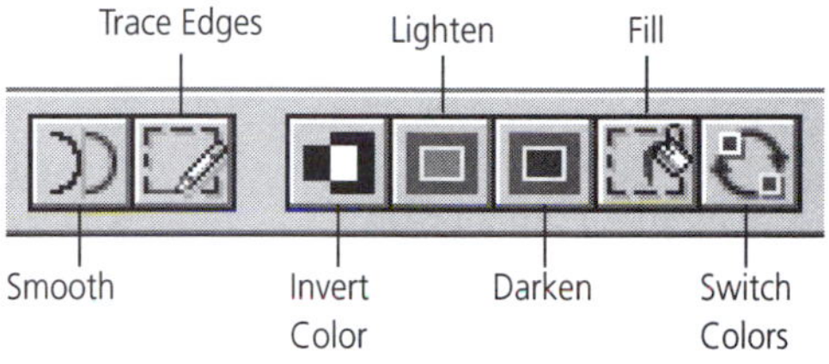

Figure 103. The **Effects** toolbar.

Figure 104. The **Smooth** command softens the edges of your artwork.

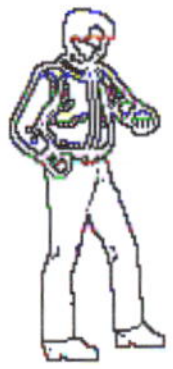

Figure 105. The **Trace Edges** command creates an outline around the edges of your selected artwork.

Figure 106. The **Invert Color** effect reverses the colors of an image.

To apply other special effects to artwork:

Smooth, Trace Edges, Invert Colors, Lighten, Darken, Fill, and Switch Colors are additional commands in the Effects toolbar that you can apply to your artwork.

1. In Director's paint window, click the Marquee or Lasso tool, and use it to select the artwork that you wish to affect (note that you cannot use the Lasso tool with the Trace Edges command).
2. Choose Smooth, Trace Edges, Invert Colors, Lighten, Darken, Fill, or Switch Colors from Director's Effects toolbar **(Figure 103)**.

The **Smooth** command softens the edges of your artwork **(Figure 104)** by adding pixels that blend the colors between edges.

The **Trace Edges** effect creates an outline around the edges of the artwork you've selected **(Figure 105)**. Select Trace Edges repeatedly to increase the number of outlines in the trace.

The **Invert Color** effect reverses all the colors in the selected artwork. If the artwork is black and white, white pixels turn to black, and vice versa, which creates a negative image **(Figure 106)**. If the artwork uses more than two colors, Director reverses the order in which the colors are displayed. The artwork's color palette is effectively flipped, so that the colors that were assigned to the top of the palette are placed at its bottom. *(See the Color in Director chapter on page 142 for details on palettes)*

The **Lighten** and **Darken** commands respectively increase and decrease the brightness of the selected artwork.

The **Fill** command fills the selected area in the paint window with the foreground color and pattern.

Switch Colors *(See page 111)*

To create a sequence of in-between images of an artwork selection:

Director's **Auto Distort** command creates a number of in-between images for artwork that you transform with the Skew, Warp, Perspective, or the Rotate commands. Let's say you use the Free Rotate command to rotate a picture by 350 degrees—almost a full circle. You can then use Auto Distort to create versions of the artwork in a number of rotated positions between 0 and 350 degrees—for instance, at 60 degrees, 120 degrees, 180, 240, and so on **(Figure 107)**. Director then places each of these in-between images into the current cast window, where they can be incorporated in your movie as an animation sequence.

1. In the paint tool palette, click the Marquee tool, and use it to select the artwork that you wish to Auto Distort.
2. Click Skew, Warp, Perspective, or the Rotate commands in the Effects toolbar. Notice that Director places little "handles" at each corner of your selection.
3. Drag one of the handles to rotate or distort the selected art.
4. While the Marquee is still active, choose Auto Distort from the Xtras menu **(Figure 108)**.
5. In the Auto Distort dialog box, type the number of in-between cast members you wish to create **(Figure 109)**. In other words, how many new cast members should be created to transform the original artwork to the altered state created in step 3 above.
6. Click Begin. Director creates the new in-between cast members and adds them into the next available positions in the cast window.

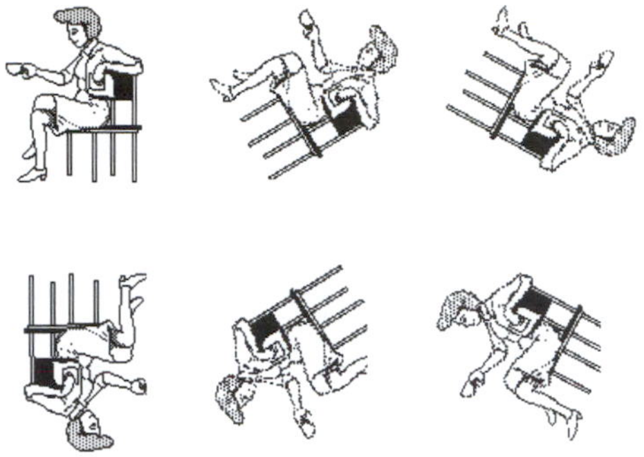

Figure 107. The **Auto Distort** command has been used here in combination with the **Free Rotate** command to create a series of in-between rotated images.

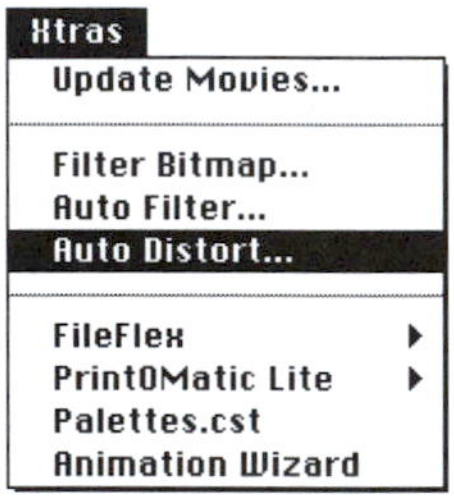

Figure 108. Choose **Auto Distort** from the **Xtras** menu.

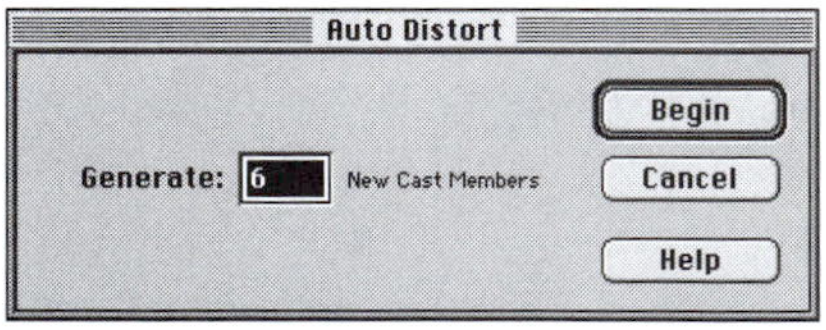

Figure 109. In the **Auto Distort** dialog box, enter the number of in-between cast members you wish to create.

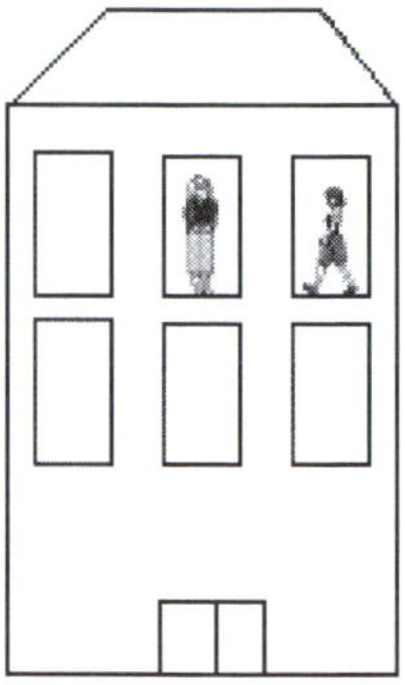

Figure 110. The windows of this house cast member are transparent, allowing you to see the characters behind them.

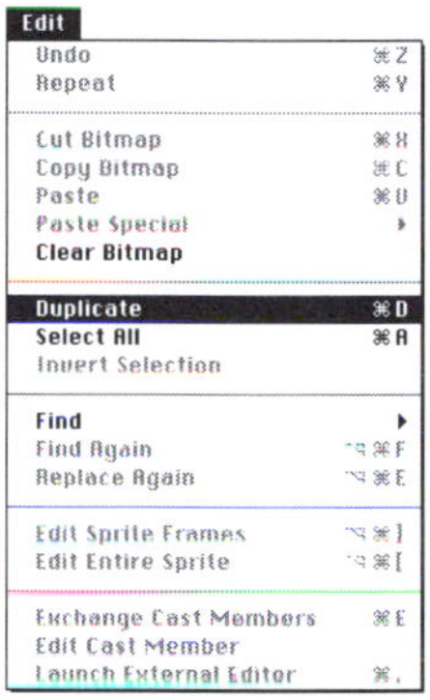

Figure 111. Choose **Duplicate** from the **Edit** menu.

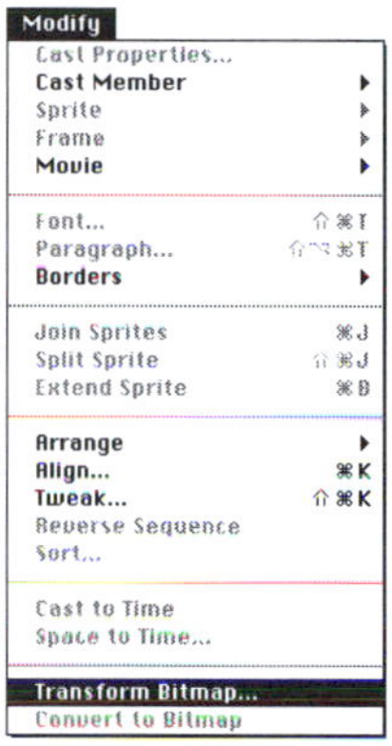

Figure 112. Choose **Transform Bitmap** from the **Modify** menu.

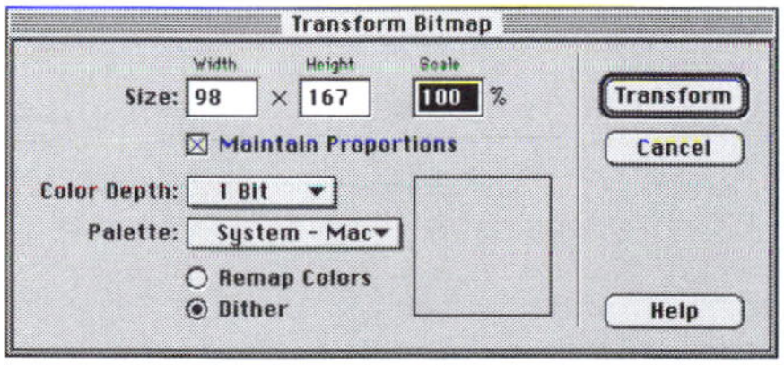

Figure 113. Select 1-Bit in the **Color Depth** pop-up menu in the **Transform Bitmap** dialog box.

INK MASKS

An ink mask allows you to make certain parts of a cast member appear transparent—in other words, you can see through it to other artwork in the background—while other parts of the cast member remain opaque. Why would you ever want a cast member to behave that way? Imagine creating a scene in which a house is viewed from outside, and animated characters can be seen through its windows **(Figure 110)**. In such a scene, the house itself would be opaque but the windows transparent, allowing you to see the characters behind them. Another good example is a scene of a moving car. The car is opaque, but its windows are transparent so that you can see the passing scenery.

To create a mask:

1. Open the cast member you wish to mask (make transparent in certain parts) in the paint window. A quick way to do this is to double-click it in the cast window.
2. Choose Duplicate from the Edit menu **(Figure 111)**.
3. While viewing the cloned cast member, choose Transform Bitmap from the Modify menu **(Figure 112)**.
4. In the Transform Bitmap dialog box, select 1-Bit in the Color Depth pop-up menu **(Figure 113)**. You are changing the cloned cast member to black and white (1-bit color depth), which is required to make a mask.
5. Click Transform.
6. From the paint tool palette, select either the Paint Bucket or Paint Brush tool.

7. Fill in the parts of the cloned cast member that should be opaque (that is, that should not be seen through). Be sure not to paint outside the borders of the cloned cast member; doing so could create a ghosting effect when you place the mask in your movie.
8. In the cast window, make sure that the cloned cast member you've created is positioned immediately following the original version of the cast member **(Figure 114)**. If it is not already there, drag the clone to the appropriate location.
9. Choose Score from the Window menu.
10. Place the cast member you wish to mask in Director's score.
11. Select the frames in the score that contain the cast member you wish to mask.
12. In the score, click and hold the Ink selector to display a pop-up menu, and choose Mask. **(Figure 115)**. Director displays your masked cast member in the selected frames.

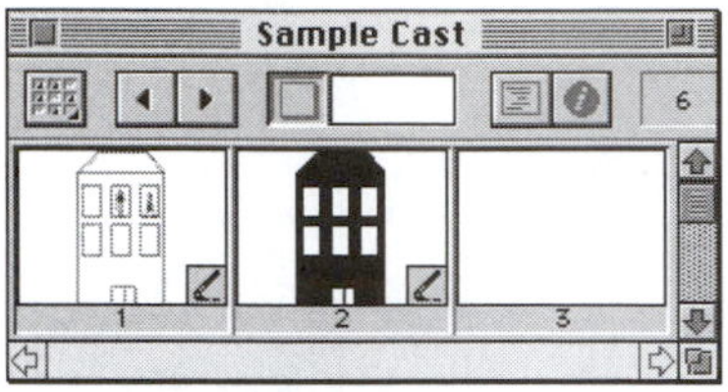

Figure 114. In the cast window, make sure the cloned cast member is positioned immediately following the original cast member.

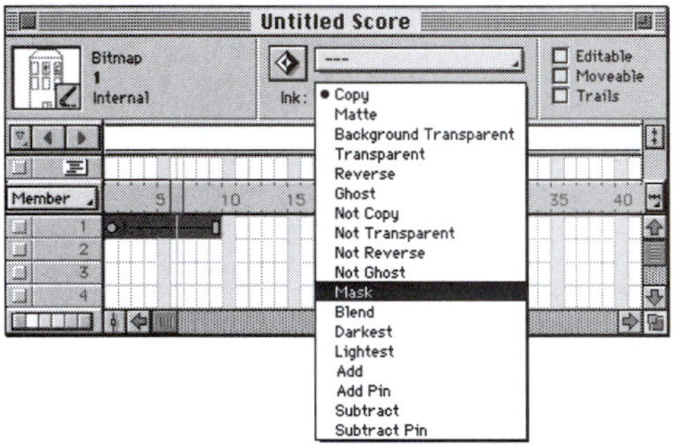

Figure 115. In the score window, choose **Mask** in the **Ink** pop-up menu.

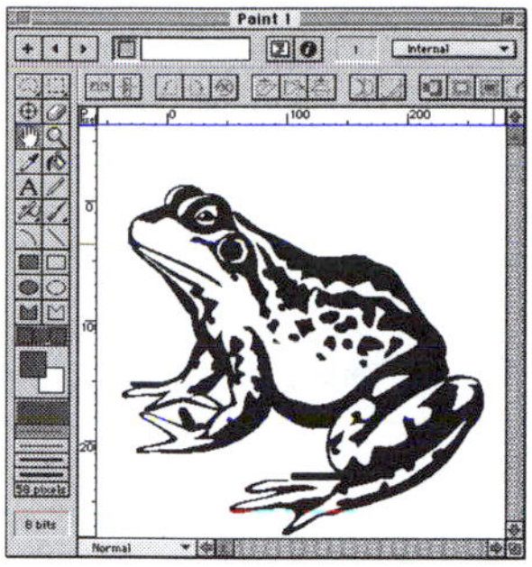

Figure 116. Open the cast member you wish to use as the background reference image in the paint window.

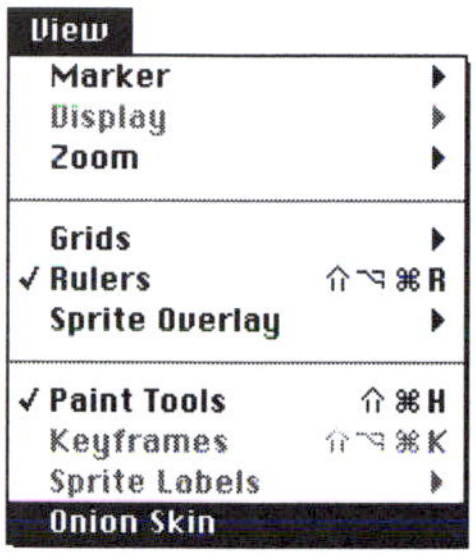

Figure 117. Choose **Onion Skin** from the **View** menu.

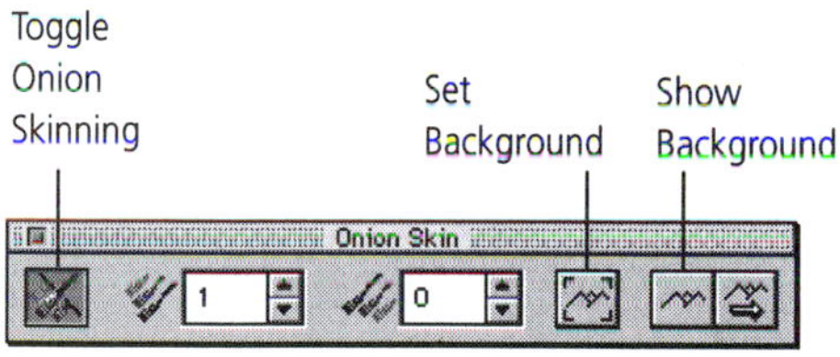

Figure 118. The **Onion Skin** toolbar.

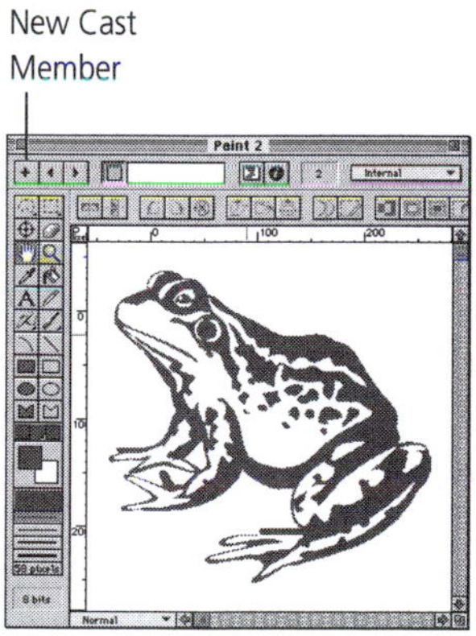

Figure 119. The reference cast member appears dimmed in the paint window. Draw your new cast member on top of this image.

ONION SKINNING

Onion Skinning is a technique which allows you to create a new cast member in the paint window while viewing one or more existing cast members as reference images which appear dimmed in the background. You effectively draw on top of these reference images, tracing the parts of their features that will carry over to the new cast member. The cast members used as references are not altered in the process.

The term onion skin refers to the very thin paper traditional animators use to trace over one or more previous images.

Onion Skinning is extremely useful for creating sequences of closely related cast members, which would be hard to generate without viewing reference images.

To use Onion Skinning:

Follow the steps below to create a new cast member while viewing one other previously rendered cast member as a background reference image:

1. Open the cast member you wish to use as the background reference image in the paint window **(Figure 116)**. You can do so by double-clicking it from its cast window.
2. Choose Onion Skin from the View menu **(Figure 117)**.
3. Click Toggle Onion Skinning in the Onion Skin toolbar **(Figure 118)**.
4. Click Set Background **(Figure 118)**.
5. Click the New Cast Member button in the paint window.
6. Click Show Background in the Onion Skin toolbar. The reference cast member appears dimmed in the paint window **(Figure 119)**. You now draw your new cast member on top of this image. The reference cast member is not altered by doing so.

To create a cast member while viewing a sequence of reference cast members:

As you create a cast member that is part of an animation sequence, it is very helpful to view several preceding frames of the sequence at the same time, so that your new cast member will fit in appropriately. With this technique, your reference cast members appear on top of each other in the paint window, with decreasing levels of brightness **(Figure 123)**. This allows you to create your new cast member in precise relation to the entire sequence.

1. Open the cast window that contains the reference cast members you wish to use. Make sure the reference cast members are grouped together.
2. In the cast window, create an empty position immediately following or preceding your reference cast members, and select it **(Figure 120)**.
3. Choose Media Element from the Insert menu and select Bitmap from the pop-up menu **(Figure 121)**. The paint window is opened.
4. Choose Onion Skin from the View menu.
5. Click Toggle Onion Skinning in the Onion Skin toolbar to turn it on **(Figure 122)**.
6. Click the arrows in the Preceding or Following Cast Members setting in the Onion Skin toolbar **(Figure 122)** to display your reference cast members. You can display as many of them as you have by setting the appropriate value. They are displayed on top of each other in the paint window **(Figure 123)**. The further away your reference cast members are from your new cast member in the cast window, the dimmer they appear.
7. Draw your new cast member on top of your reference images.

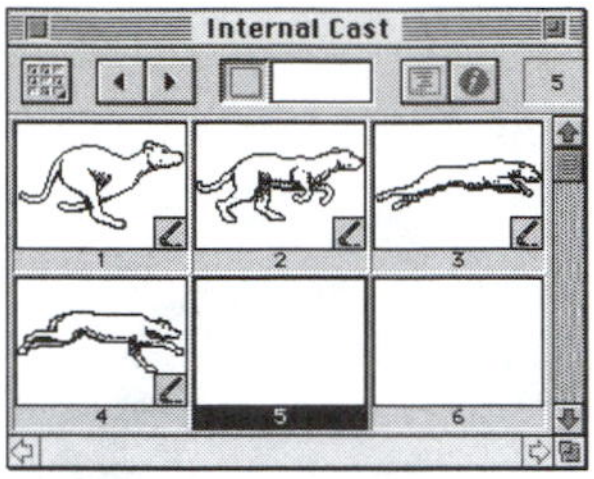

Figure 120. Create an empty position in the cast window immediately following or preceding your reference cast members. Select it.

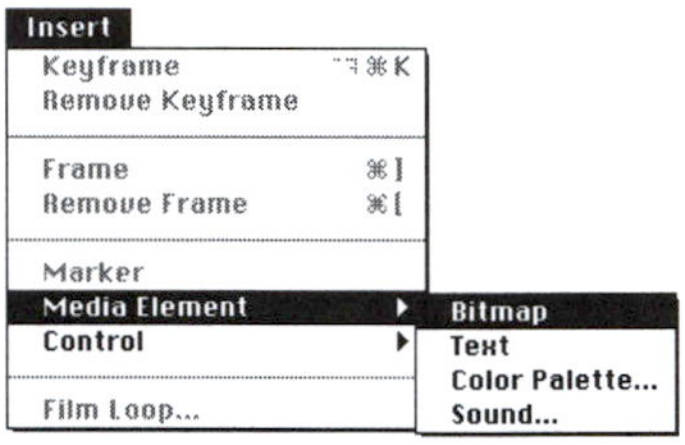

Figure 121. Choose **Media Element** from the **Insert** menu and select **Bitmap** from the pop-up menu.

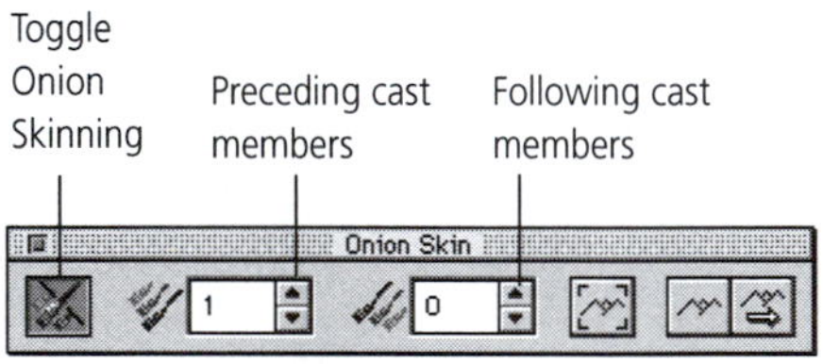

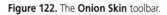

Figure 122. The **Onion Skin** toolbar.

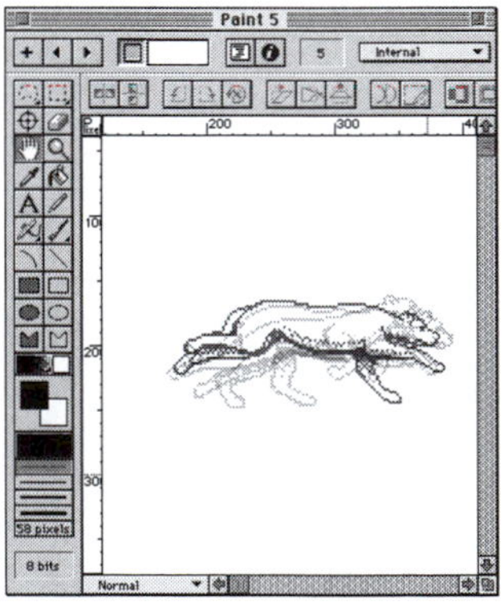

Figure 123. Your reference cast members appear on top of each other in the paint window.

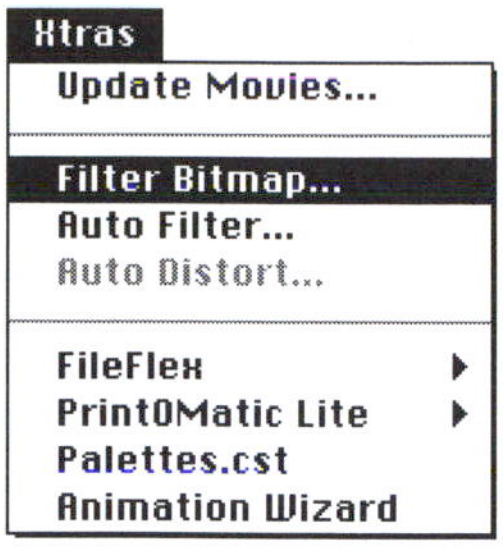

Figure 124. Choose **Filter Bitmap** from the **Xtras** menu.

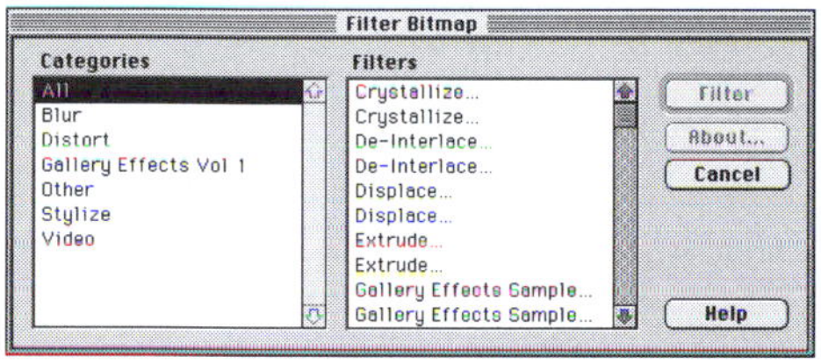

Figure 125. On the left side of the **Filter Bitmap** dialog box, select the category of filters you wish to view. On the right side, select the filter you wish to apply to your cast member and click **Filter**.

IMAGE FILTERS

Director allows you to apply Photoshop or Premiere image filters to your bitmapped cast members. In order for Director to have access to such filters, you must first place them in the Xtras folder in the Director application folder *(see page 223 in the Xtras chapter for more details on installing Xtras).* You can then apply a filter to modify a portion of a bitmapped cast member, or to modify multiple cast members at once. Image filters are applied in either the cast window or paint window.

To apply a filter to a portion of a bitmapped cast member:

1. Open the cast member in the paint window.
2. Use the Marquee or Lasso tool to select the part of the cast member you wish to modify.
3. Choose Filter Bitmap from the Xtras menu **(Figure 124)**.
4. On the left side of the Filter Bitmap dialog box, select the category of filters you wish to view **(Figure 125)**. Select All to view every available filter.
5. On the right side of the Filter Bitmap dialog box, select the filter you wish to apply to your cast member and click Filter. At this point, your filter will most likely display its own custom dialog box which allows you to enter filter settings. Make the appropriate selections and apply the filter. If your filter doesn't have a custom dialog box, it will be immediately applied after you click Filter.

✓ Tip

■ You can apply a filter to a multiple cast member selection in a cast window. Select the appropriate cast members in a cast window and choose Filter Bitmap from the Xtras menu.

TOOL PALETTE 8

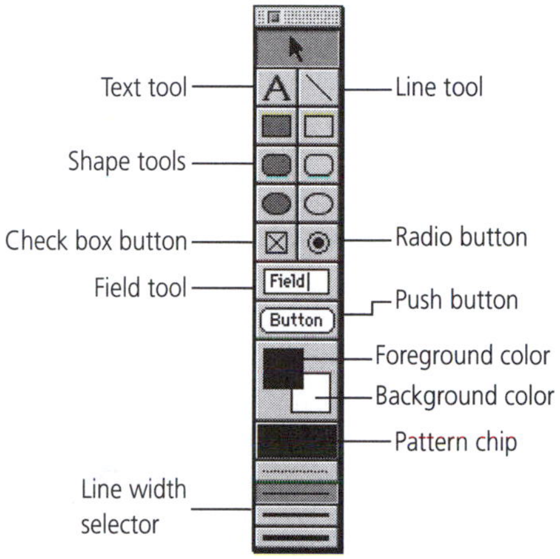

Figure 1. The Tool Palette.

Director's Tool Palette allows you to create text, shapes, and buttons directly on the stage **(Figure 1)**. These objects are automatically placed in the cast and score windows. Open the Tool Palette by choosing Tool Palette from the Window menu **(Figure 2)**.

Shapes created with the Tool Palette are called **QuickDraw** graphics. They offer several advantages over bitmap graphics created in Director's paint window: QuickDraw shapes (including lines) can be resized and edited on the stage. They consume a lot less memory than bitmap images, and print much better to laser printers. On the down side, QuickDraw graphics animate slower, so if speed is an issue, use bitmaps. You cannot edit QuickDraw graphics in the paint window.

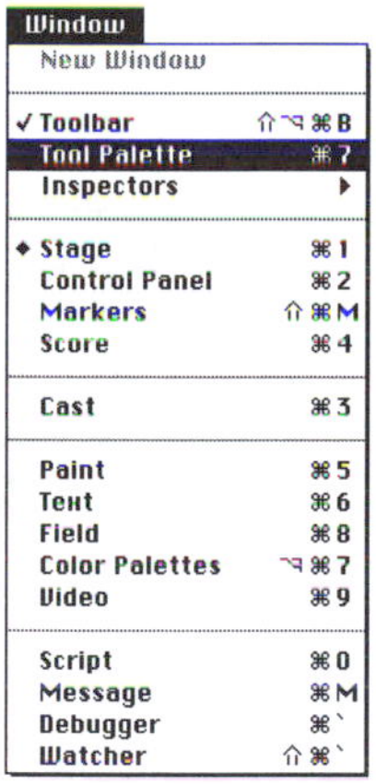

Figure 2. Choose **Tool Palette** from the **Window** menu.

Text tool

Use the Text tool **(Figure 3)** to create text as an alternative to using the text window under the Window menu. Text created with the Text tool is visible in the text and cast windows.

Select the Text tool, then click the stage where you wish to create and position some text. Click the arrow in the Tool Palette to select text on the stage that you wish to edit. *(See pages 172–175 in the Creating Text in Director chapter for more information on the Text tool and creating text with the text window)*

Field tool

The Field tool **(Figure 4)** also allows you to create text on the stage, except this text has the feature of being editable during movie playback. *(See page 177 for more information about using the Field tool)*

Figure 3. The Text tool.

Figure 4. The Field tool.

Line tool

Use the Line tool to draw lines on Director's stage **(Figure 5)**. Drag it to size your line. The line width can be changed by using the Line width selector at the bottom of the Tool Palette.

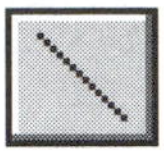

Figure 5. The Line tool.

Shape tools

The shape tools in the Tool Palette work very much like the shape tools in the paint window **(Figure 6)**. Click a hollow shape tool to draw an outline of that shape on the stage by dragging (you can set the thickness of the outline by using the Line width selector at the bottom of the Tool Palette). The shaded shape tools produce solid shapes using the current foreground color and pattern.

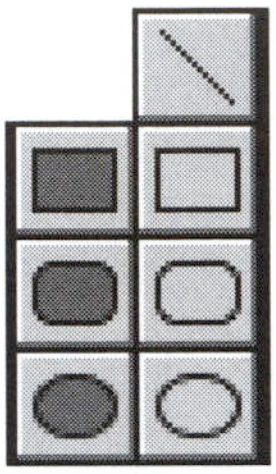

Figure 6. The shape tools.

✔ Tip

- Hold the Shift key while dragging a shape tool on the stage to constrain it to a perfect square or circle. Hold the Shift key while dragging the Line tool to constrain it to 45-degree lines.

Button tools

Director allows you to create push buttons, check boxes, and radio buttons by using the button tools provided in the Tool Palette **(Figure 7)**. Select the appropriate button tool, then drag a rectangle on the stage where the button should be placed. You can then type in the text that should appear on or next to your button. The font, size, and style of the button text can be set in the Font dialog box (choose Font from the Modify menu), or by using the Text Inspector *(see page 175 for info about the Text Inspector)*. Once placed onto the stage, a button cast member is created. Button text can be edited directly on the stage.

Figure 7. The button tools.

During movie playback, buttons appear to respond when clicked, but cause no special action unless they have a Lingo script attached to them. *(See page 202 for information on scripts)*

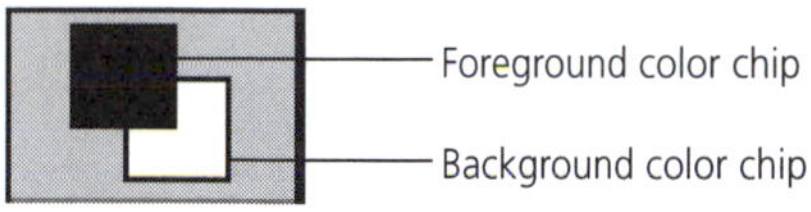

Figure 8. The Foreground and Background color chips.

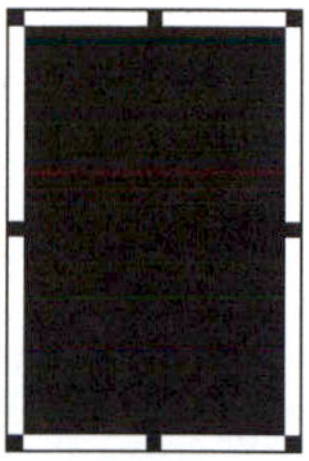

Figure 9. Select a QuickDraw line or shape on the stage.

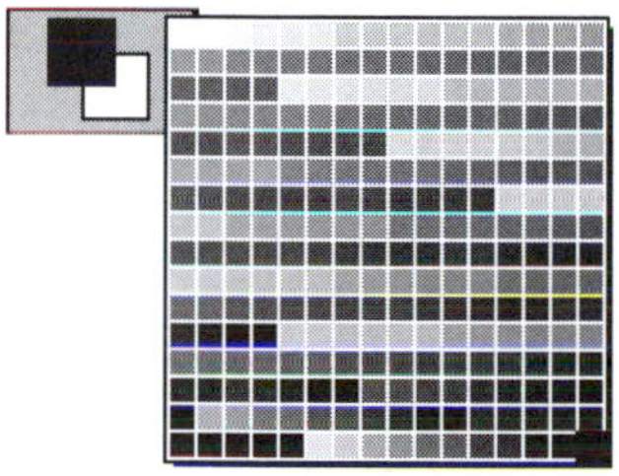

Figure 10. Click and hold the Foreground or Background color chips to select a new color from the pop-up menu.

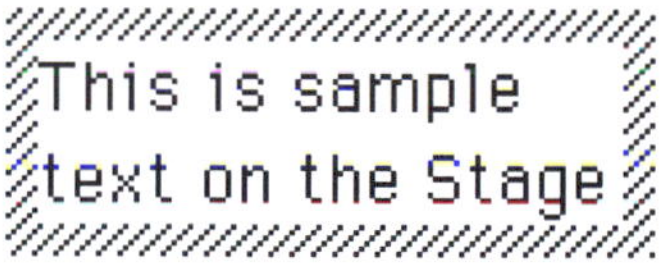

Figure 11. Double-click a text cast member on the stage.

FOREGROUND AND BACKGROUND COLOR CHIPS

Use the Foreground and Background color chips in the Tool Palette **(Figure 8)** to set the colors of QuickDraw lines, QuickDraw shapes, and sprites. Use them to also set the color of text on the stage, as well as text in text and script windows.

To set the color of QuickDraw lines or shapes:

1. Select a QuickDraw line or shape on the stage **(Figure 9)**.
2. Click and hold the Foreground or Background color chips in the Tool Palette to select a new color from the pop-up menu for the foreground or background colors **(Figure 10)**. The background color has no effect on a QuickDraw line, but does effect the color of solid QuickDraw shapes if a pattern for them is selected.

To set the color of text on the stage:

1. In the score, select the frame that contains the text cast member whose color you wish to change. Double-click the text cast member on the stage (a thick border appears around it) **(Figure 11)**.
2. Select a foreground color using the Foreground color chip **(Figure 10)**. Additional text now typed will have this color, but to change existing text color, select the actual text first by dragging across it, and then click the Foreground color chip.
3. Select a background color for the text block by using the Background color chip.

To set the color of text in text and script windows:

1. Select a text or script window so that it is the active window **(Figure 12)**.
2. Select a foreground color using the Foreground color chip in the Tool Palette **(Figure 13)**. Additional text now typed will have this color, but to change the color of existing text, select the actual text first by dragging across it and then click the Foreground color chip.
3. Select a background color for the text or script window by using the Background color chip in the Tool Palette.

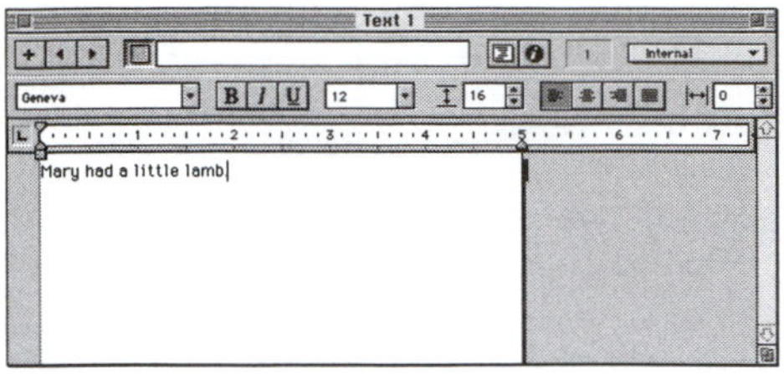

Figure 12. Make a text or script window active.

To set the color of sprites:

1. Select a sprite on the stage or in the score.
2. Choose a new foreground or background color using the Foreground and Background color chips in the Tool Palette **(Figure 13)**. Unless the foreground color of the sprite is originally black, changing its foreground color in this manner can result in unpredictable colors.

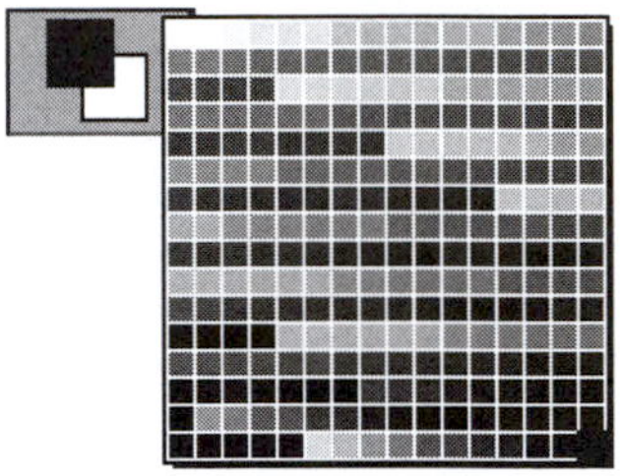

Figure 13. Click and hold the Foreground or Background color chips to select a new color from the pop-up menu.

Pattern chip

Click and hold the Pattern chip to select a new pattern from the pop-up menu **(Figure 14)**.

Figure 14. The Pattern chip.

Line width selector

Allows you to set the line width that's used with the Line tool and hollow shape tools **(Figure 15)**.

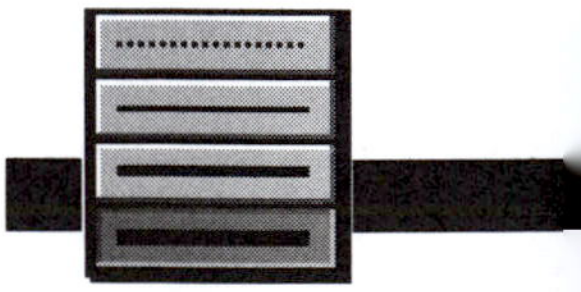

Figure 15. The Line width selector.

COLOR IN DIRECTOR 9

Color Palette

The Color Palette is used throughout this chapter. Choose Color Palettes from the Window menu to display it (**Figure 1**).

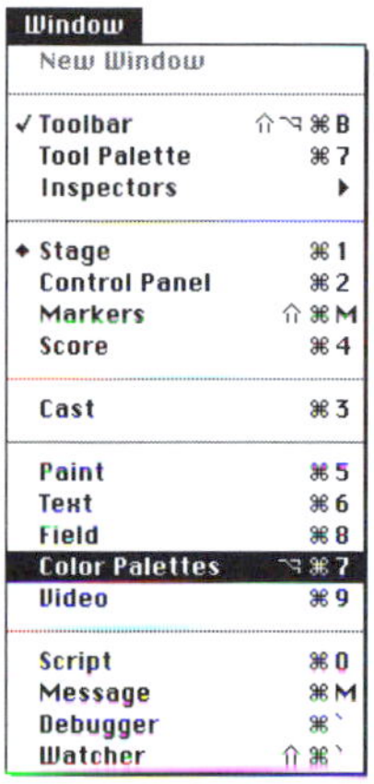

Figure 1. Choose **Color Palettes** from the **Window** menu.

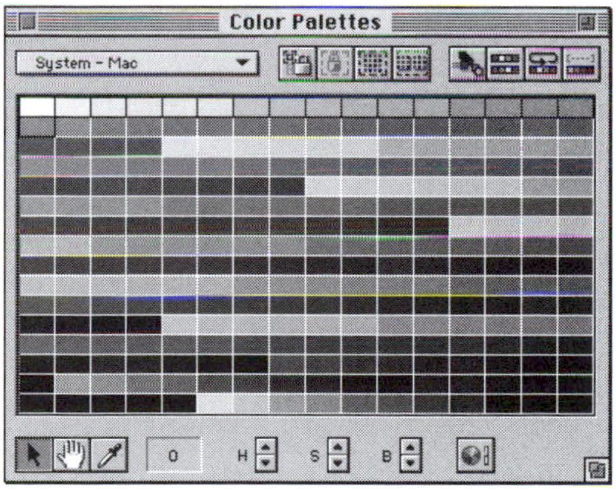

Figure 2. The color palettes window.

If you plan on creating Director movies that use 8-bit color depth or less *(see Color Depth on the next page)*, it is especially important to understand the nature of color palettes in Director and how to work around their limitations. This knowledge will enhance your ability to create visually pleasing movies.

In this chapter you'll learn about movie and cast member color depth and how these settings relate to color palettes. You will learn how to create and edit color palettes using the color palettes window **(Figure 2)**. And you'll learn how to take the most commonly used colors from a variety of cast members and arrange them into a new "optimal" palette that all cast members can use simultaneously. You will also discover how to create impressive visual effects through palette transitions and a special technique called "color cycling" that makes cast members appear to animate and pulse.

COLOR DEPTH

The first thing to know about color in Director is color depth. Color depth generally refers to the number of colors that your computer can display on the screen at the same time. The maximum depends on the type of graphics hardware installed in your Macintosh.

Color depth is expressed in bits per pixel. 1-bit color depth corresponds to black and white, 2-bit is 4 colors, 4-bit is 16 colors, 8-bit is 256 colors, 16-bit is 32,768 colors, and 32-bit is 16.7 million colors.

In Director, there are two types of color depth settings: The first is the color depth of your overall movie, and the second is the individual color depth setting of each of your cast members.

Movie color depth

Your movie's color depth corresponds to the color depth setting of your monitor. Movie color depth determines the maximum number of colors that can be displayed by any image in Director. This setting takes precedence over cast member color depth. For example, if your movie is set to 8-bit color depth, a 16-bit or 32-bit cast member will be displayed in 8-bit color (256 colors).

To change movie color depth:

1. Choose Control Panels from the Apple menu **(Figure 3)**, and double-click the Monitors icon.
2. In the Monitors dialog box, set your monitor to display the number of colors you wish to have available in Director **(Figure 4)**. This affects all other open applications.
3. Save your Director movie.

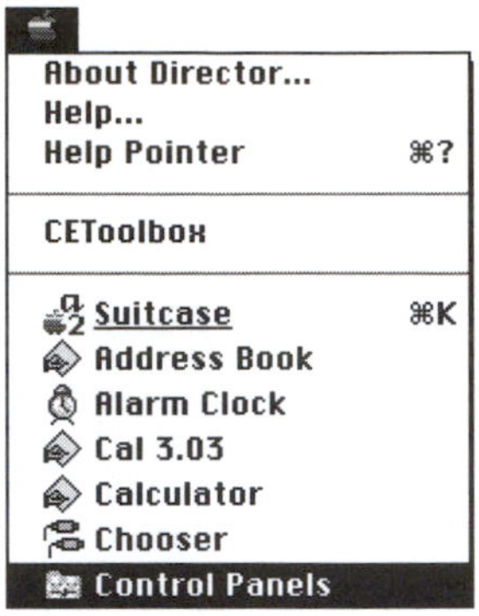

Figure 3. Choose **Control Panels** from the **Apple** menu.

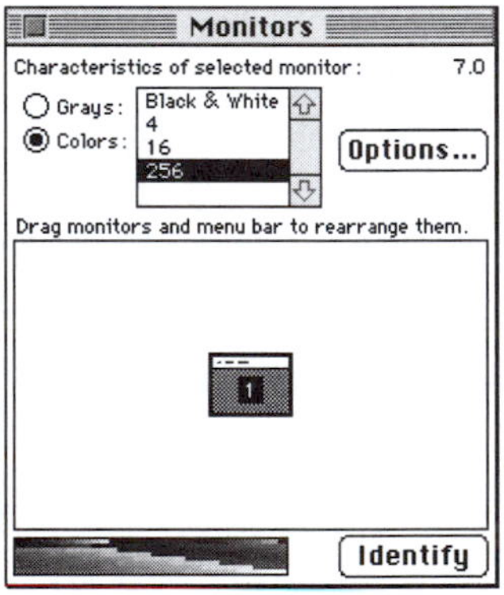

Figure 4. In the **Monitors** dialog box, select a new color depth for your monitor. This setting is also the new color depth for your Director movie.

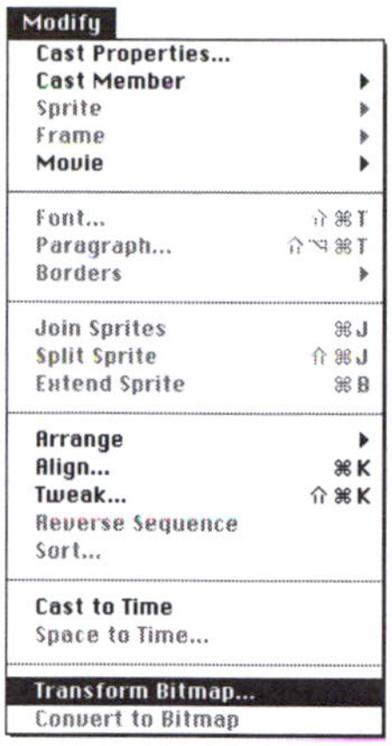

Figure 5. Choose **Transform Bitmap** from the **Modify** menu.

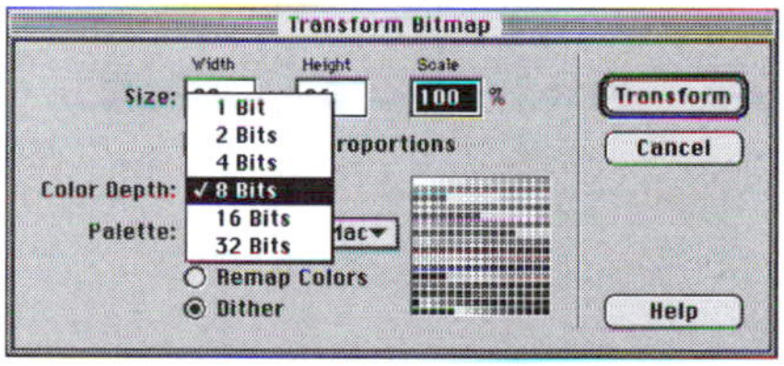

Figure 6. In the **Transform Bitmap** dialog box, use the **Color Depth** pop-up menu to select the desired cast member color depth.

Cast member color depth

Each bitmap cast member in Director has its own color depth setting, which can differ from the movie color depth. You can view this setting for any bitmap cast member by selecting it in a cast window, and choosing Transform Bitmap from the Modify menu, or by clicking the Cast Member Properties button.

The larger a cast member's color depth, the more memory it requires, and the slower it animates. If your movie will be playing on a wide variety of systems, 8-bit color depth is still the safest choice.

In order for a cast member to display its entire range of colors in your movie, the movie color depth setting must be set at least as high as the cast member color depth. For example, if you want to accurately display a 16-bit cast member (32,768 colors), the movie color depth setting must be at least 16-bits.

Note: If your cast members have higher color depth settings than your movie, the extra colors will not be displayed, but they will still animate slowly, as if all their colors were being displayed. In most cases, you should transform these cast members to the color depth setting of your movie, or lower.

To change a cast member's color depth:

You cannot undo this operation. Make sure you have a copy of the original cast member before proceeding.

1. Select the cast member in the cast window whose color depth you wish to change.
2. Choose Transform Bitmap from the Modify menu **(Figure 5)**.
3. In the Transform Bitmap dialog box, use the Color Depth pop-up menu to select the new depth for the cast member **(Figure 6)**.
4. Click Transform.

COLOR PALETTES

A **color palette** is a collection of all possible colors that can be displayed on the screen at any one time **(Figure 7)**. When your movie color depth is set to 8-bits (256 colors) or lower, the colors that Director can display (including colors in its user interface) are limited to those which are contained in color palettes. On the other hand, colors you can display in 16-bit or higher movies are not restricted to limited choices in color palettes since Director has a continuous spectrum of colors to work with (in such movies, you use color palettes only for the purpose of selecting colors to paint with).

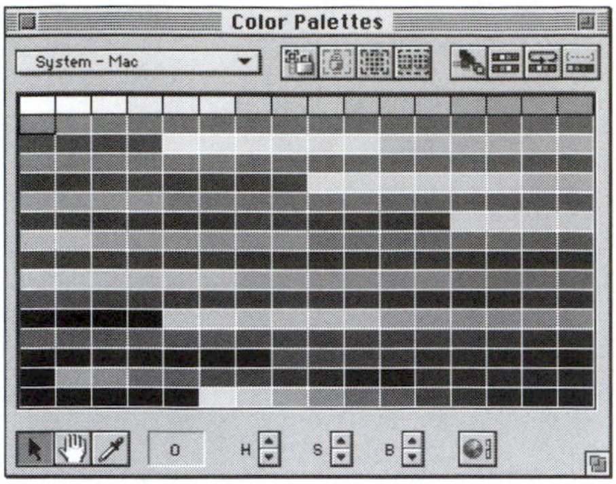

Figure 7. This is an 8-bit (256 colors) color palette.

Director has a number of standard built-in 8-bit color palettes you can choose from *(see page 145)*, or you can create your own color palettes. You can also import color palettes into Director *(see page 148)*. Palettes you create or import become cast members.

The current color palette

Only one color palette is active in any single frame of your movie and this palette is called the **current color palette**. All cast members are displayed in the colors of the current palette. A different current palette can be set for each frame of your movie by using the score's palette channel **(Figure 8)** *(see page 145)*. The colors that can simultaneously appear in any single frame of your movie must be in the current color palette set for that given frame. An 8-bit Director movie can display more than 256 unique colors, but not in any single frame. It can do so over a range of frames, by switching the current palette in those frames.

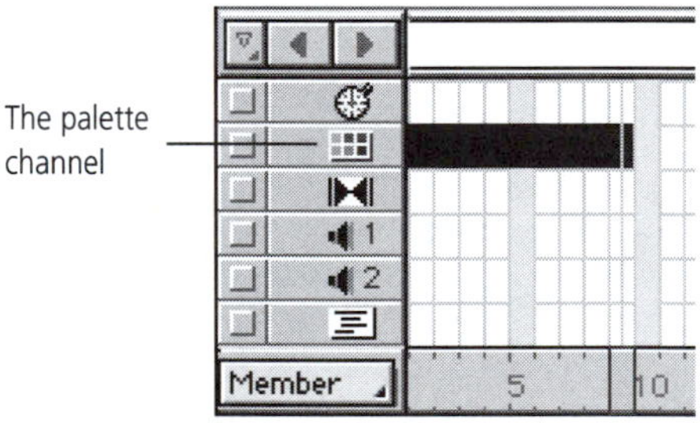

Figure 8. Use the palette channel to set the current color palette for any frame.

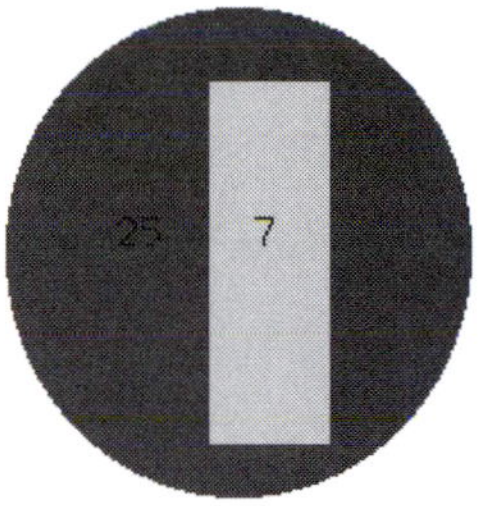

Figure 9. In an 8-bit or lower bitmap cast member, each pixel is mapped to a specific color palette position and the colors which occupy those positions in the current palette determine the pixels' coloring.
In the sample cast member above, the color of pixels in the circle are mapped to the 25th color palette position while the pixels in the rectangle are mapped to the 7th position (shown in Figure 10).

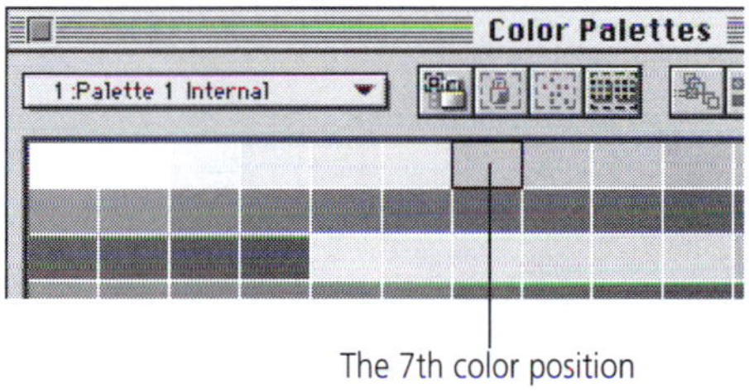

Figure 10. The color mapping of the cast member in Figure 9 is such that the pixels in its rectangular section are mapped to the seventh color palette position. If you change the color in the seventh color position of the current palette to green in this example, the rectangular section in figure 9 will turn green.

Cast members and color palettes

When you create a 2-, 4-, or 8-bit image in any graphics application such as Photoshop, a color palette is used to describe all colors in that image. This color palette is linked to the image file. When you import such an image into Director, you can import its linked color palette *(see page 148)*. In order for Director to display any 2-, 4-, or 8-bit cast member in its proper colors, the color palette used to create the original image should be set as the current palette. Another way to ensure that a cast member's colors are displayed accurately is to remap it to a new color palette that has similar colors to its original palette *(see page 149)*, and then use that palette as the current palette.

Each 2-, 4-, and 8-bit bitmap cast member in Director is mapped to a particular color palette. This means that the color of each pixel in such a cast member is determined by referencing a specific color position in the cast member's mapped palette. For example, if a section of a cast member is red, the pixels in that section reference (or are mapped to) the color position in the palette which holds the same color. If you display a cast member using a current palette that's different from the palette its mapped to, the cast member will probably be displayed in the wrong colors. This is because the cast member's pixels are still mapped to its assigned palette, but this mapping is used to reference colors in a different current palette, and this results in colors being shown improperly.

You can see which palette a cast member is mapped to and remap the cast member to a new palette by using the Transform Bitmap command (see page 149).

Figures 9–10 give an example as to how a set of pixels in a cast member is mapped to a specific color position.

ASSIGNING COLOR PALETTES TO FRAMES AND CAST MEMBERS

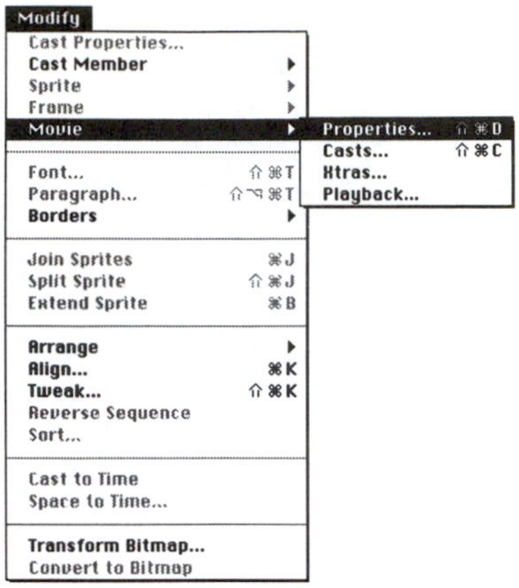

Figure 11. Choose **Movie** from the **Modify** menu and select **Properties** from the pop-up menu.

To set a default color palette:

You can set a default color palette that is used automatically when you create a new Director movie. This default palette is used as the current color palette in your frames until a new palette is set in the palette channel. *(See page 145)*

1. Choose Movie from the Modify menu and select Properties from the pop-up menu **(Figure 11)**.
2. Use the Default Palette pop-up menu to select the palette you wish to use as your movie's default palette **(Figure 12)**.
3. Click OK.

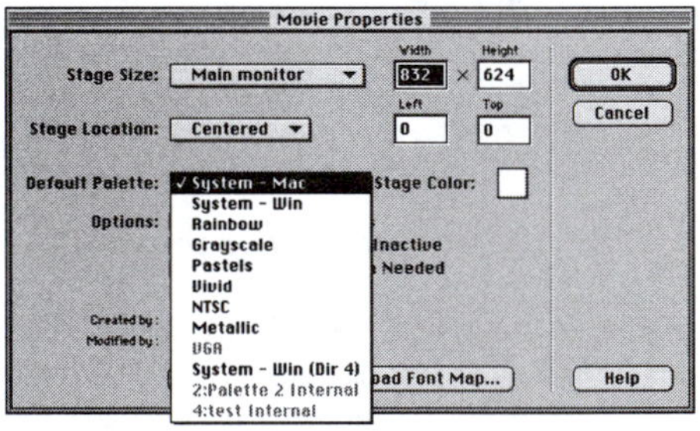

Figure 12. Select your movie's default palette from the pop-up menu.

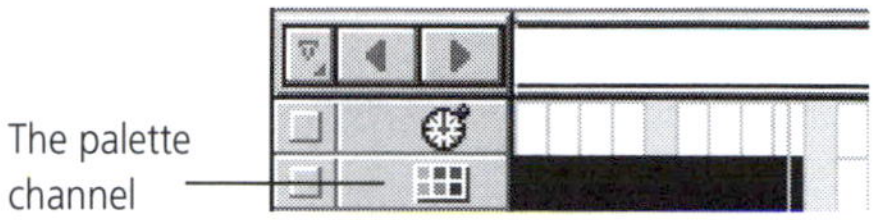

Figure 13. In the palette channel, select the frame or series of frames whose palette you would like to set.

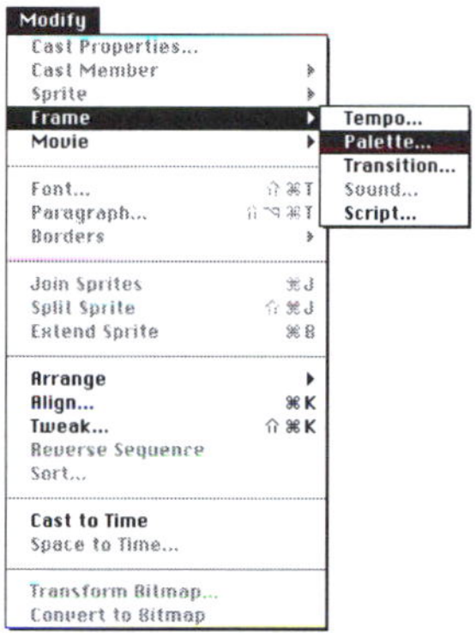

Figure 14. Choose **Frame** from the **Modify** menu and select **Palette** from the pop-up menu.

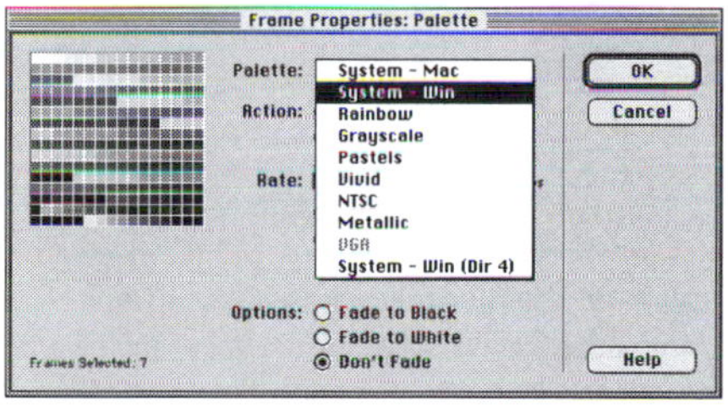

Figure 15. In the **Frame Properties** dialog box, use the **Palette** pop-up menu to choose a palette you wish to apply to the selected frames.

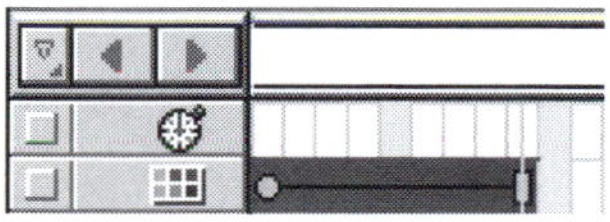

Figure 16. Click OK in the **Frame Properties** dialog box and Director sets the new palette in selected frames.

To set the current color palette in the palette channel:

When Director plays a movie, it displays its cast members using a color palette specified in the palette channel of the score. These settings override any default palette set through the Movie command *(see page 144)*. Like all of Director's score channels, the palette channel **(Figure 13)** can be controlled on a frame-by-frame basis—for instance, frame 1 can employ palette A to display cast members, while frame 5 switches to palette B, and frame 15 switches to palette C. By swapping palettes like this, you can display a sequence of distinct cast members in their original palettes, and create unique visual effects by changing between palettes over time.

When you are placing a cast member on the stage that uses a palette different from the currently active palette, Director automatically assigns that cast member's palette to the palette channel and uses it for all subsequent frames until a new palette is set in the channel. Setting a new palette in the palette channel is easy.

1. In the palette channel, select the frame or frames where you wish to set a new color palette **(Figure 13)**.
2. Choose Frame from the Modify menu and select Palette from the pop-up menu **(Figure 14)**.
3. In the Frame Properties dialog box, use the Palette pop-up menu to choose the palette you wish to apply to the selected frames. Your choices include all of Director's core palettes (System, Rainbow, Pastels, etc.), plus any you've created **(Figure 15)**.
4. Click OK. Director sets the new palette in the selected frames **(Figure 16)**. Don't be surprised if the cast members in those frames suddenly change colors—they are now displayed in the colors of your new palette.

✔ **Tip**

- You can double-click a frame in the palette channel to open the Frame Properties dialog box.

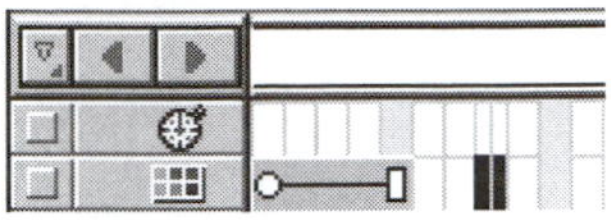

Figure 17. Select the cell in the palette channel where the palette transition should take place.

To set a color palette transition over a single frame:

Switching palettes in a scene can be a little jarring: You see a particular set of colors in one frame, and in the next frame the set is entirely different. Director lets you use a palette transition to control the speed at which colors change, smoothing the switch from one palette to the next.

1. In the palette channel of the score window, select the cell where you would like your palette transition to take place **(Figure 17)**.
2. Choose Frame from the Modify menu and select Palette from the pop-up menu **(Figure 18)**.
3. In the Frame Properties dialog box, use the Palette pop-up menu to choose the palette to which you wish to make a transition **(Figure 19)**. Remember that the palette you set in this frame should be different from the palette used in the channel's previous frames.
4. In the Frame Properties dialog box, adjust the Rate scroll bar to determine how fast the transition between the old and new palettes will be. The speed can be set anywhere between 1 and 30 frames per second **(Figure 20)**. During playback, your movie will pause in this frame while the transition takes place.
5. Click OK to apply the new palette with its transition.

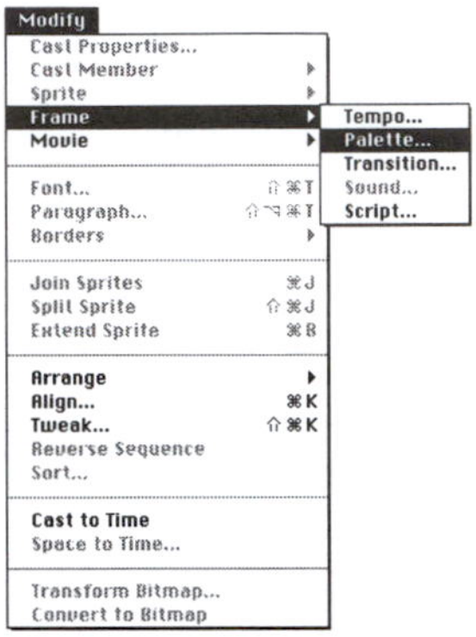

Figure 18. Choose **Frame** from the **Modify** menu and select **Palette** from the pop-up menu.

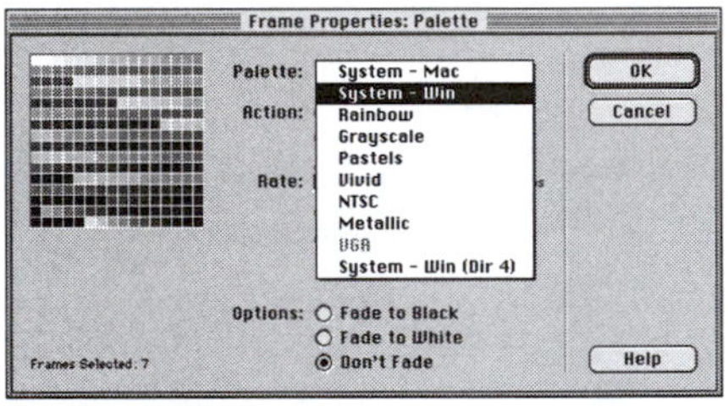

Figure 19. Use the **Palette** pop-up menu in the **Frame Properties** dialog box to choose the palette to transition to.

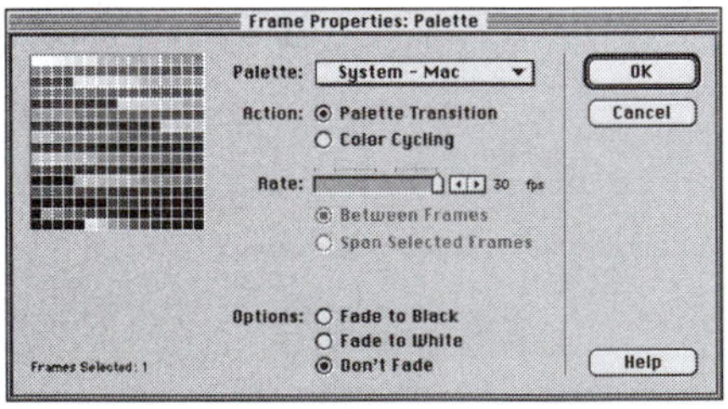

Figure 20. Adjust the Rate scroll bar to set how fast the transition between the palettes should be.

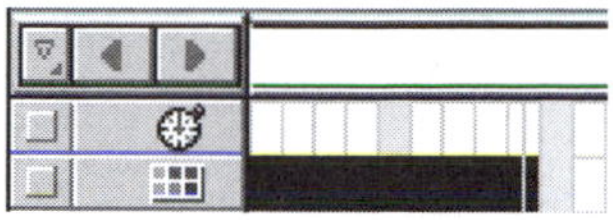

Figure 21. Select a series of cells in the palette channel in which your palette transition will occur.

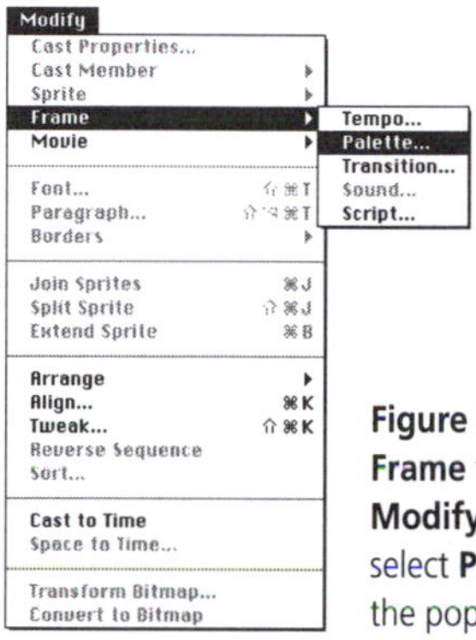

Figure 22. Choose **Frame** from the **Modify** menu and select **Palette** from the pop-up menu.

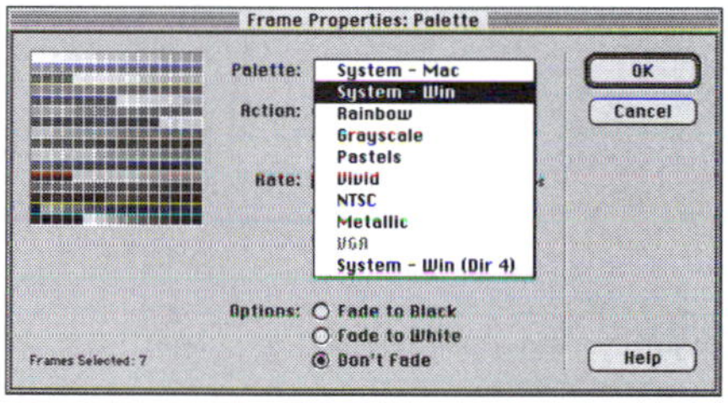

Figure 23. In the **Frame Properties** dialog box, select the transition palette in the **Palette** pop-up menu.

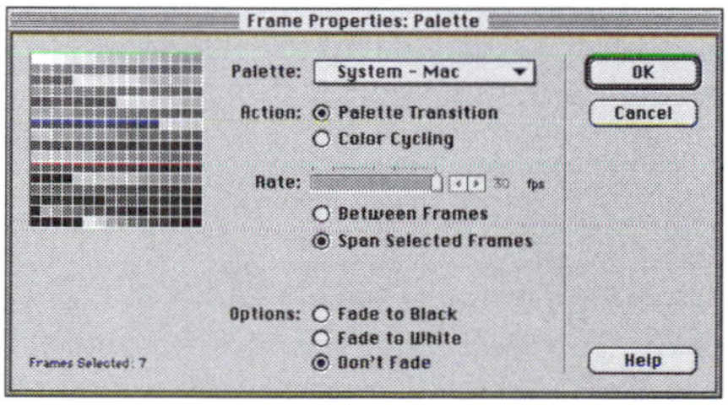

Figure 24. Select the **Span Selected Frames** option.

To set a color palette transition over a series of frames:

Just as you can set a smooth palette transition over one frame, you can set a transition to last over a series of frames. This will make the transition between color palettes more subtle, and your animation can continue without interruption.

1. In the palette channel, select the series of cells in which your palette transition will occur **(Figure 21)**.
2. Choose Frame from the Modify menu and select Palette from the pop-up menu **(Figure 22)**.
3. In the Frame Properties dialog box, use the Palette pop-up menu to select the palette to which you want to make a transition **(Figure 23)**.
4. Select the Span Selected Frames option **(Figure 24)**.
5. Click OK to apply the new palette with its transition.

To import a new color palette into Director:

You import a color palette into Director for Macintosh by importing an image that was created with the desired palette.

1. Choose Import from the File menu **(Figure 25)**.
2. In the Import dialog box, select the image file that uses the color palette you wish to import and click Import **(Figure 26)**. The Image Options dialog box appears if the image's color palette is different from the currently active color palette.
3. Click the Import radio button **(Figure 27)** in the Image Options dialog box and click OK to import the image's color palette. The color palette is placed into the active cast window. *(See page 29 in the Cast Windows chapter for more details on the Image Options dialog box)*

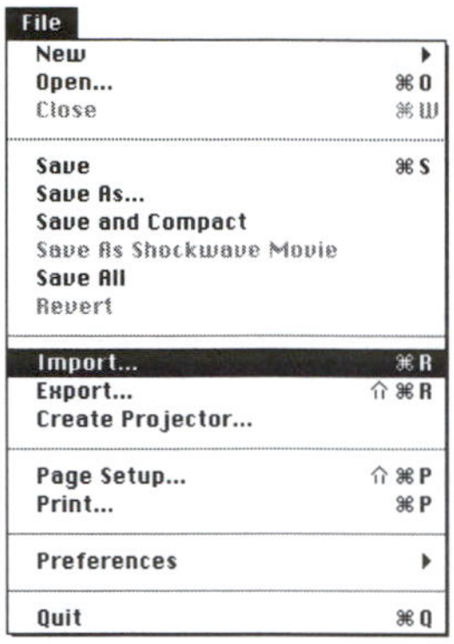

Figure 25. Choose **Import** from the **File** menu.

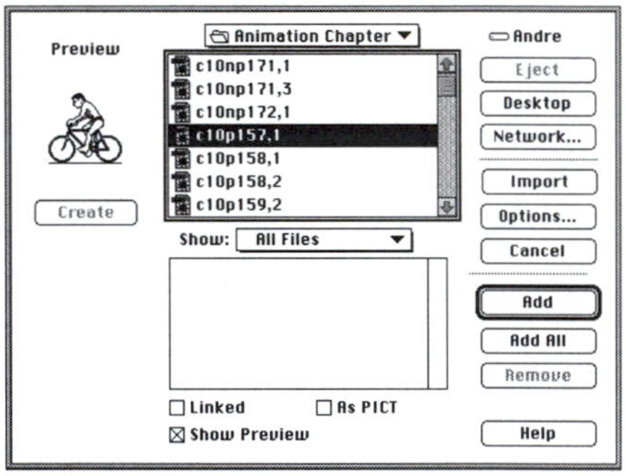

Figure 26. Select the desired cast member and click Import.

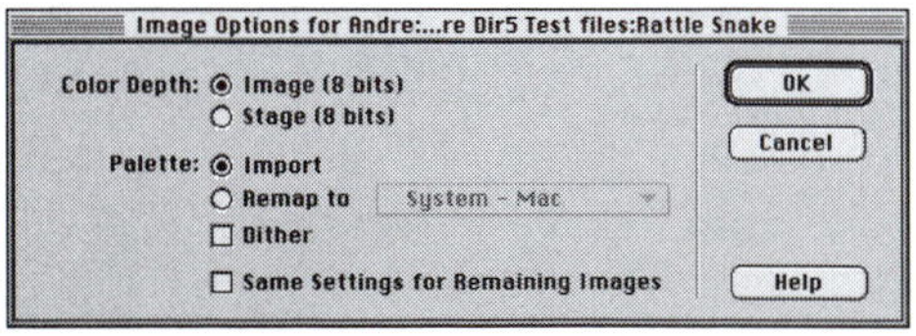

Figure 27. Click the **Import** radio button in the **Image Options** dialog box, then click **OK** to import the image's original color palette.

Figure 28. Select the cast member you'd like to remap.

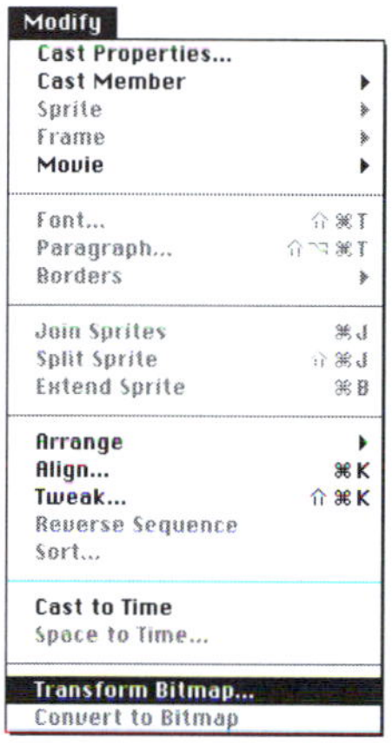

Figure 29. Choose **Transform Bitmap** from the **Modify** menu.

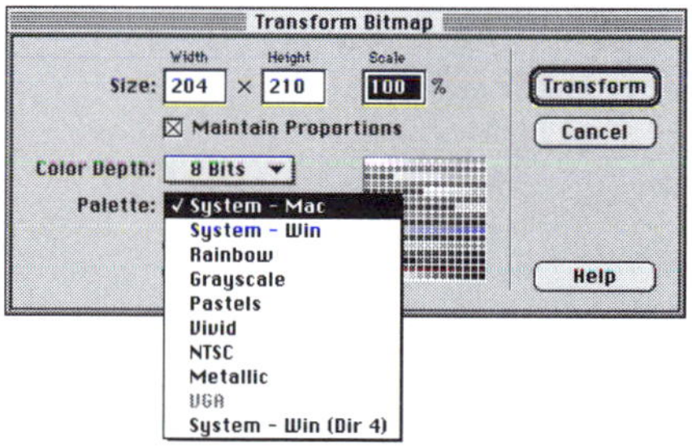

Figure 30. In the **Transform Bitmap** dialog box, select a palette from the **Palette** pop-up menu to which the cast member should be remapped.

To remap a cast member to a different color palette:

Director lets you "remap" a cast member to a different palette. When you remap a cast member to a new palette, Director examines the cast member's original colors (actually examines which color each pixel is currently mapped to), and remaps its pixels to new color positions in the new palette which contain colors that best match the original. This often leads to a close, but not identical match of colors. To improve results, the palette you are remapping to should have a similar set of colors compared to the cast member's currently assigned palette.

1. In a cast window, select the cast member you would like to remap **(Figure 28)**.
2. Choose Transform Bitmap from the Modify menu **(Figure 29)**.
3. In the Transform Bitmap dialog box, use the Palette pop-up menu to choose the palette to which the cast member should be remapped **(Figure 30)**.
4. Click the Remap Colors radio button in the Transform Bitmap dialog box.
5. Click Transform to remap the cast member to the new palette. Now play your movie back to see how the cast member looks in its new color scheme, or examine the cast member more closely in Director's paint window.

✓ Tip

- Since remapping a cast member can distort its colors, it's a good idea to perform your first remap on a copy of the cast member. This way, you can still revert to an earlier color scheme. To copy a cast member, select it in the cast window, and choose Copy from the Edit menu; then select an empty cast member position and choose Paste from the Edit menu.

To remap cast members on the stage to the current palette:

When you have cast members on the stage that are assigned color palettes different from the current palette, these cast members will not appear in their accurate colors. Director can automatically remap all such cast members on the fly to the current color palette. Note that this feature only affects the appearance of cast members on the stage, and does not permanently remap the actual cast members.

1. Choose Movie from the Modify menu and select Properties from the pop-up menu **(Figure 31)**.
2. In the Movie Properties dialog box, check the Remap Palettes When Needed box **(Figure 32)**.
3. Click OK.

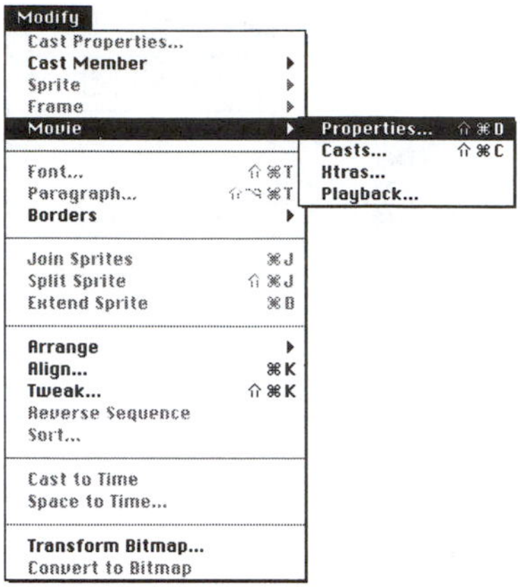

Figure 31. Choose **Movie** from the **Modify** menu and select **Properties** from the pop-up menu.

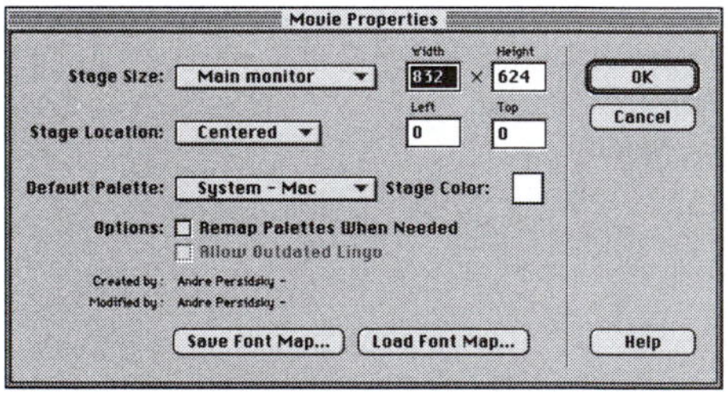

Figure 32. In the **Movie Properties** dialog box, check the **Remap Palettes When Needed** box.

Figure 33. Select the cast member whose palette you wish to use as the basis for your optimal palette.

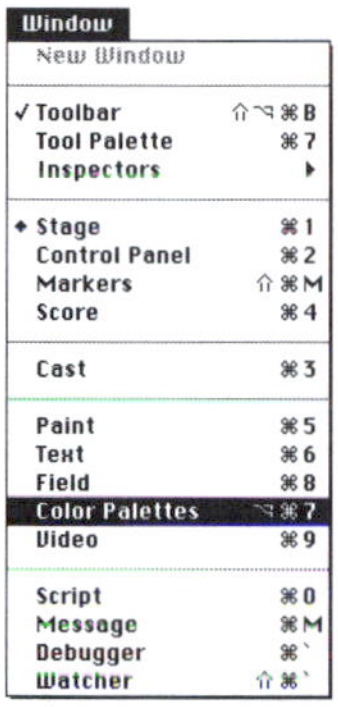

Figure 34. Choose **Color Palettes** from the **Window** menu.

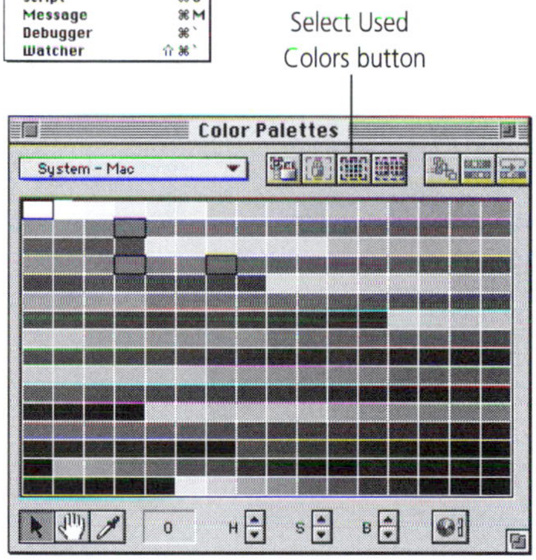

Figure 35. Click the **Select Used Colors** button in the color palettes window.

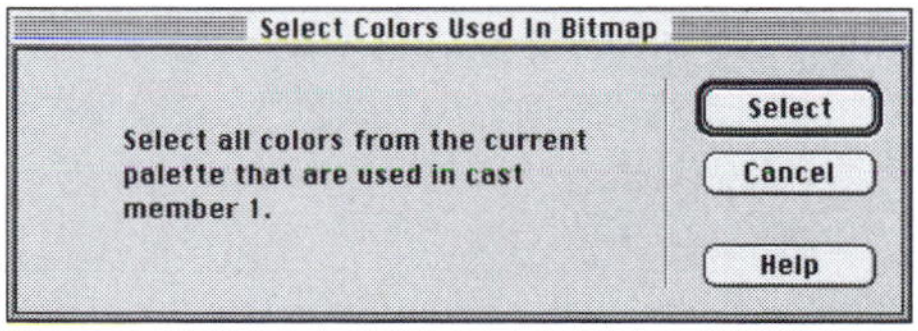

Figure 36. In the **Select Colors Used in Bitmap** dialog box, click the **Select** button to highlight all colors used by the selected cast member.

CREATE AN OPTIMAL COLOR PALETTE

It's possible to create a single, specialized palette that incorporates many of the same colors, or similar ones, shared by your entire cast. Once you've created this "optimal" palette, you can remap all of your cast members to it using the steps outlined on page 149. This approach allows your movie to operate from a single common palette, keeping colors consistent throughout.

Remember, however, that if your optimal palette does not contain all the same colors used in any given cast member, remapping such a cast member to this new palette may lead to a close but not identical match of colors.

To create an optimal color palette for all cast members:

1. In a cast window, select one of the cast members that you will later remap to your optimal palette **(Figure 33)**. It's preferable to choose a cast member that uses only a small number of the colors available in its palette.
2. Click the Cast Member Properties button in the cast window to make the cast member's assigned palette the current palette. Click cancel.
3. Choose Color Palettes from the Window menu **(Figure 34)**.
4. In the color palettes window, click the Select Used Colors button **(Figure 35)**.
5. In the Select Colors Used in Bitmap dialog box, click the Select button **(Figure 36)**. Director will highlight all the colors used by the cast member you selected earlier. It's often difficult to tell which of the palette's colors are selected. Selected colors have a thin black border, while unselected colors have thin white borders **(Figure 35)**.

6. Choose Duplicate from the Edit menu **(Figure 37)**. By copying the original palette, you're free to work without disturbing the cast member's current coloring.
7. In the Create Palette dialog box, type the name you wish to give this palette **(Figure 38)**. You might want to use something descriptive, such as "Optimal Palette". Click OK.
8. With all the used colors still highlighted in the color palettes window, click the Hand tool and then drag one of the highlighted colors to the second color position in the first row of colors (the position immediately to the right of white). Director rearranges the selected colors into a continuous range **(Figure 39)**.

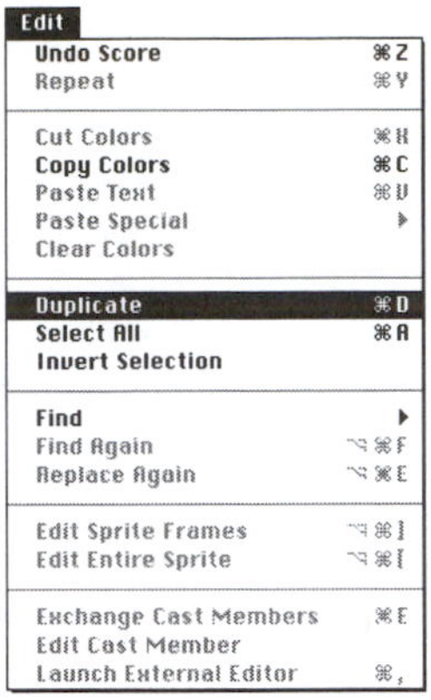

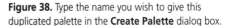

Figure 37. Choose **Duplicate** from the **Edit** menu.

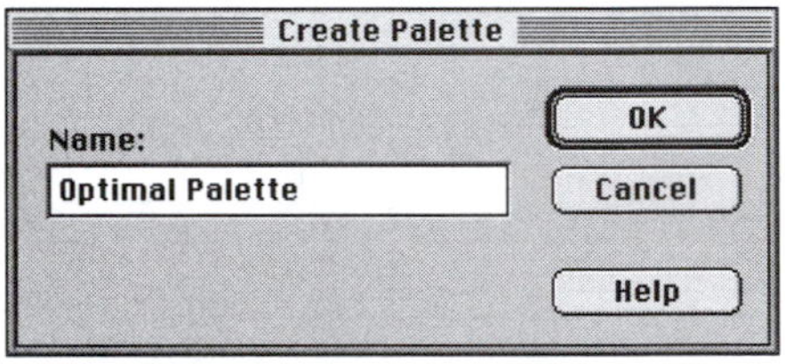

Figure 38. Type the name you wish to give this duplicated palette in the **Create Palette** dialog box.

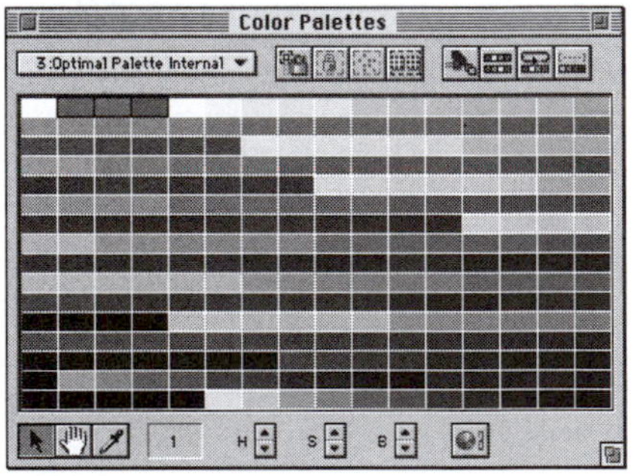

Figure 39. Drag one of the highlighted colors to the second position in the first row. Director rearranges the selected colors into a continuous range.

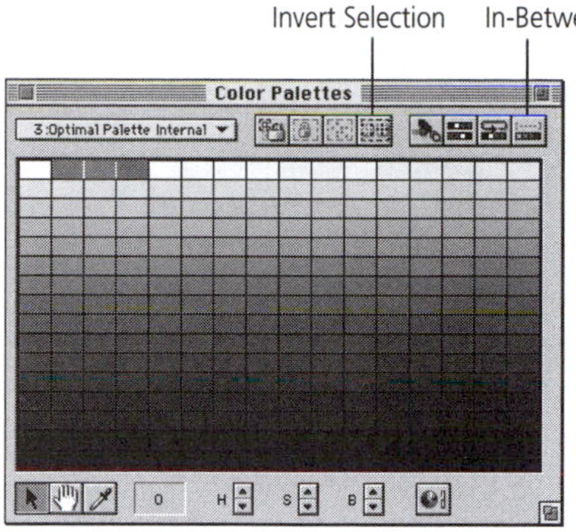

Figure 40. In-Betweening a range of colors changes them into a continuous blend of similar colors, so you can easily tell them apart from the used colors.

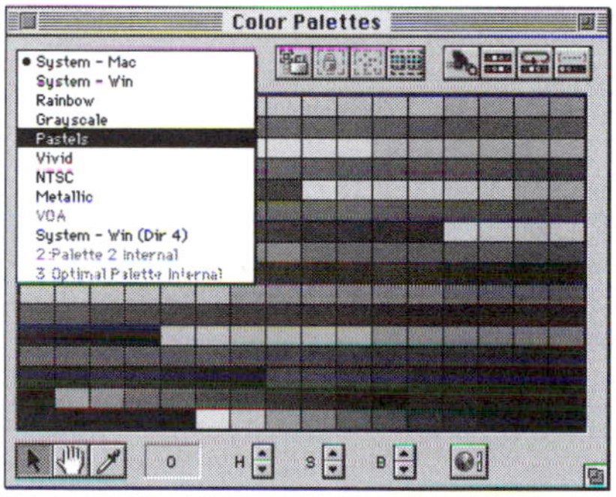

Figure 41. In the color palettes window, click the **Palette** pop-up menu and select another palette used by other cast members in your movie.

9. Click the Invert Selection button in the color palettes window. This selects all the *unused* colors in the palette.

10. Click the In-Between button in the color palettes window **(Figure 40)**. Director changes all unused colors into a continuous blend of similar colors so you can easily tell them apart from the used colors that will be the backbone of your optimal palette **(Figure 40)**. In this area of blended colors (which you don't need, since these colors are not used by the cast member selected in step 1) you can paste additional colors from other color palettes.

11. You are now ready to collect additional colors used by your cast members from other color palettes. In the color palettes window, click the Palette pop-up menu and select another palette used by other cast members in your movie **(Figure 41)**.

12. In the color palettes window, click each color chip that you'd like to add to your optimal palette **(Figure 42)**. Hold down the Command key to make multiple, discontinuous selections, or the Shift key to select a range. You can also select a cast member in the cast window that uses this palette and then click the Select Used Colors button in the color palettes window to highlight all the colors the cast member uses. Try to select a handful of colors that best represent the color range of the palette. For instance, pick a couple of reds, a couple of blues, a few grays, greens, and so on.
13. Choose Copy Colors from the Edit menu **(Figure 43)**.
14. In the color palettes window, click the Palette pop-up menu and select the optimal palette you created earlier **(Figure 44)**.

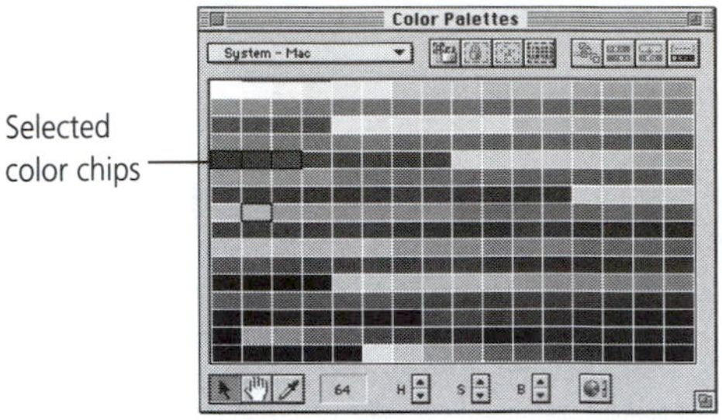

Figure 42. In the color palettes window, select the color chips to be added to your optimal palette.

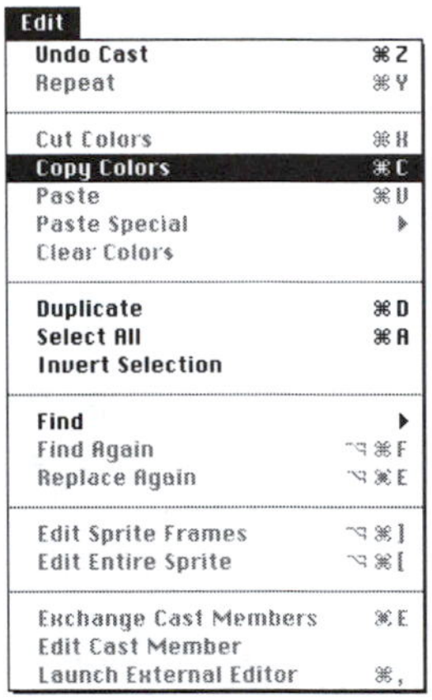

Figure 43. Choose **Copy Colors** from the **Edit** menu.

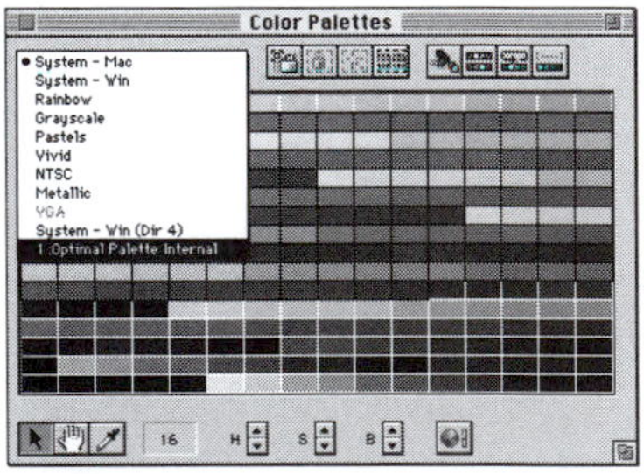

Figure 44. In the color palettes window, click the **Palette** pop-up menu and select the optimal palette you created earlier.

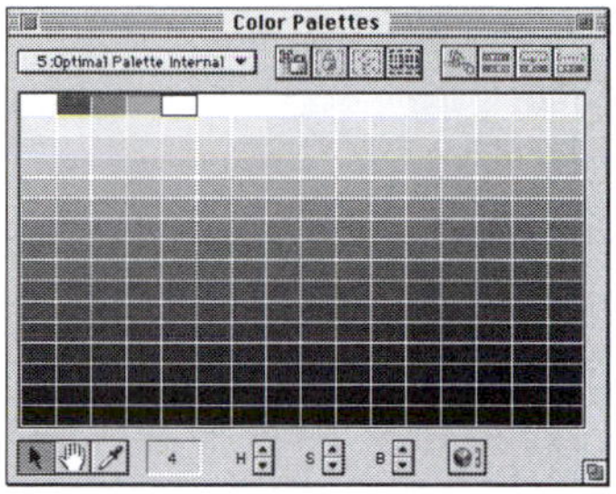

Figure 45. In the optimal palette, highlight one of the blended, unused color chips.

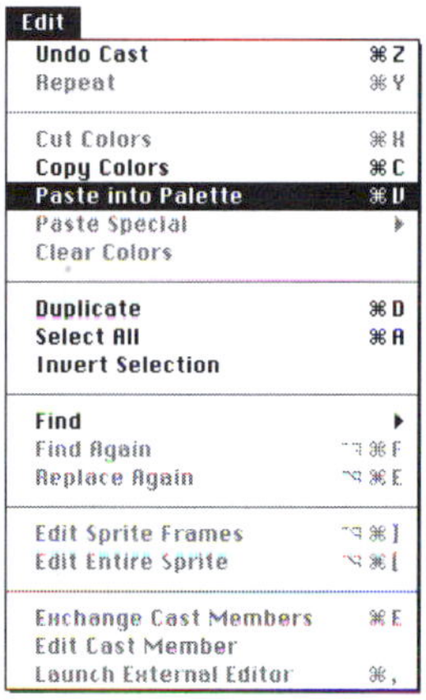

Figure 46. Choose **Paste Into Palette** from the **Edit** menu.

15. In the optimal palette **(Figure 45)**, select the first blended chip that immediately follows the last used color in the palette. Make sure that you have enough blended, unused color chips to accommodate the new colors.

16. Choose Paste Into Palette from the Edit menu to add the new colors to your optimal palette **(Figure 46)**.

17. Repeat steps 11 through 16 to continue adding colors from other color palettes.

18. Close the color palettes window when you've filled up your optimal palette.

19. Now you're ready to remap your movie's cast members to the optimal palette you've just created. To do so, follow the steps outlined on page 149, under the heading "*To remap a cast member to a different palette*".

✓ Tip

- Creating an optimal palette can sometimes require a lot of trial and error. After your first attempt, you may find that the optimal palette's colors are still not true enough to your cast member's original colors. In that case, simply open the optimal palette (choose Color Palettes from the Window menu) and adjust or replace the colors that affect your cast members. *(See page 156 for more details about editing the colors in a palette)*

CREATING CUSTOM COLOR PALETTES

If you wish to create a custom color palette, the first step is to create a duplicate of one of Director's standard palettes, since they cannot be modified. You are then free to edit any color in this duplicate palette, or even replace the colors all together.

To duplicate a color palette:

1. Choose Color Palettes from the Window menu **(Figure 47)**.
2. In the color palettes window, use the Palette pop-up menu to select the color palette you'd like to duplicate **(Figure 49)**.
3. Choose Duplicate from the Edit menu **(Figure 48)**.
4. In the Create Palette dialog box **(Figure 50)**, type a name for the duplicate palette and click OK. The palette is placed in the active cast window.

To edit colors in the color palettes window:

1. Choose Color Palettes from the Window menu **(Figure 47)**.
2. In the color palettes window, use the Palette pop-up menu to select the color palette you'd like to edit **(Figure 49)**. Since you cannot modify the standard preset Director palettes, you will be prompted with the Create Palette dialog box when you try to change a standard palette.
3. With the Pointer tool click the color chip you want to edit. The chip is highlighted by a black border.

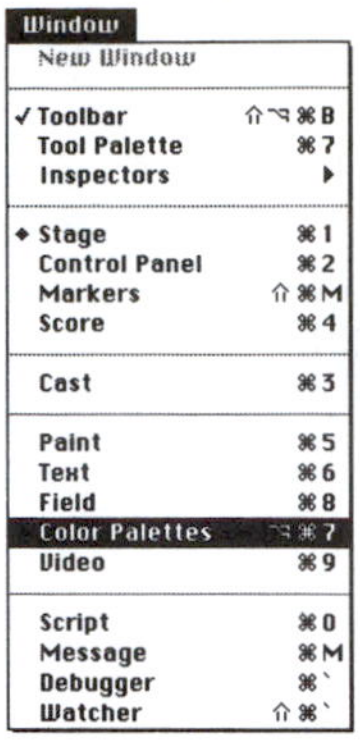

Figure 47. Choose **Color Palettes** from the **Window** menu.

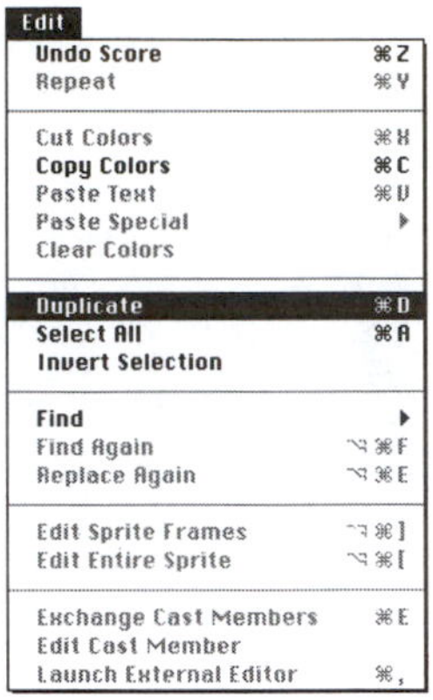

Figure 48. Choose **Duplicate** from the **Edit** menu.

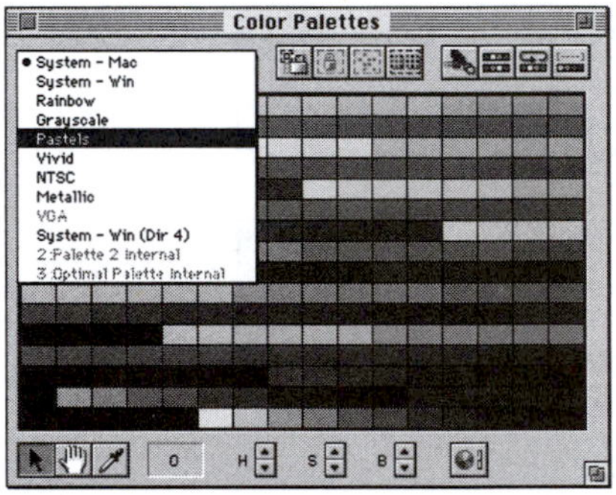

Figure 49. In the color palettes window, select a palette from the **Palette** pop-up menu.

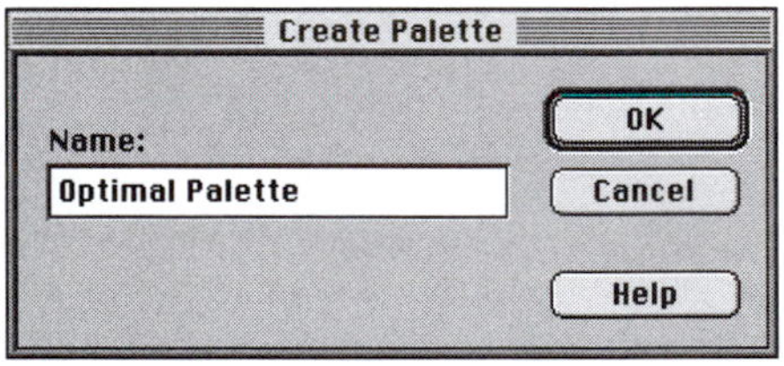

Figure 50. Type the name you wish to give this duplicate palette in the **Create Palette** dialog box.

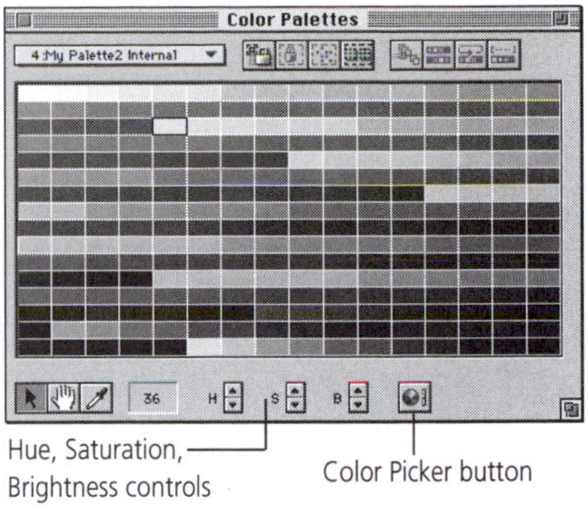

Figure 51. Click the color chip you want to edit.

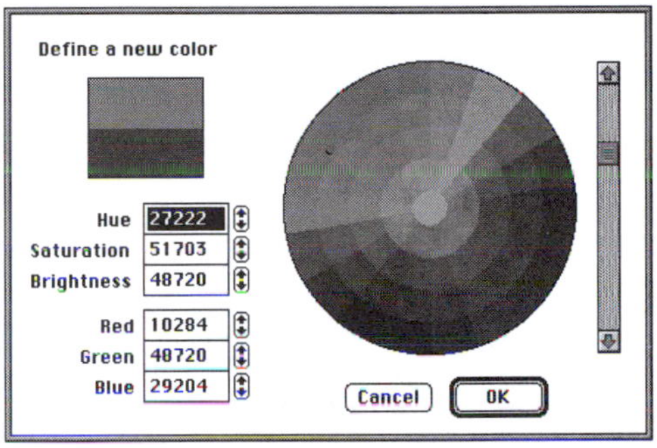

Figure 52. In the **Color Picker** dialog box, click inside the color wheel to select a color, or type values into the Hue, Saturation, Brightness, or Red, Green, Blue boxes for a precise selection.

In the **HSB** color model, **hue** refers to the basic color that is created by mixing two primary colors, such as red and green. **Saturation** refers to the amount of white that's mixed into any given color—a fully saturated color is vivid, containing no white, while a less saturated color appears lighter, more pastel. **Brightness** measures how much black is mixed into a color. Lowering the brightness value adds more black, making the color darker and muddier. A brightness value of 0 makes a color solid black.

The **RGB** model is simpler, defining colors by mixing varying degrees of red, green, and blue. Each color has over 65,000 possible degrees.

You can create one of the more than 16 million colors that your Macintosh can display with either of these color models.

4. Use the hue, saturation, and brightness controls (labeled H, S, and B, respectively) at the bottom of the color palettes window to adjust the color. Clicking the up and down arrows steps through new values for the color **(Figure 51)**.

or

4. For greater accuracy in your color selection, use the Color Picker. The Color Picker allows you to describe a new color by using precise numeric values or simply by clicking the color wheel. With a color chip selected in the color palettes window, click the Color Picker button **(Figure 51)**.

5. In the Color Picker dialog box, click a desired color on the color wheel **(Figure 52)**. Use the Color Picker's scroll bar to control brightness. To make a precise selection, type values in the Hue, Saturation, and Brightness boxes, or the Red, Green, and Blue boxes.

6. When you're satisfied with the selected color, click OK. Director places the new color in the palette.

✔ Tip

- When editing a color chip, you may want to work with a copy of it. This way you can easily return to the original color if you have to, since only its copy will have been changed. To copy a color, select it in the palette and choose Copy Colors from the Edit menu. Then select an unused color chip in the palette and choose Paste into Palette from the Edit menu.

To copy and paste colors in a palette:

You can use Director's Copy and Paste features to move colors from one palette to another or to rearrange colors within a single palette.

1. Choose Color Palettes from the Window menu.
2. In the color palettes window, use the pointer or Hand tool to select the color chips you wish to copy. Hold down the Command key to make multiple, discontinuous selections, or Shift-click to select a range between two color chips **(Figure 53)**.
3. Choose Copy Colors from the Edit menu **(Figure 54)**.
4. If you are copying the colors to a new palette, use the Palette pop-up menu in the color palettes window to choose the destination palette.
5. Click the new color chip position in which to paste the copied colors **(Figure 55)**.
6. Choose Paste into Palette from the Edit menu to place the copied colors **(Figure 56)**.

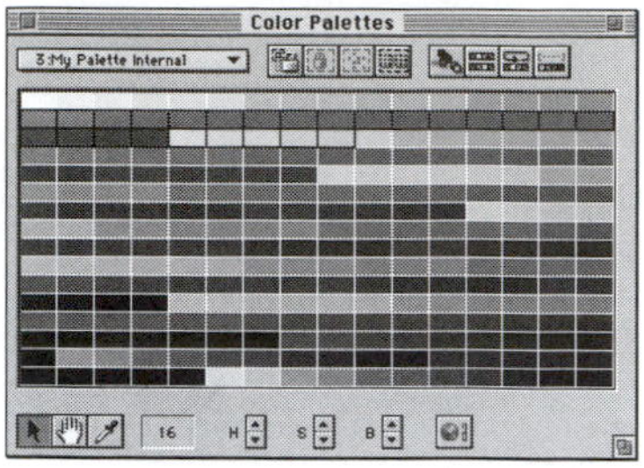

Figure 53. In the color palettes window, use the pointer or Hand tool to select the color chips you wish to copy.

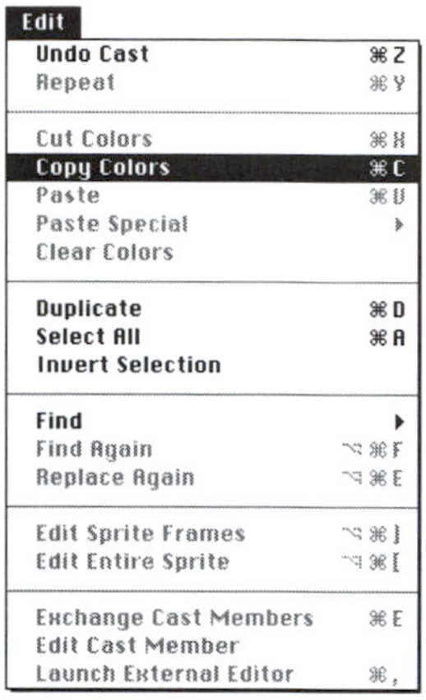

Figure 54. Choose **Copy Colors** from the **Edit** menu.

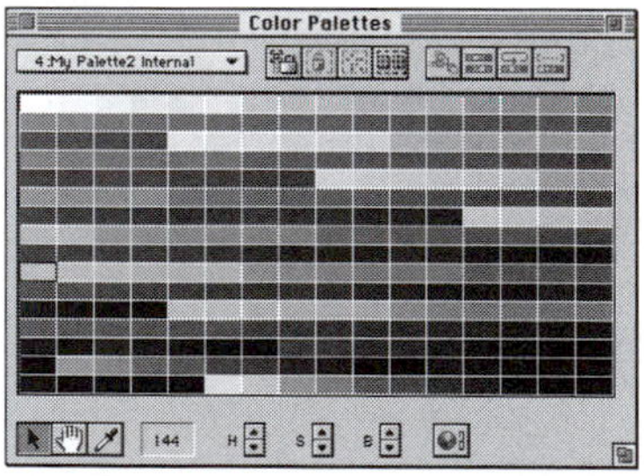

Figure 55. Click the new color chip position where the copied color(s) will be pasted.

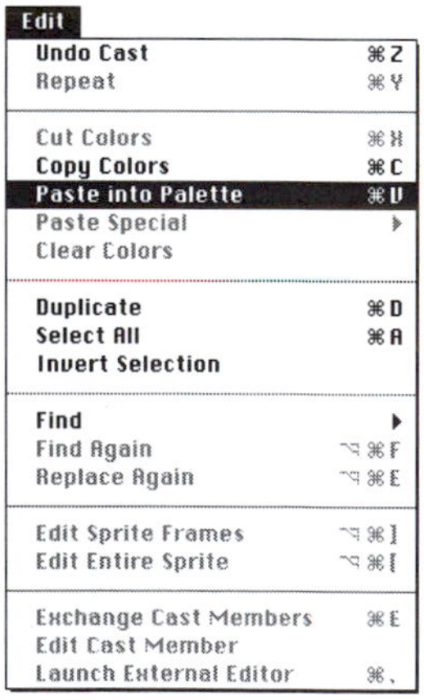

Figure 56. Choose **Paste Into Palette** from the **Edit** menu.

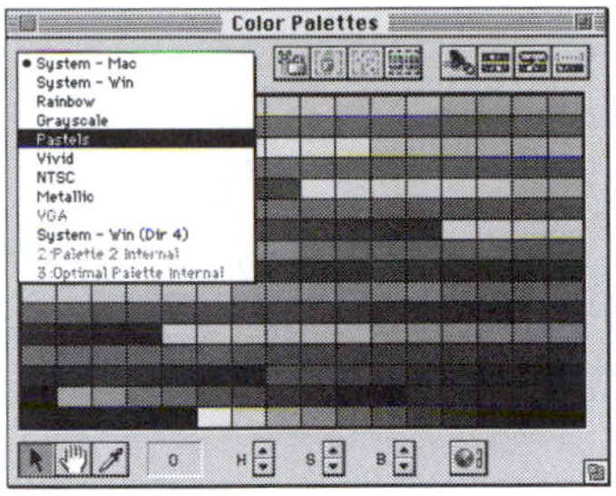

Figure 57. In the color palettes window, use the **Palette** pop-up menu to select the desired palette.

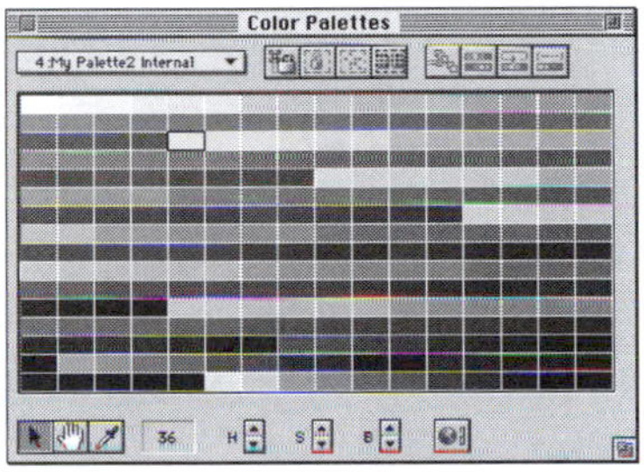

Figure 58. With the Pointer tool, select the first color in your blend.

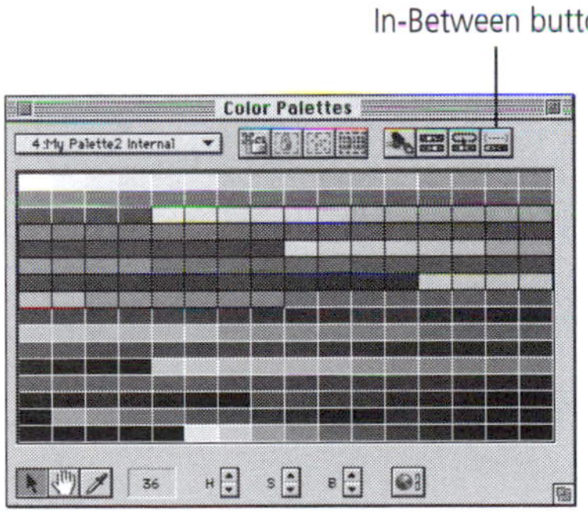

Figure 59. Hold down the Shift key and select your blend's destination color to highlight all colors in this range.

To blend colors within a palette:

You can create a range of colors that blends from one color to a second color. For example, if you were creating a sunset backdrop, you might need a blend of colors from red to yellow. Blending colors is especially useful for creating subtle gradient fills and smooth color cycling.

1. Choose Color Palettes from the Window menu.
2. In the color palettes window, use the Palette pop-up menu to select the desired palette **(Figure 57)**.
3. With the Pointer tool, select the first color in your blend **(Figure 58)**. For instance, if you want to blend the palette from red to yellow, you would first click the red color chip.
4. Hold down the Shift key and select your blend's destination color **(Figure 59)**. If blending from red to yellow, you'd select the yellow color chip.
5. Click the In-Between button in the color palettes window **(Figure 59)**. The palette will blend in a continuous tone from the first selected color to the second.

✓ Tip

- Sometimes you'll want to control the number of color chips over which your blend occurs—for instance, you may want a blend to occupy only fifteen or twenty color chips, rather than taking up a hundred valuable chips in an already limited palette. To do this, you may have to move the two blended colors closer together in their palette so that they are separated by the desired number of color chips. To move a color chip, use the palette window's Hand tool to drag it to a new position in the palette.
- You may want to work with a duplicate of your original palette, since creating a blend can radically change it.

To sample colors directly from artwork:

Director's Eyedropper tool makes it easy to identify specific colors that appear in a cast member on the stage. With the Eyedropper, you can click any color you see on the stage, and Director automatically highlights that color in the color palettes window. This is especially useful when you want to isolate certain colors, either for modification or for copying into another custom palette that you're building, such as an optimal palette.

1. In the score, select the cell that contains the cast member sprite whose colors you'd like to identify with the Eyedropper. The sprite should appear on the stage **(Figure 60)**.
2. Choose Color Palettes from the Window menu **(Figure 61)**.
3. In the color palettes window, select the Eyedropper tool **(Figure 62)**.
4. With the Eyedropper tool, click the sprite on the stage to sample its color at any point **(Figure 60)**. This color becomes highlighted in the color palettes window **(Figure 62)**. You can now modify the color or copy it to a new palette.

Figure 60. Use the Eyedropper tool to sample the colors of a cast member sprite on the stage.

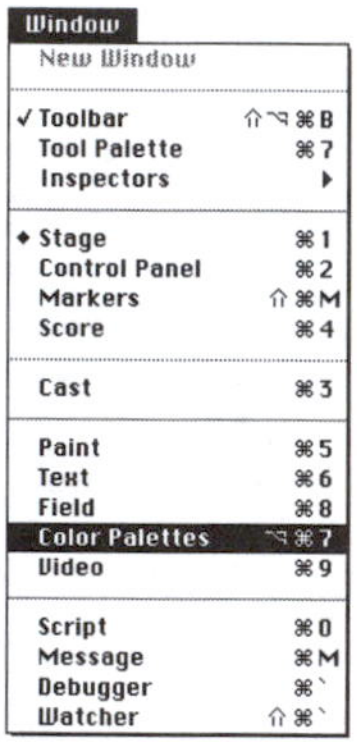

Figure 61. Choose **Color Palettes** from the **Window** menu.

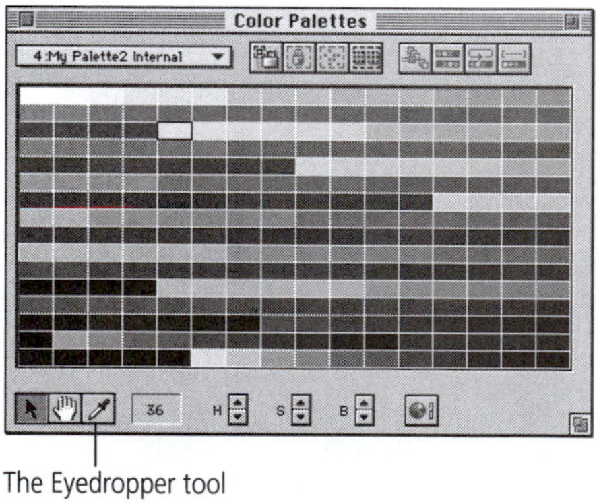

Figure 62. In the color palettes window, select the Eyedropper tool.

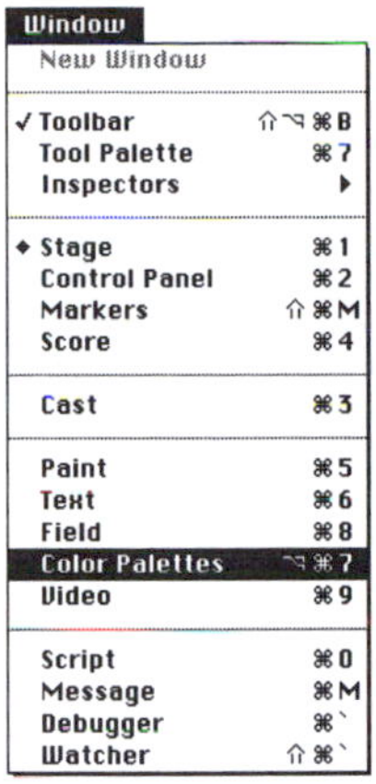

Figure 63. Choose **Color Palettes** from the **Window** menu.

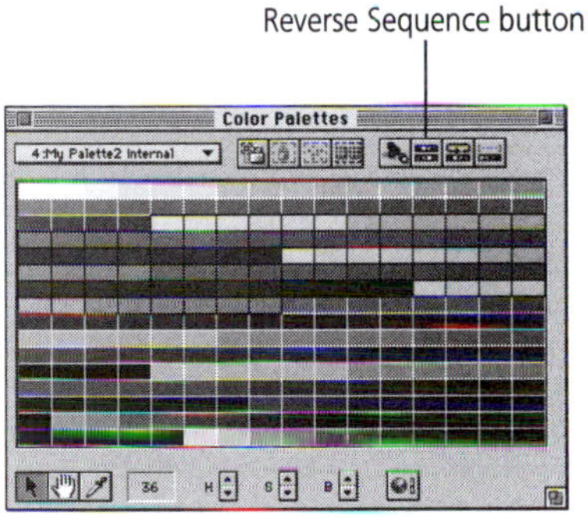

Figure 64. In the color palettes window, select a range of colors to be reversed.

To reverse the order of a palette's colors:

You can reverse the order of all the colors in a palette, or just within a select range. Reversing colors causes the chips positioned toward the end of the palette to be moved toward the palette's beginning. Doing so can change the coloring of cast members that are based on that particular palette.

1. Choose Color Palettes from the Window menu **(Figure 63)**.
2. In the color palettes window, select the first color chip in the range **(Figure 64)**.
3. Hold down the Shift key and select the last color chip in the range. All color chips between the two colors will be selected.
4. Click the Reverse Sequence button in the color palettes window. Director reverses the order of all the colors selected **(Figure 64)**.

✓ Tip

■ Reversing the color order in a palette will adversely affect the coloring of cast members using that palette. Consequently you may want to work with a duplicate of the palette, and then apply the new palette to cast members selectively.

To sort colors in a palette:

Director can sort the colors in a color palette by their hue, saturation, or brightness values. This feature is helpful when you would like to compare related colors in a palette.

1. Choose Color Palettes from the Window menu.
2. In the color palettes window, select a range of colors to sort **(Figure 65)**. Using the Pointer tool, select the first color chip in the range.
3. Hold down the Shift key and select the last color chip in the range. All color chips between the two selections will be selected.
4. Click the Sort button in the color palettes window **(Figure 65)**.
5. In the Sort Colors dialog box, click either Hue, Saturation, or Brightness to indicate which color attribute you'd like to sort by **(Figure 66)**. Sorting by hue is recommended, since it arranges similar colors together in the palette.

✔ **Tip**

- Like most other changes to a color palette, sorting the color order will affect the coloring of cast members using that palette. Consequently you may want to create a duplicate of the palette, sort your colors in the copied palette, and then apply the new palette to cast members selectively.

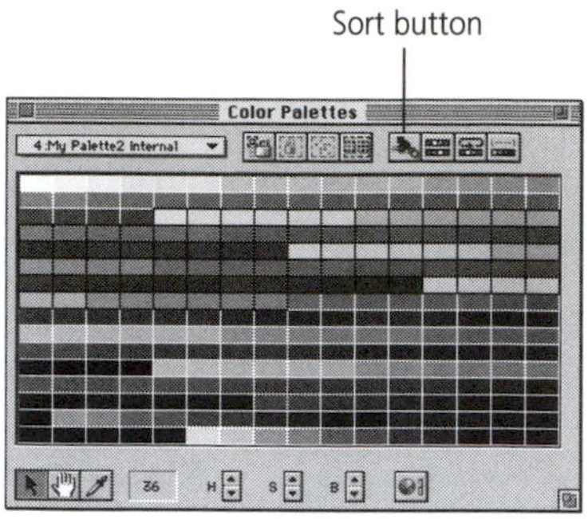

Figure 65. In the color palettes window, select a range of colors to sort.

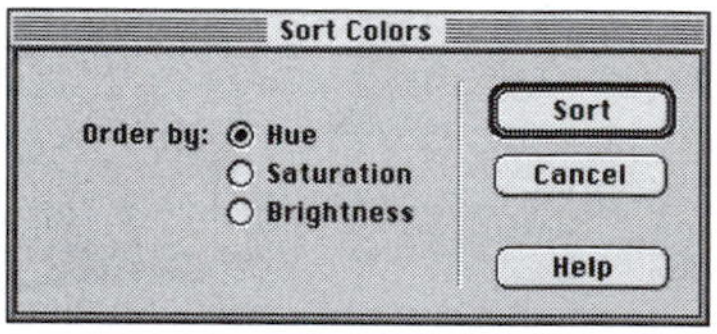

Figure 66. In the **Sort Colors** dialog box, click Hue, Saturation, or Brightness to indicate which color attribute to sort by.

COLOR CYCLING

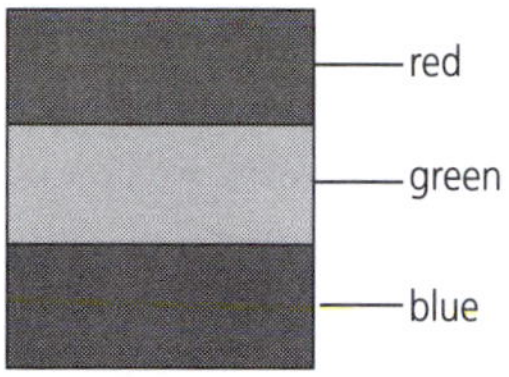

Figure 67. Color cycling, initial colors.

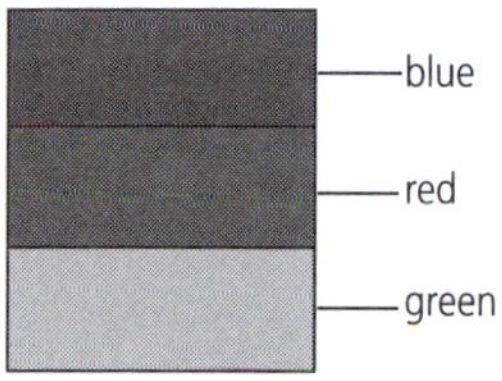

Figure 68. Color cycling, first step.

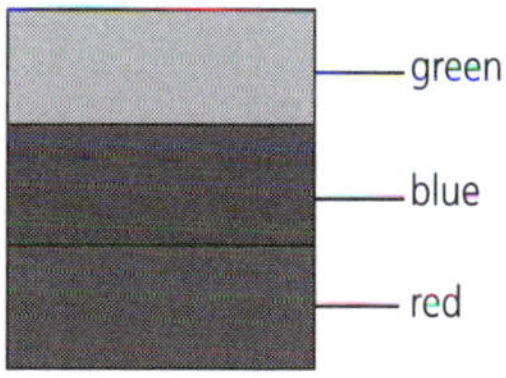

Figure 69. Color cycling, last step.

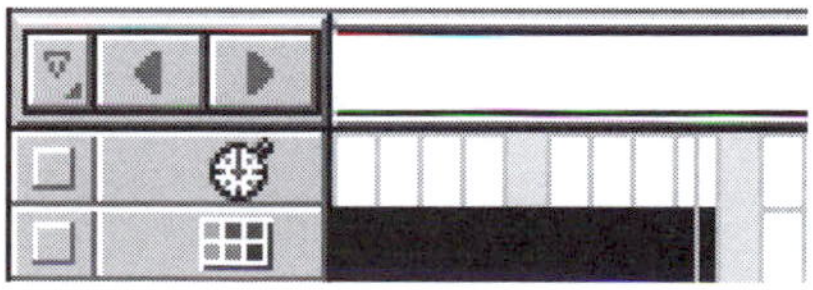

Figure 70. In the score's palette channel, select the frame or series of frames that contain the sprite(s) you wish to color cycle.

The technique known as **color cycling** achieves the illusion of animation by rotating a selected range of colors in a palette over time. For instance, let's take a cast member that is painted red on top, green in the middle, and blue at its base **(Figure 67)**. Let's assume these three colors are grouped sequentially in a color palette, and that they have been selected for color cycling. Color cycling rotates these colors so that in the first step of the cycle, the red color will shift to the cast member's middle, the green to its base, and the blue to its top. In the next step of the cycle, the red will shift to the cast member's base, the green to its top, and blue to the middle **(Figures 68–69)**.

Cycling colors is the process used to animate TV weather maps, where a storm front appears to pulsate through a range of dark and light shades of blue. It's also handy for effects such as fire and explosions, where color pulses through a series of reds, yellows, and oranges.

Color cycling in Director is applied to a selected range of colors over a series of frames. Within those frames, any cast members painted in the selected colors will be cycled.

To cycle colors in a palette:

1. Place the cast members that you wish to color cycle in the desired animation channels and frames of Director's score.
2. In the score's palette channel, select the frame or series of frames that contain the sprite(s) you wish to color cycle **(Figure 70)**. You can select a single frame if you would like to color cycle a stationary sprite (in other words, one that won't move while being cycled). You can cycle throughout an animation by selecting a range of sprites.

3. Choose Frame from the Modify menu and select Palette from the pop-up menu **(Figure 71)**.
4. In the Frame Properties dialog box, click the Color Cycling radio button to select it **(Figure 72)**.
5. Use the Palette pop-up menu to select the palette you wish to apply and cycle in the frames selected in the score.
6. In the Frame Properties dialog box, select a range of colors in its palette that you wish to cycle. You can Shift-click two color chips to select the range of colors between them **(Figure 72)**.
7. Type the number of cycles in the Cycles box if you wish to make complete color cycles per frame. A cycle is achieved each time Director rotates through all the colors selected in step 6.
8. Click the Loop radio button if you want the color cycle to start from the beginning when it reaches the end.

or

8. Click the Auto Reverse radio button if you wish the color cycling to reverse itself at the end of a cycle—for instance, to cycle colors from red to blue in the first cycle, and then from blue to red in the second.
9. Click OK to apply your color cycling to the selected frames in the score.

Note: Color cycling can occur only over a continuous range of colors in a palette. If you wish to cycle only through several colors that are scattered throughout the palette, you will have to group them first in the palette. *(See page 158 on "To copy and paste colors in a palette")*

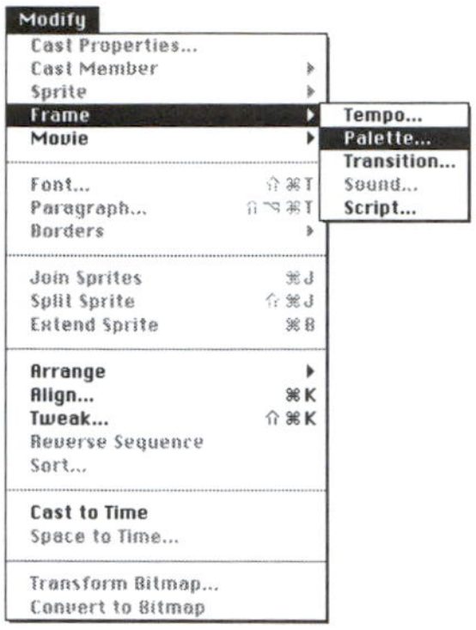

Figure 71. Choose **Frame** from the **Modify** menu and select **Palette** from the pop-up menu.

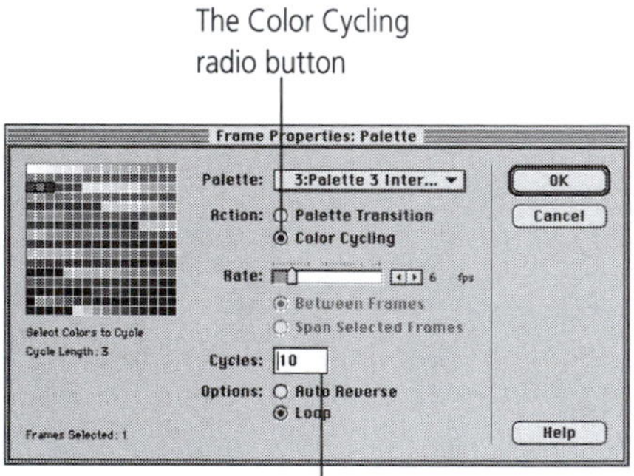

Figure 72. The **Frame Properties** dialog box.

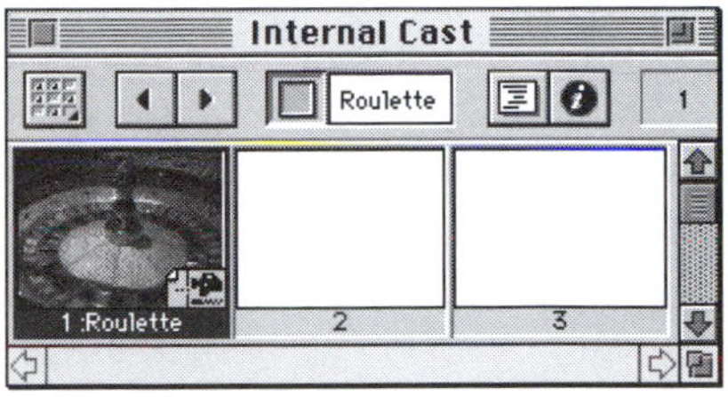

Figure 1. QuickTime movies become digital video cast members when imported.

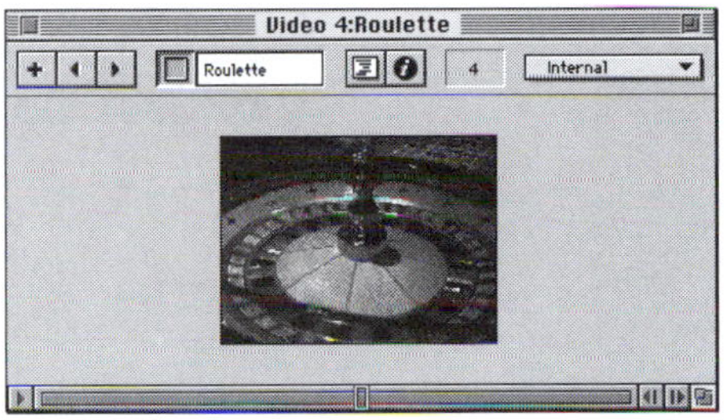

Figure 2. The video window.

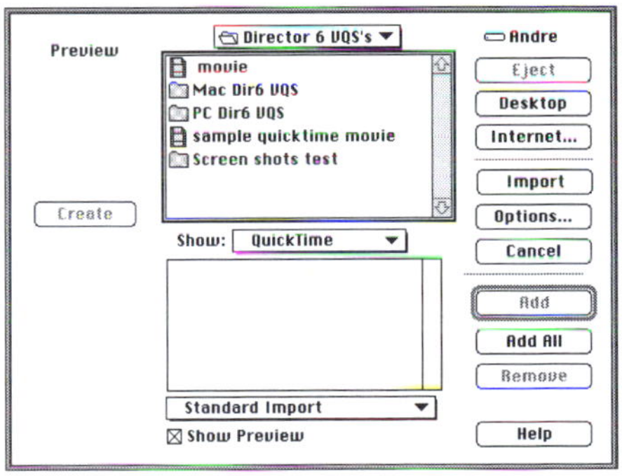

Figure 3. Choose **QuickTime** from the **Show** pop-up menu in the **Import** dialog box.

Director for Macintosh allows you to import QuickTime movies, which are referred to as digital video throughout the Director application. Once imported, a QuickTime movie becomes a digital video cast member in a cast window **(Figure 1)**. You incorporate a digital video cast member into your Director movie as you would any other graphical cast member, by placing it on the stage through an appropriate range of frames.

Director provides very basic editing capability for digital video inside the video window **(Figure 2)**. You are limited to rearranging frames by cutting, copying, and pasting. For more extensive editing features, you will need to use a video editing application.

To import a digital video:

1. Choose Import from the File menu.
2. Choose QuickTime from the Show pop-up menu **(Figure 3)**, and add the desired files to be imported.
3. Click Import.

Note: Digital videos are always imported linked to their original files. This means that if you edit a digital video in Director, you will permanently change the original file. Also, any changes you make to a digital video file outside Director are automatically reflected in Director. When you transfer your Director movie or projector to another system, all digital video files must be included.

To place a digital video into a Director movie:

A digital video cast member is placed into your movie the same way in which you incorporate any other graphical cast member, by dragging it from a cast window onto the stage, or directly into the cells of the score.

1. Open the cast window which contains your digital video cast member **(Figure 4)**.
2. Choose Score from the Window menu **(Figure 5)**.
3. Drag your digital video cast member from its cast window into a sprite channel in the score and into the appropriate frame where the video should begin playing.
4. Position the sprite on the stage as it should appear in your movie by dragging it to the desired location.

Note: Director starts to play your video when the playback head reaches the frame in which it is contained. But in order for the video to play to completion, it must be extended over enough frames in the score to match its playing length, otherwise it will end without finishing, much like a sound. For example, if you know the duration of your video to be 5 seconds, and your movie frame rate is 30 FPS (frames-per-second), then your digital video should occupy approximately 150 frames. The best way to determine the appropriate number of frames is to first extend the video over more frames than necessary using the Extend command *(see page 50)*. Second, play your movie back with the score window open, and note in which frame your video finishes playing.

Note: You can set your video to loop by checking the Loop option in its Cast Member Properties box **(Figure 6)**.

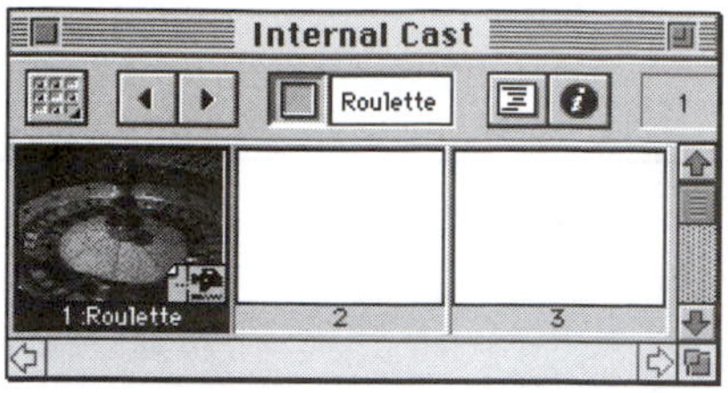

Figure 4. Open the cast window which contains your digital video.

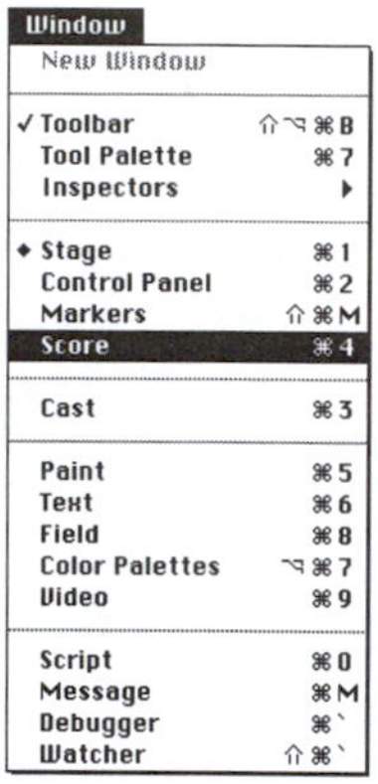

Figure 5. Choose **Score** from the **Window** menu.

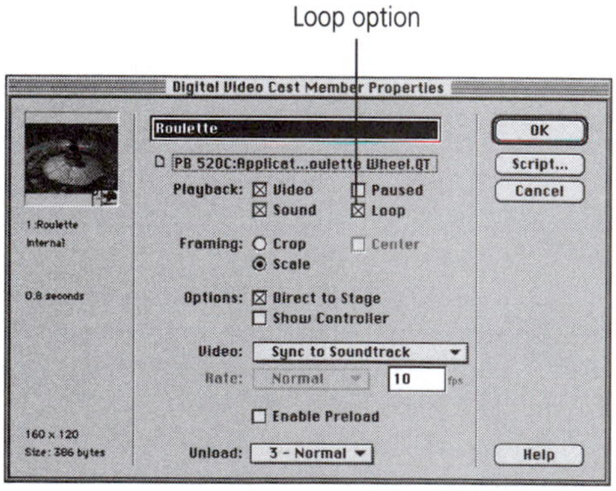

Figure 6. Check the **Loop** option in the **Digital Video Cast Member Properties** dialog box.

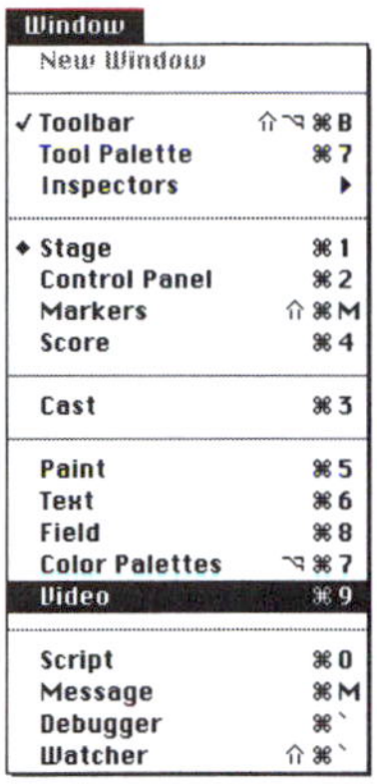

Figure 7. Choose **Video** from the **Window** menu.

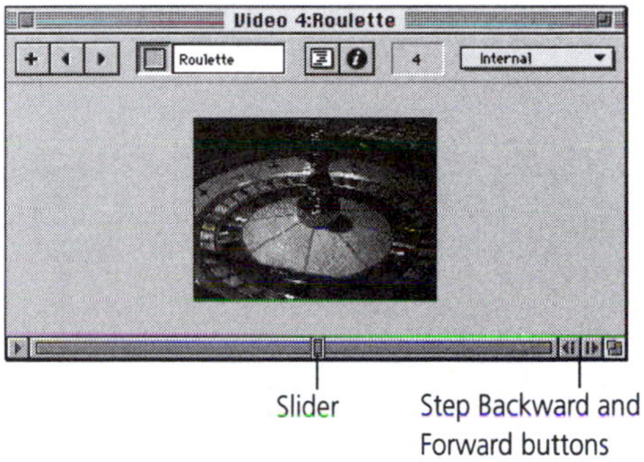

Figure 8. In the video window, use the slider or the **Step Backward** and **Forward** buttons to display the first frame in the range of frames you wish to copy or cut.

Figure 9. Hold the Shift key and drag the slider to select a range of frames in the video window.

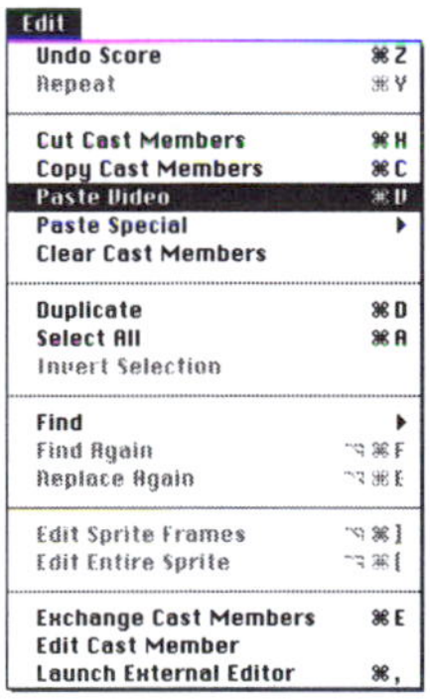

Figure 10. Choose **Paste Video** from the **Edit** menu.

If the Loop option is checked, your video will repeat from the beginning when it reaches its end, assuming that the video occupies enough frames in the score.

✔ **Tip**

■ You can ensure that a video finishes playing by setting a tempo in the tempo channel using the Wait for Cue Point option. *(See page 191 in the Movie Tempo Chapter)*

To cut, copy, or clear video frames:

1. Choose Video from the Window menu **(Figure 7)**.
2. Go to the first frame in the range of frames you wish to copy or cut by using the Step backward and forward buttons, or by dragging the slider bar in the video window **(Figure 8)**.
3. If you want to select a range of frames, hold down the Shift key and drag the slider until the last frame in your range is displayed. The portion of the slider which corresponds to your range turns black **(Figure 9)**.
4. Choose either Cut Video, Copy Video, or Clear Video from the Edit menu.

To paste a frame or frames into a digital video:

1. Use the Previous and Next cast member buttons in the video window to display the digital video cast member into which you wish to paste video frames. If you are pasting into a new digital video, Director prompts you to enter a file name for this new cast member when you paste.
2. Using the slider, display the frame in the video window that precedes the frame in which you want your frame or range of frames to be pasted. Your frame(s) will be inserted at this point.
3. Choose Paste Video from the Edit menu **(Figure 10)**.

To crop a digital video:

You can crop a video so that only a portion of its rectangular area is visible during play. Doing so hides a section of your video, but does not permanently delete it.

1. In the cast window, select the digital video cast member that you wish to crop **(Figure 11)**.
2. Click the Cast Member Properties button in the cast window **(Figure 11)**.
3. Check the Crop option in the Digital Video Cast Member Properties dialog box **(Figure 12)**. Check the Center option if you want your cropped video centered in its new rectangular area.
4. Click OK.
5. Open the score window and select the sprite which contains the video.
6. On the stage, drag the handles that surround your video to crop it.

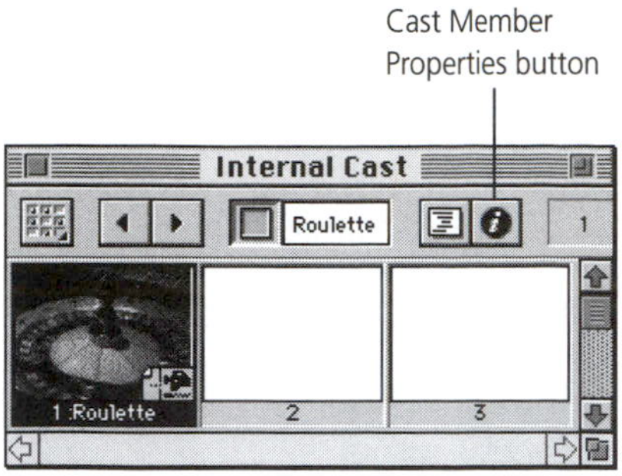

Figure 11. Select the digital video cast member you wish to crop in the cast window and click the **Cast Member Properties** button.

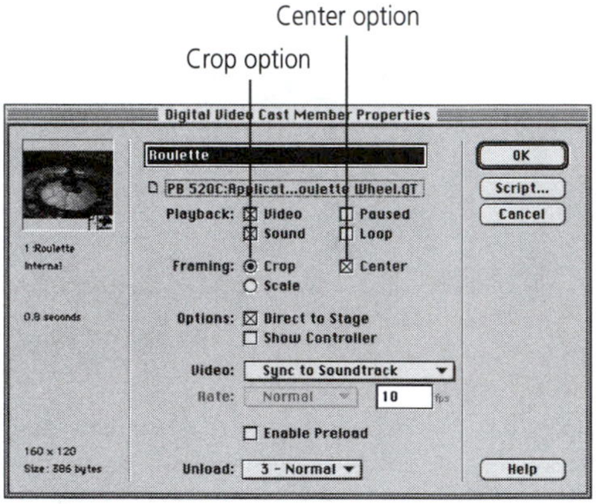

Figure 12. Check the **Crop** option in the **Digital Video Cast Member Properties** dialog box.

To scale a digital video:

You can scale a video so that it takes on the dimensions of any rectangular area.

1. Select the video in the cast.
2. Click the Cast Member Properties button in the cast window.
3. Check the Scale option in the Digital Video Cast Member Properties dialog box **(Figure 13)**.
4. Click OK.
5. Open the score window and select the sprite which contains the video.
6. On the stage, drag the handles that surround your video to scale it.

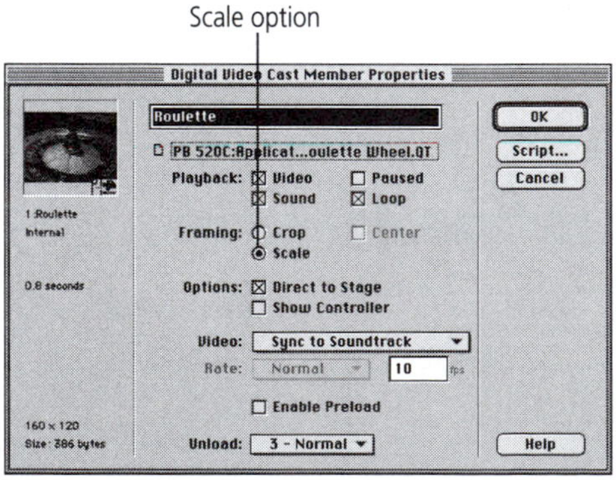

Figure 13. Check the **Scale** option in the **Digital Video Cast Member Properties** dialog box.

CREATING TEXT IN DIRECTOR 11

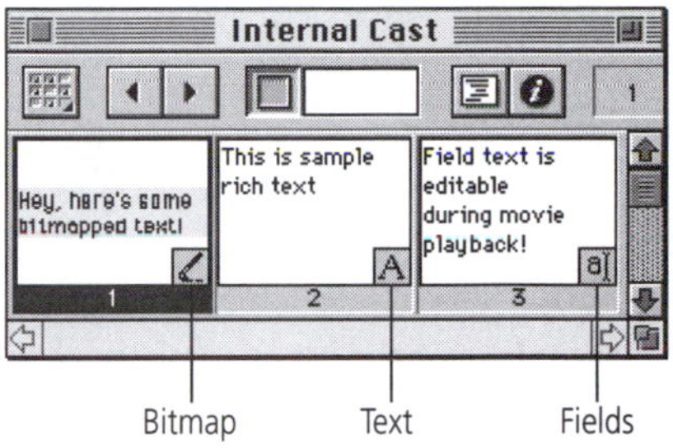

Figure 1. Director supports three different types of text: bitmapped, rich text (or simply text cast members), and fields.

Director supports three different types of text that you can incorporate in your movies. These are bitmapped text, rich text, and fields **(Figure 1)**. Each type has its advantages. A summary of each is given below.

Bitmapped text is created in Director's paint window. You can apply all the effects and tools in the paint window to bitmapped text, as you would to any other painted image. Bitmapped text animates the fastest. The down side is that bitmapped text cannot be edited once it is created and placed into a cast window (words cannot be rearranged, new fonts can't be applied, and so on).

Rich text (simply referred to as "text" throughout Director) is created using Director's text window, or with the Text tool found in the Tool Palette. Of the three text types, rich text has the most extensive formatting controls. Unlike bitmapped text, rich text can be edited after it has been created. The text window provides the features of an elementary word processor, offering definable tabs, margins, paragraph formatting, line spacing, and other controls. Rich text can also be edited directly on the stage.

A **Field** cast member is created with the Field tool in the Tool Palette, or in the field window. The distinguishing feature of a field cast member is that its text can be edited while a movie is playing. This is useful in an interactive movie, where users type in data. Field cast members should only be used when absolutely necessary since they animate the slowest, and require that the same fonts be installed on any system that will be running your movie.

BITMAPPED TEXT

Bitmapped text is created in Director's paint window. The most notable feature of bitmapped text is that it cannot be edited once it's created. If you decide you want to change a word, a typeface, the text's spacing, and so on, you must erase the original text and start over again. On the other hand, like any other bitmap image, bitmapped text can be selected and then modified with a variety of Director's paint window effects—for instance, it can be rotated, warped, flipped, and so on *(see page 125 in the Paint window chapter)*. It can also be easily incorporated into other painted artwork you might have. The print quality of bitmapped text is poor. Fields offer the best print quality *(see page 177)*. Bitmapped text requires more storage space than rich text or fields.

When you create text in the paint window, that text automatically becomes a bitmap cast member, where it can be dragged to the stage and assigned to the score like any other cast member.

With bitmapped text, it is not required to have the same fonts installed on those systems where you play the movie.

To create bitmapped text:

1. Choose Paint from the Window menu to open Director's paint window **(Figure 2)**.
2. Click the Text tool icon in the paint tool palette to select it **(Figure 3)**.
3. Click the mouse anywhere in the paint window to select the location where your text will be placed. A text box containing a blinking insertion point appears at this spot.
4. Choose Font from the Modify menu to open the Font dialog box, where you can select the desired font, size, and style **(Figures 4–5)**.

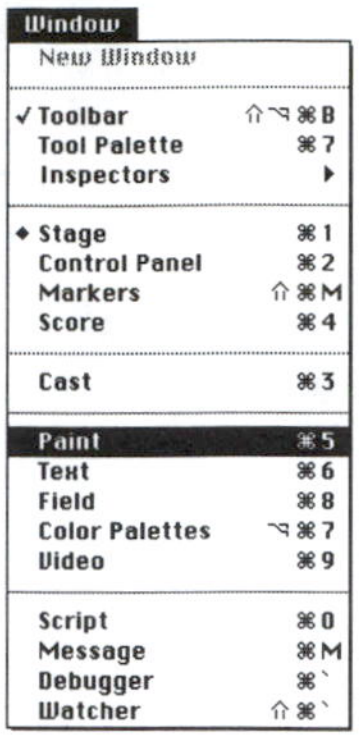

Figure 2. Choose **Paint** from the **Window** menu.

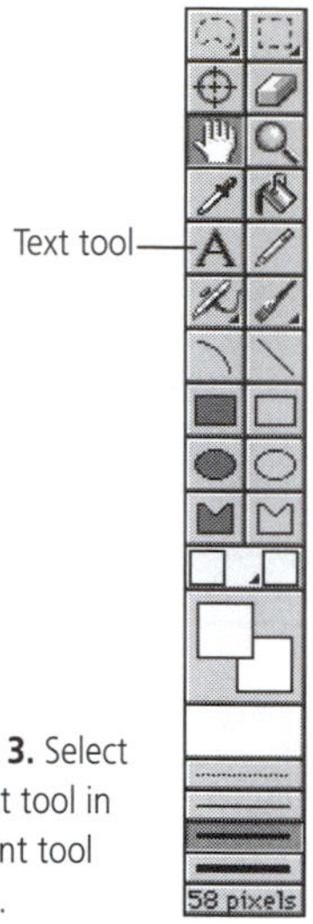

Figure 3. Select the Text tool in the paint tool palette.

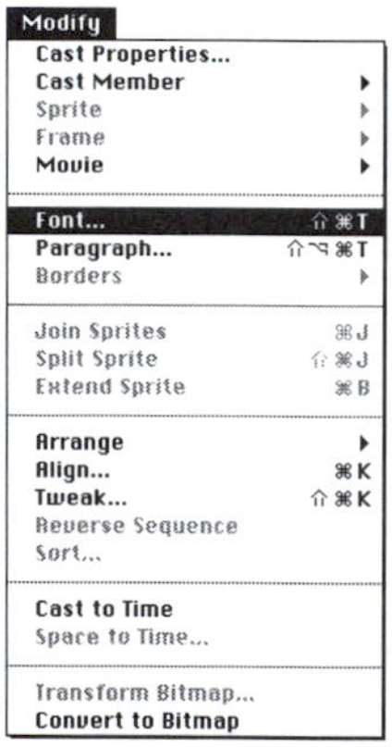

Figure 4. Choose **Font** from the **Modify** menu.

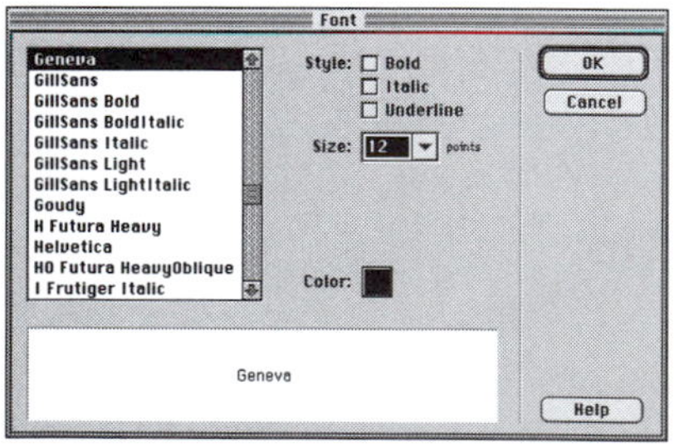

Figure 5. Set the desired font, size, and style in the **Font** dialog box.

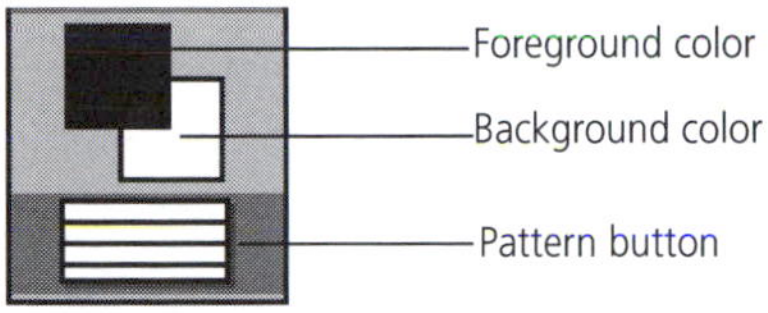

Figure 6. Select the text colors by clicking the **Foreground** and **Background** color chips. Apply a pattern to the text by clicking the **Pattern** button.

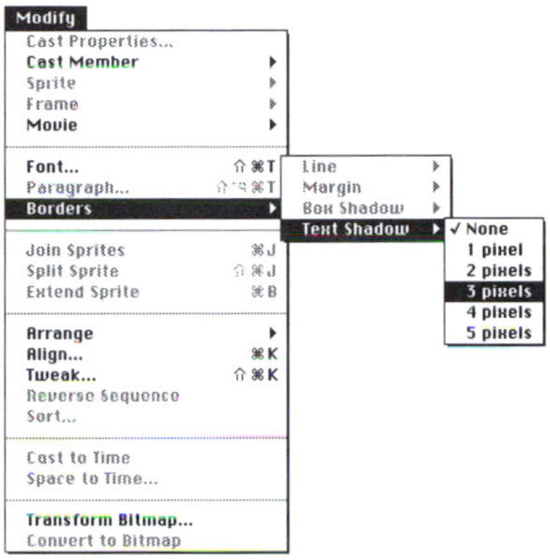

Figure 7. Add a drop shadow to the text by selecting **Borders** from the **Modify** menu, and selecting **Text Shadow** from the pop-up menu.

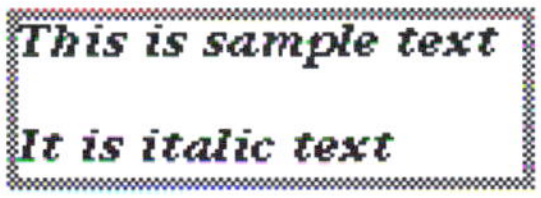

Figure 8. A text box with sample text.

Figure 9. The **Warp** effect from the **Effects** toolbar was used to alter this bitmapped text.

5. Click the Foreground and Background color chips in the paint tool palette to color the text. The Foreground chip sets the color of the text itself, while the Background chip sets the color of the box that surrounds the text. You can also apply a pattern to the text by clicking the Pattern button in the tool palette **(Figure 6)**.
6. To add a drop shadow to the text, choose Borders from the Modify menu, and select Text Shadow from the pop-up menu. In the Text Shadow submenu, choose the number of pixels by which the shadow should offset the text **(Figure 7)**.
7. Type in your text **(Figure 8)**. Press Return to start a new line.
8. Click outside of the text box to finalize your text bitmap. If you wish to move the text to a new location, drag the text box before finalizing the entry.

✔ Tips

- Remember that bitmapped text can be altered with the variety of effects in the paint window's Effects toolbar. Director's Warp effect was used to make the text sample in **Figure 9** appear to have dimension.
- From the cast window, you can double-click a bitmapped text cast member and Director automatically opens the image in its paint window.

RICH TEXT

All the limitations of bitmapped text—the fact that once you place the text, you can no longer edit it, and that such text prints poorly to laser printers—are overcome by rich text (simply referred to as "text" throughout Director). The benefit of rich text is that it can easily be edited, resized, and otherwise altered after it becomes a cast member in your movie, making it more flexible than the bitmapped text created in the paint window. On the downside, this variety of text can't be rotated or otherwise distorted for special effect, as bitmapped text can. Also, Director animates rich text more slowly than bitmapped text.

There are two ways to create rich text cast members in Director. The first is to create and position the text directly on the stage, using the Text tool **(Figure 10)** in the Tool Palette. The second approach is to type your text into Director's text window **(Figure 11)**, and then drag the corresponding text cast member to the stage at a later time. The first approach is the quickest, most straightforward method of incorporating rich text into a movie. The second is best if you need more extensive formatting controls, or would like to create a number of text cast members at one time, and place them throughout your movie later on.

If you create a projector, rich text is converted into bitmaps, so you don't need to have the same fonts installed on those systems where you play the movie.

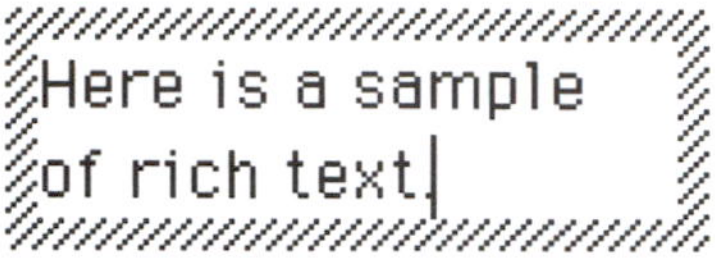

Figure 10. The Text tool in the Tool Palette is used to create and position a rich text cast member directly on the stage.

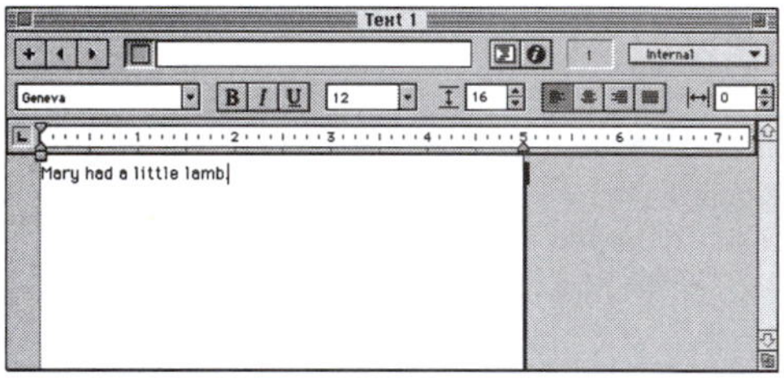

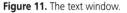

Figure 11. The text window.

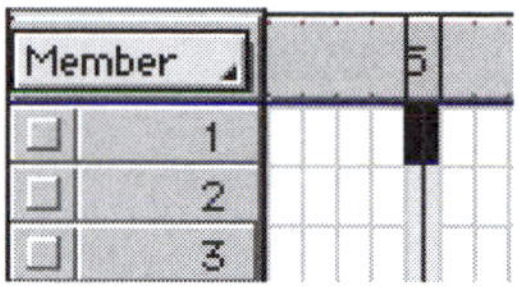

Figure 12. Select a cell in the desired sprite channel where you wish to place a rich text cast member.

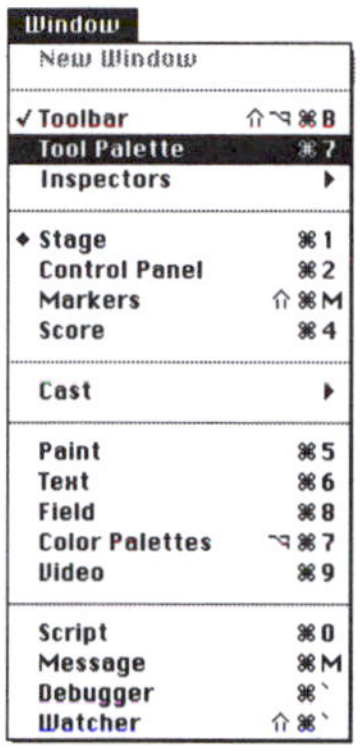

Figure 13. Choose **Tool Palette** from the **Window** menu.

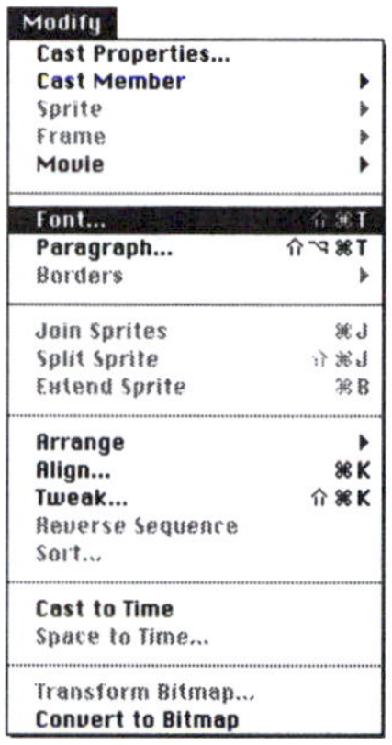

Figure 14. Choose **Font** from the **Modify** menu.

Figure 15. Click the Text tool in the Tool Palette.

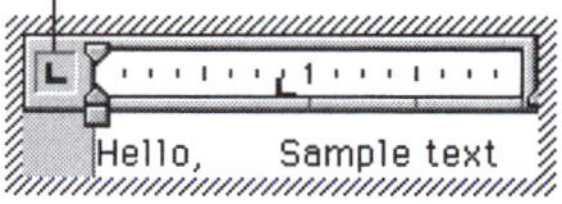

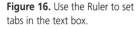

Figure 16. Use the Ruler to set tabs in the text box.

To create rich text directly on the stage:

1. In Director's score window, select the cell in the desired sprite channel where you wish to place a rich text cast member **(Figure 12)**.
2. Choose Tool Palette from the Window **(Figure 13)**.
3. In the Tool Palette, click the Text tool **(Figure 15)**.
4. Position the crosshair pointer on the stage, and click the mouse to place a text box there.
5. You can set the text's font, size, and style by choosing Font from the Modify menu **(Figure 14)**, and making the appropriate selections in the Font dialog box.
6. In the Tool Palette, click the Foreground and Background color chips to assign color to your text. The Foreground color applies to the text itself, while the Background color applies to the text box **(Figure 15)**.
7. Type your text into the text box. Text wraps around to a new line automatically as you type.
8. When you've finished typing, click outside the text box to make it final. The text is placed on the stage and in the active cast window.

✓ Tips

- After step 4 above, choose Rulers from the View menu to display a ruler over the text box, which allows you to set tabs **(Figure 16)**. Click the tab well repeatedly to select the type of tab you wish to set. Click on the ruler to set a tab. To remove a tab, drag it off the ruler.
- You can convert rich text and field cast members into bitmap cast members (but not the other way around). Select the text or field cast member in a cast window and choose Convert to Bitmap from the Modify menu.

To create rich text with the text window:

1. Choose Text from Director's Window menu **(Figure 17)**.
2. Use the controls in the text window to set the font, style, size, alignment, spacing, and kerning settings for your text **(Figure 18)**,
3. To set a tab, first click the tab well repeatedly to select the type of tab you wish to set **(Figure 19)**. Click on the ruler to set a new tab. To remove a tab, drag it off the ruler.
4. To set margins, drag the indent markers (left, first-line, or right indents) on the ruler **(Figure 19)**.
5. Type your text in the text window. The text will be formatted automatically in the style that you specified. Text wraps around to a new line as you type. You can also press Return to begin a new line.

   The text that you type will automatically be entered as a cast member in Director's cast window, where you can drag it to the stage and assign it to the score.
6. When you've finished typing, you can either close the text window, or, if you would like to create more text cast members, click the New cast member button at the top of the text window **(Figure 18)**. Director will clear the window, and create another cast member position in the cast window to accommodate the new text.

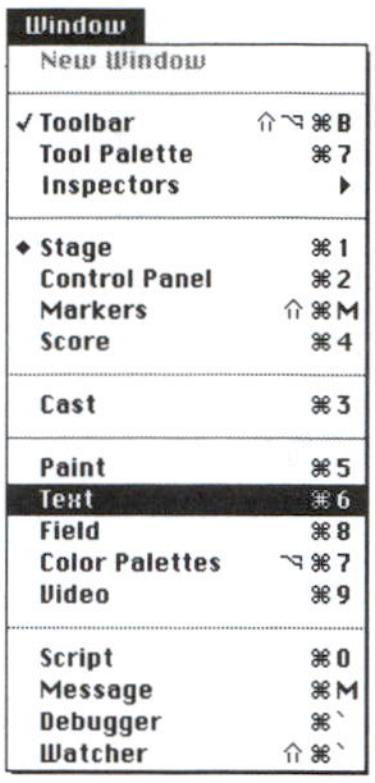

Figure 17. Choose **Text** from the **Window** menu.

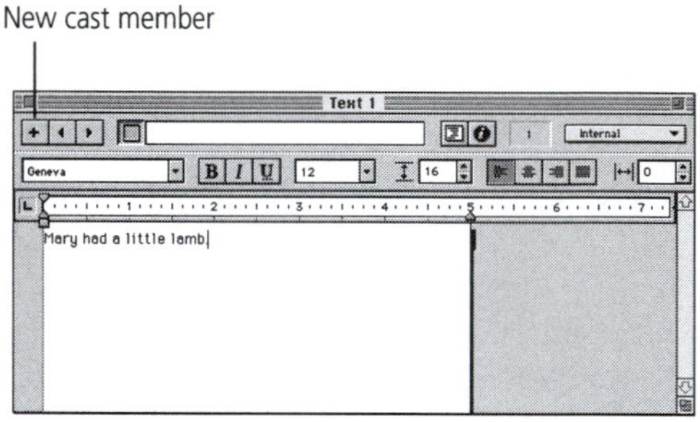

Figure 18. Use the controls in the text window to set the font, style, size, alignment, spacing, and kerning settings for your text.

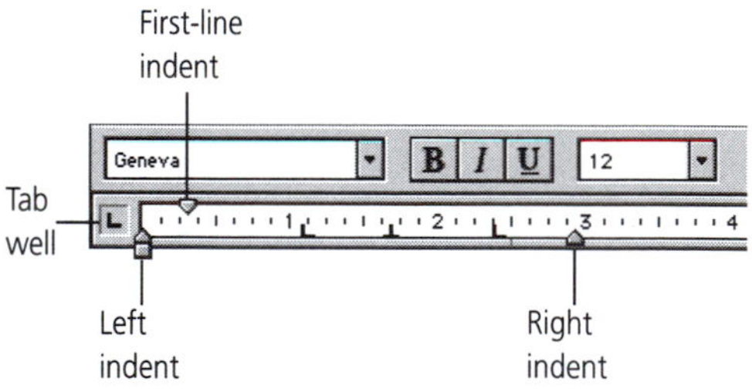

Figure 19. Set tabs and margins in the text window's ruler.

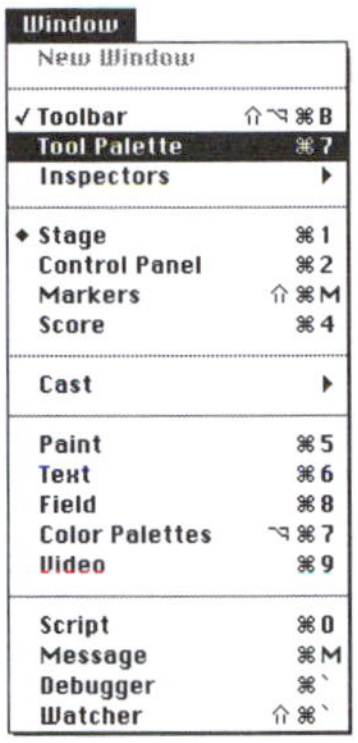

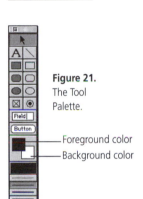

Figure 20. Choose **Tool Palette** from the **Window** menu.

Figure 21. The Tool Palette.

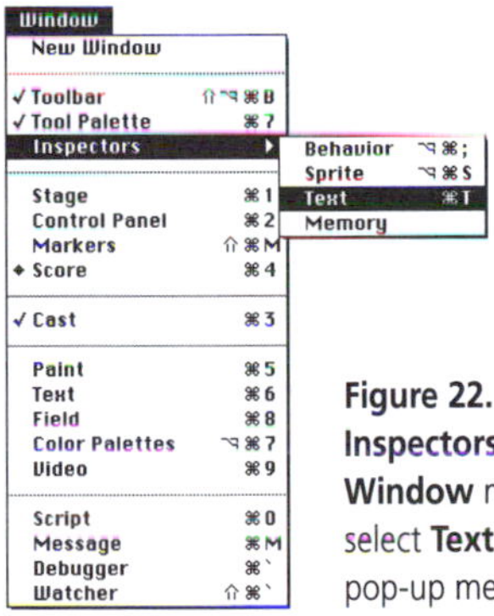

Figure 22. Choose **Inspectors** from the **Window** menu and select **Text** from the pop-up menu.

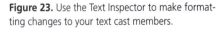

Figure 23. Use the Text Inspector to make formatting changes to your text cast members.

optional

7. If you would like to add color to your text or the box surrounding it, choose Tool Palette from the Window menu **(Figure 20)**.

8. To change the color of text, first select the section of text you wish to color by dragging across it in the text window. Then click the Foreground color chip in the Tool Palette **(Figure 21)** and select a color.

9. To change the color of the text box, click the Background color chip in the Tool Palette and select a color from the pop-up menu.

To edit text in the text window:

Once you place a text cast member into the score, you can edit the text directly from the stage by double-clicking its sprite and dragging across the portion of text you wish to edit. You can also edit text by opening a cast window, selecting a text cast member, and choosing Text from the Window menu to open the text window for the selected cast member.

Using the Text Inspector

The Text Inspector is simply another tool for changing the formatting of your text. It has most of the controls found in the text window. The convenience of the Text Inspector is that you can change the formatting of text directly on the stage without having to open the text cast member in the text window.

1. Choose Inspectors from the Window menu, and select Text from the pop-up menu **(Figure 22)**.

2. Select the sprite in the score that contains the text cast member you wish to change on the stage.

3. Make the desired formatting adjustments in the Text Inspector window **(Figure 23)**.

Anti-alias text feature

Anti-aliasing reduces the jagged edges and curves of text. It is most useful for larger point sizes where rough edges can be noticeable. The anti-alias feature is available only for rich text, and is on by default.

To change the anti-alias setting for text:

1. In the cast window, select the text cast member whose anti-aliasing setting you wish to change.
2. Choose Cast Member from the Modify menu and select Properties from the pop-up menu **(Figure 24)**.
3. In the Text Cast Member Properties dialog box, click on the appropriate anti-alias option **(Figure 25)**.

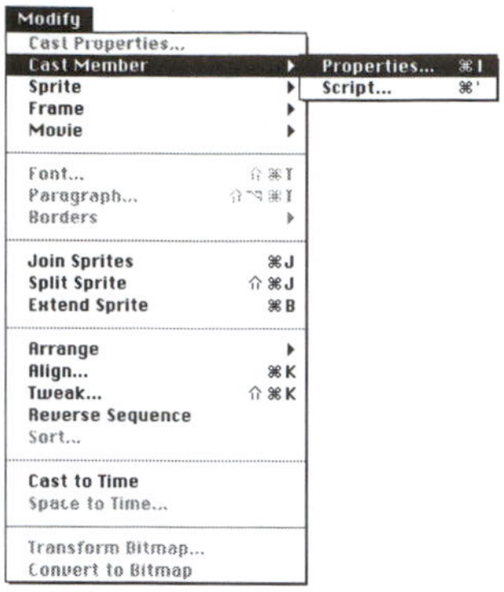

Figure 24. Choose **Cast Member** from the **Modify** menu and select **Properties** from the pop-up menu.

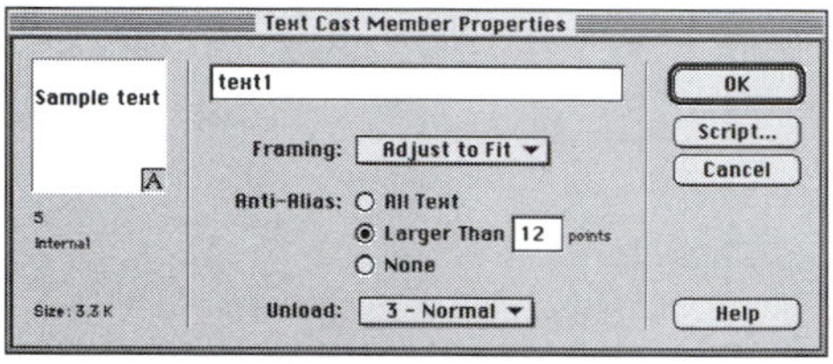

Figure 25. Click on the appropriate anti-alias option in the **Text Cast Member Properties** dialog box.

To import text:

Director allows you to import text files saved in the rich text format (RTF).

1. Choose Import from the File menu **(Figure 26)**.
2. In the Import dialog box, choose text as the file type to import.
3. Add the text file and click Import. The text file is imported as a single cast member unless the file contains page or column breaks. Each time Director encounters a page or column break, it creates a new cast member for the text.

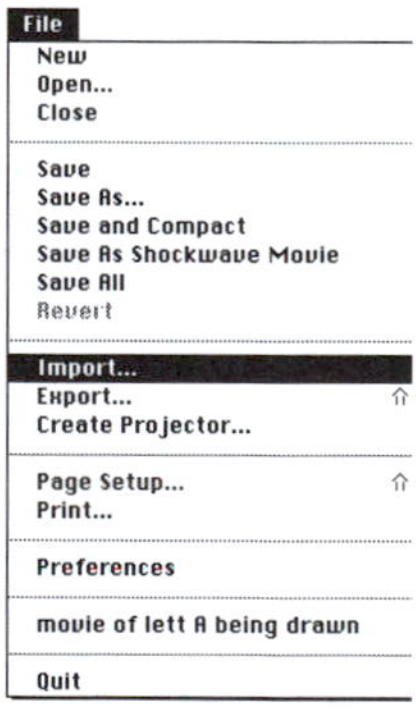

Figure 26. Choose **Import** from the **File** menu.

✔ Tip

- You can apply three of Director's score ink effects to rich text, namely Copy, Background Transparent, and Blend. In the score window, select the cell or range of cells that contains the desired text sprites, and then click the Ink pop-up menu to make an ink selection **(Figure 27)**.

Figure 27. Use the **Ink** pop-up menu in the score to apply one of three ink effects to your text sprites.

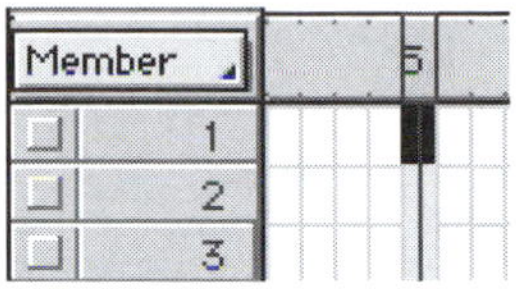

Figure 28. Select a cell in the desired sprite channel where you wish to place your field cast member.

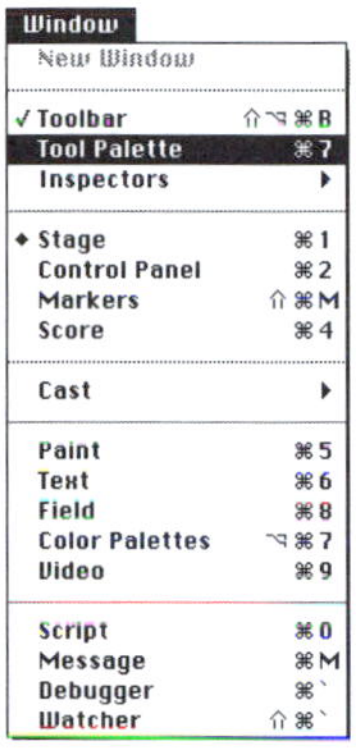

Figure 29. Choose **Tool Palette** from the **Window** menu.

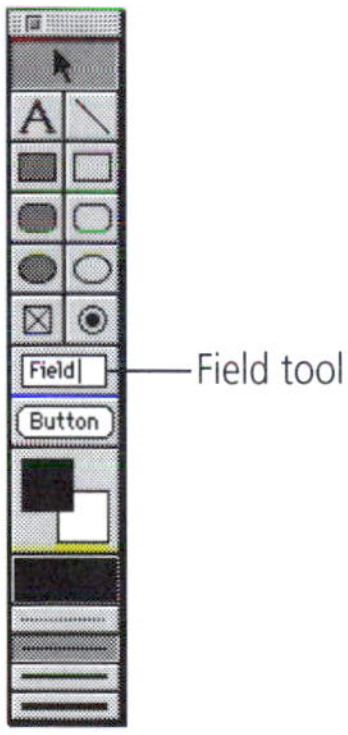

Figure 30. Click the Field tool in the Tool Palette.

FIELDS

Working with fields in Director is very similar to working with text cast members. The main difference with field cast members is that their text is editable during movie playback, adding an interactive dimension. This allows you to create movies where your users change and enter text data on the stage. For example, you might want to incorporate your user's name into the actual movie, by asking him or her to enter it during the course.

Another feature of fields is that their print quality is higher than either bitmapped or rich text.

You should only use fields if you need either editable text during playback, or high print quality, since there are several important disadvantages: Of the three text types, fields animate the slowest; fields require that any system which plays your movie have the same fonts installed, even if your movie is played as a Projector; formatting controls are more limited with fields than with text cast members.

To create a field directly on the stage:

Creating a field on the stage is very similar to creating a text cast member on the stage. *(See page 173)*

1. In the score, select the cell in the desired animation channel where you wish to place your field cast member **(Figure 28)**.
2. Choose Tool Palette from the Window menu **(Figure 29)**.
3. Click the Field tool in the Tool Palette **(Figure 30)**.
4. Position the crosshair pointer on the stage, and click the mouse to place a field text box there.
5. Choose Font from the Modify menu to set the field's font, style, and size.

To make a field editable during movie playback:

1. Select the field cast member in the cast window.
2. Click the Cast Member Properties button in the cast window.
3. In the Field Cast Member Properties dialog box, check the Editable option **(Figure 31)**.

✔ **Tip**

- If you want a field cast member to be editable only during certain frames in your movie, select the appropriate cells in the score and check the editable check box in the score **(Figure 32)**. If the Editable option in the Field Cast Member Properties dialog box is set, the score's editable option is ignored, and the field will be editable in every frame where it is present.

To edit a field during playback:

Whenever your movie is playing and an editable field sprite is present on the stage, you can click on it and then type to edit its contents. Its parent cast member in the cast window *is* changed as you type.

To create a field cast member using the field window:

The field window is similar to the text window, except that the ruler (tabs and indents) as well as spacing and kerning controls are not available.

1. Choose Field from the Window menu **(Figure 33)**.
2. Type your text in the field window **(Figure 34)**. When you close the field window, a field cast member is created in the current cast window, from where it can be dragged and placed onto the stage.

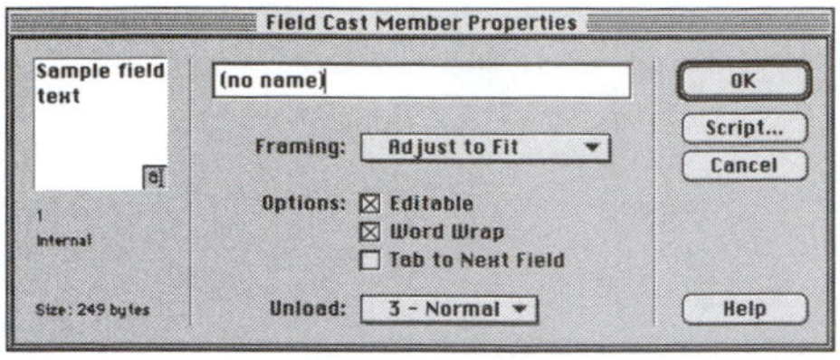

Figure 31. Check the **Editable** check box in the **Field Cast Member Properties** dialog box.

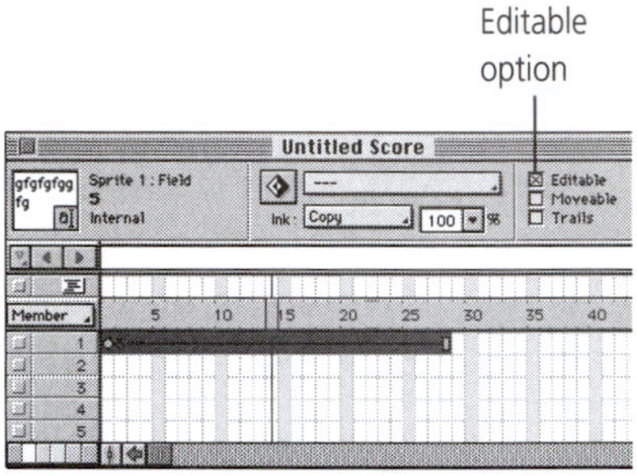

Figure 32. Check the **Editable** check box in the score.

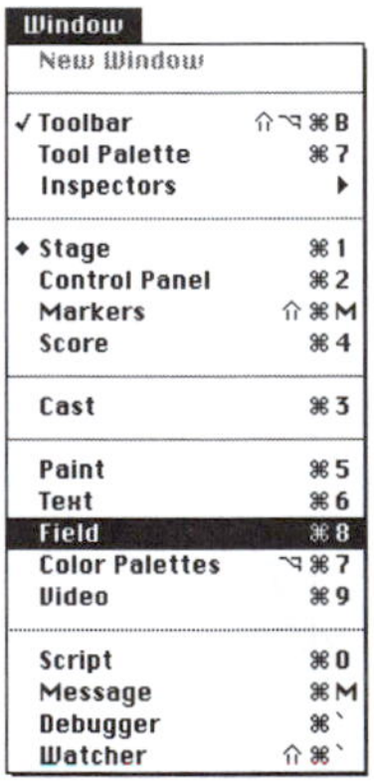

Figure 33. Choose **Field** from the **Window** menu.

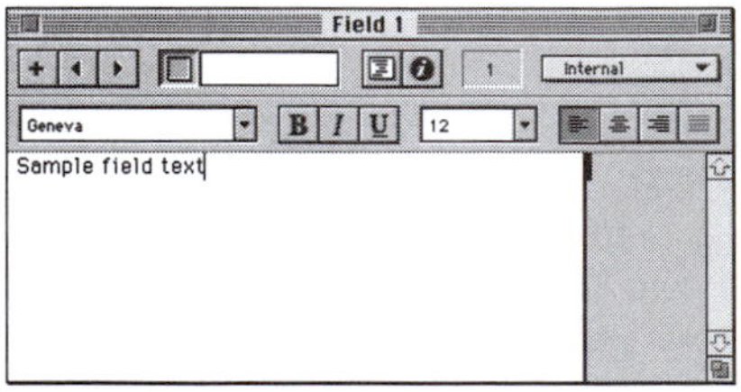

Figure 34. The field window.

SOUND IN DIRECTOR 12

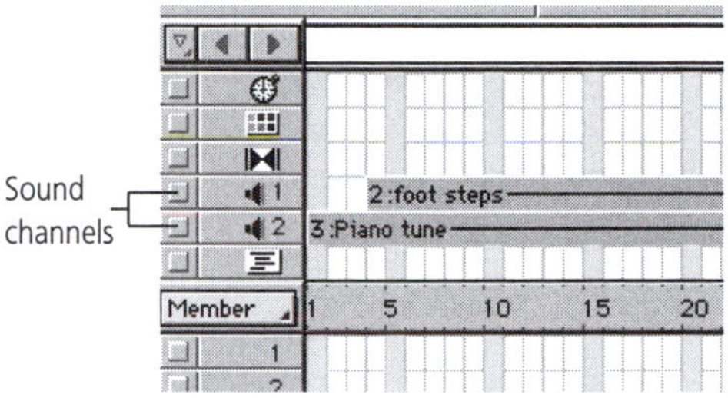

Figure 1. Sounds are placed in one of two sound channels in the score.

Adding musical scores, sound effects, and voice overs to Director movies is easy. Simply import a sound file, and place its cast member in a range of frames in one of Director's sound channels **(Figure 1)**. If there's any trick to this, it's deciding which frames the sound should play in. For example, if you want Director to play the sound of footsteps as a character walks across the screen, you'd first animate the character and then note in which frames his feet touch the ground. You'd then place your footstep sound in these frames, assigning it to one of the score's two sound channels. Another movie might call for playing a musical score throughout an entire animation rather than timing it to specific events. In this case you would place the music into a sound channel through a range of frames.

Director for Macintosh actually has eight sound channels available, so you can mix up to eight sounds. Only two of these channels are accessible from the score, and this chapter focuses on their use. You can access the additional channels by using special Lingo commands, or by playing sounds through digital videos.

IMPORTING AND CREATING SOUND

To import a sound into a cast window:

1. In a cast window, select the cast member position into which you'll import your sound. If you do not select a particular cast position, Director will place your sound in the first available slot **(Figure 2)**.
2. Choose Import from the File menu **(Figure 3)**.
3. In the Import dialog box, choose Sound from the Show pop-up menu **(Figure 4)**. This tells Director to display only Sounds in the file selector box.
4. Add the desired sound, and click Import. Director places your sound in the cast window. Now it's ready to be assigned to the score.

✔ Tips

- Ordinarily when you import a sound, Director copies the contents of the sound file into your movie. This can significantly increase the disk size and memory requirements of the movie. To avoid this, select the Link to External File option in the pop-up menu at the bottom of the Import dialog box before importing a sound file. This tells Director to link to the sound file, rather than copying its entire contents into your movie.
- When you import a sound into Director, the sound can only be played *as is*. Other than volume, Director has no controls for editing the sound's various attributes, such as pitch. You can't even use Director's tempo channel to alter the sound's playback speed. Changes made to Director's tempo will affect the animation rate, but not the sound.

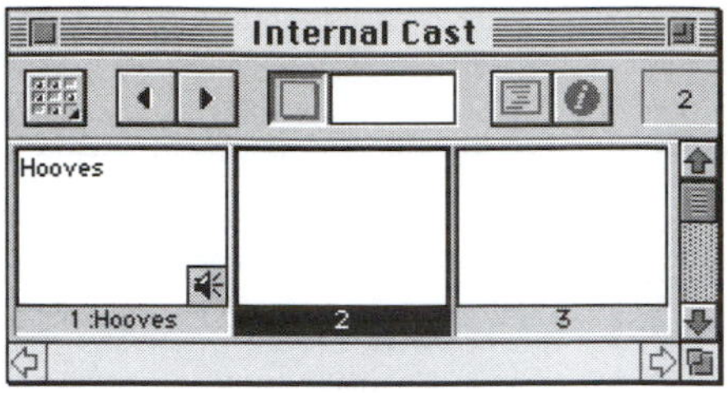

Figure 2. Select a cast member position in a cast window into which you'll import a sound.

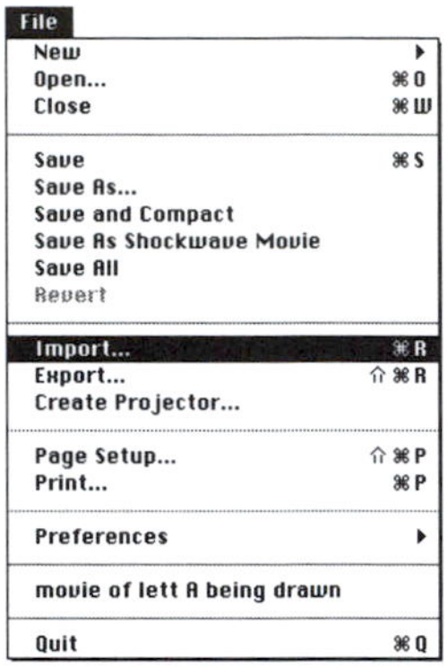

Figure 3. Choose **Import** from the **File** menu.

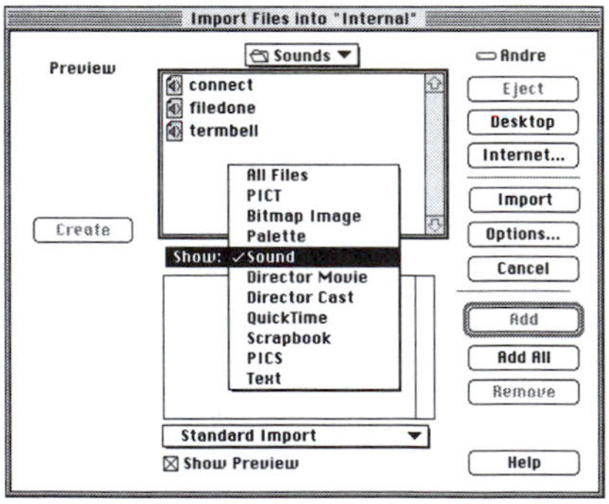

Figure 4. Choose **Sound** from the **Show** pop-up menu in the **Import** dialog box.

About MIDI

Besides playing digitized sound files, Director can also play sound effects and music by controlling a MIDI instrument such as a keyboard synthesizer, drum machine, or sequencer that has been attached to your Macintosh. Using these types of instruments allows your movie to play a very rich and intricate musical score; it is, however, a complex process. First, your Macintosh needs a special MIDI interface that allows it to work with MIDI equipment. Second, Director requires that you use a series of somewhat cryptic commands to control the instruments properly. This topic falls beyond the scope of this book. For more information consult your Director reference manual.

✔ Tips

- Director accepts sounds saved either as AIFF, AIFC, or System 7 files. These formats are standards supported by most, if not all, sound digitizers and editors for the Macintosh. Most libraries of prerecorded "clip-sounds" support these formats as well.
- An intricate soundtrack—especially one with long-lasting sounds such as voice overs and musical scores—can slow your entire movie down. This is a particularly important issue if you intend to play your movie on a wide variety of Macintosh models; while a top-of-the-line PowerPC may keep pace, a run-of-the-mill LC model might be overtaxed and slow your movie significantly. So try to think ahead about the types of Macintoshes likely to play your movie, and design your soundtrack accordingly.

To record a sound in Director:

You can record (or "digitize") sounds within Director by using the Sound command in combination with the hand-held microphone that ships with most Macintosh models. Although Director doesn't have sophisticated controls for top-notch sound production, it does offer a quick and easy way to engineer short sounds for your movies.

1. Make sure that you have a microphone attached to your Macintosh.
2. Choose Media Element from the Insert menu, and select Sound from the pop-up menu **(Figure 5)**.
3. From the Sound dialog box, click the Record button to begin recording a sound via the attached microphone **(Figure 6)**.
4. Click Pause to pause a recording session, or the Stop button when you have finished recording a sound.
5. Click Play to listen to your recorded sound.
6. Click the Save button to place the recorded sound into the active cast window.

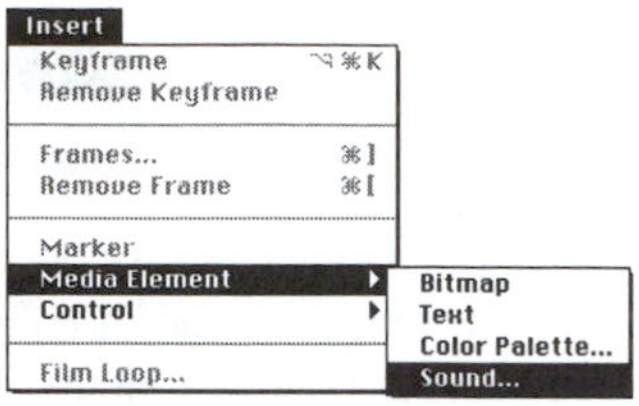

Figure 5. Choose **Media Element** from the **Insert** menu, and select **Sound** from the pop-up menu.

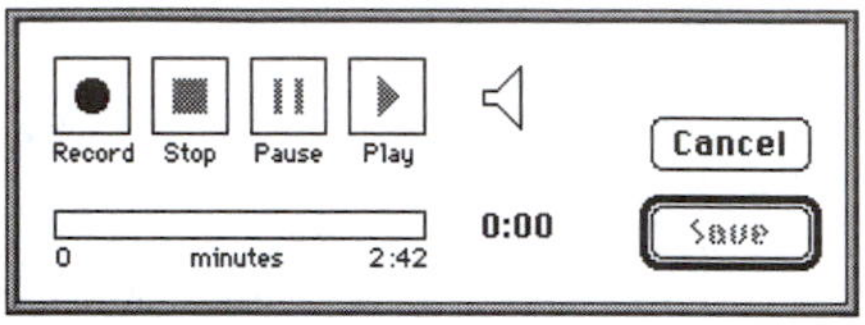

Figure 6. Click the **Record** button to begin recording a sound.

To set the volume of your movie:

1. Choose Control Panel from the Window menu **(Figure 7)**.
2. Click the Volume button in the control panel **(Figure 8)**, and select the desired volume level from the pop-up menu. This setting controls the volume of your entire movie.

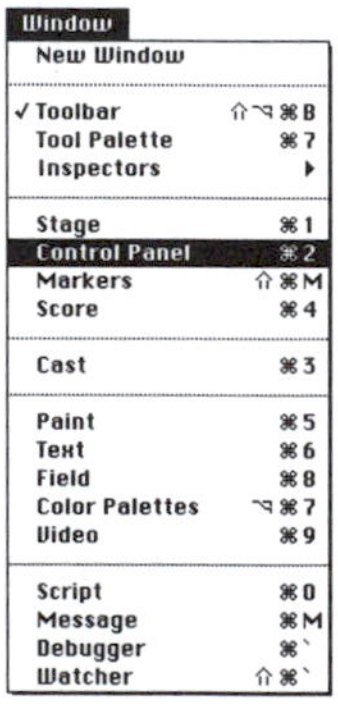

Figure 7. Choose **Control Panel** from the **Window** menu.

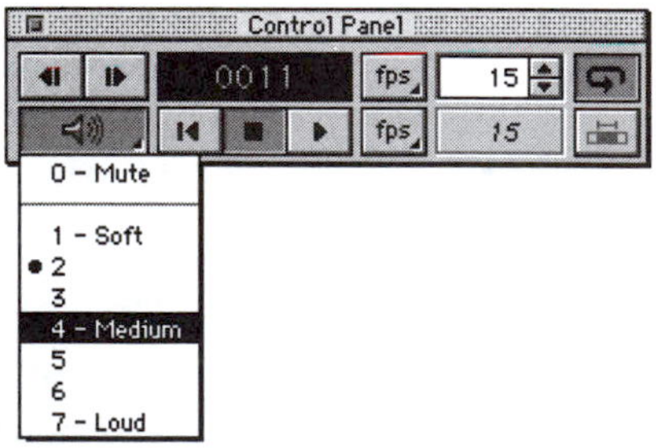

Figure 8. Click the **Volume** button in the control panel, and select the desired level from the pop-up menu.

Sound production outside Director

The process of making ambitious movies in Director will inevitably require custom sounds that you'll have to create from scratch. Unfortunately, the quality of sounds recorded in Director is often too low for polished movies.

For serious sound production you'll want to use a third-party digitizer that can record sounds at high resolutions from a variety of sources, such as microphones, tapedecks, and musical synthesizers. Digitizers also allow you to edit sounds, cutting out unwanted noise and adjusting pitch, volume, and other characteristics. One of the most popular digitizers available is Macromedia's SoundEdit Pro, which offers solid features for a reasonable price. Another excellent choice, if you see yourself heading heavily into sound production, is PassPort Design's SoundPro card, which provides a sophisticated set of software tools for tweaking and mixing sounds in almost every imaginable way.

Note: However you create your custom sounds, make sure that they are saved as AIFF, AIFC, or System 7 files, since these are the only sound formats that Director accepts.

PLACING SOUND

To place sounds in the score:

1. In the score window, click the frame (or drag across a range of frames) in the desired sound channel to indicate where your sound should be placed **(Figure 9)**.
2. Choose Frame from the Modify menu and select Sound from the pop-up menu **(Figure 10)**.
3. In the Frame Properties: Sound dialog box, select the sound you'd like to place in the score (a sound must have already been imported into Director's cast window to appear in this list). With a sound selected, click the Play button to hear a preview, or click OK to place it in the score **(Figure 11)**.

✔ Tip

■ You can place a sound into the score by dragging it from a cast window directly into one of the sound channels. The number of frames your sound sprite is assigned to is determined by the Span Duration setting in the Sprite Preferences dialog box.

To extend sounds to play completely:

Most sounds need to be assigned to a range of frames in order to play completely—a laser blast, for instance, might require 20 frames, while a musical score could fill hundreds. If a sound is assigned to fewer frames than its duration demands, it will cut off prematurely. For instance, if a sound is designed to last two seconds, and the movie tempo is set at 30 fps, then the sound needs to be assigned to at least 60 frames. If it's assigned to only 45 frames, it will end in its last frame without finishing. If you find that your sound is ending prematurely,

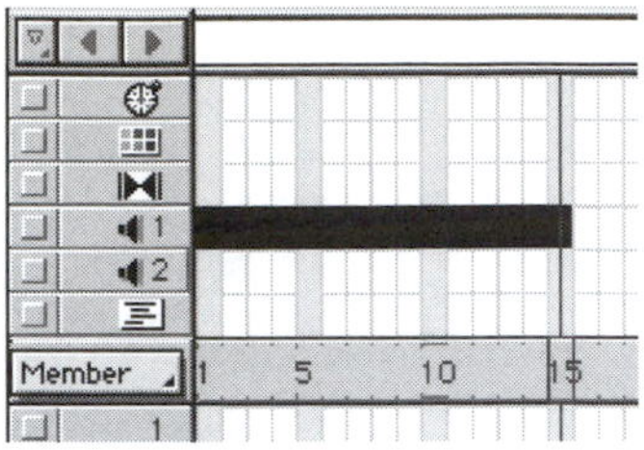

Figure 9. Select a frame or range of frames in a sound channel in which your sound will be placed.

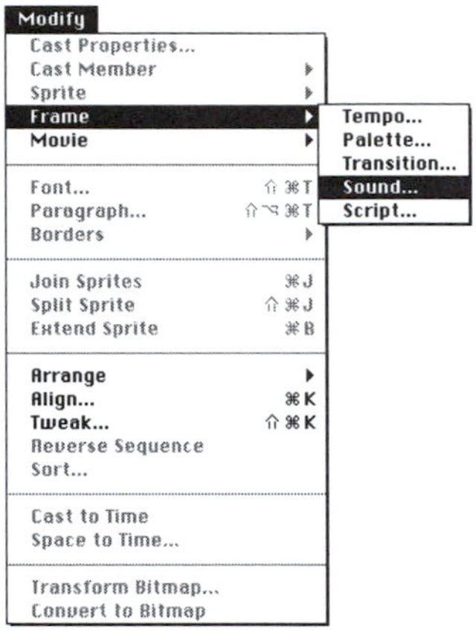

Figure 10. Choose **Frame** from the **Modify** menu and select **Sound** from the pop-up menu.

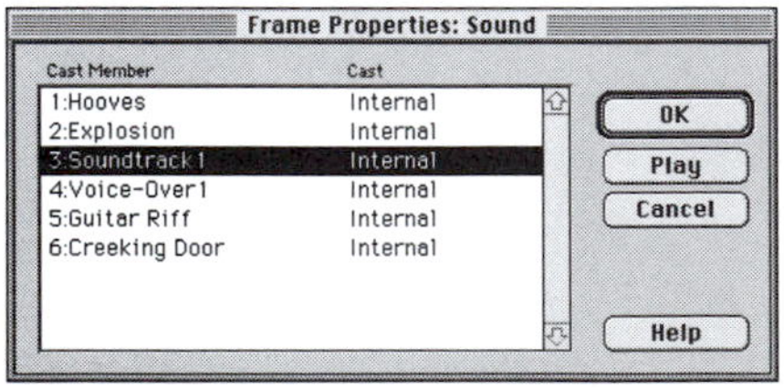

Figure 11. Select a sound to be placed in a sound channel.

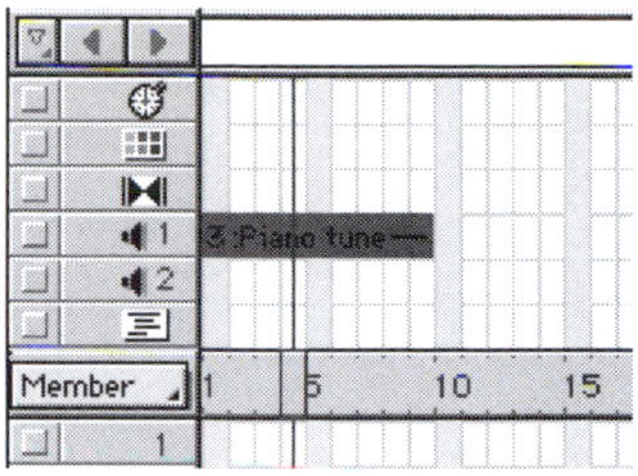

Figure 12. Click the sound sprite you wish to extend.

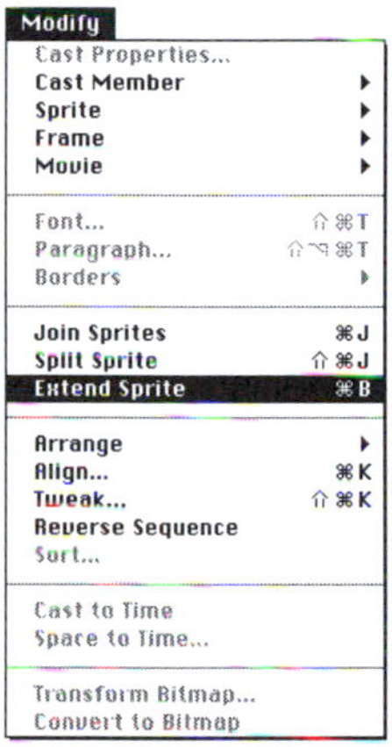

Figure 13. Choose **Extend Sprite** from the **Modify** menu.

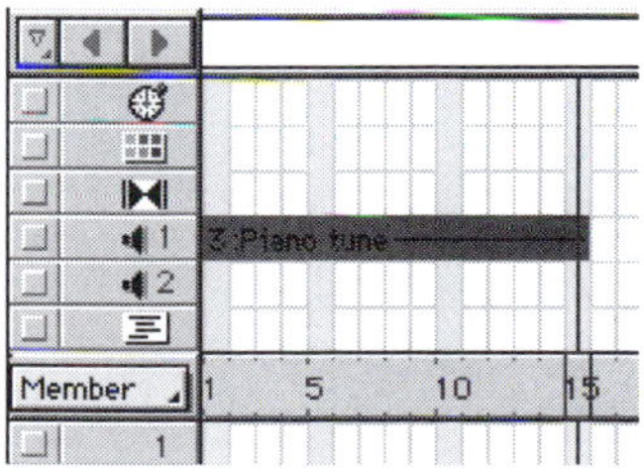

Figure 14. The sound is extended through all the highlighted frames.

you simply have to extend the sound to occupy additional frames in the score.

1. In the score, click the sound sprite you wish to extend **(Figure 12)**.
2. Click the frame in the frame channel to where you wish to extend your sound sprite.
3. Choose Extend Sprite from the Modify menu **(Figure 13)** to extend the sprite **(Figure 14)**.
4. Play back the movie to confirm that your sound now plays completely. If it still cuts off, simply extend the sound sprite into additional frames by repeating the steps above.

✔ Tips

- If you assign a sound to more frames than it requires, the sound will not repeat, unless it has been set to loop. *(See the section "To loop a sound" on page 186 for more info)*
- To quickly determine the number of frames a sound requires, use the steps above to extend it into more frames than it can possibly require (for example, if you know that a laser blast sound effect will require roughly 20 frames, then extend it to 40 or 50). Then play back your movie with the score window open and visible. As the movie plays, Director will highlight each frame it moves through. Simply listen for your sound, and note at which frame in the score it finishes. Now you know how many frames the sound really requires, and can cut out any extra frames it occupies.
- You can also ensure that a sound finishes playing by setting a pause in the tempo channel that waits until the end of a sound. *(See the section "To set a pause in the movie's tempo" on page 191 in the Movie Tempo chapter)*

To loop a sound:

Often you'll want a particular sound to play repeatedly throughout your movie. For example, you might want the sound of a chirping bird to play over and over, or you might want the sound of background music to loop continuously. Setting up such repetitions is easy.

1. Place your sound cast member into the score and extend it through as many frames as you wish it to play **(Figure 15)**. When you extend the sound, you should account for the number of repetitions desired. For instance, if a sound normally requires 10 frames to play completely, and you want it to repeat five times, then you should extend it through 50 frames.

2. In the cast window, select the sound cast member that you placed into the score.

3. Choose Cast Member from the Modify menu and select Properties from the pop-up menu **(Figure 16)**.

4. In the Sound Cast Member Properties dialog box, click the Loop check box **(Figure 17)**.

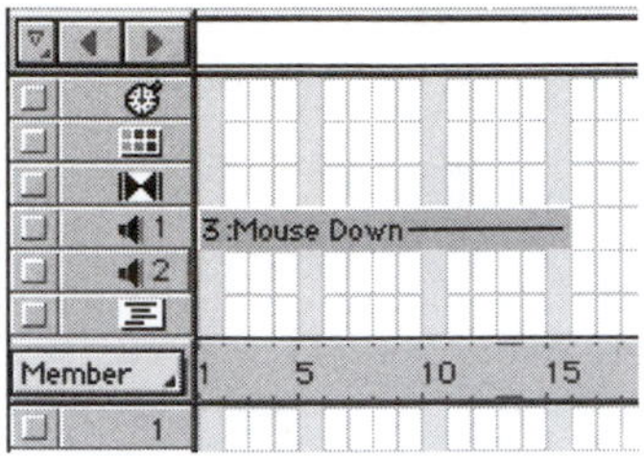

Figure 15. Extend your sound sprite through the range of frames you wish it to play in.

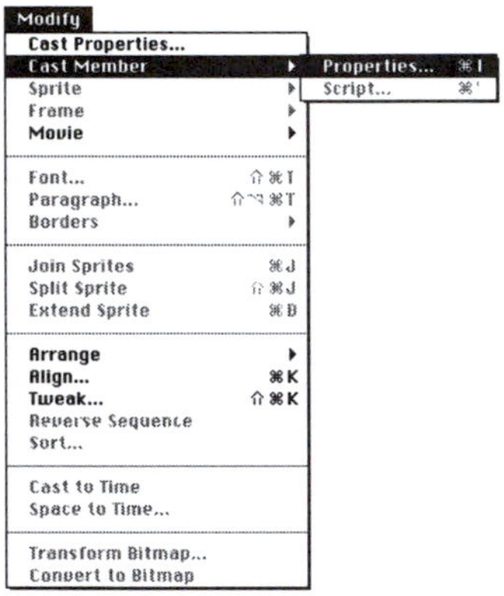

Figure 16. Choose **Cast Member** from the **Modify** menu and select **Properties** from the pop-up menu.

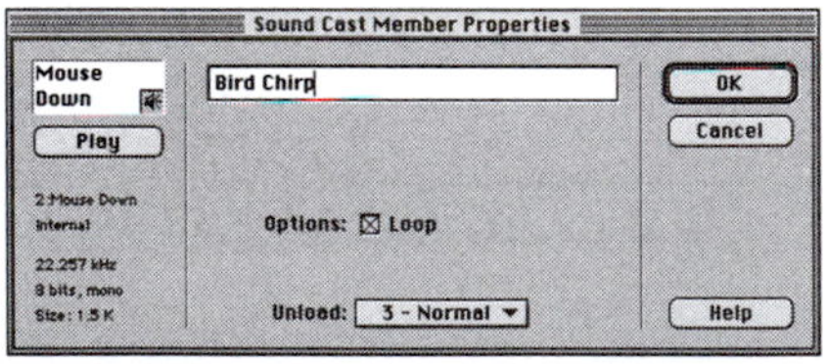

Figure 17. Click the **Loop** option in the **Sound Cast Member Properties** dialog box.

Setting Scene Transitions 13

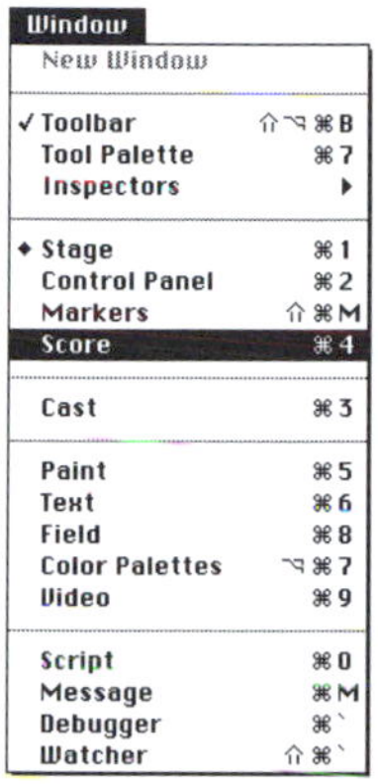

Figure 1. Choose **Score** from the **Window** menu.

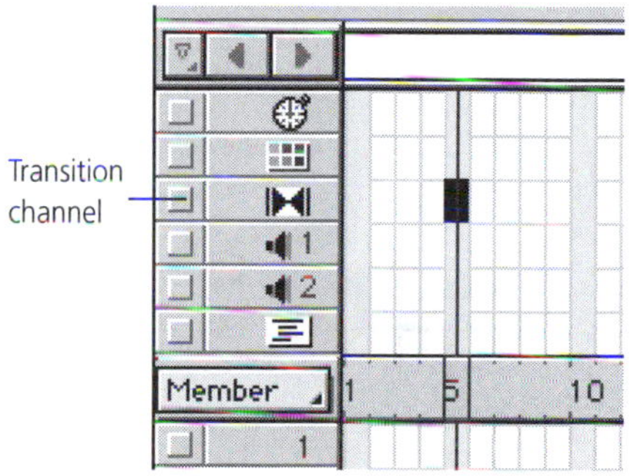

Figure 2. Select a cell in the transition channel where you want a transition to occur.

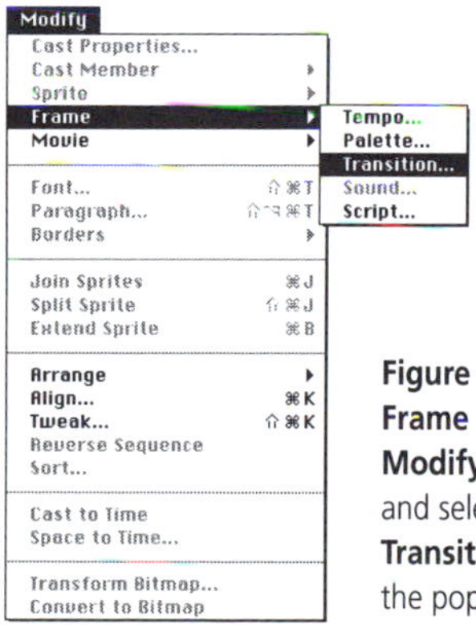

Figure 3. Choose **Frame** from the **Modify** menu and select **Transition** from the pop-up menu.

Director offers more than 50 special effects **transitions** such as dissolves, wipes, and fades that you can use to smoothly move from one scene in a movie to another (a scene is a sequence of related action that takes place on Director's stage). Without transitions, scenes simply cut abruptly from one to another, often creating a jarring effect for the viewer.

Transitions are placed into the transition channel of Director's score, at the particular frame where you wish the transition to occur.

To set a transition:

1. Choose Score from the Window menu to open Director's score **(Figure 1)**.
2. In the transition channel, select the cell at the particular frame in which the transition should occur **(Figure 2)**. The transition begins between the frame that you select, and the frame that precedes it. To transition between two scenes, you'd set the transition at the first frame of the second scene and not at the last frame of the first scene.
3. Choose Frame from the Modify menu, and select Transition from the pop-up menu **(Figure 3)**, or double-click the cell you've selected in the transition channel.

4. In the Frame Properties:Transition dialog box, click the transition that you wish to apply **(Figure 4)**. Use the dialog box's scroll bars to move throughout all of the transition types. ***Note:*** Director features too many transition types to cover here. Fortunately, each type is identified with a descriptive name. Experiment with the different transition types before selecting one for your scene.
5. Click the Entire Stage radio button if the transition should apply to Director's entire stage. Click the Changing Area Only button if the transition should apply only to areas of the stage that are changing from one scene to the next (in other words, where sprites are present, but then are not, or vice versa).
6. Use the Duration and Smoothness slider bars to give the transition a custom duration time and smoothness (smoothness refers to the size of pixel "chunks" used to dissolve one scene or introduce another).
7. Click OK to apply the selected transition to your score. The transition is placed into the active cast window as a transition cast member **(Figure 5)**.

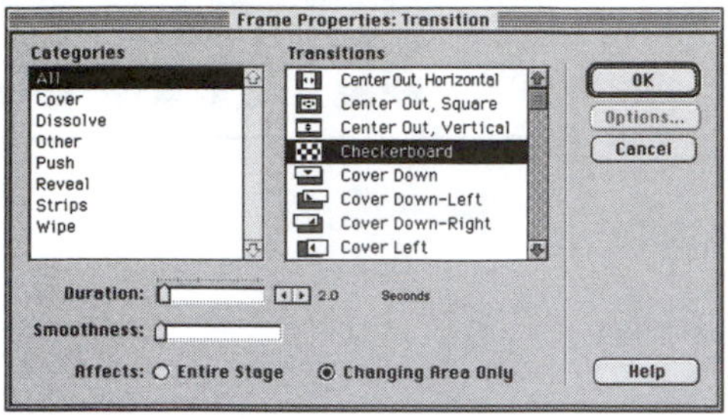

Figure 4. Select the desired transition in the **Frame Properties:Transition** dialog box.

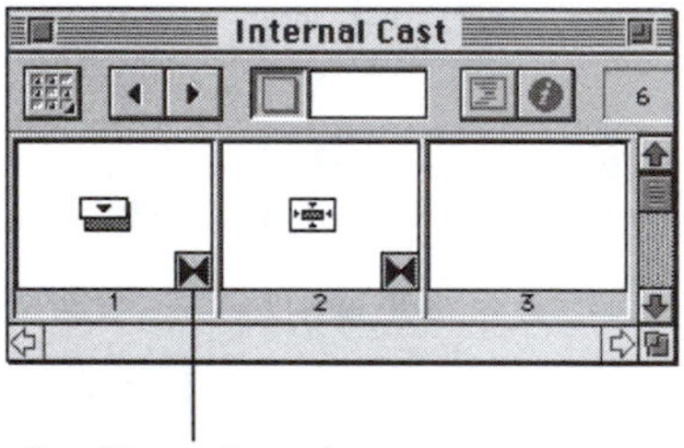

Transition cast member

Figure 5. The transition becomes a cast member.

To add Xtra transitions to Director:

You can add new transitions to Director by installing them as Xtras. *(Also see the Xtras chapter on page 223)*

1. Copy your Xtra transition file into the Xtras folder in the Director application folder. This installs the new transition.
2. Double-click the cell in the transition channel in the score where you wish a transition to occur.
3. In the Frame Properties:Transition dialog box, your Xtra transition appears as a special icon.

MOVIE TEMPO

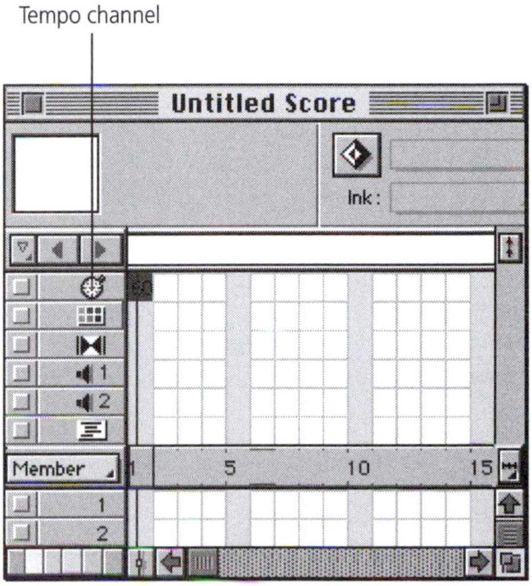

Figure 1. The tempo of your movie is set in the tempo channel of the score.

Director plays your movie at a particular **tempo**, or speed, which you can easily adjust. The movie's tempo is measured in **frames-per-second** (fps), which means the higher the tempo rate (15 fps, 24 fps, 30 fps, etc.), the faster Director plays back animation. With a high tempo (say, 60 fps), you can make sprites zoom across the stage, while you can use a low tempo (perhaps 7 fps) to create a slow-motion effect.

Your movie's tempo is set in the tempo channel of Director's score **(Figure 1)**. Although one tempo can apply to an entire movie, you can also vary your tempo on a frame-by-frame basis.

There are two important things to know about the effects that tempo settings have on your movie: First of all, while the tempo you set affects the speed at which cast member sprites are animated on stage, it does not affect the playback rate of sounds or digital videos.

Secondly, while you may set a high tempo in a movie, the Macintosh that Director is running on must be advanced enough to keep up with that pace. If a particular scene calls for the animation of a large number of sprites, or if it features special ink effects, or if cast members are painted at high color depths (such as 32-bit color), or if there are complex transitions or color palette manipulation at work, your Macintosh may simply not be able to manage all this without slowing the scene's tempo. If this is the case, you must either settle for this slow playback speed, buy a faster Macintosh, or redesign the movie's scene so that it is less demanding.

To set a new movie tempo:

When you set a new tempo in the tempo channel, that tempo applies to all the following frames of your movie (until you set another tempo change).

1. Choose Score from the Window menu to open Director's score **(Figure 2)**.
2. In the tempo channel, select the cell where you would like a new tempo to occur **(Figure 4)**.
3. Choose Frame from the Modify menu, and select Tempo from the pop-up menu **(Figure 3)**.
4. In the Frame Properties:Tempo dialog box, click the Tempo radio button and slide the Tempo scroll bar to set the movie's tempo in frames per second **(Figure 5)**.
5. Click OK to apply the tempo change to the score. Director now uses this tempo setting to play the frame you selected in step 2, and all the frames to the right of it (until, that is, you set a new tempo).

✔ Tips

- You can also open the Frame Properties:Tempo dialog box by double-clicking a cell in the tempo channel.
- If your movie will be played on a variety of Macintosh models (for instance, if it's an educational game), try to set a tempo that even low-end Macintoshes will be able to keep up with. Otherwise, owners of low-end Macintoshes such as LC's may be disappointed with your movie's playback performance. The best way to determine how well a particular Macintosh will play your movie is to play it on that machine and compare the movie's set tempo to its actual playback tempo. *(See page 192)*

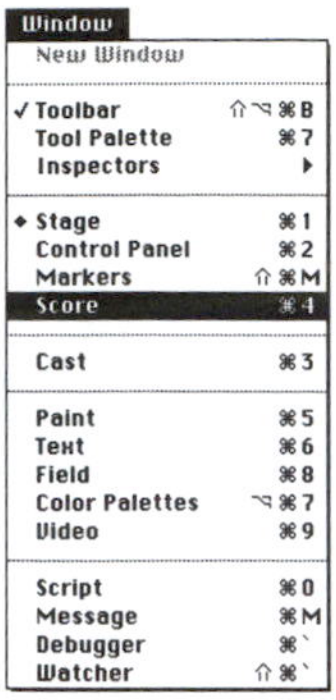

Figure 2. Choose **Score** from the **Window** menu.

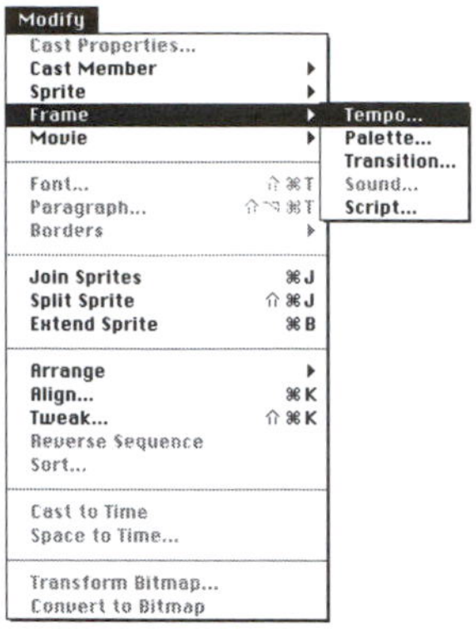

Figure 3. Choose **Frame** from the **Modify** menu, and select **Tempo** from the pop-up menu.

Figure 4. Select a cell in the tempo channel where you would like a new tempo to occur.

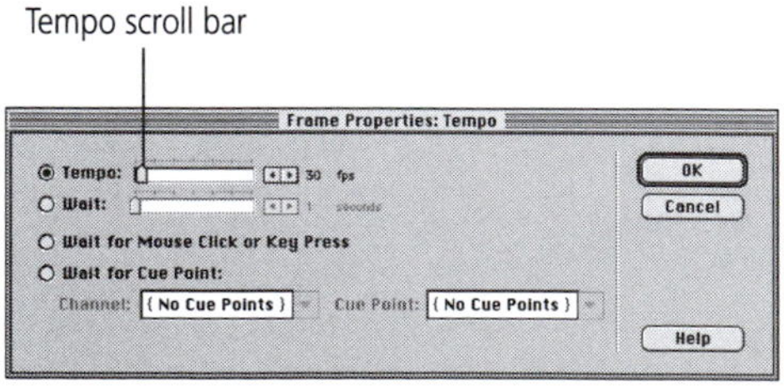

Figure 5. Use the **Frame Properties:Tempo** dialog box to set the movie's tempo in frames-per-second.

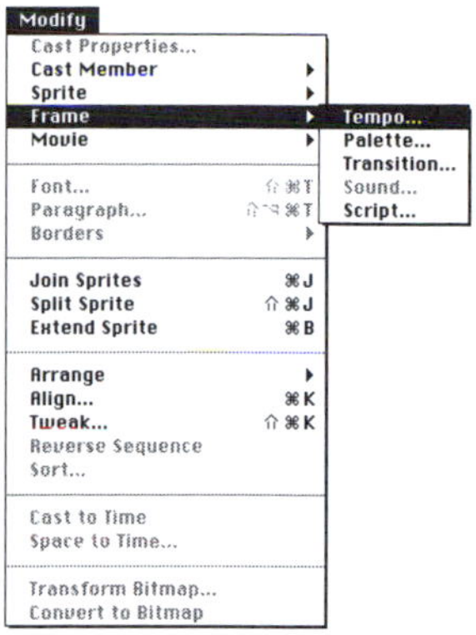

Figure 6. Choose **Frame** from the **Modify** menu, and select **Tempo** from the pop-up menu.

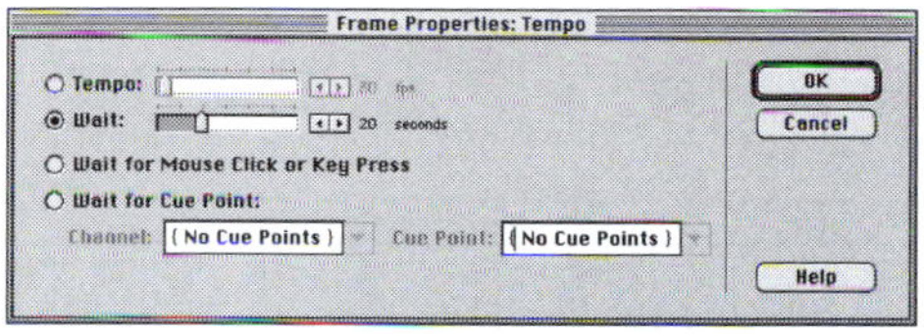

Figure 7. Select the **Wait** option in the **Frame Properties:Tempo** dialog box to create a timed pause in your movie. Select the second Wait option to pause your movie until a mouse click or key press occurs.

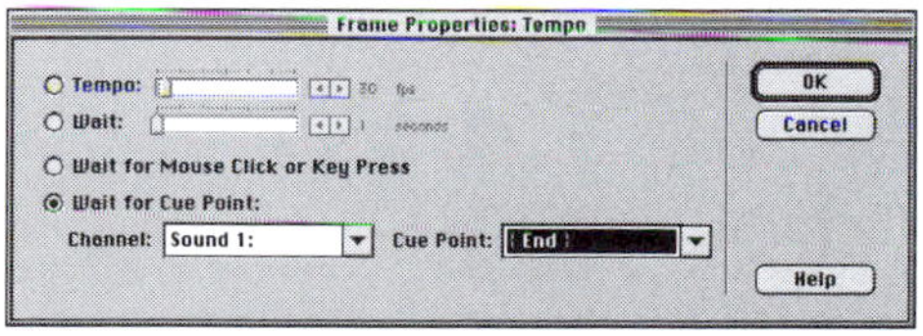

Figure 8. Select the **Wait for Cue Point** option in the **Frame Properties:Tempo** dialog box to pause your movie until a specified cue point is reached in either a sound or digital video.

To set a pause in a movie:

You can use the tempo channel to create a pause in the playback of your movie. You can pause your movie for a specified number of seconds, create a pause until a mouse click or key press occurs, or set a pause that waits for a specific cue point to be reached in either a sound or digital video cast member.

1. In the tempo channel, select the frame where you would like to set a pause.
2. Choose Frame from the Modify menu, and select Tempo from the pop-up menu **(Figure 6)**.
3. In the Frame Properties:Tempo dialog box, select the first Wait option if you are creating a timed pause, and use the adjacent scroll bar to specify the duration in seconds **(Figure 7)**. Select the Wait for Mouse Click or Key Press option for your movie to remain paused until the mouse or a key is pressed.

or

3. If you wish to pause your movie until a specific cue point is reached in a sound or a digital video, select the Wait for Cue Point option **(Figure 8)**. Use the channel pop-up menu to select the channel where your sound or digital video is located. Then use the Cue Point pop-up menu to select a cue point in either the sound or digital video that you wish to wait for. Cue points for both sound and digital video files can be set using Macromedia's Sound Edit 16.
4. Click OK to set the pause in the selected frame.

Note: If you create a pause that waits for a cue point in a sound or digital video, make sure that the sound or video clip begins playing before the frame where the pause takes place.

To compare actual playback tempo versus the set tempo:

Director tries to play a movie at the particular tempo you've set in the tempo channel. Unfortunately, the actual playback speed may fall short when complex animations are featured. This is very likely on a low-end Macintosh. Fortunately, Director makes it easy to compare this actual tempo to the tempo you've set on a frame-by-frame basis.

1. Set the desired tempo for your movie as outlined on page 190.
2. Choose Control Panel from the Window menu to open the control panel **(Figure 9)**.
3. Click Rewind in the control panel.
4. Click the control panel's Step forward button to step through your movie one frame at a time.
5. In the control panel, compare the Actual Tempo to the Tempo display setting for each frame in your movie **(Figure 10)**. The Actual Tempo value is how fast the computer has managed to play back the given frame. The Tempo display setting shows the target frame rate you've set in the tempo channel for the given frame.

✔ **Tip**

■ You can adjust the target tempo for each frame by clicking the arrows in the Tempo display in the control panel **(Figure 9)**. The effect is the same as setting a tempo in the tempo channel for the given frame. A tempo you set in the tempo channel overrides any value you set in the control panel's Tempo display.

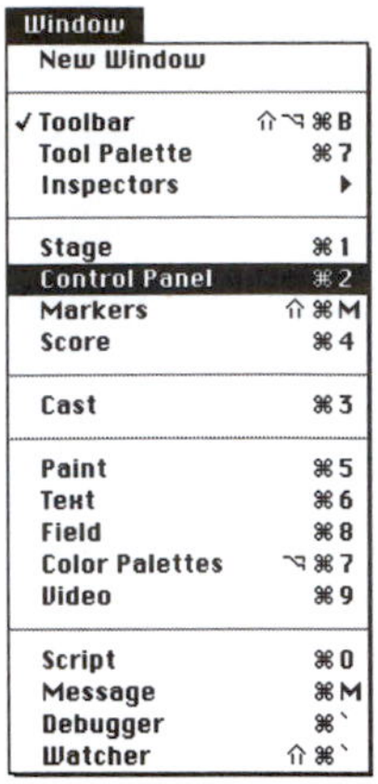

Figure 9. Choose **Control Panel** from the **Window** menu.

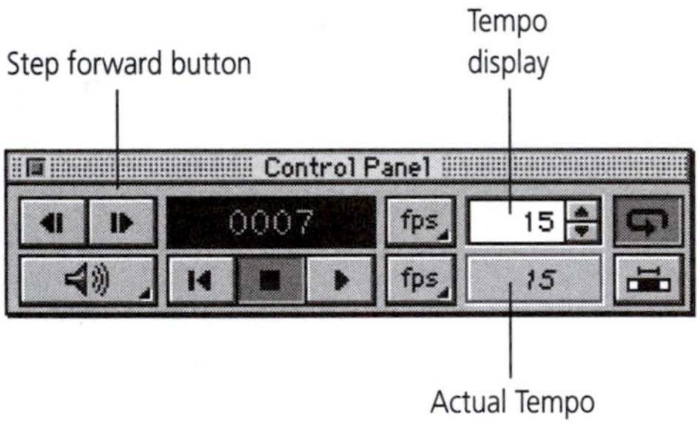

Figure 10. The control panel shows the Actual Tempo of a single frame, and the Tempo display setting for that frame.

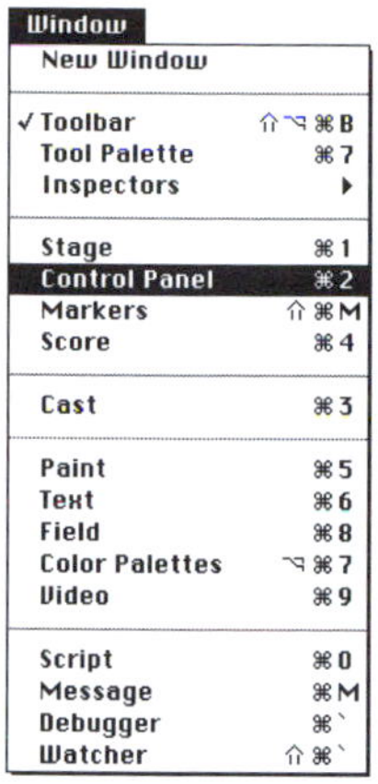

Figure 11. Choose **Control Panel** from the **Window** menu.

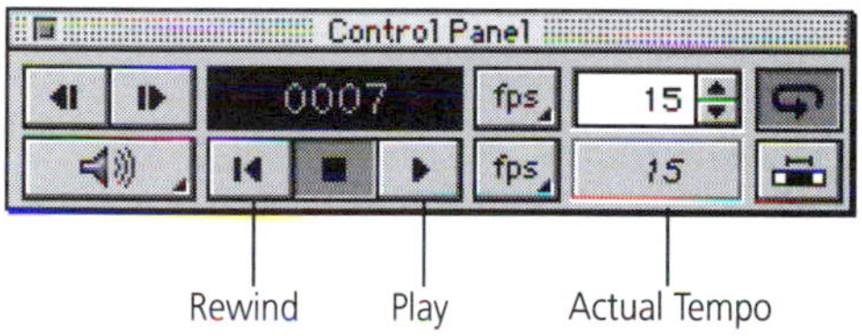

Figure 12. The control panel.

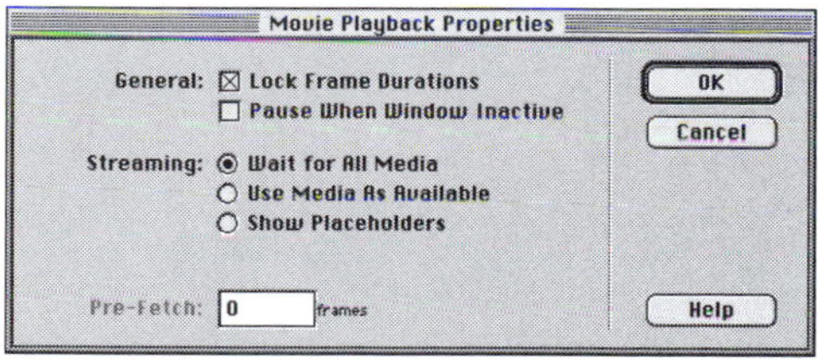

Figure 13. Check the **Lock Frame Durations** option in the **Movie Playback Properties** dialog box.

Locking playback speed

When you've determined the proper tempo for your movie, you can then "lock" that speed so that it's used by whatever Macintosh your movie happens to play on. Doing so guards against your movie being played too fast on more advanced Macintoshes but does not prevent the movie from playing back *slower* when run on less sophisticated Macintoshes. If you're trying to set the movie's tempo to play workably on even low-end Macintoshes, you should establish a tempo that even those Macs can keep up with, and then lock it in.

To lock your movie's playback speed:

1. Set the desired tempo for your movie as outlined on page 190.
2. Choose Control Panel from the Window menu **(Figure 11)**.
3. Use the control panel to rewind and then play back your movie from beginning to end **(Figure 12)**. In doing so, Director records the actual speed at which it plays each frame, and stores these values in the Actual Tempo display in the control panel. If the movie branches off into multiple segments (for instance, in an interactive presentation), make sure you play through all of these segments.
4. Choose Movie from the Modify menu and select Playback from the pop-up menu. In the Movie Playback Properties dialog box, check the Lock Frame Durations option **(Figure 13)**. Each frame is now locked to play at the actual speed that was recorded in step 3. To unlock the movie's playback speed, uncheck the Lock Frames Duration option.

CREATE A PROJECTOR 15

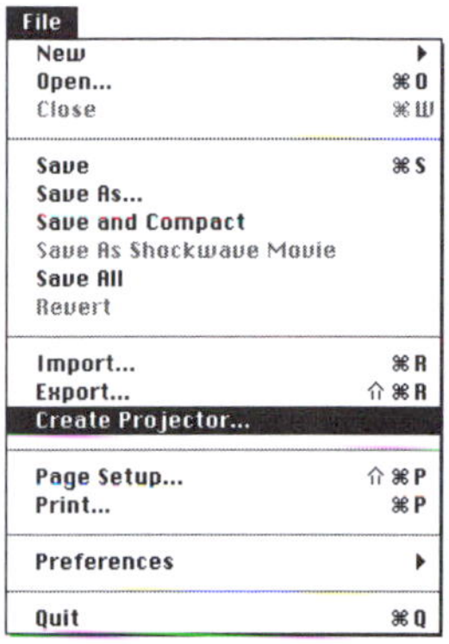

Figure 1. Choose **Create Projector** from the **File** menu.

When you wish to distribute your Director movie to the public, you need to create a projector—a play-only version of your movie (or sequence of movies) that runs like any application from the Finder. Your users don't need to own a copy of Director to run your projector. Anyone can watch your projector movie as long as their computer meets the minimum hardware requirements.

A projector file can't be opened or edited in Director, preventing users from modifying your movie. Only the original source movie files can be opened in Director.

To create a projector:

1. Choose Create Projector from the File menu **(Figure 1)**.
2. Select the movie or external cast file that you wish to include in your projector **(Figure 2)**. You can include Xtras in your projector by selecting the Check Movies for Xtras option in the Projector Options dialog box. *(See page 198)*
3. Click the Add button. You can add as many movies and external casts as you wish to a single projector file by repeating steps 2–3. When you play the projector, its movies will play one after the other, in the order in which they appear in the play list, assuming that you have selected the Play Every Movie option in the Projector Options dialog box. *(See page 198)*
4. Click the Options button to set projector options in the Options dialog box. *(See page 198)*
5. Click Create. The Save dialog box appears.
6. Type the name of your projector and click Save.

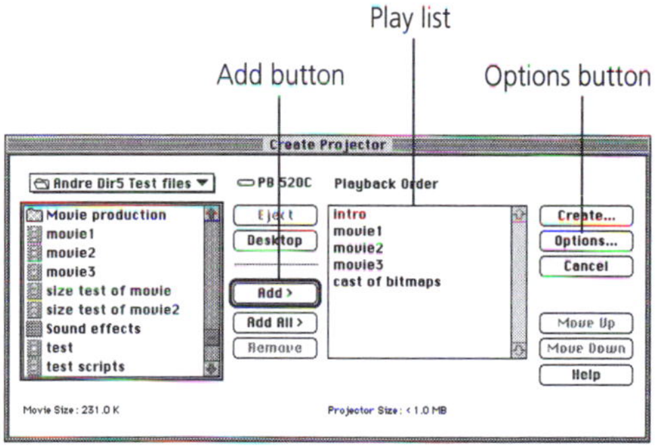

Figure 2. Select and add movie and cast files to your projector play list from the left side of the **Create Projector** dialog box.

7. To play a projector, double-click its icon from the Finder.

Note: If any of the movies included in your projector have links to external files which are not part of a cast in the projector play list, then those files must be included in the same folder along with the projector file in order for your users to be able to properly run the projector.

How to organize files for distribution

Creating a projector that consists of many movie files in its play list has its drawback. If you wish to change a single movie in the play list, you must re-create the entire projector each time. A more efficient way to organize your production is to create a projector that consists of a single short movie, which launches all the other movie files that form your multimedia production. This is accomplished by incorporating a Lingo script in the short projector movie, such as in **Figure 3**, that branches to each of your movies *(see page 218 in the Lingo through Interactivity chapter for details on scripts that branch)*. These other movie files are not projectors, but are Director movies. You can protect them from being opened and edited by using the Update Movies command. *(See page 197)*

The other movie files that your projector launches should be included in the same folder as the projector file **(Figure 4)**, as well as any external casts and linked files. With this type of organization, you are free to edit any of the movies that your projector launches, without having to re-create the projector file.

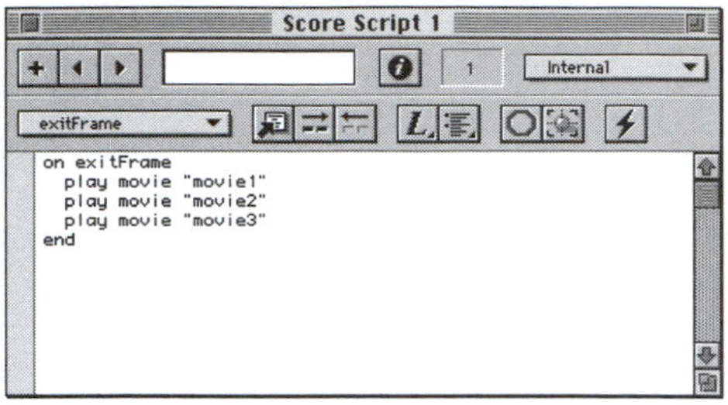

Figure 3. A frame script that launches three other Director movies. You can keep your projector file small, and your production more manageable, by using a projector to launch your movies, rather than incorporating all of your movies in a single large projector file.

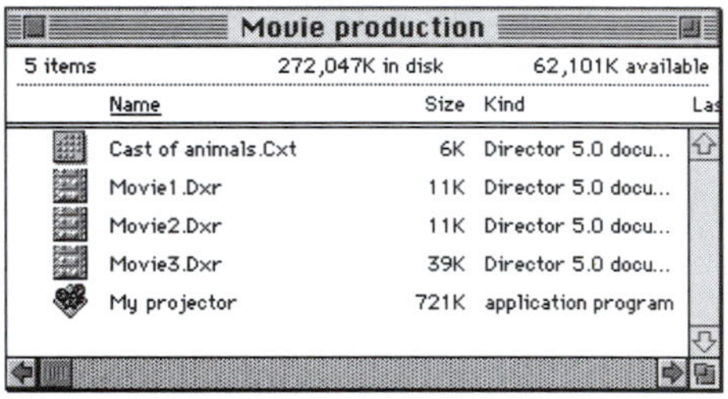

Figure 4. A good way to organize your files for distribution. The movie and cast files here have been protected using the **Update Movies** command, as indicated by the file extensions.

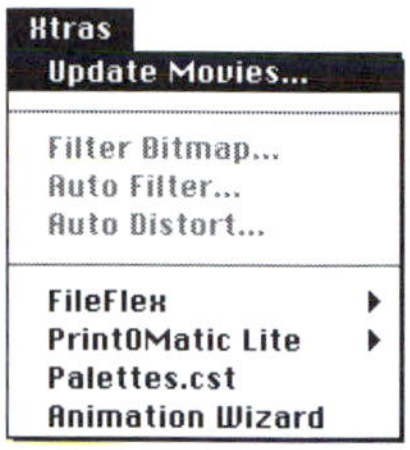

Figure 5. Choose **Update Movies** from the **Xtras** menu.

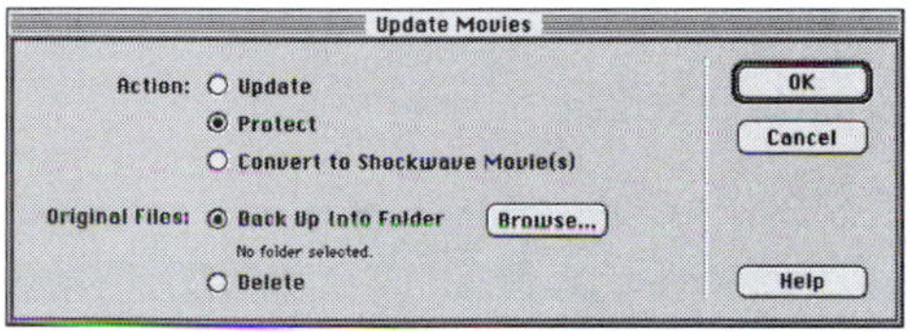

Figure 6. Click the **Protect** radio button in the **Update Movies** dialog box.

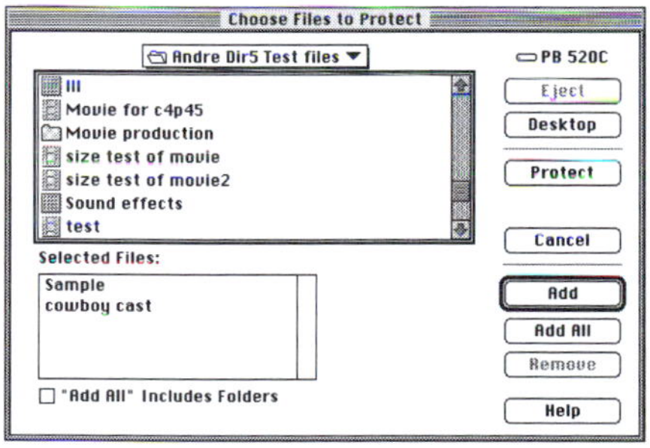

Figure 7. Select the movie and cast files you wish to protect by selecting them individually in the file box, and then clicking **Add**.

To protect movie and cast files using Update Movies:

You can use the Update Movies command under the Xtras menu to protect movie and cast files from being opened and edited in Director. When you create a projector file that launches other movies, you may want to protect those other movie files, which are not themselves projectors. You will very likely want to do this if you will be distributing your multimedia production.

The Update Movies command is also used to update older versions of Director movies.*(See page 12 in the Basics chapter)*

1. Choose Update Movies from the Xtras menu **(Figure 5)**.
2. Click the Protect radio button in the Update Movie dialog box **(Figure 6)**.
3. Click the Back Up into Folder radio button if you wish to place the original movie and cast files into a specified folder. Click the Browse button to select the folder in which to place these original files.

Or

3. Click the Delete button if you wish the new protected files to overwrite the originals. Make sure that you have backed up the original files since you cannot unprotect them.
4. Click OK
5. In the Choose Files to Protect dialog box **(Figure 7)**, select a movie or cast file you wish to protect and click Add. Repeat this step to add all the files you wish to protect to the list at the bottom of the dialog box. Click Add All to add all the files in the current folder to the list of files to protect.
6. Click Protect.

Note: There is no way to unprotect a movie or cast file once it has been protected. Make sure to back up the original files before you protect them.

Projector Options

The Projector Options dialog box allows you to set some general settings that affect all the movies in your projector. Click Options from the Create Projector dialog box to open it **(Figure 8)**.

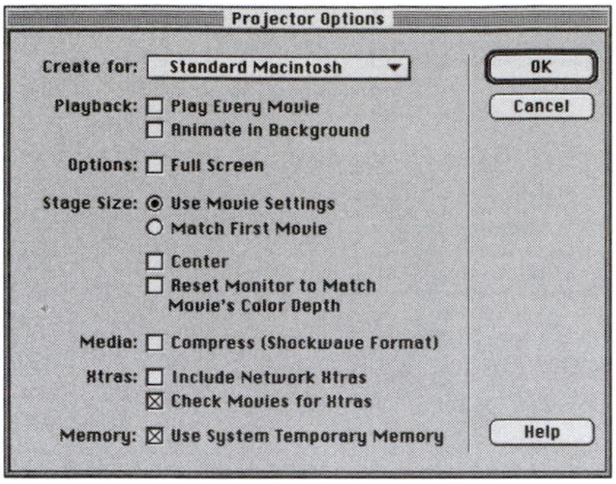

Figure 8. Click the **Options** button in the **Create Projector** dialog box to open the **Projector Options** dialog box.

Create for:

Click the Create for pop-up menu to select the type of computer system your projector will play on. On the Macintosh platform, your options are: Power Macintosh Native, Standard Macintosh, and All Macintosh models **(Figure 9)**. To ensure that your projector plays at optimal speed on all Macintosh models, select the All Macintosh models option. Keep in mind that this option creates a larger projector file than the other two options.

Figure 9. Click the **Create for** pop-up menu to select the type of computer system your projector will play on.

Playback:

If you check the Play Every Movie option, all the movies you add to the projector play list will be played in the order they are listed. If not checked, only the first movie on the list is played. This first movie can activate other movies, regardless of whether this option is set, by branching to them using Lingo.

Check the Animate in Background option if you wish your projector to continue playing even if you click outside of it on the desktop. If not checked, the projector stops playing if you click outside of it.

Options:

Check the Full Screen option if you wish your movie to occupy the full screen when playing. The desktop is hidden, and any menu bar used in your movie is displayed at the top of the stage.

Stage Size:

If the Use Movie Settings radio button is selected, the stage size takes on the dimensions of each new movie that is opened in the projector play list. If the Match First Movie radio button is clicked, the stage size retains the dimensions of the first movie in the play list.

If the Center option is checked, the stage is automatically centered on the screen (this comes in handy when the stage is smaller than the full screen dimensions). If not checked, the position of the stage is determined by the movies in the play list.

If the Reset Monitor to Match Movie's Color Depth option is checked, you're monitor's color depth changes to match the color depth of each movie listed in the projector play list.

Media:

Check the Compress (Shockwave Format) option if your projector will be played back over the Internet.

Xtras:

Check the Check Movies for Xtras option if you wish to include any Xtras your movie uses in the projector file. You can determine which Xtras your movie uses by choosing Movie from the Modify menu, and selecting Xtras from the pop-up menu.

Memory:

Check the Use System Temporary Memory option if you wish Director to be able to use system memory when its own memory partition is full. This option is disabled when virtual memory is turned on.

INTERACTIVITY THROUGH LINGO 16

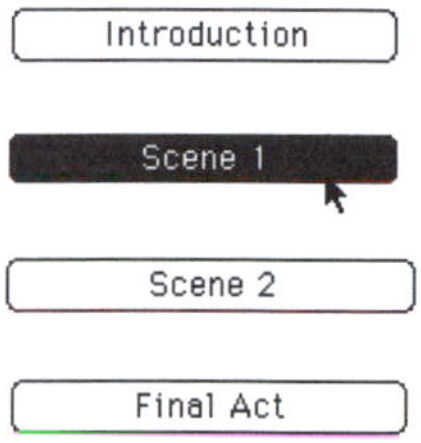

Figure 1. A menu of scene choices, composed of four interactive buttons.

Lingo is Director's scripting language that adds the intelligent, interactive dimension to your multimedia productions. Through Lingo, you enable users to communicate with your movie; they can type in text, click on sprites, and your movie can respond to these inputs in limitless ways.

Lingo allows your movie to go beyond what is normally possible when authoring only through the score. For instance, you can use Lingo to offer your users navigational control over the order in which scenes of your movie are played. A common example of this involves a multimedia presentation that offers a menu of scene choices **(Figure 1)**.

This chapter introduces you to the basics of writing Lingo scripts. It is organized into the following four sections:

Introduction to scripts and script windows defines scripts, script types, and explains how to create scripts in script windows.

Making sprites and cast members interactive teaches you how to make your sprites and cast members respond to mouse input.

Navigation explains how to write scripts that allow users to navigate through the scenes of your movie in a non-sequential order.

Handlers, messages, and events explains how Director knows which scripts to run and when.

If you want to avoid learning about writing Lingo scripts, but still wish to incorporate basic interactivity in your movies, you can do so by using a new feature in Director 6 called drag and drop behaviors. *(See page 227 in the Drag and Drop Behaviors chapter)*

INTRODUCTION TO SCRIPTS AND SCRIPT WINDOWS

What is a Lingo script?

A Lingo script is a set of instructions written in Lingo code that tells Director how your movie should respond when specific events occur during play. Examples of events include user input through the mouse and keyboard. Other events are non-input oriented such as the playback head entering a new frame (events are described in detail on page 219).

Suppose a user clicks the mouse on a particular sprite in your movie. Should something happen? If you want your movie to respond to an event such as a mouse click, you need to write a script. Your movie can respond in many ways. For example, you can write a script that causes a sprite's color to change when a user clicks on it. In fact, scripts can be written that allow user inputs to affect virtually every aspect of your movie, such as sound, positions of sprites, the path the playback head follows through a movie, text output, and many other attributes for limitless interactive possibilities.

The instructions in a Lingo script are organized into handlers. A **handler** is a set of Lingo instructions that is activated by an event in your movie (technically, a handler is activated by a message which is sent when an event occurs). One script can contain multiple handlers. Handlers, messages, and events are described in detail on pages 219–222.

All handlers start with the word **on**, and end with the word **end** **(Figure 2)**. The word after **on** is the message the handler should respond to. The instructions inside a handler (between **on** and **end**) are executed when the handler receives a matching message.

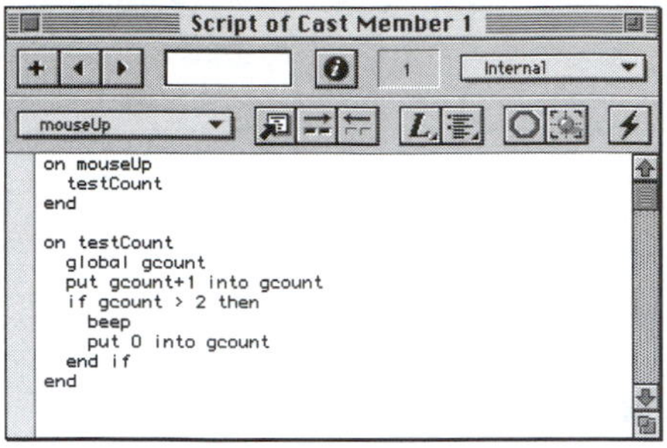

Figure 2. This script is composed of two handlers: the mouseUp handler and the testCount handler.

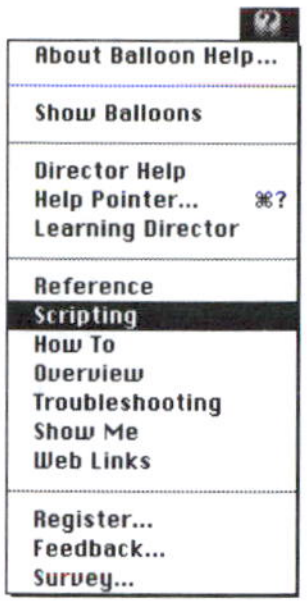

Figure 3. Choose **Scripting** from the **Help** menu.

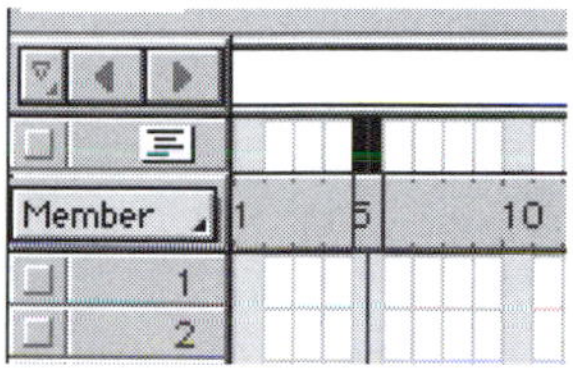

Figure 4. Select the fifth frame in the script channel.

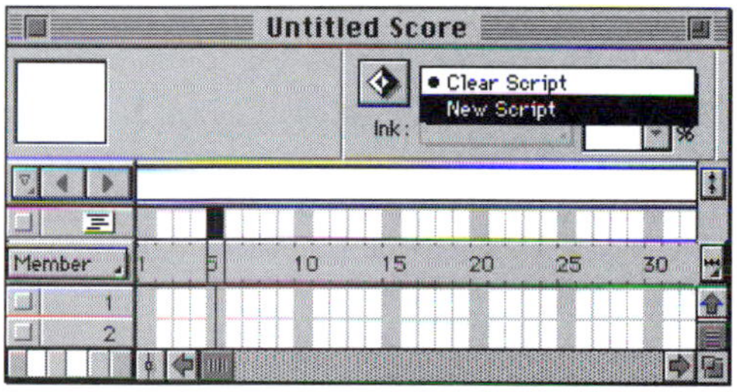

Figure 5. Choose **New Script** from the **Script** pop-up menu in the score window.

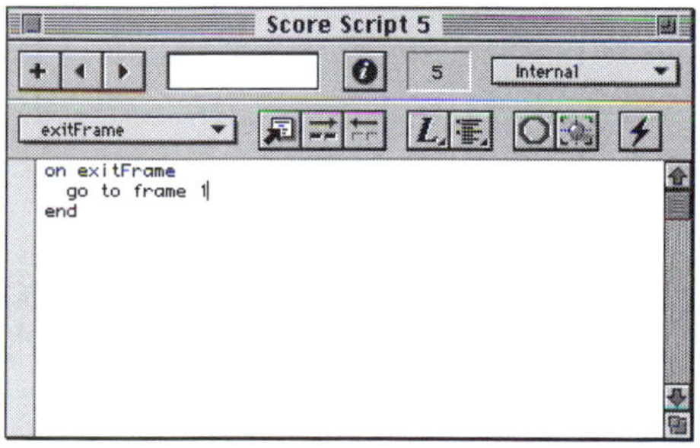

Figure 6. Example script 1.

Writing a script

Lingo scripts are written in script windows, which can be opened in several ways in Director. How you open a script window is important since it determines the type of script it will contain. A script window's type is indicated in its title bar. *(See pages 205–207 for a description of the five script types, and how to open the corresponding script windows)*

The Lingo instructions written in scripts need to conform to the language rules of Lingo. Lingo instructions are valid combinations of Lingo elements, which are introduced throughout this chapter in sample scripts. All Lingo elements are defined in Director's Lingo online help. Open it by choosing Scripting from the Help menu **(Figure 3)**, and selecting the Lingo category from the help window.

Example script 1

The following steps create a handler that causes the playback head to jump to frame 1 each time it reaches frame 5 as your movie is playing. The script that contains this handler is called a frame script since it is assigned to a frame in the script channel.

1. Choose Score from the Window menu.
2. Select the fifth frame in the script channel **(Figure 4)**.
3. Choose New Script from the Script pop-up menu in the score window to open a script window **(Figure 5)**.
4. In the script window that opens, type **go to frame 1** on the middle line **(Figure 6)**. The first and last lines are automatically provided.
5. Close the script window.
6. Choose Control Panel from the Window menu.
7. Rewind the movie to frame 1.
8. Click Play in the control panel. You can see the playback head looping between frames 1 and 5 in the score.

Analysis of Example script 1

You wrote a handler in a frame script that causes your movie to loop between frames 1 and 5. The first line of the handler **on exitFrame** tells Director to run the instructions in the body of the handler when the playback head exits the frame which contains the script, in this case, the fifth frame. The body of the handler holds the statement **go to frame 1**, which tells Director to move the playback head to frame 1, thus creating a loop in your movie. The **end** keyword is required at the last line of each handler.

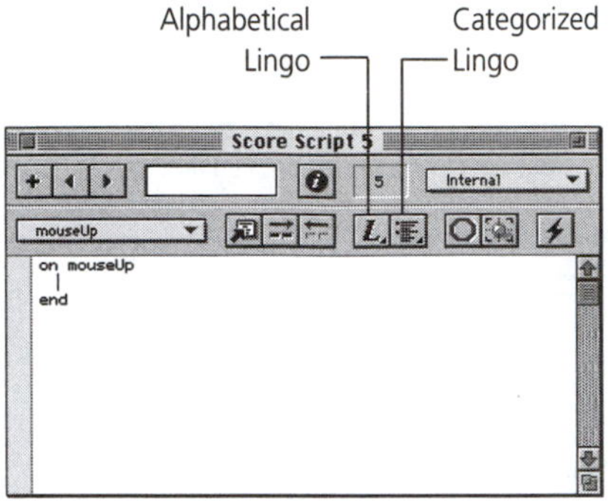

Figure 7. The **Alphabetical** and **Categorized** Lingo buttons allow you to insert Lingo elements automatically into your scripts.

To automatically insert Lingo elements into a script window:

The Alphabetical Lingo and Categorized Lingo buttons **(Figure 7)** in the script window allow you to select and insert Lingo elements into your script.

1. Click the Alphabetical Lingo button and select the Lingo element from the pop-up menu **(Figure 8)** that you wish to insert into your script at the cursor.

Or

2. Click the Categorized Lingo button and select the Lingo element by category from the pop-up menu **(Figure 9)** that you wish to insert into your script.

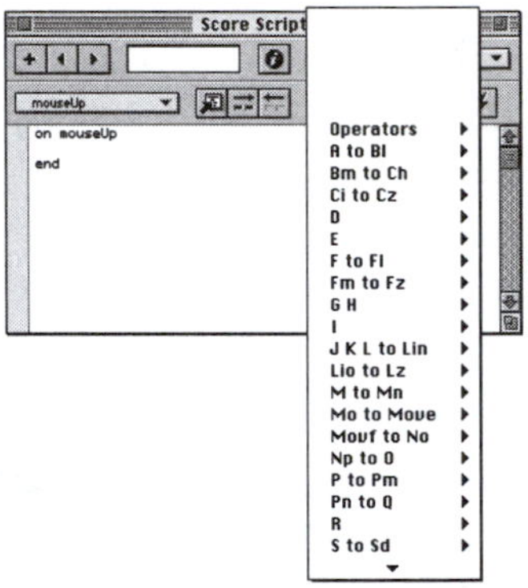

Figure 8. Click the **Alphabetical** Lingo button to select a Lingo element for insertion into your script.

✔ Tip

- Lingo is not case-sensitive. However, it is wise for the sake of readability to be consistent with case in your scripts. Follow the conventions used in the Lingo online help, as well as those provided in the example scripts throughout this chapter.

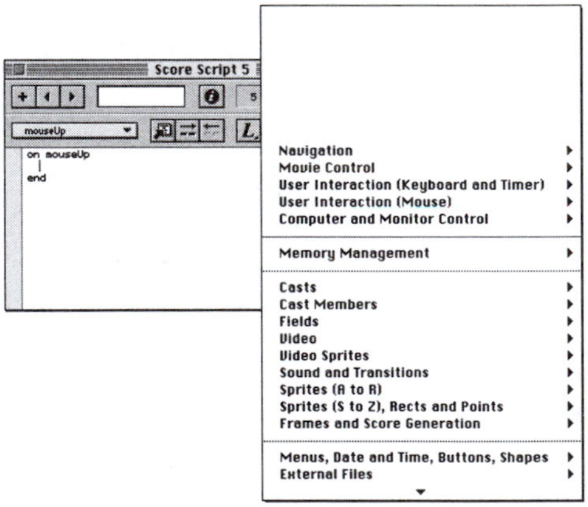

Figure 9. Click the **Categorized** Lingo button to select a Lingo element by category for insertion into your script.

Frame scripts are assigned to frames via the script channel.

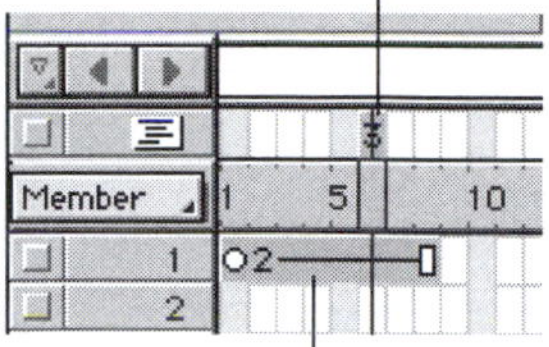

Sprite scripts are assigned to sprites.

Figure 10. Frame and sprite scripts are assigned in the score. They are also referred to as score scripts.

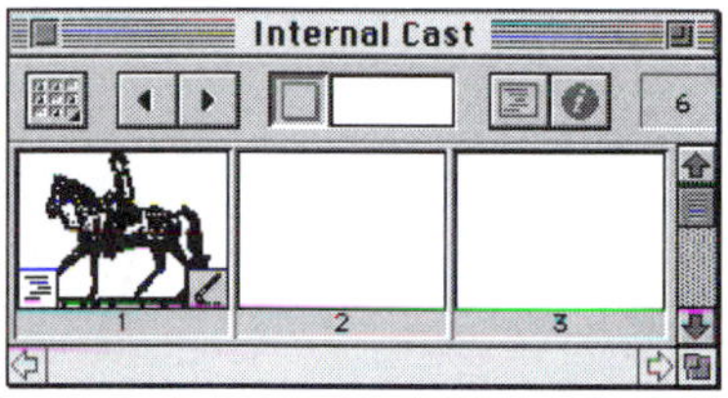

Figure 11. A cast member script is assigned to a cast member. A script symbol appears in the bottom-left corner of a cast member thumbnail when it has an assigned script.

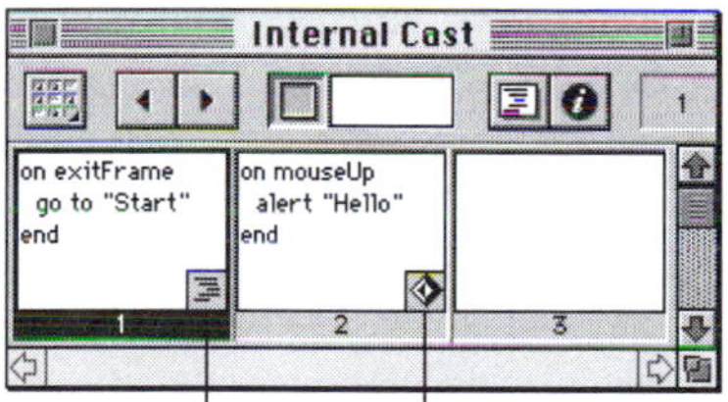

Movie script Score script

Figure 12. Movie, score, and parent scripts are themselves cast members and are stored in cast windows.

Script types

There are five script types in Director. These are sprite scripts, frame scripts, cast member scripts, movie scripts, and parent scripts (parent scripts are an advanced Lingo topic beyond the scope of this book). Sprite, cast member, and frame script types are described in detail on pages 209, 210, and 214 respectively.

A script type is determined by the object the script is assigned to in Director **(Figures 10–11)**. Sprite scripts are assigned to sprites, frame scripts are assigned to frames in the score's script channel, cast member scripts are assigned to cast members, and movie scripts are assigned to the entire movie—not to an individual object. Sprite and frame scripts are referred to as score scripts since they are both assigned in the score window.

Which script type you choose to write handlers in determines how accessible those handlers are to your movie. Handlers in a cast member script are available to be executed only when the corresponding cast member is clicked or receives input through the keyboard during playback. Likewise, handlers in a sprite script are available to be executed only when you click on the corresponding sprite, or the sprite receives input through the keyboard.

Handlers in a frame script are available to be executed only when Director is entering or exiting the frame where the script is assigned.

Handlers in movie scripts are the most accessible since they are available at anytime during playback.

All script types except cast member scripts are themselves cast members, and are stored in cast windows **(Figure 12)**.

To change a script's type to another script type:

You can change any movie, score, or parent script's type. You cannot change a cast member script's type.

1. Select the script in the cast window whose type you wish to change **(Figure 13)**.
2. Click the Cast Member Properties button in the cast window.
3. Click the Type pop-up menu in the Cast Member Properties dialog box **(Figure 14)**, and select a new type.

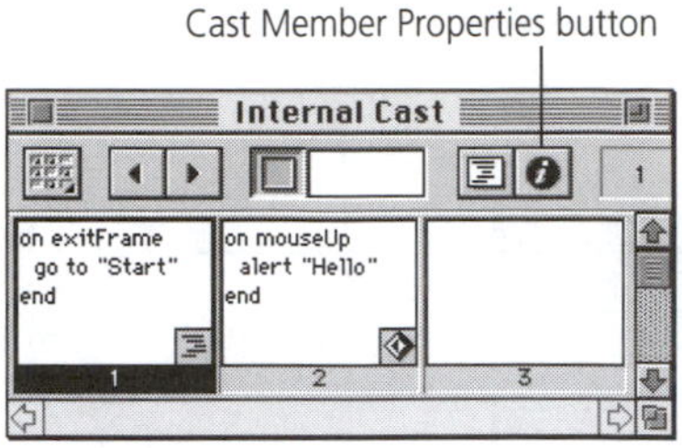

Figure 13. Select the script whose type you wish to change and click the **Cast Member Properties** button.

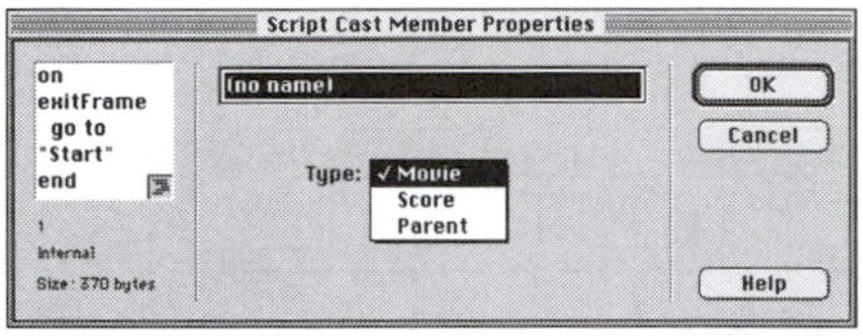

Figure 14. Click the **Type** pop-up menu in the **Cast Member Properties** dialog box and select a new type.

Script windows

Lingo scripts are edited in script windows. The title bar in a script window indicates the type of script being edited. A cast member script is edited in a script of a cast member window. Sprite and frame scripts are edited in score script windows (remember that they are classified as score scripts). And a movie script is edited in a movie script window. The only difference between script window types is how they are opened in Director. *(See below)*

To open a new score script window:

Sprite and frame scripts are created in score script windows.

1. Open the score window.
2. Select a sprite or a cell in the script channel.
3. Choose New from the Script pop-up menu in the score window **(Figure 15)**. A score script window appears.

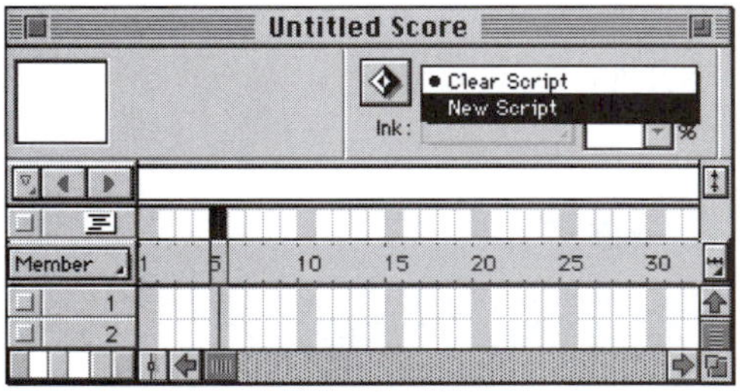

Figure 15. Choose **New Script** from the **Script** pop-up menu in the score window.

To open a cast member script window:

1. Open the cast window.
2. Select a cast member that you wish to attach a script to, or edit its existing script **(Figure 16)**. These are limited to graphical cast member types.

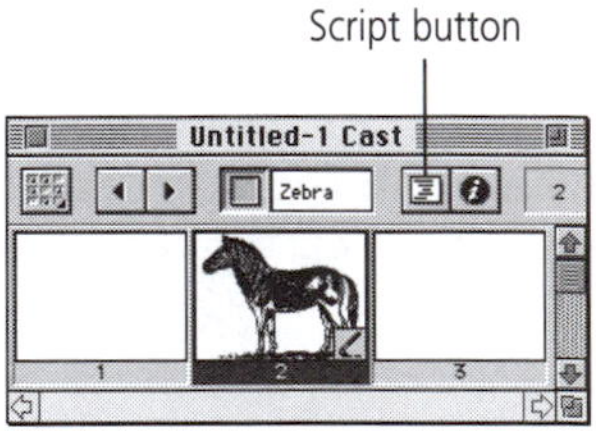

Figure 16. Open a cast member script window by selecting a cast member, then clicking the **Script** button.

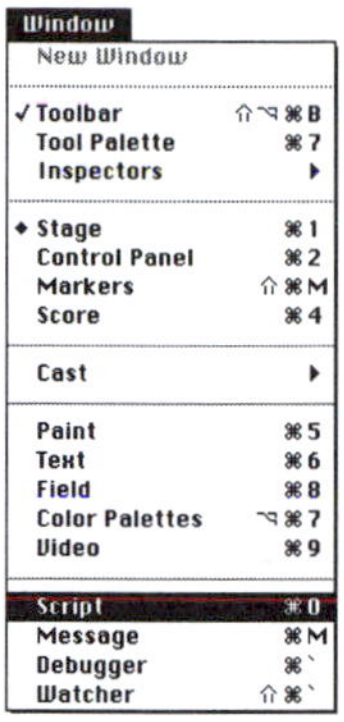

Figure 17. Choose **Script** from the **Window** menu.

3. Click the script button in the cast window to open the cast member script window. A cast member that has a script already attached to it displays a script symbol in the lower left corner of its thumbnail.

✔ **Tip**

■ You can also open a cast member script window by clicking the Script button in the cast member properties dialog box for a selected cast member.

To open a new movie script window:

1. Choose Script from the Window menu **(Figure 17)**.

Or

2. Click the New script button in any opened score, cast member, or movie script window **(Figure 18)**. *(See page 206 on opening score and cast member script windows.)*

New Script

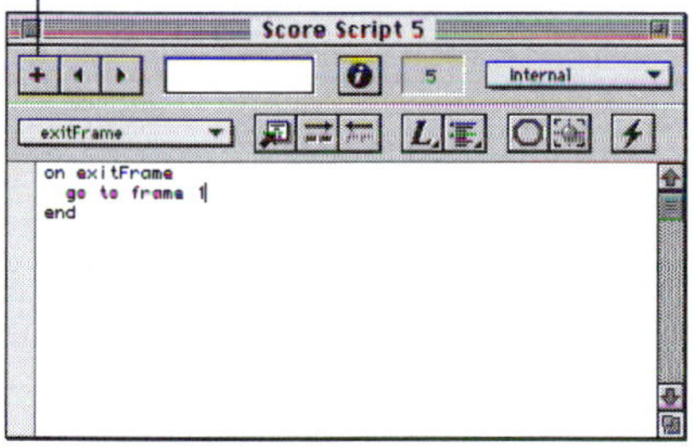

Figure 18. Click the **New Script** button in any opened score, cast member, or movie script window to open a new movie script window.

MAKING SPRITES AND CAST MEMBERS INTERACTIVE

A very direct way in which a user can interact with your movie is by clicking on sprites. What your movie does in response to such input is entirely up to you, the author. For instance, you may want to set up a sprite so that its size, color, or position changes when it is clicked. You can even change the cast member a sprite is based on when clicked, as you might want to do for a customized button that changes appearance when clicked.

This section explains how to write scripts that make sprites and cast members respond to mouse clicks. In the process, sprite and cast member script types are described in detail.

Example script 2

The following script sets up a sprite so that when it is clicked, your movie produces a beep sound. This is an example of a sprite script (defined on next page).

1. Choose New from the File menu and select Movie from the pop-up to create a new movie.
2. Create a cast member using one of the shape tools in the paint window.
3. Place the cast member starting in frame 1, channel 1 of the score.
4. With the sprite selected, choose New Script from the Script pop-up in the score.
5. In the script window that opens, type **beep** in the middle line of the script **(Figure 19)**. The other two lines are automatically provided.
6. Close the script window.
7. Choose Loop Playback under the Control menu **(Figure 20)** to set it.
8. Play back your movie. Notice that when you click within the sprite on the stage, you hear a beep.

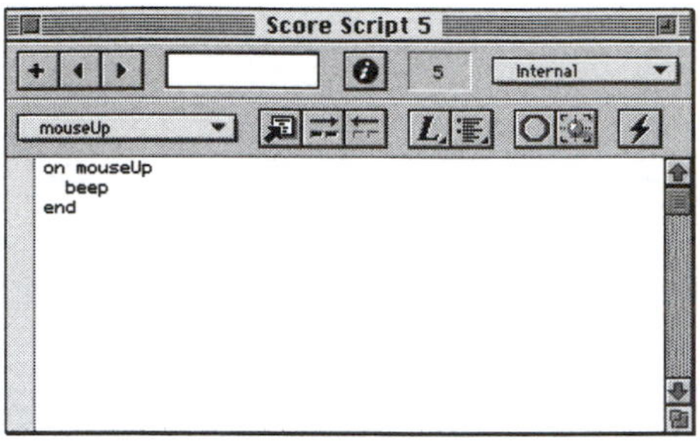

Figure 19. Example script 2.

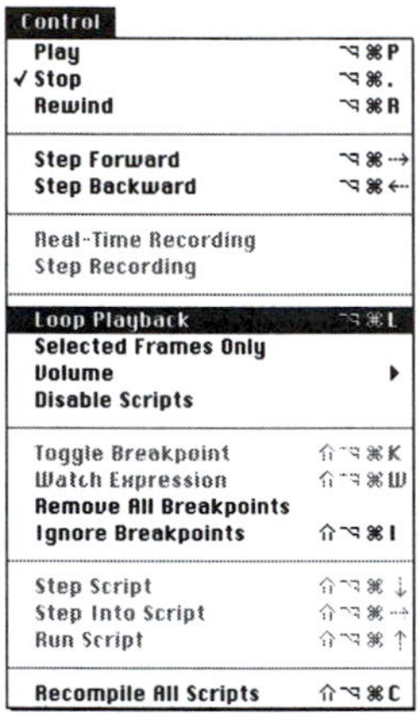

Figure 20. Choose **Loop Playback** from the **Control** menu.

Analysis of Example script 2

The first line **on mouseUp** tells Director that when the mouse is clicked and released over the sprite, the instructions in the body of the script should be executed, in this case, the **beep** command. You can change the first line to **on mouseDown** and the beep will be heard as soon as the mouse is clicked on the sprite.

This script is assigned to a single sprite. The script becomes activated only when the particular sprite in the particular range of frames is clicked. The script does not apply to other sprites based on the same cast member unless it has been assigned to them as well.

Figure 21. Sample score script.

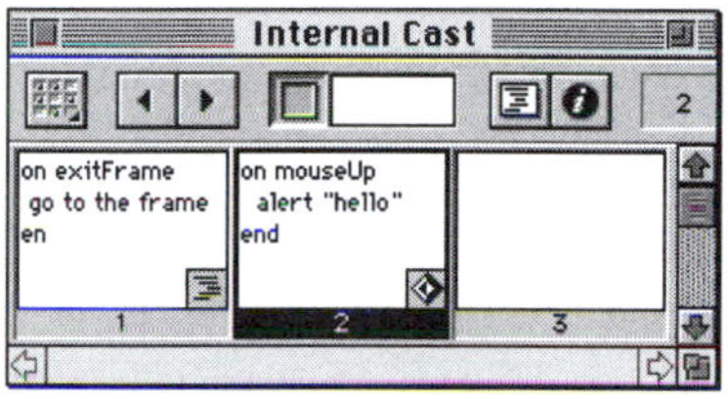

Figure 22. Select the desired score script cast member you wish to edit and click the script button in the cast window.

Behavior Inspector button

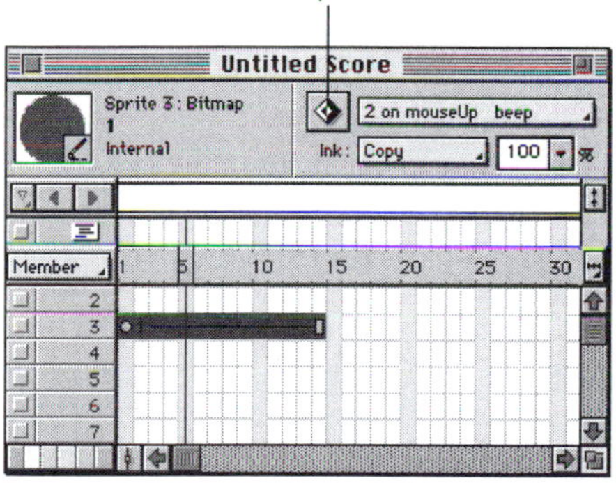

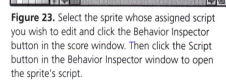

Figure 23. Select the sprite whose assigned script you wish to edit and click the Behavior Inspector button in the score window. Then click the Script button in the Behavior Inspector window to open the sprite's script.

Sprite Scripts

Sprite scripts are scripts that are assigned to sprites *(see page 46 for a definition of sprites)*. Sprite scripts are also referred to as **score** scripts **(Figure 21)**. Sprite scripts are created and edited in score script windows. Sprite scripts are themselves cast members, and are stored in cast windows. A sprite script is assigned to an entire sprite, and cannot be assigned to a partial range of frames in a sprite.

Sprite scripts require user input through the keyboard or mouse in order for their instructions to be executed. Generally, a user must click on a sprite during playback in order for its script to run.

A sprite script applies only to the particular sprite it has been assigned to. Other sprites which are based on the same cast member will not respond unless the script is assigned to them as well. Use a cast member script if you wish all sprites based on the same cast member to respond the same way. *(See page 210)*

By assigning different sprite scripts to sprites based on the same cast member throughout your movie, a single cast member, such as a button, can perform multiple functions depending on which frame during your movie it is clicked.

To edit an existing sprite script:

1. Open the cast window.
2. Select the desired score script cast member you wish to edit **(Figure 22)**. Click the script button in the cast window and the score script window appears.

✓ Tip

- You can open and edit a score script that is already assigned to a particular sprite by selecting the sprite in the score and clicking the Behavior Inspector button in the score **(Figure 23)**. Then click the Script button in the Behavior Inspector window.

To assign scripts to sprites:

1. Open the score window
2. Select the sprite you wish to assign a script to.
3. In the Script pop-up menu, choose an existing score script to assign to your selected sprite(s) **(Figure 24)**. Score scripts are listed in the pop-up menu by numbers, which correspond to their positions in the cast window, and by their first line of Lingo code.

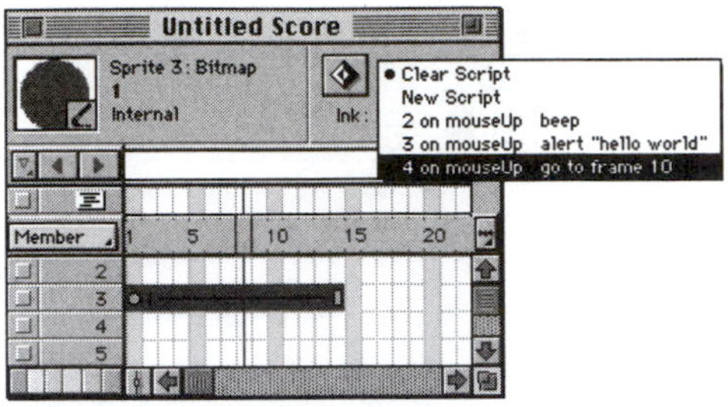

Figure 24. Choose an existing score script from the **Script** pop-up menu to assign to your selected sprite.

Cast member scripts

A cast member script is a script that is attached to a cast member **(Figure 25)**. The instructions in a cast member script are usually set up to execute when a sprite based on a cast member with an attached script is clicked on the stage.

The usefulness of a cast member script is that its Lingo instructions will run in any frame where the cast member is activated, unlike a sprite script. For example, you may want a button cast member to always produce the same response when clicked, regardless of which frame it is clicked in.

If a sprite has both a cast member script and a sprite script associated with it, the sprite script takes precedence. This is important to keep in mind when you are determining which type of script to use. If a cast member should always perform the same function throughout your movie, such as causing a jump to a certain movie segment, then use a cast member script. On the other hand, if your cast member responds differently depending on where it is activated in your movie, assign sprite scripts to the sprites based on the cast member.

Unlike movie, score, and parent scripts, cast member scripts are not cast members; instead, they are attached to cast members.

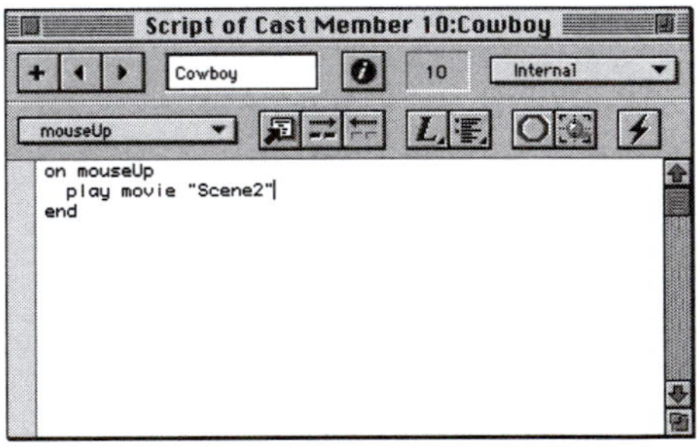

Figure 25. A sample cast member script.

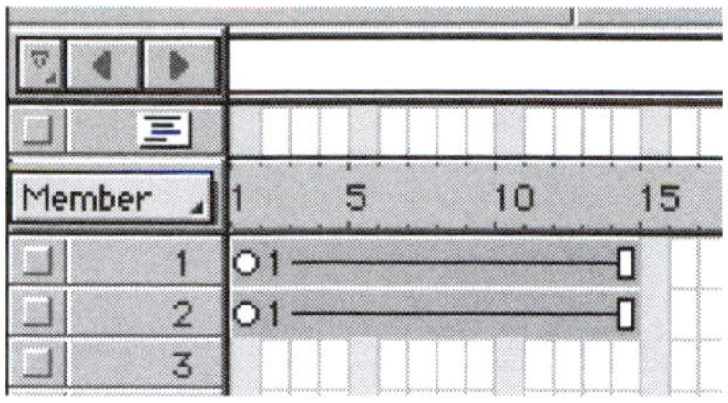

Figure 26. Create two sprites based on the same cast member by dragging the cast member into channels one and two in the score.

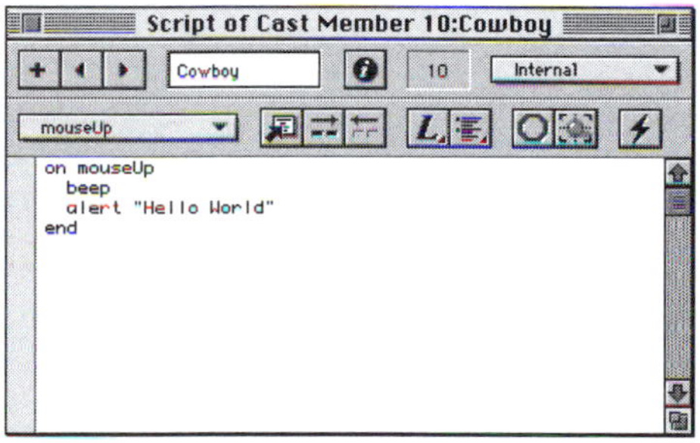

Figure 27. Example script 3.

Example script 3

The following script is very similar to the script in example 2, except that it is a cast member script. You can click any sprite based on the cast member in any frame, and this script will run and produce a beep sound and a short message.

1. Create two sprites based on the same cast member by dragging the cast member into channels one and two in the score **(Figure 26)**. Make sure that the sprites are in different locations on the stage.
2. Open the cast window and select the cast member in step 1.
3. Click the Script button at the top of the cast window.
4. In the script window that opens, type **beep** in the middle line of the script. Type **alert "Hello World"** on the line beneath it so that your script is identical to the one in **Figure 27**. The first and last lines are provided automatically.
5. Close the script window.
6. Choose Loop Playback under the Control menu to set it.
7. Play back your movie. Notice that when you click either sprite based on the same cast member, you hear a beep and see the message "Hello World".

Analysis of Example script 3

You created a cast member script and attached it to a cast member. The first line **on mouseUp** tells Director that when the mouse is clicked and released over the cast member, the instructions in the cast member script's mouseUp handler should be executed, in this case, the **beep** command, and **alert** command. The **alert** command prints the message Hello World to the screen.

Example Script 3

NAVIGATION

You can offer your movie viewers the choice of being able to jump to various segments of your movie while it is being played—they are not limited to watching from start to finish. This is accomplished by writing scripts that move the playback head to different frames in a movie. These scripts are typically set up to respond to user input, such as clicking the mouse on a particular sprite (such as a button), or pressing a certain key. This section describes steps for writing scripts for very common situations involving navigation, including scripts for pausing a movie. In the process, frame scripts are described in detail, as well as some additional language elements of Lingo.

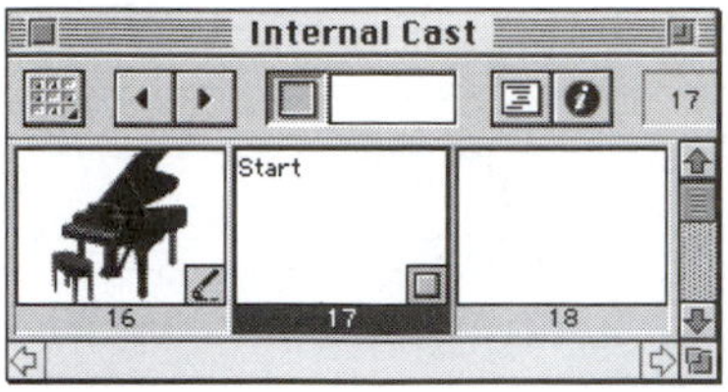

Figure 28. Select the cast member to which you will attach a script.

Example script 4

The following steps create an interactive cast member, which causes your movie to jump to a new frame when it is clicked.

1. Open the cast window and select a cast member that appears in your movie **(Figures 28)**.
2. Click the Script button at the top of the cast window. A script window appears.
3. On the middle line of this script, type **go to frame number (Figure 29)**. In the **number** field, enter the actual frame number that you wish the playback head to jump to (e.g. **go to frame 57**).
4. Close the script window to enter the script. When you play back your movie, clicking this cast member whenever it appears on the stage causes Director to jump to the frame you specified in the script.

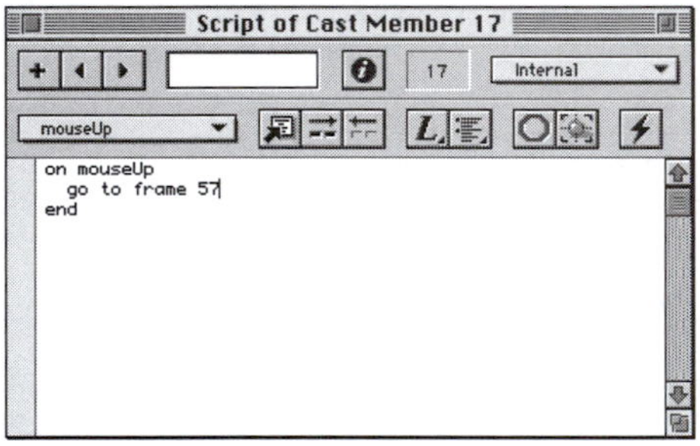

Figure 29. Example script 4.

Figure 30. Select a sprite to which you will assign a score script.

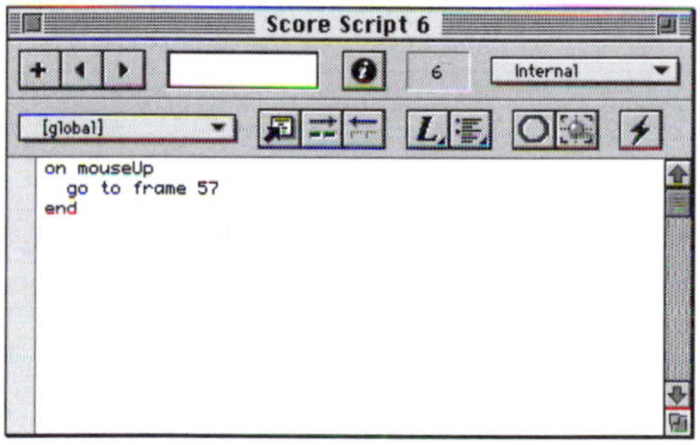

Figure 31. Example script 5.

Analysis of Example script 4

You created a cast member script. The first line of the script **on mouseup** instructs Director that whenever the mouse is pressed and released on this cast member, this mouseUp handler should be executed. In this case, the result is that the **go to** command is executed, which causes the playback head to jump to the specified frame number.

Example script 5

The following steps create an interactive sprite that causes your movie to jump to a new frame when it is clicked. This is similar to example script 4, except that it applies to a single sprite.

1. Open the score window.
2. Select the sprite that you wish to assign this score script to (remember a sprite script is a type of score script) **(Figure 30)**.
3. Choose New from the Script pop-up menu in the score. The lines **on mouseup** and **end** automatically appear in the script **(Figure 31)**.
4. On the middle line of this script, type **go to frame number**. In the **number** field, enter the actual frame number that you wish the playback head to jump to (e.g. **go to frame 57**). Don't change the rest of the script.
5. Close the script window to enter the script. To activate this script, click this specific sprite during your movie.

Frame scripts

Frame scripts are scripts which are assigned to cells in the script channel of Director's score. Unlike sprite and cast member scripts, frame scripts don't require user input to be activated. Frame scripts are generally used when you want Lingo instructions to be available for activation in a certain frame or range of frames. A frame script handler is executed when the playback head is in the frame where the script is assigned, and the appropriate message is sent to trigger the handler. *(See page 219 for an explanation of messages)*

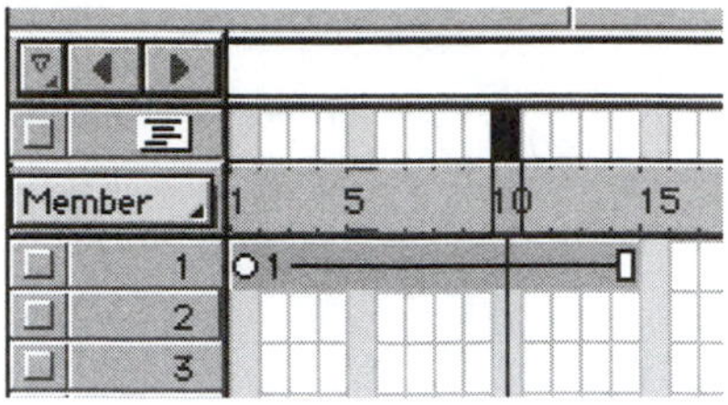

Figure 32. Select the frame in the script channel where you wish to set a pause for your movie.

Example script 6

The following steps create a frame script which causes your movie to pause in a specific frame during playback.

1. Open the score window and select the frame in the script channel where you wish your movie to pause **(Figure 32)**.
2. Choose New from the Script pop-up menu in the score. A script window appears with the text **on exitFrame** and **end** already in place.
3. Type **go to the frame (Figure 33)**.
4. Close the script window.

Figure 33. Example script 6.

✔ Tip

- You can create a loop in your movie by typing **go to frame number** in step 3 above, where **number** refers to a frame number that precedes the current frame. During playback, when Director reaches the frame with this frame script, your movie jumps back to the specified frame and will start looping within this movie segment.

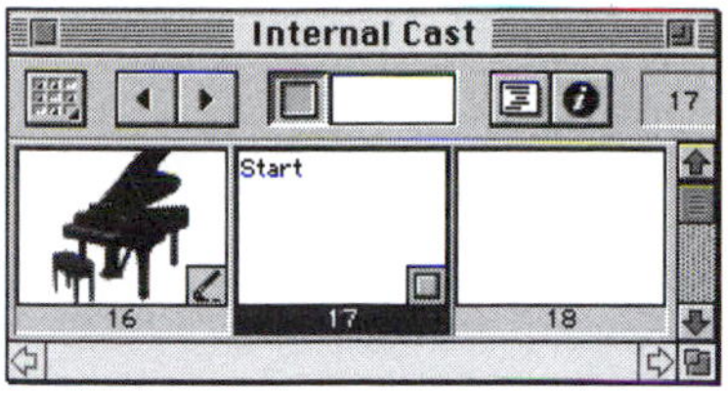

Figure 34. Select the cast member to which you will attach a script.

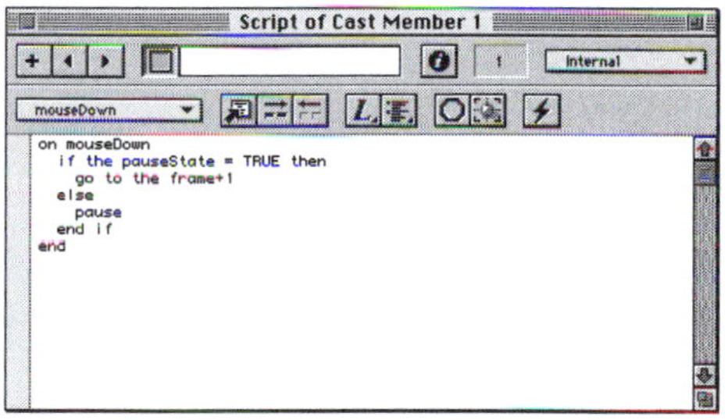

Figure 35. Example script 7.

Analysis of example script 6

You created a frame script which causes your movie to pause in the frame where you assigned the script. During playback, when Director reaches this frame, the Lingo handler **on exitFrame** tells Director to run the body of the script when the playback head exits the frame (the Lingo handler **on enterFrame** would cause the script to run at the start of the frame). In this case the **go to the frame** command is executed which tells Director to stay in the current frame. Your movie will remain paused until you stop the movie, or another script becomes activated that moves the playback head to a new frame. Such a script could be attached to a sprite in this frame, which causes the movie to jump to a new frame when the sprite is clicked.

Example script 7

The following steps create an interactive cast member, which functions as a pause button. When the cast member is clicked, the movie pauses. When the cast member is clicked again, the movie resumes play.

1. Open the cast window and select a cast member that appears in your movie **(Figure 34)**.
2. Click the Script button at the top of the cast window.
3. Type in this script **(Figure 35)**.

```
on mouseDown
 if the pauseState = TRUE then
  go to the frame+1
 else
  pause
 end if
end
```

4. Close the script window to enter the script.

Analysis of example script 7

You wrote a cast member script. The first line **on mouseDown** causes Director to execute this handler whenever the cast member is clicked. The next line **If the pauseState = TRUE then go to frame+1** checks to see if the movie is currently paused. If it is paused, the **go to frame+1** command is executed and the movie resumes play. If the movie is not paused, then the command after the **else** statement is executed, which is **pause**.

PauseState is a Lingo function that returns the **TRUE** value when the movie is paused, and **FALSE** when it is not.

The If-then structure evaluates a statement, and then acts in one of two ways. If the statement is true, the command after **then** is executed. If the statement is false, the command after the **else** is executed (look up the **If** keyword entry in the Lingo online help for more details on the if-then structure).

To use the go to command to jump to a frame relative to the current frame:

You can use the Lingo **go to** command to jump to a frame that is a certain number of frames before or after the current frame. To jump to a frame that lies before the current frame, include the statement **go to the frame -x** in your handler **(Figure 36)**, where **x** is the number of frames before the current frame that you wish to jump to. Similarly, to jump to a frame after the current frame, include the statement **go to the frame +x**.

Figure 36. When this script handler is activated, it causes your movie to jump to the frame which is five frames before the current frame.

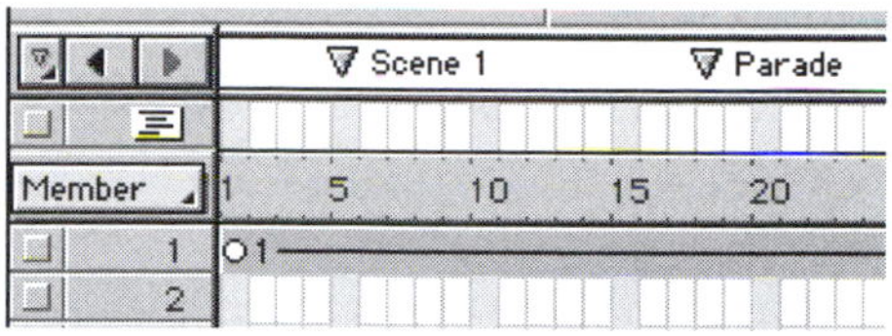

Figure 37. Markers are used to label different segments of your movie.

Figure 38. This Lingo statement go to "Parade" jumps to the segment of the movie labeled Parade.

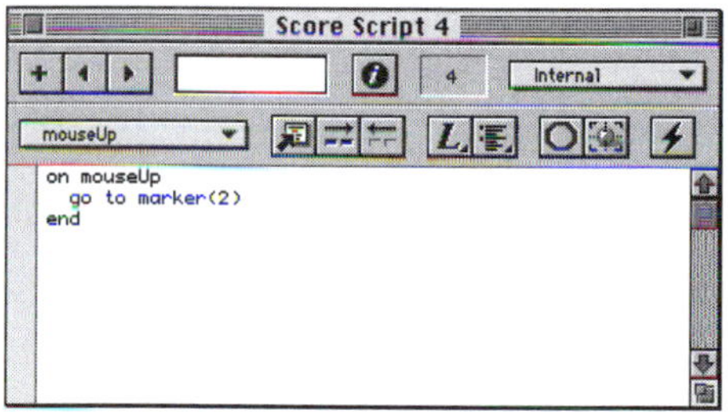

Figure 39. The Lingo statement go to marker(n) jumps to the nth marker ahead of the current frame.

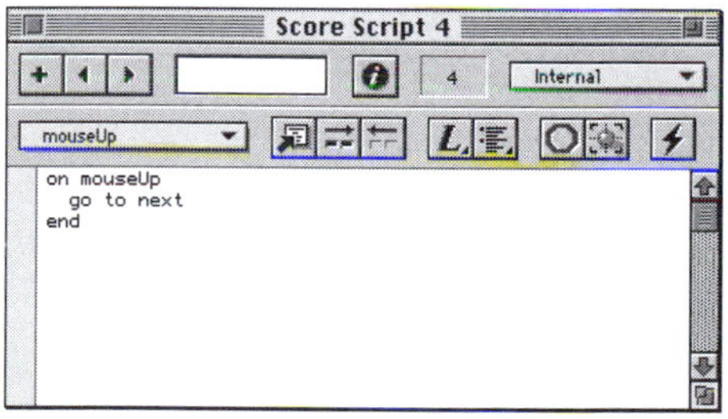

Figure 40. The Lingo statement go to next jumps to the next marker after the current frame.

To use the go to command to jump to a marker label:

You can use the **go to** command to move the playback head to a specific marker instead of to a frame number. Markers are used to label different segments of your movie **(Figure 37)**. *(See page 66 in the Score and Sprite Basics chapter for more information on creating markers)*

The advantage of using markers rather than frame numbers with the **go to** command is that frame numbers often change while you're editing in the score, whereas a marker name marks a specific movie segment independently of any frame number.

Use the **go to** command to jump to a marker by typing **go to "marker"** in your handler, where **marker** is the name of the marker you wish to jump to **(Figure 38)**.

To jump to a marker relative to the current frame:

Lingo allows you to refer to a marker in relation to how many markers it is ahead of or behind the current frame. To jump to the nth marker ahead of the current frame, include the statement **go to marker(n)** in your script, such as **go to marker(2) (Figure 39)**. This tells Director to jump to the second marker after the current frame. Similarly, to jump to the nth marker before the current frame, include the same statement, but make **n** a negative number. You can also jump to the next marker after the current frame by using the statement **go to next (Figure 40)**. To jump to the marker immediately before the current frame, use **go to previous**. These commands are equivalent to **go to marker(1)**, and **go to marker(-1)**.

Branching

In Director, **branching** is the process where the playback head jumps to a certain movie segment, plays that segment, and then returns back to the original frame that caused the jump. Suppose your movie offers a tour of different restaurants. Let's say that this movie starts with a main menu of button sprites, each corresponding to a specific restaurant you can view. When you click a button, Director jumps to a particular restaurant segment, plays that segment, and returns back to the main menu. This branching is best accomplished by using the Lingo branch command **play** in your scripts.

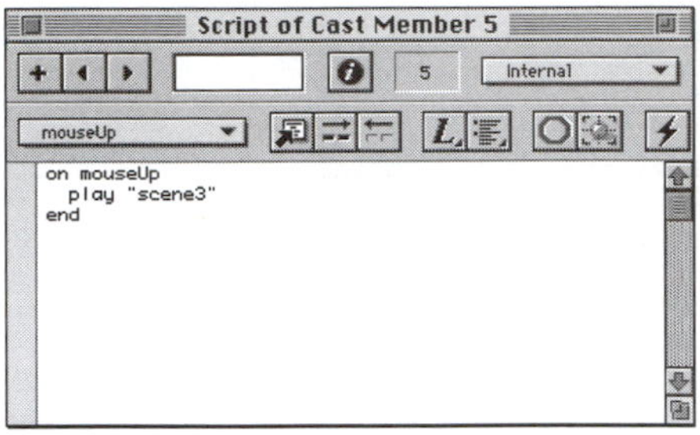

Figure 41. Type play "marker", and include the marker name you wish to branch to.

To write a script that branches to a marker or frame:

1. Open a script window for the script where a branch should take place.
2. Type **play "marker"**, and include the marker name you wish to branch to **(Figure 41)**. You can also type **play frame number** where **number** is the frame to branch to.
3. At the end of the movie segment that is branched to in step 2, place the command **play done** in the appropriate script. This command returns the playback head back to the original frame from where the branch occurred **(Figure 42)**.

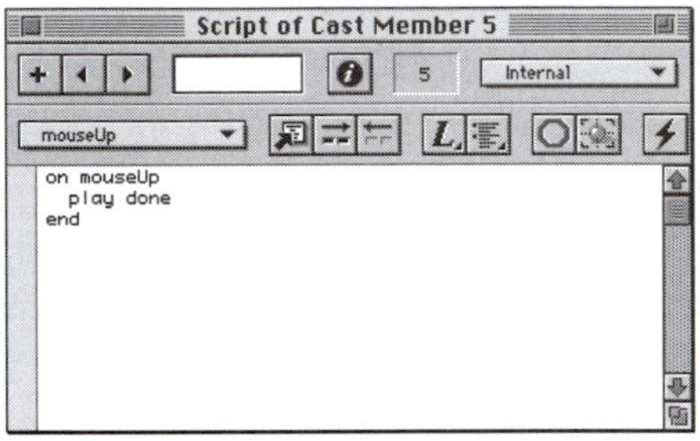

Figure 42. The play done command returns the playback head to the frame where the branch occurred.

✔ Tip

- You can branch to a different movie by using the Lingo statement **play movie "moviename"**, where **moviename** is the name of the movie file **(Figure 43)**. To branch to a specific frame in a different movie, use the statement **play frame "frame" of movie "moviename"**, like in **(Figure 44)**.

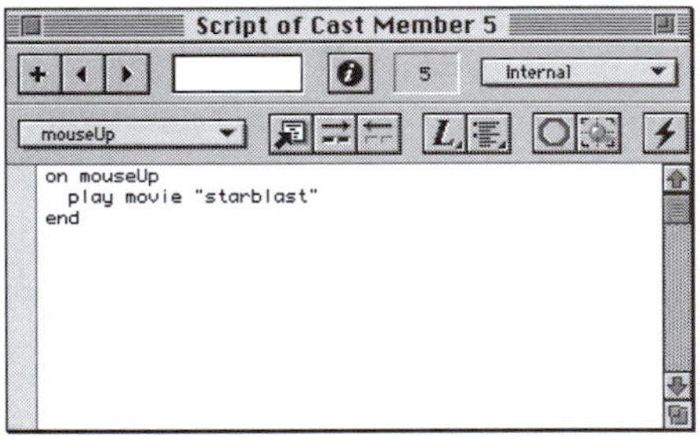

Figure 43. The play movie command branches to a different movie.

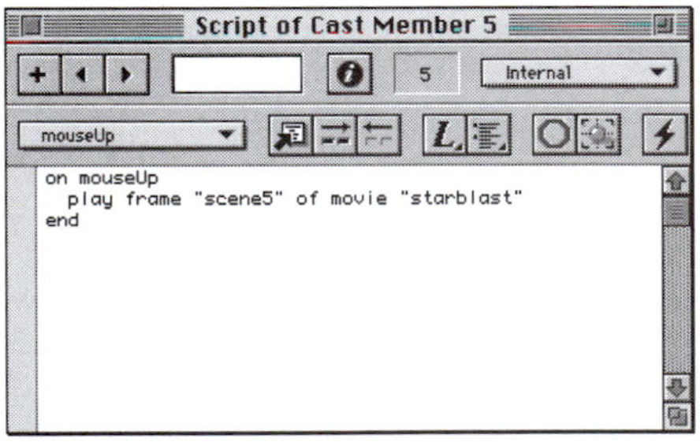

Figure 44. This script branches to a specific frame in a different movie.

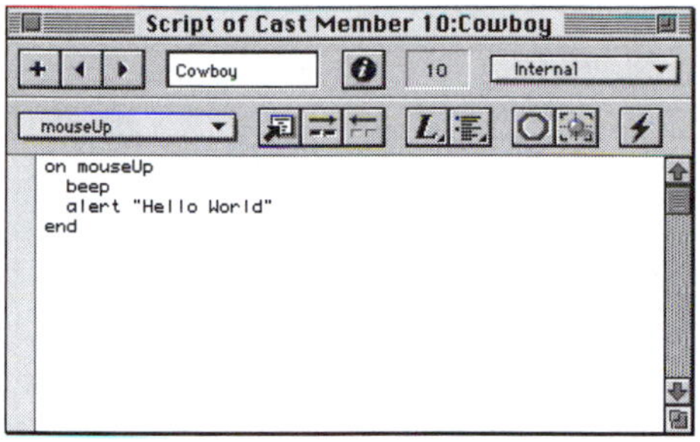

Figure 45. This script contains a mouseUp handler.

Event	Message
A window is activated	activateWindow
A window is closed	closeWindow
A window is deactivated	deactivateWindow
Playback head enters current frame	enterFrame
Playback head exits the current frame	exitFrame
No event occurred	idle
A key is pressed	keyDown
A key is released	KeyUp
Mouse button pressed	mouseDown
Mouse button released	mouseUp
Pointer entered sprite's region	mouseEnter
Pointer left sprite's region	mouseLeave
Pointer within sprite's region	mouseWithin
Message received from script or behavior	newEvent
Playback head has left previous frame but has not entered next frame	prepareFrame
Movie starts playing	startMovie
Movie stops playing	stopMovie
A window is maximized or minimized	zoomWindow

Figure 46. These are built-in events that can occur while a movie is playing, and the corresponding messages that they send. You can write handlers which respond to any of these messages. You can also create handlers which respond to messages that you define (these types of handlers operate very much like functions. This topic is beyond the scope of this book.)

HANDLERS, MESSAGES, AND EVENTS

Handlers

A Lingo script is composed of one or more handlers. A handler is a set of Lingo instructions that is activated by a specific event during the playback of your movie (technically, by a message which is sent in response to an event, *see section below*).

A handler always starts with the word **on** followed by the name of the message the handler should respond to. For example:

```
on mouseUp
  beep
  alert "Hello World"
end
```

This handler **(Figure 45)** responds to the mouseUp message, which is sent when the mouse button is released. The body of the handler script, which is the indented part, contains the commands which are executed when the handler is triggered by the matching message. These commands are run in the order they are listed.

Handlers can be stored in any of the five script types discussed on page 205. Which script type you place a handler or handlers in is important since it directly affects when those handlers are available to receive messages for activation. *(See How handlers receive messages, page 220)*

What are events and messages?

Events are the actions that occur in your movie that cause messages to be sent. Handlers in turn respond to these messages. Director features a set of built-in events that can occur while a movie is playing **(Figure 46)**. About half of these events are caused by inputs from the user, such as clicking the mouse button, pressing a key, activating a window, or closing a window. The other half of the built-in events are actions that occur in your movie which don't directly relate to user input, but are nonetheless events that you may want a handler to respond to. Such events include a frame being entered or exited, and the movie being started or stopped. For example, when the following handler **(Figure 47)** receives the exitFrame message, it causes the movie to jump to frame 1.

```
On exitFrame
  go to frame 1
end
```

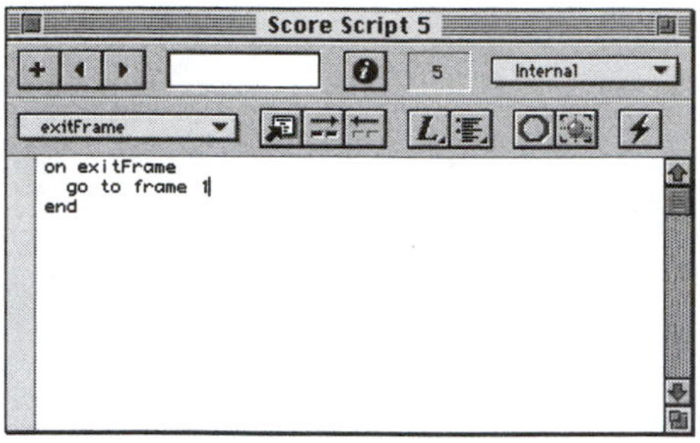

Figure 47. This script contains a handler which responds to the exitFrame message.

How do handlers receive messages?

When an event occurs, its corresponding message is sent in a specific order to a group of objects in Director. Director checks to see if any one of these objects has a script attached to it which contains a matching handler. If so, that handler is executed.

The objects that messages are sent to in general are a primary event handler (defined on page 222), an activated sprite, an activated sprite's cast member, the current frame, and the movie. Which of these objects a message is sent to and in what order depends on the type of message.

Generally, when an object receives a message and its script contains a matching handler for that message, this handler is executed, and the message does not continue on to other objects (the exception to this is the primary event handler, which passes a message along).

The order in which Director sends messages to objects

MouseUp, **mouseDown**, **keyUp**, and **keyDown** messages are sent to objects in one of two possible orders. If the mouse pointer is positioned over a sprite (includ-

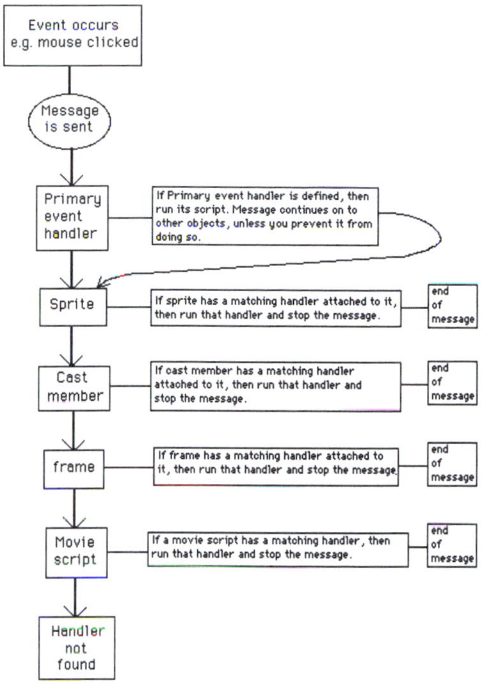

Figure 48. This chart shows where mouseUp, mouseDown, keyUp, and keyDown messages get sent when the mouse pointer is positioned over a sprite.

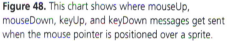

ing field sprites) when any one of these messages is generated, then the message is sent to objects in the following order: **(Figure 48)** primary event handler, activated sprite, the activated sprite's cast member, the current frame, and the movie (which can have many movie scripts, all of which are checked for a matching handler). If the mouse pointer is not positioned over a sprite when the message is generated, then the order is as follows: primary event handler, the current frame, and movie scripts.

Both the **enterFrame** and **exitFrame** messages are sent to the current frame (technically, to the script channel in the current frame), and then to movie scripts. If the current frame has a script assigned to it that contains a handler for one of these messages, that handler is executed.

The **idle**, **activateWindow**, **closeWindow**, **deactivateWindow**, **startMovie**, **stopMovie**, and **zoomWindow** messages are directly sent to movie scripts.

Where to place handlers

Understanding the order in which messages are sent to objects is important, since it will affect where you place your handlers. For example, if a mouseUp message is generated when the mouse pointer is positioned over a sprite, the message first goes to the sprite script before it goes to the cast member script. Therefore, if the sprite and cast member both have handlers attached to them, the sprite handler takes precedence. You can use this to your advantage. For example, you can have many sprites in your movie all based on the same cast member, yet each can perform a different function when clicked.

Primary event handlers

There are four events for which you can define a primary event handler. The messages that correspond to these events are mouseUp, mouseDown, keyDown, and timeOut. Primary event handlers provide the first opportunity for your movie to respond to these messages.

You need to define a primary event handler in order for it to respond to one of these messages. Following are the Lingo terms you use in defining a primary event handler, and the messages they correspond to:

Term	Message
keydownScript	keyDown
mousedownScript	mouseDown
mouseupScript	mouseUp
timeoutScript	timeOut

The following handler sets up a primary event handler for a mouseDown message:

```
on startMovie
set the mousedownScript to "go to frame 5"
end
```

This handler would be placed in a movie script **(Figure 49)**, since the startMovie message is sent exclusively to these types of scripts. Movie scripts are a good place to initialize variables and properties.

After this script is executed, anytime a mouseDown message occurs, the playback head will jump to frame 5, regardless of what frame the mouse click occurs in, or where the mouse pointer is positioned.

To turn off the primary event handler for the mouseDown message, you would use the following Lingo statement:

```
set the mousedownScript to EMPTY
```

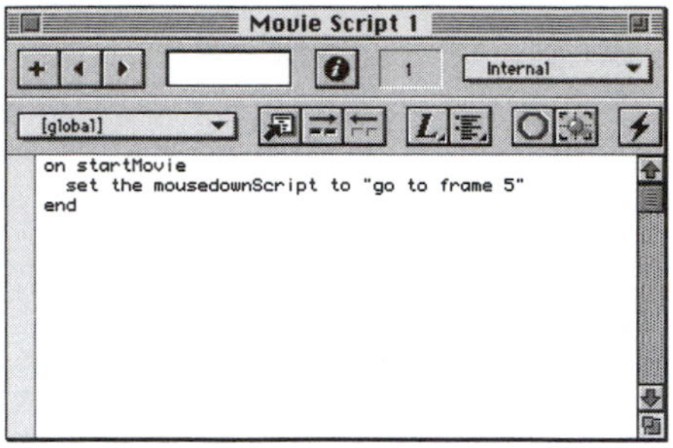

Figure 49. This script defines a primary event handler for a mouseDown message.

Figure 1. Install Xtras by placing them into the Xtras folder in the Director application folder, or in the System:Macromedia:Xtras folder.

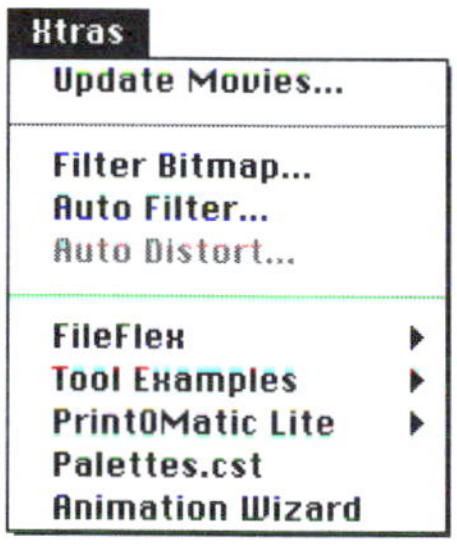

Figure 2. The **Filter Bitmap** and **Auto Filter** commands under the **Xtras** menu are used to apply image filters to bitmapped images.

Director's open architecture design allows you to incorporate third party software modules called Xtras, which extend Director's functionality in many different ways. For example, you can add new cast member types, expand Director's built-in set of transition effects, and even add new authoring tools—all by installing Xtras in Director.

There are five types of Xtras in Director: image filters, transition Xtras, cast member Xtras, Lingo Xtras, and tool Xtras. Each is described in this chapter.

To install an Xtra:

An Xtra (any type) is installed into Director for Macintosh by placing its file into one of two possible locations: the Xtras folder in the Director application folder **(Figure 1)**, or the Xtras folder in the Macromedia folder, which should be in your System folder. You can place the Xtra file up to five layers deep in these locations. Relaunch Director in order for it to recognize the newly installed Xtra. An Xtra file can contain more than one Xtra.

In Director 6, Xtras can be embedded into a projector file, so you no longer need to provide the Xtras separately. *(See pages 195 and 199 in the Create a Projector chapter for details on embedding Xtras into a projector)*

Image filters

You can use image filters from Adobe Photoshop or Premiere to modify your bitmapped cast members in Director. These filters must be installed as Xtras. Image filter Xtras are accessed using the Filter Bitmap and Auto Filter commands **(Figure 2)** under the Xtras menu. *(See page 133 in the Paint Window chapter on using image filters)*

Transition Xtras

You can add new transitions to the standard choices available in Director's Frame Properties:Transition dialog box by installing transition Xtras. When you apply a transition Xtra in the transition channel, the transition Xtra becomes a transition Xtra cast member in a cast window **(Figure 3)**. *(See page 188 in the Setting Scene Transitions chapter on how to set an Xtra transition)*

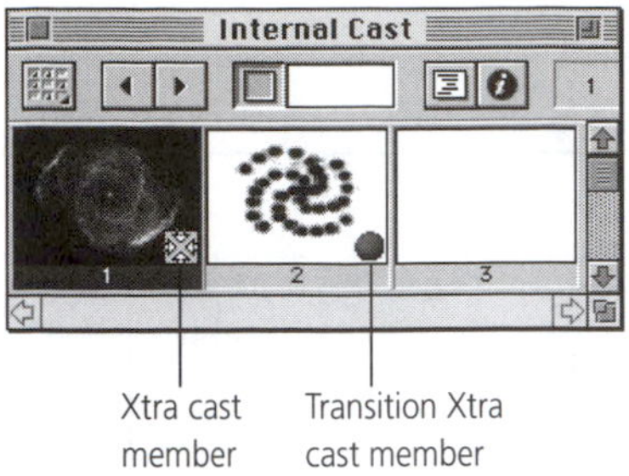

Figure 3. Xtra and transition Xtra cast member types are shown.

Xtra cast members

Xtra cast members can be many different objects. They don't have to be a specific media type like a bitmap or text. Their type can be quite abstract. For example, an Xtra cast member can be an interactive digital video, a database, or even a utility program that aids you in generating cast members, like the Auto Distort command.

When Xtra cast members are installed, they appear under the Insert menu **(Figure 4)**. When you choose an Xtra cast member from the Insert menu, it is placed into a cast window from where it can be assigned to the score.

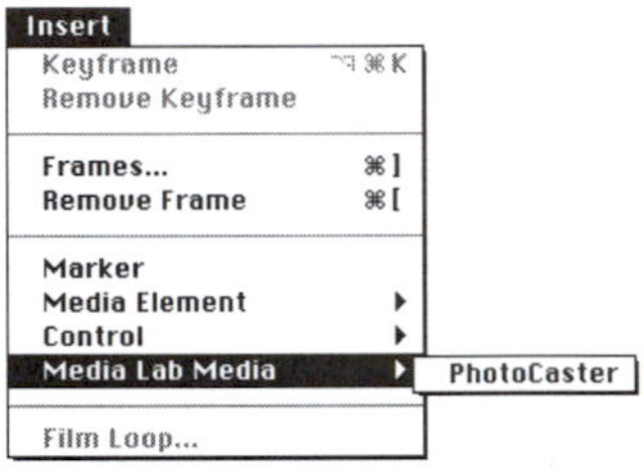

Figure 4. Insert an Xtra cast member into a cast window by choosing it from the Insert menu.

An Xtra cast member can have its own custom Options dialog box and About box. If these are defined, they are accessed from the Xtra Cast Member Properties dialog box **(Figure 5)**. Open it by selecting the Xtra cast member in the cast window and clicking the Cast Member Properties button.

An Xtra cast member can also have its own media editor, which you can open by double-clicking the Xtra in the cast window.

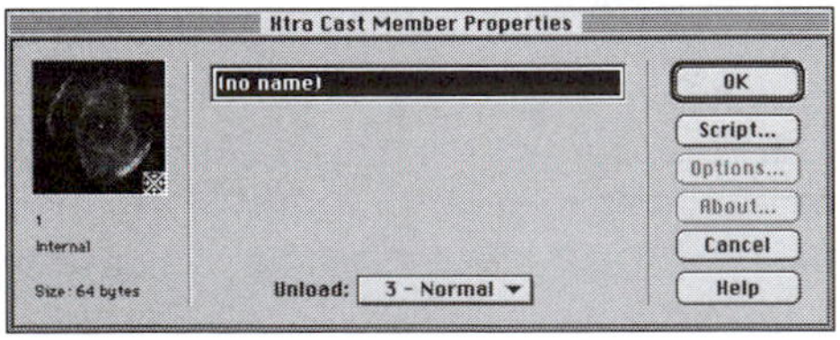

Figure 5. An Xtra cast member may have a custom **Options** dialog box and an **About** box, both of which are opened from the **Xtra Cast Member Properties** dialog box.

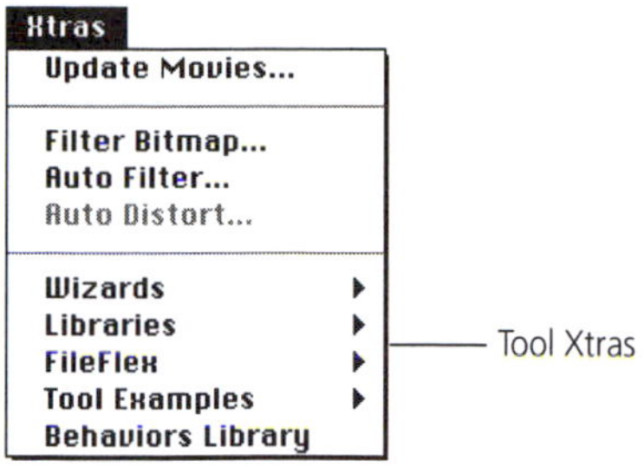

Figure 6. Tool Xtras are located under the **Xtras** menu.

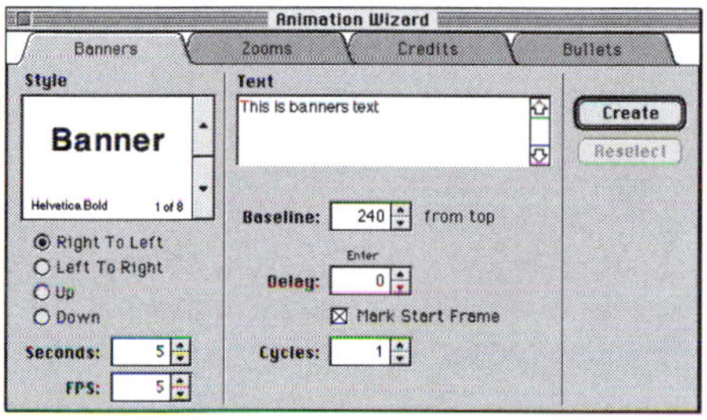

Figure 7. Animation Wizard is an example of a tool Xtra.

Lingo Xtras

Lingo Xtras add new language elements to Lingo—Director's scripting language. By adding Lingo Xtras, you expand the power of Lingo without having to wait for the next release of Director. You can open Lingo Xtras by using the Lingo openXlib command. *(See the online Lingo help for this entry)*

Tool Xtras

Tool Xtras are software modules that aid in the authoring of a Director movie. When you install a tool Xtra, it is accessible from the Xtras menu **(Figure 6)**. Director 6 comes with several preinstalled Tool Xtras. One is called Animation Wizard.

Animation Wizard **(Figure 7)** allows you to quickly create moving banners, zoom effects, scrolling credits, and bullets. Animation Wizard inserts these effects directly into your score, saving you a lot of time. Open Animation Wizard by choosing it from the Xtras menu.

Developing Xtras

Xtras are usually written in C language. If you are interested in creating Xtras, see the Xtras Developer Kit (XDK) on your Director 6 CD-ROM.

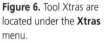

DRAG AND DROP BEHAVIORS 18

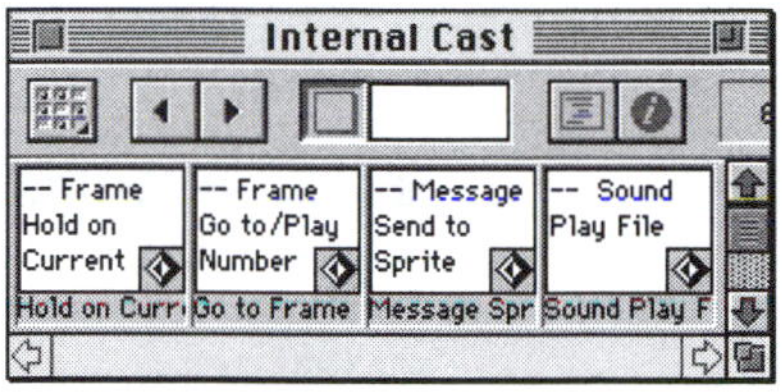

Figure 1. Behaviors are special cast members which you can assign to sprites and frames to make them perform certain actions in response to specific events.

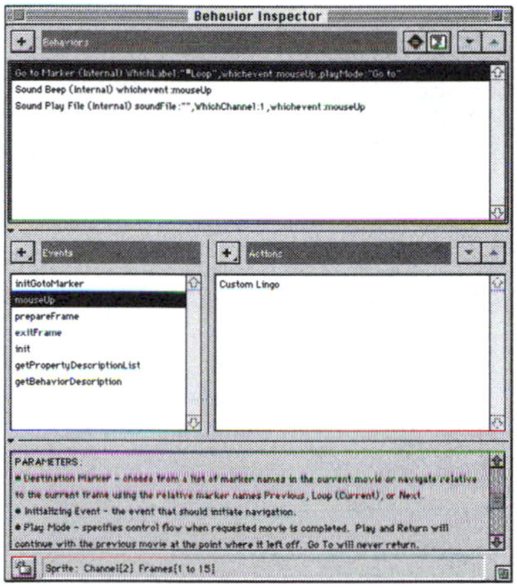

Figure 2. Use the **Behavior Inspector** window to create behaviors or modify existing ones.

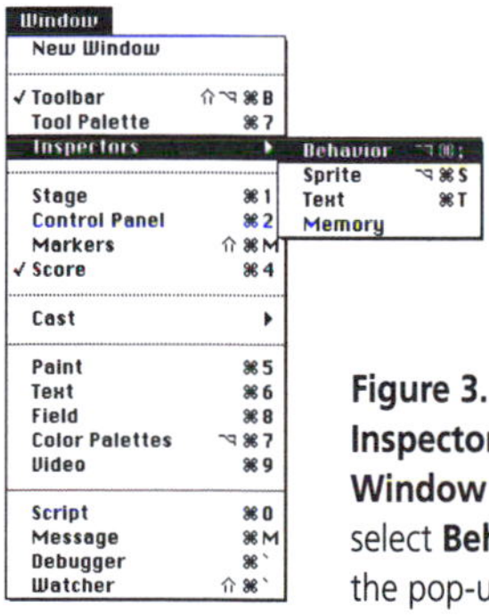

Figure 3. Choose **Inspectors** from the **Window** menu and select **Behavior** from the pop-up menu.

You can use Director's drag and drop behaviors to add interactive features to your movies without having to write Lingo scripts.

Behaviors are special cast members **(Figure 1)** which you assign to sprites and frames to make them perform certain actions in response to specific events. For example, you can assign a built-in behavior called Go to Frame to a sprite, in order to make that sprite change the playback head position in your movie when clicked.

Director 6 includes a library of built-in behaviors that appear in their own cast window. These behaviors can be literally dragged and dropped onto sprites and frames in the score to add interactive controls and Lingo logic to your movie without ever having to open a script window.

You can create your own behaviors as well as modify existing ones by using the Behavior Inspector window **(Figure 2)**. Open it by choosing Inspectors from the Window menu and Behavior from the pop-up menu **(Figure 3)**.

To open the built-in Behavior library:

You open the behavior library by choosing Behavior Library from the Xtras menu **(Figure 4)**. A set of built-in behaviors appears in its own cast **(Figure 5).**

The behaviors in this library perform a wide range of functions. For instance, the Go to Maker behavior can be used to cause your movie to jump to a designated marker label in the score when a specific event occurs, such as a sprite click. The Sound Play File behavior can be used to play an external sound file when a specific event occurs.

Figure 4. Choose **Behavior Library** from the **Xtras** menu.

ASSIGNING BEHAVIORS

Behaviors are assigned to either sprites or frames in the script channel. This is how you incorporate behaviors into your movie.

To assign a behavior to a sprite:

1. Open the score window.
2. Open the cast window which contains your behavior. If you are assigning a behavior from the built-in library, choose Behavior Library from the Xtras menu **(Figure 4)**.
3. Drag a behavior from a cast window onto a sprite in the score or onto a sprite on the stage. You can assign as many behaviors as you want to a single sprite. If the behavior you are assigning is from the built-in library, Director copies it to the active internal cast to prevent you from inadvertently modifying the original.
4. If a Parameters window appears, this means that you need to provide additional information to customize how the behavior works. For example, if you assign the Go to Marker behavior, you need to enter the parameters shown in **Figure 6**. Doing so does not change the original behavior, only the specific instance.

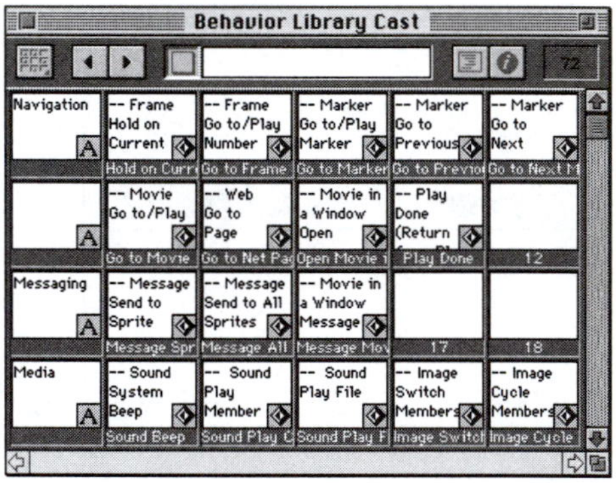

Figure 5. The Behavior Library Cast offers a set of built-in behaviors, which perform a wide range of functions.

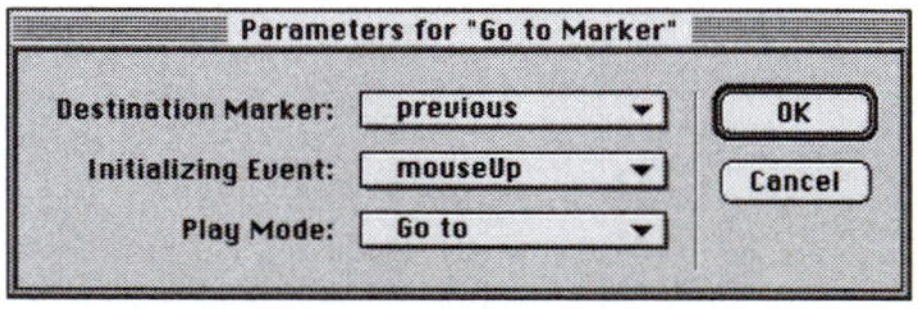

Figure 6. The **Parameters** window for the Go to Marker Behavior.

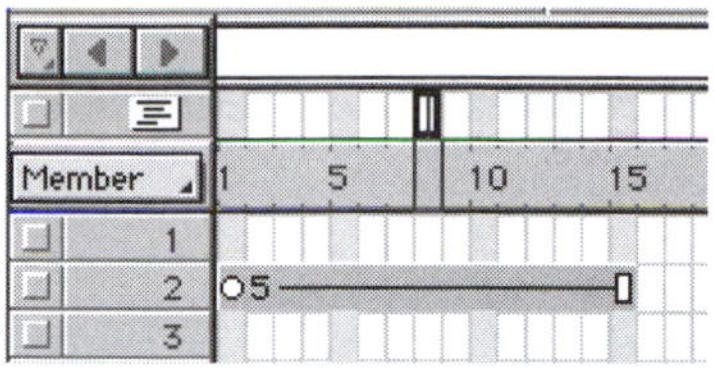

Figure 7. Drag a behavior from a cast window into a frame in the script channel in the score.

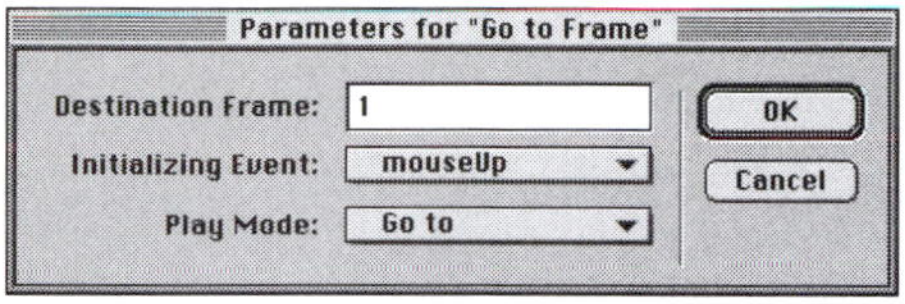

Figure 8. This is the **Parameters** window for the Go to Frame Behavior.

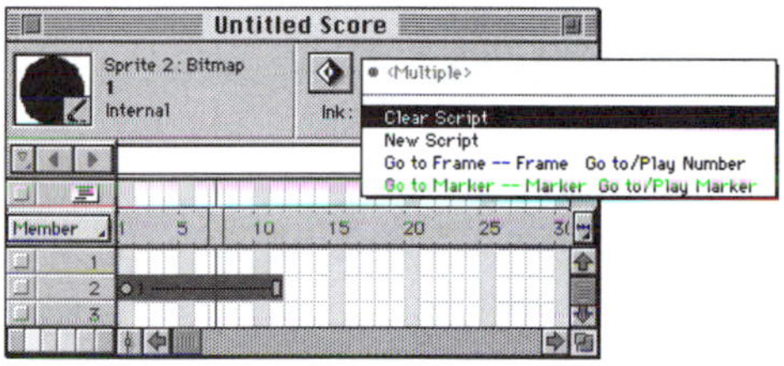

Figure 9. You can delete all behaviors assigned to either a sprite or a frame by selecting the sprite or frame and choosing **Clear Script** from the **Script** pop-up menu in the **Sprite Toolbar**.

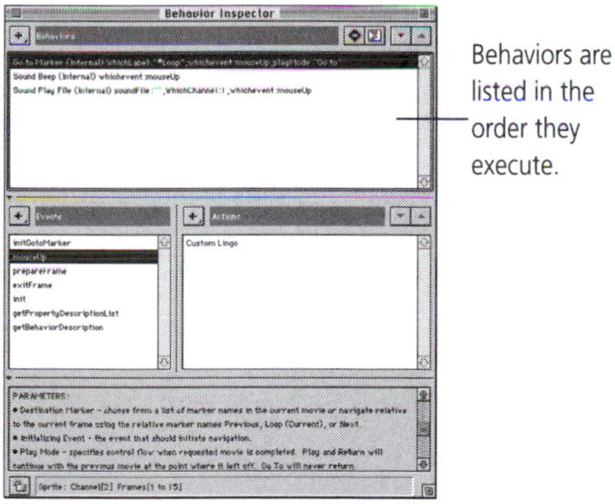

Figure 10. The **Behavior Inspector** window.

To assign a behavior to a frame:

1. Open the score window.
2. Open the cast window which contains your behavior. If you are using a behavior from the built-in library, choose Behavior Library from the Xtras menu.
3. Drag a behavior from a cast window into a frame within the script channel in the score **(Figure 7)**. You can assign only one behavior to a specific frame. If the behavior you are assigning is from the built-in library, Director copies it to an internal cast to prevent you from inadvertently modifying the original.
4. If a Parameters window appears, enter additional information to customize how the behavior works **(Figure 8)**.

✔ Tip

- You can delete all behaviors assigned to a sprite or a frame by selecting the sprite or frame and choosing Clear Scripts from the Script pop-up menu in the Sprite Toolbar **(Figure 9)**.

BEHAVIOR INSPECTOR

Use the Behavior Inspector window when you wish to create a new behavior, modify an existing one, or change the order in which behaviors are executed for a given sprite or frame **(Figure 10)**. Open it by choosing Inspectors from the Window menu and selecting Behavior from the pop-up menu.

When you select a sprite or a frame in the script channel, and then open the Behavior Inspector window, the top of the window lists all of the behaviors which have been assigned to the sprite or frame. Behaviors are listed in the order in which they execute.

The Behavior Inspector has two expandable regions in it, which are expanded or collapsed by clicking the small triangular buttons on the left side **(Figure 11)**. The first region is called the editing pane **(Figure 12)**, which you use when modifying or creating a behavior. The second region is the description pane which contains a description of the behavior currently selected at the top of the window.

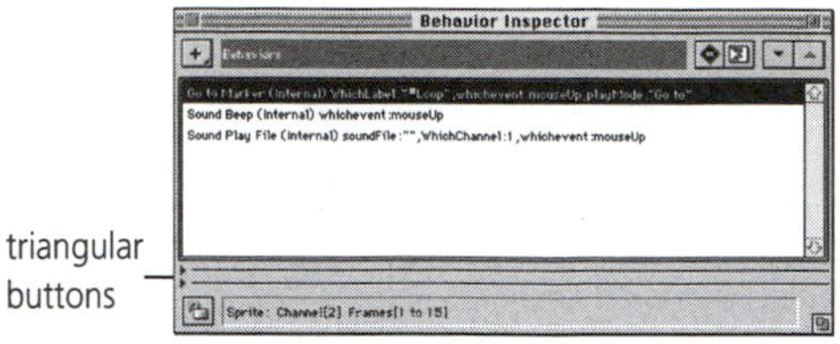

Figure 11. Click the small triangular buttons at the left of the **Behavior Inspector** window to open the editing and description panes.

To modify an existing behavior:

1. Double-click a behavior in the cast window to open it in the Behavior Inspector window.
2. Open the editing pane by clicking the small triangular button.
3. In the editing pane, use the Event and Action pop-up menus **(Figure 12)** to specify which actions are executed in response to which events *(see pages 202 and 219 in the Lingo Through Interactivity chapter for a description of events)*. First select an event from the Event pop-up menu. Then select an action from the Action pop-up menu, such as Go to Frame, which should occur in response to the selected event. You can assign multiple actions to a single event. Director executes the actions in the order they are listed. You can reorder the actions by using the Shuffle Up and Shuffle Down buttons **(Figure 12)**. Delete an action by selecting it in the list and pressing delete.

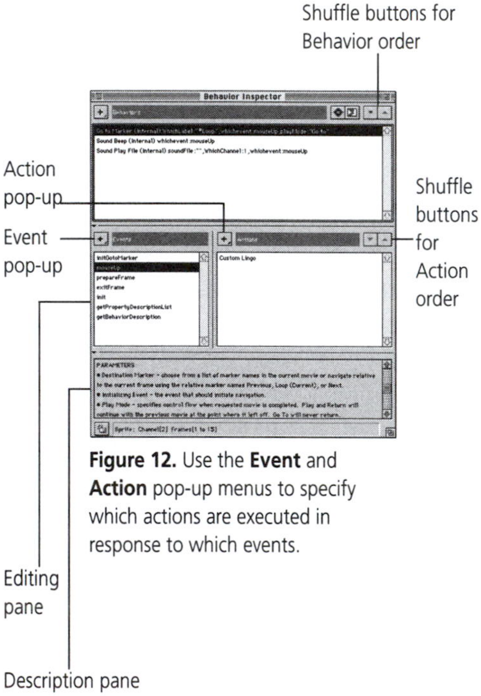

Figure 12. Use the **Event** and **Action** pop-up menus to specify which actions are executed in response to which events.

To change the order of behaviors assigned to a sprite:

1. Select the sprite which has behaviors assigned to it that you wish to reorder.
2. Click the Behavior Inspector button in the Sprite Toolbar.
3. In the Behavior Inspector, use the Shuffle Up and Shuffle Down buttons **(Figure 12)** at the top of the window to change the order of the listed behaviors.

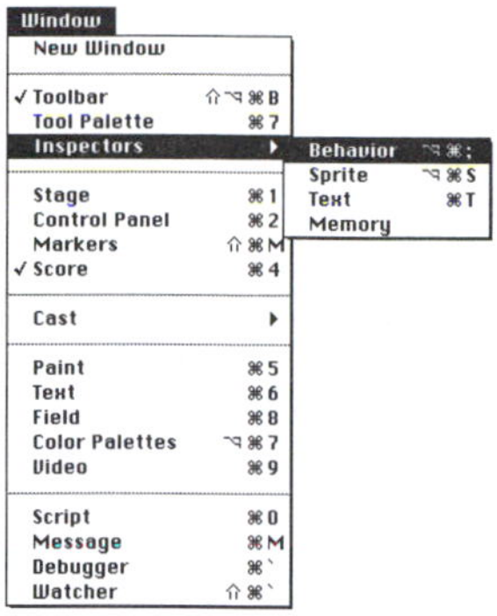

Figure 13. Choose **Inspectors** from the **Window** menu and select **Behavior** from the pop-up menu.

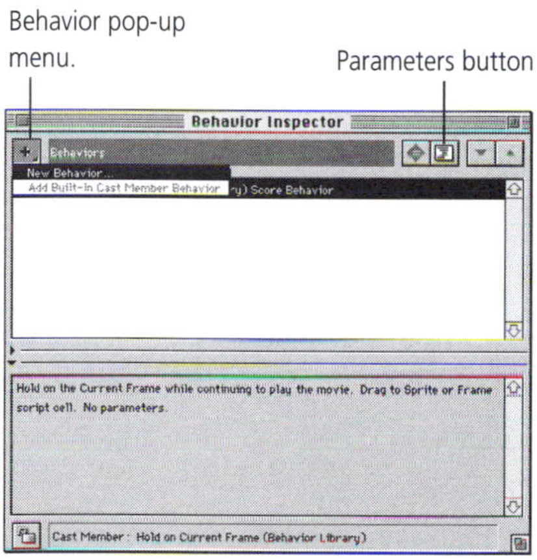

Figure 14. Choose **New Behavior** from the **Behavior** pop-up menu in the **Behavior Inspector**.

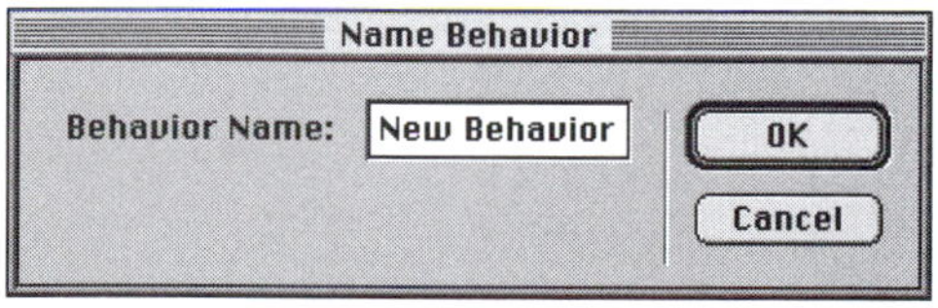

Figure 15. Enter a name for the new behavior in the **Name Behavior** dialog box.

To create a new behavior:

You can create a new behavior which executes a unique set of actions in response to a certain set of events.

1. Choose Inspectors from the Window menu and select Behavior from the pop-up menu **(Figure 13)**.
2. Choose New Behavior from the Behavior pop-up menu in the Behavior Inspector **(Figure 14)**.
3. Enter a name in the Name Behavior dialog box and click OK **(Figure 15)**. The behavior is added to the cast window.
4. Open the editing pane in the Behavior Inspector.
5. Use the Event and Action pop-up menus to specify which actions are executed in response to which events. A single behavior can respond to many events, and many actions can occur in response to a single event. The actions occur in the order they are listed.

To re-enter parameters for an assigned behavior:

You can re-enter the parameters for a behavior already assigned to a sprite or frame.

1. In the score, select a sprite or frame with an assigned behavior.
2. Click the Behavior Inspector button in the Sprite Toolbar.
3. In the Behavior Inspector, click the Parameters button **(Figure 14)**.

To edit a behavior in a script window:

Since a behavior is technically a score script, you can edit its Lingo code in a script window.

1. Select a behavior in a cast window.
2. Click the script button in the cast window.

Appendix A: Glossary

Anti-aliasing Removes or reduces the rough and jagged edges around an image.

Bit depth The number of bits used to display each pixel. In Director, bit depth can be set to 1, 2, 4, 8, 16, 24, and 32-bit color.

Cast window A Cast window is the storage area in Director that contains your multimedia elements, such as graphics, sounds, color palettes, film loops, buttons, QuickTime movies, and scripts.

Control Panel Provides VCR-type control over the playback of your movie, including Rewind, Play, and Step Forward buttons.

Cast member An individual multimedia element that can be incorporated into your movie, such as a graphic, sound, film loop, color palette, or QuickTime movie.

Cell The individual storage units that make up the Score. Each cell contains information about one cast member.

Channel A row of cells in the Score window. Each channel holds a specific cast member type. There are 48 animations channels, five effects channels (Tempo, Palette, Transition, Sound 1 & 2) and a script channel.

Color cycling A color effect, where colors are rotated through a specified range in a color palette. Cast members that appear in these colors appear to pulsate and change color.

Color depth The bit depth of a cast member, indicating how many colors it can display.

Common palette A specially constructed palette that incorporates many of the colors shared by your entire cast. Its purpose is to replace the many cast member palettes your movie may be using with a single palette that can display your entire cast in approximately accurate colors.

Current frame The frame that is currently displayed on the Stage. You can change the current frame by using the frame counter in the Control Panel, or the Playback head in the Score window.

Current palette
The color palette used to display the colors of the cast members in the current frame on the Stage. You can change the current palette in the Palette channel of the Score.

Foreground
Sprites that appear to be in front of other sprites on the Stage are in the foreground. A sprite's foreground priority is determined by its placement in the animation channels. A sprite closer to the bottom animation channel (channel 48) is closer to the foreground.

Foreground color
The main color used to paint artwork in the Paint window, and to paint QuickDraw shapes and text in the Tool Palette. It is selected using the Foreground color chip.

Frame
A column of cells in the Score window that represents a segment of time in your movie. Each frame contains information about what your cast members are doing in that time segment.

Film loop
A cast member that is composed of a sequence of graphical cast members to form a looping animation.

In-Between
A command in Director that helps create an animation sequence, by filling in the frames between two key frames that you specify.

Ink Effects
Ink effects determine how your sprites appear when they overlap each other and background artwork on the Stage. Ink effects are applied to sprites using the Score window's ink pop-up menu. Ink effects can also be applied to cast members to permanently affect their colors, by using the paint window's Ink pop-up menu.

Mask
An image that allows you to control which parts of an artwork selection are transparent (you can see background artwork through these parts) and which parts are opaque. A mask could be used to make the windows in a house transparent, and the rest of the house opaque.

Movie
The term used to describe any multimedia animation created in Director.

Palette
A subset of colors used to display your cast members. Only one color palette can be active at a time.

Playback head
The position of the Playback head in the Score window indicates which frame is currently displayed on the Stage. You can drag the Playback head to display different frames on the Stage.

Projector A play-only version of a Director movie. Projectors cannot be opened or edited in Director and are the best way to distribute your movies to the public. It is not necessary to own a copy of Director to run a projector movie.

Real-time recording A feature in Director that allows you to record the path of mouse movements, and then substitute any graphical cast member to follow this path to form an animation.

Registration point A reference point used to align the positions of cast members in an animation sequence.

Score A frame-by-frame record of your movie, used to direct all your cast members. The Score is organized into 48 animation channels, five effects channels (Tempo, Palette, Transitions, 1 & 2), and one script channel.

Stage The background upon which your movie animations are played and viewed.

Step Recording The most basic animation technique in Director, where you arrange and record each frame on an individual basis to create an animation sequence.

Tempo The rate at which the frames of your movie are played. Tempo is measured in frames-per-second.

Appendix B: List of Keyboard Shortcuts by Menu

File Menu

New Movie	Command-N
New Cast	Command-Option-N
Open	Command-O
Close	Command-W
Save	Command-S
Import	Command-R
Export	Command-Shift-R
Page Setup	Command-Shift-P
Print	Command-P
Quit	Command-Q

Edit Menu

Undo	Command-Z
Repeat	Command-Y
Cut	Command-X
Copy	Command-C
Paste	Command-V
Clear	Delete
Duplicate	Command-D
Select All	Command-A
Find Text	Command-F
Find Handler	Command-Shift-;
Find Cast Member	Command-;
Find Selection	Command-H
Find Again	Command-Option-F
Replace Again	Command-Option-E
Edit Sprite Frames	Command-Option-]
Edit Entire Sprite	Command-Option-[
Exchange Cast Members	Command-E
Launch External Editor	Command-,

View Menu

Next Marker	Command-right arrow
Previous Marker	Command-left arrow
Zoom in	Command-+
Zoom out	Command--(minus)
Show Grid	Command-Shift-Option-G
Snap to Grid	Command-Option-G
Show Info	Command-Shift-Option-O
Show Paths	Command-Shift-Option-H
Sprite Toolbar	Command-Shift-H
Keyframes	Command-Shift-Option-K

Insert Menu

Keyframe	Command-Option-K
Insert Frame	Command-]
Remove Frame	Command-[

Modify Menu

Cast Member Properties	Command-I
Cast Member Script	Command-' (apostrophe)
Sprite Properties	Command-Shift-I
Sprite Script	Command-Shift-' (apostrophe)
Tweening	Command-Shift-B
Movie Properties	Command-Shift-D
Movie Casts	Command-Shift-C
Font	Command-Shift-T
Paragraph	Command-Shift-Option-T
Join Sprites	Command-J
Split Sprite	Command-Shift-J
Extend Sprite	Command-B
Bring to Front	Command-Shift-up arrow
Move Forward	Command-up arrow
Move Backward	Command-down arrow
Send to Back	Command-Shift-down arrow
Align	Command-K
Tweak	Command-Shift-K

Control Menu

Play	Command-Option-P
Stop	Command-Option-. (period)
Rewind	Command-Option-R
Step Forward	Command-Option-right arrow
Step Backward	Command-Option-left arrow
Loop Playback	Command-Option-L
Volume:Mute	Command-Option-M
Toggle Breakpoint	Command-Shift-Option-K
Watch Expression	Command-Shift-Option-W
Ignore Breakpoints	Command-Shift-Option-I
Step Script	Command-Shift-Option-down arrow
Step into Script	Command-Shift-Option-right arrow
Run Script	Command-Shift-Option-up arrow
Recompile All Scripts	Command-Shift-Option-C

Window Menu

Toolbar	Command-Shift-Option-B
Tool Palette	Command-7
Behavior Inspector	Command-Option-;
Sprite Inspector	Command-Option-S
Text Inspector	Command-T
Stage	Command-1
Control Panel	Command-2
Markers	Command-Shift-M
Score	Command-4
Cast	Command-3
Paint	Command-5
Text	Command-6
Field	Command-8
Color Palettes	Command-Option-7
Video	Command-9
Script	Command-0
Message	Command-M
Debugger	Command-` (back single quote)
Watcher	Command-Shift-` (back single quote)

S

T

U

V

W

X

Z

More from Peachpit Press

A Day with Biff

Ron Romain and Joe Crabtree

It's a dog-eat-dog world. Just ask Biff, a protagonist pooch who's leapt paws first into the puzzling, amusing world of humans at work. Superb usable, original clip art makes this whimsical interactive book/disk package a joy. Like any good bad dog, Biff takes his job—distracting you from the task at hand—very seriously. His weapons: a maze, a treasure hunt, and more. Now play! $24.95
(96 pages, w/Macintosh disk)

Animation and 3D Modeling on the Mac

Don Foley and Melora Foley

The world isn't flat. Your animations needn't be, either. This visual, instructional volume guides experienced and novice animators through the exhilarating but complex challenge of designing in 3D. More than 1,000 striking, full-color illustrations demonstrate work from the world's best modelers and animators. Plus you'll learn the software you need most, including Director, Photoshop, Premiere, Infini-D, Ray Dream Designer, KPT Bryce, and more.
$34.95 (144 pages)

A Blip in the continuum

Robin Williams and John Tollett

In this full-color book, author Robin Williams and illustrator John Tollett celebrate the new wave of type design known as "grunge" typography. The book consists of famous and not-so-famous quotes about type and design set in a range of grunge fonts, using rule-breaking layouts. The illustrations, created in Fractal Design Painter, complement the text. Includes a companion disk with 21 of the best freeware and shareware grunge fonts, several of which were newly created for this book. *$22.95 (96 pages)*

ColorCourse Interactive Training CDs

ColorExpert

ColorCourse/Photography demonstrates how to evaluate, scan, and separate photos for faithful reproduction. *ColorCourse/Illustration* covers trapping, scaling, blends, scanning specifications, and proofing. *ColorCourse/Imagesetting* focuses on getting the best final output possible with tips on topics like film imaging, proofing, quality assurance, and working with service bureaus. Includes a comprehensive trouble-shooting guide. Fully indexed with text links throughout.
$49.95 each (CD-ROM)

Designing Multimedia

Lisa Lopuck

If you're interested in being part of the booming field of multimedia, this beautifully illustrated volume shows you how. It's concept-to-product approach is highly visual: with stunning, full-color samples of actual multimedia projects. Title structure, user interface, software dynamics, and many other factors that affect design decisions are explained in detail.
$34.95 144 pages

Digital Image Creation

Hisaka Kojima

This book takes you inside the studios of award-winning digital photographers. Through a series of interviews and step-by-step examples, these artists share their secrets of image creation. Heavily illustrated with stunning, full-color images. *$49.95 230 pages*

HTML: Visual QuickStart Guide

Elizabeth Castro

This step-by-step guide teaches you how to use Hypertext Markup Language to design pages for the World Wide Web. The book presumes no prior knowledge of HTML, or even the Internet, and uses clear, concise instructions for creating each element of a Web page. From the title and headers and your company's logo to complex tables and clickable graphics, this book covers it all. *$17.95 (176 pages)*

Home Sweet Home Page and the Kitchen Sink (w/ CD-ROM)

Robin Williams with Dave Mark

This exciting new book/CD-ROM combo provides all the tools you need to get online and create Web pages. *The Home Sweet Home Page* book takes a friendly, non-technical approach to planning and designing interactive Web pages with easy-to-follow instructions and delightful illustrations. The CD-ROM provides everything else you need to finish creating your pages, including connection software for AOL, CompuServe, and AT&T. *$24.95 (208 pages)*

HyperCard 2.3 in a Hurry

George Beekman

HyperCard turns mere mortals into whiz-bang programmers. Witness Myst, which was created in HyperCard. Whether you're already building multimedia applications or just nosing your mouse into the introductory stacks, *HyperCard 2.3 in a Hurry* provides an easy-to-follow, self-paced tutorial that gets results fast. Entertaining projects help you master HyperCard's more advanced features. *$24.95 (384 pages)*

The Illustrator 7 Book

Deke McClelland

Experienced Illustrator users and novices alike will learn many helpful tips and techniques from this book. Thorough and comprehensive, *The Illustrator 7 Book* gives in-depth coverage of Illustrator's latest features. *$29.95 (688 pages)*

The Illustrator Wow! Book

Sharon Steuer

Modeled on the best-selling *Photoshop Wow! Book*, this book provides step-by-step descriptions with full-color illustrations of actual commercial art produced with Adobe Illustrator. The works of over 70 of the country's best Illustrator artists are included. A unique introductory chapter, "The Zen of Illustrator," helps you understand how the program thinks. The accompanying disk includes tutorials, special filters, artist tips, and other goodies. *$39.95 224 pages (w/ disk)*

Kai's Power Tools 3

Nick Clarke

This lavish, full-color guide is a desktop designer, illustrator, and pixel lover's dream. Beginners will love the step-by-step instructions; experienced users will gain insight into the hidden power of KPT. The cross-platform CD is packed with free filters, shareware, links to KPT-related sites on the Web, plus a gallery of KPT-created images. *$39.95 120 pages*

The Macintosh Bible, 6th Edition

Edited by Jeremy Judson

This classic reference book is now completely updated. *The Macintosh Bible, 6th Edition* is crammed with tips, tricks, and shortcuts that will help you to get the most out of your Mac. Completely revised by 13 editors and over 70 contributors, this is the ultimate reference for all things Mac. It tackles every subject area with a clear vision of what Macintosh users need to know in an engaging, no-nonsense style. Includes a new section on the Internet: getting connected, sending e-mail, surfing the Web, and downloading files. *$29.95 (1,009 pages)*

Netscape 3 for Macintosh: Visual QuickStart Guide

Elizabeth Castro

This book is the perfect introduction to the latest version of Netscape, the most widely used browser of the World Wide Web. You'll learn how to transfer files, read and send e-mail, use the address book, and post to newsgroups. Additionally, the book covers Netscape Gold, with helpful information on how to format your own Web page. *$16.95 (288 pages)*

The Painter 4 Wow! Book, 2nd Edition

Cher Threinen-Pendarvis

This newly updated, full-color volume uses hundreds of stunning, original illustrations depicting Painter 4's full range of styles and effects. Step-by-step descriptions clearly explain how each piece was created. Users of all levels will find these tips and tricks easy to integrate in their own work. The dual-platform CD includes custom brushes and textures, stock photos, video clips, filters, and try-out versions of some of the hottest graphics programs available. *$44.95 264 pages (w/ CD-ROM)*

Photoshop 4 for Macintosh: Visual QuickStart Guide

Elaine Weinmann and Peter Lourekas

Completely revised for Photoshop 3, this indispensible guide is ideal for Mac users who want to get started in Adobe Photoshop without having to wade through long-winded explanations. *Photoshop 3 for Macintosh* uses illustrated, step-by-step examples to cover Photoshop fundamentals, including how to use masks, filters, colors, and more. *$19.95 (295 pages)*

The Photoshop 4 Wow! Book (Mac Edition)

Linnea Dayton and Jack Davis

This book is really two books in one: an easy-to-follow, step-by-step tutorial of Photoshop fundamentals, and over 150 pages of tips and techniques for getting the most out of Photoshop version 3. Full-color throughout, *The Photoshop Wow! Book* shows how professional artists make the best use of Photoshop. Includes a CD-ROM containing Photoshop filters and utilities. *$39.95 (286 pages, w/CD-ROM)*

Order Form

USA 800-283-9444 • 510-548-4393 • FAX 510-548-5991
CANADA 800-387-8028 • 416-447-1779 • FAX 800-456-0536 OR 416-443-0948
http://www.peachpit.com

Qty	Title	Price	Total
	SUBTOTAL		
	ADD APPLICABLE SALES TAX*		
	SHIPPING		
	TOTAL		

Shipping is by UPS ground: $4 for first item, $1 each add'l.

*We are required to pay sales tax in all states with the exceptions of AK, DE, MT, NH, and OR. Please include appropriate sales tax if you live in any state not mentioned above.

Customer Information

NAME

COMPANY

STREET ADDRESS

CITY STATE ZIP

PHONE ( ) FAX ( )
[REQUIRED FOR CREDIT CARD ORDERS]

Payment Method

❑ CHECK ENCLOSED ❑ VISA ❑ MASTERCARD ❑ AMEX

CREDIT CARD # EXP. DATE

COMPANY PURCHASE ORDER #

Tell Us What You Think

PLEASE TELL US WHAT YOU THOUGHT OF THIS BOOK: TITLE:

WHAT OTHER BOOKS WOULD YOU LIKE US TO PUBLISH?

PEACHPIT PRESS • 2414 Sixth Street • Berkeley, CA 94710